PUGIN

PUGIN

A
MEDIÆVAL
VICTORIAN

BY

MICHAEL TRAPPES-LOMAX

Domine, dilexi decorem domus tuae;
et locum habitationis gloriae tuae . . .
Pes meus stetit in directo : in ecclesiis
benedicam te, Domine. PSALM XXV.

There is nothing worth living for but
Christian Architecture and a boat.
AUGUSTUS WELBY NORTHMORE PUGIN.

LONDON
SHEED & WARD
MCMXXXII

PRINTED IN GREAT BRITAIN
BY THE WHITEFRIARS PRESS LTD.
LONDON AND TONBRIDGE
FOR SHEED AND WARD
31 PATERNOSTER ROW
LONDON, E.C.4
FIRST PUBLISHED NOVEMBER 1932

MATRI PATRIQUE

D. D. D.

M.

CONTENTS

LIST OF ILLUSTRATIONS

PUGIN

CHAPTER I

ORIGINS

" Great will your life be and troublous," said Vermund.
The Saga of Grettir the Strong.

Of the Pugin ancestry, nothing definite seems to be known.
It is said [1] to include ' a nobleman who raised a hundred
soldiers for the service of Fribourg,[2] the Senators augmenting
his arms " d'un oiseau sable," for his valour in having defeated
a hundred cavalry at Morat, when besieged by Charles Duke
of Burgundy, in 1477.' The reward hardly seems adequate ;
and in any case, ' un oiseau sable '—in modern heraldic
language, a martlet—could only detract from the fine simplicity of ' gules, a bend or.' However, the martlet remains.
Between the anonymous warrior of 1477 and Auguste-Charles,
Comte de Pugin, the father of Augustus Welby Northmore
Pugin, the subject of this essay, there is an unbridged gap of
nearly three hundred years. Two glimmerings of light alone
appear : on 30th December 1636, according to *The Notebook
of John Southcote, D.D.*,[3] ' Marquis of Pugin the ordinary
french ambassador died at Rigat ' [Reigate] ; and Mrs. A. C.
Pugin wrote to her sister, Selina Welby [4] : ' You may
remember that the family arms which Mr. Pugin's mother
burnt in the Revolution, in terror of their being discovered,
because of their being of the noblesse of Switzerland, are again

---

[1] *Ferrey* ; pp. 1–2.
[2] I.e. Fribourg in Switzerland ; not (as is stated in *Sequel* ; I., p. 83) Freiburg in
Germany.
[3] *Catholic Record Society* ; I., p. 110.   [4] *Ferrey* ; p. 140.

restored in the family ; they are very handsome in themselves, and very handsomely emblazoned, framed, and glazed. In the account pasted at the back of the frame (which account is given by the Herald's Office), they are said to have been assumed in the fourteenth century. Augustus is delighted with them, but cannot help at the same time observing that Roger de Welby died fighting at the Battle of Hastings, which clearly proves the family Saxon, and carries it up at once to William the Conqueror.' But these are only glimmerings, and they once more grow dim at the statement of Mr. Harry Sirr [1] that : ' Neither the family nor the arms [of Pugin] are recorded in published armorials of France or Switzerland.' The elder Pugin's title, in fact, like those of many lesser men, seems to have lacked official recognition. But, unlike many lesser men, he did not use it.

However, the truth or otherwise of these family traditions is a matter of no great importance : what is of importance is that they were believed. In consequence, Augustus Welby Northmore Pugin could start upon his career knowing that on both his father's and his mother's side he was at least the equal of the majority of his employers ; and the possession of aristocratic birth has at any rate one advantage in that it frees its possessor from both false pride and false humility, and helps to save him from that crime against the soul known as ' human respect.'

Pugin, then, entered upon life in a certain sense armoured.

What is of more importance than this armour, however, is the matter of immediate environment : the personalities of father and of mother, and the kind of life which they create between them. In all these three formative influences Pugin's life was exceptional, if not in all aspects exceptionally fortunate.

To start, then, with the elder Pugin. Of his early life little

[1] *Sirr, F.R.I.B.A.*

is known. Whether he fled to England because of a duel,[1] or whether the story is true [2] that he fell fighting for Louis XVI., was thrown with the bodies of the slain into a pit near the Place de la Bastille, escaped by swimming the Seine, and eventually reached England by way of Rouen, it now seems impossible to determine. What is certain is that his position on arriving in England was precarious ; for he had neither money nor connections, and was almost entirely ignorant of the language. The advertising columns of newspapers seemed his best chance of getting employment, and he studied them eagerly. At last an opportunity appeared. Mr. John Nash, Architect to the Office of Works, required a draughtsman in his office, and, sinister proviso at a time when the country contained many refugees, stated ' that the services of a foreigner would be preferred.' [3] Whether Nash was in search of cheap labour or was generously trying to help the unfortunate, does not appear. At any rate the elder Pugin, who ' was astonished to find a French nobleman, whom he had known in Paris, a candidate for the same appointment ' [3] was given the post, and, being a skilled water-colourist [4]—a skill which he increased by taking lessons from Merigot, the aquatint engraver, formerly ' a drawing-master to his father's family in France ' [5]—soon was promoted to doing more important work amid the multitudinous activities of Nash's studio. His progress was rapid, and from being Nash's ' draughtsman ' he quickly rose to the position of Nash's ' ghost ' ; more, after a few years he became an employer of ' ghosts ' himself.

The use of the word ' ghost ' must not be misunderstood. The cases were not strictly parallel with those lamentably frequent ones in literature where an unknown man writes a book and sells it at starvation price to a well-known writer

---

[1] *The Life of Charles James Mathews* ; ed. by C. Dickens ; I., p. 39.
[2] *Ferrey* ; p. 2.   [3] *Ib.*
[4] He became an Associate of the Old Water-colour Society in 1808.
[5] *Ib. ;* p. 3.

for publication under the purchaser's name. They were more
like those of barristers' ' devils,' who learn while they work
and pay for their learning partly by their work. But there is
a border-line. Nash at any rate would seem to have stepped
beyond it.

Nash, however, was too generous an employer, and the
elder Pugin too great a man, for the ghostly relationship to be
permanent. The elder Pugin's progress from *emigré* poverty
to a niche in *The Dictionary of National Biography* may be
summarised as follows. John Nash had undertaken more than
he could carry out; and part of what he had undertaken—
buildings in the Gothic style—was distinctly unpalatable. It
was necessary, then, if Nash were to carry out his Gothic
undertakings, that at least the spadework of making drawings
of ancient examples for reproduction should be done for him.
This the elder Pugin, who had architectural ability as well as
skill with water-colours, was eminently fitted to do. He
became, in fact, Nash's Gothic right hand man. It was not a
case of Nash's left hand not knowing what his right was doing:
it was a case of the right hand doing something of which the
left was incapable.

Nash, moreover, had only as it were the first serial rights in
the elder Pugin's work: after use in the Office he was at
liberty to publish the results of his labours in book form. In
consequence his fame grew, and he achieved an independent
position as a delineator of the antique. His position in
relation to his patron is well summed up in his dedication of
his own magnificent *Specimens of Gothic Architecture;
selected from various Antient Edifices in England*, &c., to
' John Nash, Esq. Architect to the Office of Works, Private
Architect to the King, &c. &c. &c.'

   ' Sir,
Soon after my arrival in this country, I was very fortunately
introduced to you, and prosecuted my architectural studies in

your office, with much gratification and advantage to myself.
It is, therefore, with no small degree of pleasure that I inscribe
to you the present volume of Specimens, which none, better
than yourself, know how to appropriate and appreciate.
Indeed, from your friendly and judicious counsel I have
already profited much ; and I trust that the present Work, as
well as any other I may hereafter be induced to undertake,
may merit the approbation of so distinguished a judge.

I remain,

With great respect and gratitude,

Your obedient servant,

A. Pugin.'

' Appropriate ' is good.

The relation of the elder Pugin to the architectural progress
of his time is clearly expressed in *The Quarterly Review* for
June 1821, with reference to Britton's *Chronological and
Historical Illustrations of the Ancient Architecture of Great
Britain* :

' Mr. Britton presents us, as usual, with pleasing and well
executed engravings. But he has not supplied the want,
which is so grievously felt, of such a collection as will enable
the architect to do his work. For this purpose, simple but
accurate outlines, on an intelligible scale, are alone required ;
highly finished plates, on a small scale, though they may be
liked by the amateur, are worse than useless to the art, as they
encourage the builder who attempts Gothic architecture, to
content himself with a general resemblance, and to blur all
the minor features. A work, professing to treat on architecture,
and wanting in plans and sections, is no better than a treatise
on anatomy which omits the representation of the bones.
Sections of mouldings are indispensable ; they vary in every
specimen, and can never be made out from the elevation.
Mr. Pugin has judiciously attended to these details, and his
book will consequently be exceedingly serviceable to the

practical architect, at the same time that it is equally satisfactory to the antiquary.'

The elder Pugin, in fact, was filling a need that was being
felt by others as well as John Nash. The result, for a man in
his position, was inevitable. As Ferrey put it [1] :

' The superior knowledge of Gothic architecture which the
elder Pugin was known to possess, led many architects whose
acquaintance with mediæval art was superficial, to apply to
him for aid. This he was always ready to afford, and through
the help of his son and his pupils he assisted others in carrying
out their works. Many buildings might in strictness claim
him as their author instead of the architect to whom they are
publickly ascribed.'

Ferrey adds a little moralising on the ' ghostly ' system,
moralising that is no more out of place to-day than it was
when written :

' It is to be feared that the system of working by other
people's hands and wits is not now wholly abandoned ; but
there is a meanness in the practice which cannot be too much
reprobated, and he is unworthy the name of a conscientious
architect who condescends to such surreptitious proceedings.'

With one eye, as it were, nervously on the origins of the
new Houses of Parliament, then approaching completion, he
goes on to say :

' This remark does not apply to those who, in the conception
and execution of large works, find it necessary to have their
ideas carried out by secondary agency, subordinate to their
own direction, but to the system of those who are in the habit
of throwing upon others the labour and study of design, and
then unworthily claim the merit of the performance.'

The elder Pugin, then, was a pioneer ; and like most
pioneers he did not reap the full reward of his labours—in so
far, that is, that he never achieved an architectural practice of

[1] *Ferrey ;* pp. 50–1.

his own in which his acquirements could be as useful to himself as they were to other people. But that was really no great loss : his real function was that of a teacher, and as such his good influence on his employers was no less than on his pupils —in particular on one pupil who was to be greater than any of his employers or other pupils, his son.

Before the elder Pugin, ' the only practical attempts in Gothic architecture, though unfortunately made on a large scale, were imitations of conventual or castellated buildings, exhibiting every kind of incongruity perpetrated in extensive masses of cement and terra cotta.' After him, his son was to show ' how applicable the genius of mediæval architecture is to all ages, and their various requirements.' [1] The gap was enormous between the work of the elder Pugin's predecessors and that of his son and his son's successors. The elder Pugin bridged the gap by his own tireless pioneer labours.

The elder Pugin, in fact, was a remarkable man. More, he seems to have been an extremely pleasant one. His portrait, drawn from recollection by Joseph Nash, shows a handsome and dignified face, relieved by the obvious presence of a sense of humour. Various glimpses vouchsafed by Ferrey fill out the portrait. In his early days in London he wore a three-cornered hat, and carried a muff and a gold-headed cane. To his repeated enquiries at the Post Office for letters he constantly received the same answer : ' I tell you there are no letters for Monsier Augustus Pugin, but plenty for Monsieur Puggen ' ; an incident which caused his friend Mathews the comedian to found upon it his character of Monsieur Malet, ' which he personated with so much feeling. " Ah ! " Pugin would often say, " people little know that Monsieur Malet should be Monsieur Pugin ".' [2] Later, when making drawings of the Pavilion at Brighton for a book commanded by George IV., he ' had scarcely time to rise when the King, passing by

---

[1] *Ferrey ;* p. 25.   [2] *Ib. ;* pp. 3–4.

him and not perceiving a stool on which a colour-box was
placed, accidently overthrew it. The King [1] stooped, and
instantly picking up the box, gave it to Pugin with an expression of apology. It may easily be imagined how fully Pugin
appreciated this act of condescension, which he never failed
to mention whenever he had opportunity.' [2] He was also
accustomed ' to animate his pupils to perseverance and
industry ' [3] by telling them tales of Nash's early struggles in
a manner which was both impassioned and amusing and contained a ' mixture of gravity and drollery.' [4] On one occasion
he was ' not a little surprised and gratified to find ' that an
enquiring stranger ' was no other than the Earl of Elgin
himself, accompanied by his son Lord Bruce.' [5] Better still,
he knew what was due to him as a *ci-devant* comte himself, and
' was very susceptible of affront, and sometimes even
threatened to show people the door if proper courtesy was
not shown him in conversation.' [6]

The impression emerges of a man both amiable and able,
making his way in difficult circumstances by sheer hard work,
rising with surprising quickness from success to hard-won
success. But perhaps the greatest triumph in his career, the
one offering most obstacles to be overcome, was his successful
wooing, when his ' position was hardly such as to make him
a desirable candidate ' [7] of ' the Belle of Islington.'

This lady, Catherine, daughter of William Welby, Barrister-
at-law of the Middle Temple, was not only a member of an
old and distinguished Lincolnshire family,[8] but was ' possessed

---

[1] ' Mindful perhaps of illustrious parallels in the past ' [*Dict. Nat. Biog.*; XLVII.,
p .6.]
[2] *Ferrey.* ; pp. 9–10.   [3] *Ib.*
[4] *Ib.* ; p. 12.   [5] *Ib.* ; pp. 24–5.
[6] *Ib.* ; p. 94.   [7] *Ib.* ; pp. 5–6.
[8] Her father was fifth in descent from William Welby (d. 1627), of Denton,
Lincolnshire, and, through the marriage of his great-grandfather with a first cousin,
Judith Welby, fourth in descent from William Welby (d. 1657), of Denton, and
third cousin of Sir William Earle Welby, 2nd Bart., M.P., of Denton. [Information
of Lt.-Col. Sir Alfred Welby, K.B.E.]

of no ordinary charms.'[1] In addition, she seems to have had both wit and literary leanings. At any rate, when a neighbour at a dinner party, ' looking her earnestly in the face,' exclaimed " Madam, how exceedingly like you are to the devil," an expression which ' caused no small surprise amongst the company,' her familiarity with *Paradise Lost* came to her rescue, and ' she gracefully bowed her thanks, and accepted the remark as a compliment to her personal appearance,' recognising ' in the seemingly rude observation an allusion to the fascinating form of Satan as there described by the great poet.'[2] Whether the remark was intended as a compliment or not remains unknown. But one may surmise that it may have been double-edged. For the Belle of Islington, in addition to position and birth and the ' charms ' which gave her her name, was possessed of a personality of terrifying intensity.

However, that did not deter the elder Pugin, and they were married, at St. Mary's Church, Islington, on 2nd February 1802.

Ten years later, on 1st March 1812, at their house at 34 Store Street, Bedford Square, their only child was born to them, Augustus Welby Northmore Pugin.[3]

[1] *Ferrey ;* p. 6.   [2] *Ib.*

[3] There seems to have been no descent from the Northmore family to bring about this baptismal use of the name. Penelope Welby, however, daughter of Sir William Earle Welby, first baronet, married Thomas Augustus Northmore, of Cleve, co. Devon ; and their son, the Rev. Thomas Welby Northmore, of Cleve, married Katherine, daughter of Sir William Earle Welby, the second baronet. One of these Thomas Northmores may have been the child's godfather.

CHAPTER II

CHILDHOOD

Grettir grew up at Bjarg until he was ten years old, when he began to develop a little. Asmund told him that he must do some work. Grettir . . . asked what he was to do.

The Saga of Grettir the Strong.

AUGUSTUS WELBY NORTHMORE PUGIN, after early instruction at his mother's hands, delicacy of health making prolonged absences from home inadvisable, became a day-boy at Christ's Hospital, Newgate Street, otherwise known as the Bluecoat School. While there he seems to have shown considerable capacity and mental energy, one of his masters remarking of him ' that whether in Greek, Latin, mathematics, or any other branch of education, he would learn in twenty-four hours what it took other boys weeks to acquire.' In addition, besides being ' gentle and refined,' he was accustomed to express ' his opinions in the most dogmatic manner with volubility and vehemence,' and ' mixed very little with other children of his own age, always preferring the company of those who were his seniors.' [1] He had also a natural skill in drawing, which he exercised from early infancy. This talent was not originally architectural in form, his inclinations lying in the direction of caricature. For the exercise of this, life in his father's office, which he entered on completing his school course, gave full scope.

This talent for caricature is significant. It implies more than mere skill with a pencil. It implies a capacity for seeing the salient points not only of physical appearances but of personalities and events. It implies a capacity for making a

---

[1] *Ferrey;* pp. 32–3

judgment on things perceived. And it implies a capacity for giving decisive expression to an idea. When these capacities are combined with abnormal quickness of mind and powers of concentration, something unusual may be expected. What actually occurred at the time was that he was able to distract his father's pupils from the misery of their lot. The elder Pugin, though he was not the cause of his pupils' painful life, 'never failed to express approval or displeasure in a very decided and graphic manner to each youth according to his merits. Augustus (for that was the Christian name by which he preferred to be called) created great amusement by illustrating the ups and downs of the pupils on a wheel of fortune. Every week the rotary machine was sketched with great spirit, each pupil being represented standing upon a projecting bracket attached to the wheel. The favourite was always at the top, capering and laughing with pencil in hand, while the one least fortunate was seen hurled to the ground by the revolution of the wheel. Others were planted on the ascent or descent, according to the degree of favour in which they stood with their master, their doleful or joyous faces being cleverly expressed by a few spirited touches. Great amusement was produced by this humorous device; and the publication of a new wheel of fortune was eagerly looked for by his fellow pupils. Though this was a favourite amusement with him he was not less successful by the droll manner in which he illustrated any passing event wherein he could find subject for fun.' [1]

Subjects for fun cannot have been too frequent in the Pugin household, and it must have been a godsend to its members to have one among them who could skim and preserve the cream of any passing jest. For the Belle of Islington had become the Dragon of Store Street, Bedford Square.

Ferrey, who suffered under Mrs. Pugin's regime, gives a

[1] *Ferrey; p. 34.*

horrifying account of the price youths had to pay for studying under the greatest living exponent of Gothic architecture ; for Mrs. Pugin's discipline ' was severe and restrictive in the extreme, unrelieved by any of those relaxations essential to the healthy education of youth, and the smallest want of punctuality or infringement of domestic rules excited the marked displeasure of the lady.' [1] It was Mrs. Pugin's custom to retire to bed at nine o'clock, and to rise again at four. On rising, she rang a bell, loudly, three times : the first, to rouse the servants ; the second, to rouse the pupils ; the third, to summon the pupils to start work in the office at six o'clock. ' A pitiable sight indeed it was,' wrote Ferrey,[2] ' to see the shivering youths reluctantly creeping down in the midst of winter to waste their time by a sleepy attempt to work before breakfast.' The sorry drudgery went on till half-past eight, when the tyranny of the office gave place to the tyranny of meal times, each pupil, on entering the room, having to bow profoundly to Mrs. Pugin, who was appropriately seated at the head of the table. After a short prayer, the meal was ' despatched in silence, after which each retired as he entered making the same obeisance.' [3] The same silence and the same respect were enforced at dinner, after which work in the office was incessant till eight o'clock. There then followed for the exhausted pupils two hours of leisure before going to bed at ten.

' Nothing,' Ferrey wrote,[4] ' could exceed the stern manner in which this routine was carried out ; and excellent as was the course of studies pursued in the office, the cold, cheerless, and unvarying round of duty, though enlivened by the cheerful manner and kind attention of the elder Pugin, was wretched and discouraging.'

As was inevitable, the cruel rigour of Mrs. Pugin's rule led

¹ *Ferrey* ; p. 26.   ² *Ib.* ; p. 27.
³ *Ib.*   ⁴ *Ib.* ; pp. 27–8.

to violent dissensions between her and her husband's pupils, and to him frequently fell the disquieting task of trying ' to calm the raging storm and mediate between the belligerent parties.' [1] Nevertheless, such was the elder Pugin's pre-eminence, his office was always filled with pupils. ' It is remarkable, however,' Ferrey somewhat naively adds [2] ' that of the many youths who were articled to him very few followed the profession of architects in after life. Some died, others changed their pursuits or succeeded to independent property.' However, ' to use one of Pugin's quaint expressions, none " *sunk into filth or perished on the scaffold*," a prediction which he was wont to make when much irritated by idleness or want of skill in any of his pupils.' [2]

The elder Pugin, in fact, like many another pleasant man, had married above his personality, and other people paid for it besides himself. The younger Pugin, of course, paid less than the others : he was an only child, and a delicate one at that, and in consequence, beyond passing through the usual elementary courses and making himself master of perspective, he underwent little of the drudgery of the school, ' as the labour of drawing out the details of building in a strictly geometrical manner from given measurements little suited his active habits or mental energy.' [3] Instead, he concentrated on sketching from nature, and, a love of architecture manifesting itself in spite of his environment, on making drawings of Westminster Abbey. It was at this period that he was accustomed to say to his mother : " My own dear mother, how happy I am ! Nobody can be happier than I." [4]

However, he was soon to discover that this was not the case, and that he himself could be happier elsewhere, with the result that on 20th August 1867, Thomas Grieve could write to Edward Pugin : ' It may be interesting to you to know that

[1] *Ferrey* ; p. 28.   [2] *Ib.*   [3] *Ib.* ; p. 35.
[4] *Ib.* ; p. 69 ; quoting letter from Mrs. Pugin to her sister, 1832.

your father, when quite a boy, left his father's office and entreated to be employed by me, to which I consented.'[1] The immediate causes of this step do not appear, Ferrey merely stating[2] that ' the duties of his father's office became utterly insupportable.' But one thing seems clear enough : that the young Pugin, at an early age, discovered that ability to make a jest of things was not sufficient, that there was a reality which had to be faced ; and in consequence directed upon that reality his capacity for seeing the salient points of events, for making a judgment on things perceived, and for giving decisive expression to an idea. As a child, he had made use of his faculties in the play of a child. But childhood ended very soon. It was as though some inner prompting had warned him that he should have but eight lustra of life in which to do what would be claimed to be the work of a hundred years, and that he could not begin the independent exercise of his faculties too soon.

In the meantime, however, life in the Pugin family was not all school drudgery combined with courageous lighthearted-ness under a well-nigh intolerable regime. It was necessary that the elder Pugin and his pupils, in the pursuit of knowledge, of materials for books, and of examples for Nash, should go on architectural tours.

At first, these tours were very much limited in extent by the problem of expense, but the success of the *Specimens of Gothic Architecture*, of which the first volume was published in 1821, encouraged the elder Pugin to extend his architectural activities to the Continent, and on some of these trips he was accompanied by his wife as well as by his pupils. Her letters, written to her only sister, Miss Selina Welby, ' whom she loved with a degree of affection hardly to be exceeded,'[3] give glimpses both of her son and of her own character. On 24th September 1824, she wrote :

---

[1] *Art-Architect ;* p. 9.   [2] *Ferrey ;* p. 61.   [3] *Ib. ;* p. 22.

'My dear boy bears up tolerably; he dislikes Paris altogether, and rejoices to think we are to set off for Fontainebleau on Saturday next week, to walk in the Forest, take sketches, and eat the finest grapes in the world; but of the latter *I* must be very cautious. I bless the kind Providence which gave me the means of obtaining them; and in this manner it seems to me we should think of all our departed joys and pleasures, not so much passing our time in regretting their loss as in gratitude and thanksgiving, that we *have* been indulged in the course of our lives with the possession of them; for seeing that ourselves, and all things around us, are *intended* to be continually changing, this mode of reasoning can alone produce that sincere resignation which is so much our duty, and is, in fact, that peace surpassing all understanding.'

In parenthesis it may be remarked that her husband's pupils would seem to have been unable, however sincere their resignation, to attain to any peace at all. But to a woman with Mrs. Pugin's capacity for doing her duty such a consideration would not occur. She continues:

'It is thus I have reasoned with my sister [1] Lafitte, who, from shutting herself up to uninterrupted sorrow and regret, began to think there were no pleasures left for her; but I got her, the other day, to go with us to dine in the country, and she seemed really to enjoy it, and the next morning, when I called to see how she was, I found her, both in health and spirits, another creature! To-morrow, if please God I am well enough, I take her to see my niece and my new little great nephew.' [2]

On another occasion she wrote of her son:

'If he understood how to dress himself I should consider him an universal genius; and a most orderly good creature, if he had not had the skin of his nose twice torn off by a battle of pillows in the suite of rooms they have above, quite out of

---

[1] I.e. sister in law.   [2] *Ib.;* pp. 22–3.

my observation; however, the second time it happened, I brought him down to a room near me. He does not dislike a little play, but he works infinitely more than he plays, while the rest play infinitely more than they work. His father calls this work of Paris [1] " Augustus's work," and well he may, for he has done more than three parts of it, and made sketches and coloured them for the first time from Nature, and written some very good descriptions. *Nevertheless the fellow cannot dress himself.* When he heard that you left Beverley without seeing the churches, he declared, had he been with you, you would have found him the most restive animal you ever posted with; nor whip, nor spurs, nor anything else would have got him on before seeing those churches.' [2]

The habit thus early formed, which was to kill him in the end, of doing infinitely more work than other people even when it was their work that he was engaged on, would seem nearly to have killed him at the age of fifteen. For in 1827 Mrs. Pugin wrote to her sister :

' My poor Augustus has latterly been very unwell, and on Thursday last alarmed us much; he went before breakfast to draw in Notre Dame, when suddenly (as he described his sensation) the whole building on every side seemed breaking and tumbling to pieces, and the pavement so agitated he could not stand; fortunately Mr. Nash was drawing with him, and got him into a coach and brought him home pale as death.' [3]

In the same letter that thus foreshadowed dimly the manner of her son's death, Mrs. Pugin delivered an unconscious prophecy :

' No sooner is a child born here of good family,' she wrote, ' than they immediately are thinking of a proper alliance. Mad[e] Lafitte told her brother and me, she had mentioned to

---

[1] *Paris and its Environs, displayed in a series of two hundred Picturesque Views, from Original Drawings, taken under the Direction of A. Pugin, Esq., The Engravings under C. Heath, Esq.* ; 1828–1831.

[2] *Ferrey* ; pp. 35–6.   [3] *Ib.* ; p. 39.

her daughter that a marriage between Clara and Augustus would be a very proper union, and hinted she would have a very good fortune; whether this was said as a matter of politeness, or more seriously, it is impossible to say, for Mad^e Lafitte is very polite. I laughed with my son about it, when he was quite indignant; "*What! marry a Catholic? that surely will never happen.*" But who can read the book of fate, fast closed, except the page that time doth hourly turn?'

And Ferrey sombrely adds: 'Who indeed could have foreseen that the boy, so indignantly repudiating the idea of marrying a Catholic, should in after years not only form such an alliance, but become one of the stoutest champions of the Roman Catholic Church.'[1]

Who indeed? Particularly as he 'had then no leaning whatever towards the Roman Catholic creed, and was loud in his denunciations of the men who, wanting in appreciation of the exquisite beauty of mediæval art, could mutilate their buildings by interpolations of incongruous character, fill their churches with altars and decorations of debased Italian design, and permit the very precincts of their sacred buildings to be defiled.'[2]

His sentiments in regard to the externals of nineteenth-century Catholic worship were to remain unchanged to the end.

In the meantime, however, if the visible form of Catholicism filled him with disgust, religion had another aspect which was even more trying to his ardent and sensitive nature: Mrs. Pugin had found the Strait Way, and was not prepared to follow it alone.

Ferrey puts the matter succinctly: 'His mother, who might be designated a woman of extraordinary intellect, though educated and brought up in warm attachment to the Church of England, was not always satisfied with the abilities of the

---

[1] *Ferrey;* pp. 39–40.   [2] *Ib.;* pp. 40–1.

clergy in the parish where she resided, and frequently wandered to neighbouring churches to hear strange preachers. A moderately eloquent sermon would not satisfy her : she needed strong stimulants. In justice,' he quaintly adds, ' it must be stated that she was possessed of considerable literary accomplishments, and frequently contributed articles to the leading periodicals.' [1]

It may be doubted whether even the possession of ' considerable literary accomplishments ' were sufficient to justify the suffering which Mrs. Pugin inflicted on her son.

The trouble was that Mrs. Pugin, in her desire ' to hear strange preachers,' had come under the influence of Edward Irving.

Even if Mrs. Pugin had remained faithful to her early upbringing, the religious lot of her son would not necessarily have been happy, as may be judged from the picture Eastlake [2] gives of established religion in the early nineteenth century :

' Who does not remember the air of grim respectability which pervaded, and in some cases still pervades, the modern town church of a certain type, with its big bleak portico, its portentous beadle, and muffin-capped charity boys ? Enter and notice the tall, neatly grained witness-boxes and jury-boxes in which the faithful are impannelled ; the " three-decker " pulpit placed in the centre of the building ; the lumbering gallery which is carried round three sides of the interior on iron columns ; the wizen-faced pew-opener eager for stray shillings ; the earnest penitent who is inspecting the inside of his hat ; the patent warming apparatus ; the velvet cushions which profane the altar ; the hassocks which no one kneels on ; the poor-box which is always empty. Hear how the clerk drones out the responses for a congregation too genteel to respond for themselves. Listen to the complicated

---

[1] *Ferrey ;* p. 41.   [2] *Eastlake ;* p. 117.

discord in which the words of the Psalmist strike the ear, after copious revision by Tate and Brady. Mark the prompt, if misdirected zeal, with which old ladies insist on testing the accuracy of the preacher's memory by turning out the text. Observe the length, the unimpeachable propriety, the overwhelming dulness of his sermon ! '

' Church ' was only too often like that. But ' Chapel ' was even worse. The young Pugin came in for his mother's ' chapel ' period.

Edward Irving, who was later to take to himself a divine prerogative and ' found ' a Holy Catholic Apostolic Church, was then at the height of his fame. ' People rushed to his meeting-house as to a theatre ; royal dukes, members of both Houses of Parliament thronged the doors of the miserably ugly building in Cross Street, Hatton Garden, where he preached, and hundreds were weekly turned away from want of room.' [1] Mrs. Pugin joined the throng. More, she made sure of being among those admitted, by hurrying through the ghastly Sunday morning breakfast before setting out, whatever the weather, accompanied by her reluctant son and perhaps one of the other pupils.

The tedium of Edward Irving's services was appalling. In his reeking conventicle he was accustomed to preach for three hours at a stretch, though ' he could bring himself down to an hour and forty minutes.' [2] But Mrs. Pugin, who realised the activity of her child's temperament and his passionate love of beauty, who ' even seconded him in the exciting projects in which he embarked, and fed his lively imagination by the relation of marvellous hair-breadth escapes and far-fetched tales ' [3] forced him to sit through those hours of misery. ' It never could have been expected,' Ferrey wrote,[4] ' that such a youth would submit to be pent up for hours together in a pew

---

[1] *Ferrey ;* p. 43.   [2] *Dict. Nat. Biog. ;* XXIX., p. 54.
[3] *Ferrey ;* p. 44.   [4] *Ib.*

like a cattle-pen when so magnificent a building as Westminster Abbey, with its beautiful and solemn services, was
within reach.'

But the young Pugin for a time submitted. He had perforce
to submit. His mind, abnormally keen and sensitive, had had
its first taste of beauty in books of chivalrous romance and in
the architecture of the Middle Ages ; and when it cried out
for more beauty, it was offered a conventicle. More, it was
forced to accept the offer. No wonder that he ' always
expressed his unmitigated disgust at the cold and sterile forms
of the Scotch Church.'[1] Ferrey suggests that ' his mother's
want of judgment . . . helped forward the change in his
religious views which subsequently took place.'[1] It may have
done so. There are many paths leading into the Road to
Rome. ' Disgust ' is the name of one of them.

There was one man who might have saved him from this
disgust, and so, if Ferrey's surmise is correct, from a first step
in the direction of the Catholic Church. But the elder Pugin
cared little about these things. ' Occasionally he attended the
services of the English Church, which he preferred to those
of any other communion.'[2] That was all. He was an amiable
man. He let ill alone. His ' preference ' was not strong
enough to cause him to fight his son's battles.

[1] *Ferrey* ; p. 45.   [2] *Ib.* ; p. 48.

CHAPTER III

CHILDHOOD PASSES

He now began to grow very big, but men did not clearly know what strength he had because he had never been tried . . .

The Saga of Grettir the Strong.

IN July 1826, having already familiarised himself with the Tower of London, the young Pugin, being then fourteen years old, set out on his first independent quest. Its object was the examination of Rochester Castle, a building which was then but little known. As companion he had a youth two years his senior, Benjamin Ferrey, an articled pupil in his father's office, who thirty-five years later was to produce a combined Biography of his friend and of his teacher.

George, fifth Earl of Jersey, the owner of the property, gave leave for all necessary excavations to be made, and the work began.

It was real work, no mere boyish holiday, for it was intended to be the first step towards a book devoted solely to the illustration of castles, and he brought to it a soundness of method and an energy of execution worthy of the magnitude of the proposed undertaking. He began by sketching and measuring every part of the Castle ; and then, having shown the Castle as it stood, he made accurate drawings showing it completely restored.

But that was not enough. Even at that age his interest in architecture went below the surface. He was not content to reconstruct and illustrate an achievement pictorially : he had to discover how that achievement had been brought about. With this end in view, he made great trenches at the base of the walls and ' ascertained the mode of their construction, which proved to be of a solidity and depth fully in keeping with the superincumbent masonry.' [1] The extent of the discovery may hardly seem to justify the exertion and danger involved (on one occasion he narrowly escaped being buried alive, having only just climbed the ladder out of his trench when the planks supporting its sides gave way), but it must be remembered that ' at that time little was known concerning the foundations of these enormous structures ' [2] and that he, a boy after all, was making an original investigation.

The episode of the collapsing trench was not his only escape from death in Rochester Castle. On another occasion, a large beam to which he was clinging while straining to take a measurement, slipped away from its fastenings, throwing him backwards from a height and narrowly missing his head on rebounding from the ground. Had it not done so, as Ferrey truly observes,[3] ' the result would have been fatal.'

In spite of his delicate health, draughtsmanship and hazardous archæology were insufficient to fill the days spent at Rochester. A tale came to his ears that there was treasure hidden in the well in the inner Keep, which communicated with every floor of the building and in which the water was under the tidal influence of the Medway. He hired men and apparatus, and had himself lowered in a bucket to the bottom where he directed the search. A considerable accumulation of rubbish was removed, but all that was found was a few pieces of Elizabethan pottery and glass. With these, the beginnings of an ever-increasing collection of antiquities, he returned to London, to the drudgery of his father's office, and the sabbatarian exactions of his mother.

It was no life for a boy of Pugin's burning intellectual activity. He had had a school career of exceptional brilliance ; he had laboured with vigour and success in a subordinate capacity ; he had carried out an independent and arduous

---

[1] *Ferrey* ; p. 37.　　　[2] *Ib.* ; p. 36.　　　[3] *Ib.* ; p. 38.

undertaking ; he had twice narrowly escaped death. It was time to start a career of his own.

In the following year, the opportunity came. He was then fifteen years old.

A member of the firm of Rundell and Bridge, goldsmiths, while examining ancient plate designs in the Print Room of the British Museum, noticed the young Pugin, with whom he was unacquainted, copying the prints of Albrecht Dürer and Israel Silvester, and had the surprising discernment to realise that the frail youth before him had exactly the genius for which his firm was seeking. The result was his immediate employment, and the production of some fine plate from his designs.

It was remarkably good fortune for so young a boy, and it was more remarkable that he should have been able to make such good use of the opportunity. But a still more surprising turn of fortune awaited him ; for almost at once, in June 1827, an opportunity of fantastic magnitude was offered. Jeffrey Wyatville [1] had nearly completed his reconstructions at Windsor Castle, and King George IV. wished for some Gothic furniture to correspond. He set about getting it by the curious method of sending the commission to a French upholsterer named Morel who had previously been employed at Carlton House. Morel, however, ' feeling the great responsibility of the task thrown upon the firm,' [2] applied to the elder Pugin for assistance ; and the elder Pugin, with a belief in his ability such as is not generally shown by parents in their children, immediately transferred the business to his son.

His confidence was not misplaced, though the task was no light one. All previous attempts to design furniture in the mediæval style had lamentably failed, and it was essential that the designs themselves should be both original and powerful.

[1] Earlier, Jeffrey Wyatt ; but a year later, on the completion of the royal apartments, to have the title of knight added by a grateful monarch to his already ' gothicly' augmented name. He was nephew of James Wyatt, the ' restorer.'

[2] *Ferrey*; p. 53.

That the furniture, in the circumstances, should be wholly successful was not to be expected. Nevertheless, the work was done by a boy of fifteen, and it was not only a marked improvement on previous work in the same style, but was probably better than anyone else then living could have produced. In Ferrey's view,[1] it ' was remarkable for great variety of form and detail, producing an expression of fitness not to be found in other modern attempts.' Pugin's own later opinion of the work was less favourable.

' A man who remains any length of time in a modern Gothic room,' he wrote,[2] ' and escapes without being wounded by some of its minutiæ, may consider himself extremely fortunate. There are often as many pinnacles and gablets about a pier-glass frame as are to be found in an ordinary church, and not unfrequently the whole canopy of a tomb has been transferred for the purpose, as at Strawberry Hill. I have perpetrated many of these enormities in the furniture I designed some years ago for Windsor Castle. At that time I had not the least idea of the principles I am now explaining ; all my knowledge of Pointed Architecture was confined to a tolerably good notion of details in the abstract ; but these I employed with so little judgment or propriety, that, although the parts were correct and exceedingly well executed, collectively they appeared a complete burlesque of pointed design.'[3]

Both criticisms are true. The furniture at Windsor was certainly the product of undirected genius. Pugin had not

<hr>

[1] *Ferrey ;* p. 53.   [2] *True Principles ;* p. 35.

[3] The twenty-four massive rosewood chairs in the Throne Room at Buckingham Palace are probably from Pugin's designs. They were made for Windsor Castle between 1828 and 1830, and were brought thence in 1834. They ' are of special interest as examples of fine furniture executed under the influence of the Gothic Revival. They are almost the only examples of " Gothic " furniture in the Royal collections ; and it is worthy of note that though the extensive alterations at Windsor Castle in 1824 by Sir Jeffrey Wyatville were in the Gothic manner, the furniture made for it by Morel & Seddon at the same time was purely classical in design.' Four more chairs of the set are in the Ante Throne Room at Windsor Castle. [*Buckingham Palace ;* H. Clifford Smith ; p. 148.]

yet discovered the principles which his genius required. That discovery, when made, was to bear good fruit.

In the meantime, he had interest and occupation enough ; for, while still engaged on the Castle furniture, he ' formed an acquaintance with a person of inferior position, who, amongst other occupations, was employed at night in a subordinate station in the management of the stage scenery at Covent Garden Theatre.' [1] In other words, Mr. George Dayes (whose father, Edward Dayes, had earned himself a position in *The Dictionary of National Biography* as a water-colour artist and mezzotint engraver before committing suicide in 1804) was gaining a precarious livelihood by doing odd jobs in Morel's office by day and acting as a scene-shifter by night. He seems, moreover, to have been a cheerful soul, undepressed by poverty and misfortune ; for, ' when Pugin required him to do anything' (among his other occupations was cleaning Pugin's drawing-boards), ' he invariably replied in a droll manner, adding gesture, and imitating the voice of some well-known actor.' [2] Pugin was amused by George Dayes, and his imagination was fired by the latter's descriptions of stage machinery. One evening he allowed himself to be persuaded to accompany his new friend behind the scenes.

It was the first time he had entered a theatre. His mother had seen to that.

The stimulus was immense, and, overburdened though he must have been by precocious intellectual activity, violent labours, and success, he responded with passionate intensity. Wonder quickly yielded to curiosity as to the working of what he saw, and curiosity to suggestions of methods of improvement to Bartley the stage-manager and Messrs. Grieve the scene-painters. He made himself sufficiently useful, in fact, for him to be allowed to continue his theatrical experiences. But that was not enough. As at Rochester, where he could

[1] *Ferrey ;* p. 57.   [2] *Ib. ;* p. 58.

not rest till he had laid bare the foundations, so now, too, he had to get to the roots of the matter. The scenery at Covent Garden, though fascinating enough to a neophyte, yet admitted of improvement in design. He went to Messrs. Grieve,[1] therefore, for lessons in the use of the scene-painter's materials, learned the art of distemper painting on canvas, and then proceeded to produce better designs than his teachers ; for Messrs. Grieve and their contemporaries, though capable of producing fine landscapes, were hopelessly at sea when architecture had to be represented, ' the most absurd incongruities ' being called Gothic, and ' compositions full of the grossest anachronisms ' being shown as genuine architecture.[2]

His efforts as a scenic artist, though he did not allow them to interfere with more serious architectural study,[3] were crowned with success, and in 1831, when he was nineteen, he reached the climax of his new career. In that year the ballet of *Kenilworth* [4] was produced, and all the scenery was designed by Pugin and executed under his control. The production ' created a great sensation, presenting as it did in all its features one of the most gorgeous and correct representations which had hitherto been witnessed.' [5]   In addition, ' the architectural portion of this spectacle, which was considerable, showed great originality of treatment, being in striking contrast with the old and ill-painted scenes, wings, and sky-pieces which formed the staple for all scenery no matter in what age or country the story of the opera might be laid.' [5]   *Kenilworth*, in fact, was an outstanding success, and Pugin was responsible.[6]

---

[1] Thomas (1799–1882) and William (1800–1844), whose father also had been a scene-painter. Accounts of them are in *Dict. Nat. Biog.*

[2] *Ferrey ;* p. 59.

[3] In 1829 he ' made the most elaborate drawings of Hatfield House.' (*Ferrey ;* p. 97.) His diary states : ' September 21. Went to Hatfield House with my friend Ferrey to make sketches.' ' October 1st. Started with Ferrey for Hurstmonceaux Castle, to make sketches for Gothic examples.'

[4] He also did the scenery and decorations for *La Juive* and *Count Ory* in Paris. [*Art-Architect ;* p. 3.]

[5] *Ferrey ;* p. 60.

[6] Its music, however, was harshly criticised in *The Athenæum* of July 9, 1831,

This success did not come without hard work. He started by reading everything that had been published on the subject, and then passed on to making innumerable experiments for himself. His parents, seeing him set on his career and making a success of it, handed over to his use the upper floor of their house in Great Russell Street. This, at considerable cost, he converted into a model theatre, ' removing the attic ceiling, cutting away the roof, constructing cisterns, and adapting everything necessary to his object.' [1]

There was nothing of the toy about Pugin's model theatre. It was a serious piece of work with a serious object : the making of experiments and the study of compositions before adoption on the stage ; and for it ' he designed the most exquisite scenery, with fountains, tricks, traps, drop-scenes, wings, soffites, hilly scenes, flats, open flats, and every magic change of which stage mechanism is capable.' [2]

And then, as suddenly as it had begun, his interest in theatrical matters ended. It was not enough to have large parties coming to see his performances ; it was not enough to have mechanism ' so admirably adjusted that the changes in the scenes, wings, and sky-pieces were effected with marvellous rapidity ' [2] ; it was not enough to have what was probably the best model theatre in the world. For his model theatre was but a means to an end, and that end was only scenic representation. Pugin's mind, fed on past magnificence, cried out for reality. His model theatre was as it were only the shadow of a shadow. He put both it and his career aside.

Instead, he bought a boat.

The immediate reasons for the purchase are not known ; but the underlying psychological causes are clear enough.

---

wherein, too, an error of Pugin's was carefully noted : ' King's Theatre. With the " Othello " was coupled the ballet of " Kenilworth." Pour l'amour des convenances, it would not be amiss to inform the scene-painter that ships do not usually lie at anchor with their topsails set.' In such matters, also, Pugin's knowledge was shortly to increase.

[1] *Ferrey ;* pp. 60–1.   [2] *Ib. ;* p. 61.

He bought a boat under the same impulsion which caused
Turner and Prout to draw boats. As Ruskin was later to
write [1] : ' both Turner and Prout had in them an untaught,
inherent perception of what was great and pictorial. They
could not find it in the buildings or in the scenes immediately
around them. But they saw some element of real power in
the boats.'

Pugin, too, ' saw some element of real power in the boats.'
His life, precocious, vivid, and arduous as it had been, and
offering as it did the promise of an eminent position, yet had
never offered the one thing that he required. It had offered
him a shadow, and the reward of producing shadows. He
wished for the substance, and the reward of producing the
substance. But what that substance was—in what artistic
reality consisted—he did not know. He might never know.
But in the meantime, delicate in health, worn by his own
activity in pursuit of the shadow, there was one aspect of
reality within his reach. There was the sea.

The passion for the sea thus engendered was to remain
with him all his life. Years later he made the statement [2] :
" There is nothing worth living for but Christian Architecture
and a boat." But when he first took to the sea his life had not
been fortified by realisation—in his sense of the term—of
Christian Architecture. In the meantime, however, there was
some element of real power in a boat.

---

[1] *The Harbours of England;* 1895 edn. ; p. 46.
[2] Quoted in *The Builder;* Sept. 1852 ; art. by Talbot Bury.

CHAPTER IV

A MAN STOOD UP

It will not be easy to go against this man's luck ; for he is destined to great things.
The Saga of Grettir the Strong.

PUGIN's boats—his first was quite small, but he later became possessed in turn of a smack and of a schooner—gave him more than this ' element of real power ' which his personality required. They fixed in him the slovenliness of dress of which his mother had complained during the French trip of 1827, leading him ' to asume the dress and habits of a sailor, with the exception of his innate horror of tobacco and beer.' [1] They hardened his early delicacy into enormous strength.

The benefits to spring from this mode of life—though even the strength thus acquired was to prove inadequate to the strain later imposed upon it—were naturally not at once appreciated by his parents. They were gentlefolk, and moved in an atmosphere of art and refinement, and they were seeing their delicate and only son, after a childhood of great promise, taking up a career of which they strongly disapproved ; and then, to their even greater disapproval, throwing it away when it was achieving success, and instead (with the exceptions of tobacco and beer) assuming the dress and habits of a sailor. It is little wonder that on one occasion his father, ' on meeting a friend, exclaimed with much grief, " God bless my soul, it was but this morning I met my boy Auguste in the disguise of a common sailor, carrying on his shoulder a tub of water which he had took from the pompe of St. Dunstan ".' [2] And Ferrey sympathetically adds : ' Few things probably could

---

[1] *Ferrey ;* p. 63.   [2] *Ib.*

have so severely shocked the finely poised susceptibilities of the elder Pugin.' [1]

The younger Pugin, however, was not to be deterred by any shocks to the refined tastes of his father. He had other things to which to attend. He had found the sea. He had found an enthralling hobby. He had found that a little money could be made by independent coastwise trading.[2] He had found that his collection of antiquities could be increased by extending his voyages to the Continent. He was free and he was happy, and whenever his voyages brought him within reach of interesting buildings he could stay and make drawings.

This happy-go-lucky life was not to last. In 1830 he was shipwrecked, ' on the Scotch coast, some distance below Leith, where he and his men all but perished,' [3] and in consequence arrived in Edinburgh in a destitute condition. There he made himself known to an architect named Graham, who, ' to use his own expression, completely " *rigged him out*," provided him with money, and what was more to the point gave him sound advice.' [4] This advice was that he should stop squandering his small substance on the sea, and, instead, return to the serious pursuit of that profession for which he was so clearly fitted. As a reminder, Mr. Graham added his own pocket compasses. Pugin took the compasses and the advice. On the compasses was engraved : *James Gillespie Graham, architect, Edinburgh*, 1830. Pugin made use of them for the rest of his life. They appear—though incorrectly drawn—in the portrait of him painted, years later, by his friend John Rogers Herbert, R.A.

---

[1] Perhaps one thing might have done so ; to hear his son ' burst into a fit of laughter when accosted as an egg-merchant by some of his friends, in allusion to his freight.' [*Ferrey ;* p. 59.]

[2] Samuel Smiles, in his zeal for materialistic edification, fell into error in the case of Pugin (as well as in other cases) in his *Self-help, with Illustrations of Character and Conduct*. Pugin did not go to sea with the idea of gaining profit either from ' the discipline of labour ' or from petty trading. He went to sea because he liked it ; and the rest followed. Similarly, he did not go to the theatre because he wished to become a scenic artist : he became a scenic artist because he liked going to the theatre.

[3] *Ferrey ;* p. 62.   [4] *Ib.*

It was indeed time that Pugin settled down to serious work. He was eighteen years old. He had unbounded energy and ability. The increasing movement of the Gothic Revival was flowing past him like a tide.

The steps which he took to settle himself in life were characteristic of the thoroughness of his nature : he started a business of his own ; and he got married.

The business arose from the nature of his father's ' ghostly ' occupation. For the elder Pugin was chiefly occupied as an architectural draughtsman. That is to say, he and his pupils made accurate drawings from the rough sketches of architects whose knowledge of Gothic was not equal to their intentions. The younger Pugin, on his return from his interview with Mr. Graham, joined in this work and soon became known ' as the great authority in his special department,' with the result that ' many leading architects placed their rough sketches in his hands in order to have the detail drawings accurately prepared.' [1]

The trouble, however, was that, while the Pugins could supply architects with the designs which they required, ' very few carvers could execute a foliated string-course or spandril with correct feeling, and the general notion amongst workmen was that anything grotesque would do for Gothic decorations, as grace and beauty were supposed by them to be alien to the style.' [1] The British workman, in fact, as a result of long training, could produce sham Grecian ; but he could not produce sham Gothic—a fact likely to be detrimental to the Pugins' reputation as delineators—and he did not know how to set about learning.

But the young Pugin knew how to produce it, and he saw his opportunity. He leased extensive premises in Hart Street, Covent Garden, having still ' a lingering affection for his old haunts,' [2] enlisted one or two clever carvers whom he himself

---

[1] *Ferrey ; p. 64.*　　　　[2] *Ib. ; p. 65.*

had taught, and let it be known that he would ' supply all the ornamental portions of buildings which could by possibility be executed apart from the structure and be fixed afterwards.' [1]

At first the venture was a success, for Pugin had studied genuine mediæval work and could produce sound stuff to correspond with the architects' drawings. Orders came in extensively, particularly from Scotland and Ireland, where adequate artificers were even scarcer than in England. It looked as though he were solidly established. He took the next step towards settling down. He married.

One result of choosing Covent Garden for the site of his factory had been that he was able to keep in touch with his former theatrical friends, occasionally going to the theatre ' to see how matters were going on, and to enjoy a little conversation with the Messrs. Grieve.' [2] It was probably owing to this circumstance that he met Miss Anne Garnet, for she was a grand-niece of Edward Dayes—the father of the man who first took him behind the scenes. The courtship was short, and in 1831, to his parents' displeasure, though ' they did not withhold their sanction to the match, fearing to thwart him in a matter of such delicate nature,' [2] they were married.

After the marriage, they returned to live with his parents at their house in Great Russell Street, a circumstance hardly likely to make matters easier. The marriage, however, while it lasted, was happy, and his wife ' showed a most affectionate regard, and exercised a beneficial influence over him.' [2] He was to need her affectionate regard. For it was while they were living there that the crash came.

The cause of the disaster was that, while Pugin was a Gothicist by nature and by training, he was a business man by neither. In consequence, he was incapable ' of estimating the sufficient profit to be attached to labour and materials in order to secure a proper return for his invested capital,' and could

---

[1] *Ferrey;* p. 65.   [2] *Ib.;* p. 68.

not exercise ' sufficient check over the art-workmen in his employ.' [1] The financial state of the business rapidly grew worse, and in the summer of 1831 non-payment of rent led to his being seized and placed in a spongeing house near Chancery Lane.

Late the same evening, his father, who had pursuaded a Mr. Weale and a Mr. Hogarth, architectural publishers, to go with him to Cursitor Street and become security for payment of the debts, managed to obtain his release. Bankruptcy, nevertheless, would almost certainly have followed but for the generosity of Miss Selina Welby—that sister whom his mother ' loved with a degree of affection hardly to be exceeded.' According to Ferrey,[2] she paid off all his debts. This, however, is contradicted by a letter from J. R. Herbert to Edward Welby Pugin dated 29th October, 1867,[3] in which he states that Pugin gave notes of hand to all creditors and later paid them in full. But Miss Welby's part must not be minimised. She at least seems to have relieved him of pressure and set him on his feet again ; and Pugin profited by her generosity, for ' he had sense enough to see that he was not fitted for commercial enterprise ' and determined ' henceforward to stick closely to the exercise of his profession in a regular manner.' [4] Next year, however, an even more overwhelming blow was to fall.

On 27th May, 1832, at the house in Great Russell Street, Anne Pugin died, a week after the birth of her only child.

The shock was terrible, ' a fearful blow to his sensitive mind,' [4] and he was overcome with grief.

' I feel somewhat desolate to-day,' his mother wrote to Selina Welby,[5] ' for I am without either father or son. My son travelled by the night coach for Christchurch, and my husband went this morning ; the funeral, which will be

---

[1] *Ferrey* ; p. 66.   [2] *Ib.* ; p. 68.   [3] *Art-Architect* ; p. 100.
[4] *Ferrey* ; p. 68.   [5] *Ib.* ; pp. 68–9.

merely placing my poor Anne in the vault, will, I suppose, take place on Friday. It was my intention, as a consolation to Augustus, to have attended myself, but I feel the journey would be beyond my strength. He is to sleep in a double-bedded room with his father, so he will not be left alone at night, that is the dread hour. I have never left his bedside since the death of his wife, nor known what an unbroken night's rest was before last night. Wretched he will be, grieved to the soul, but in this world, where fortitude is so necessary, he must strive to obtain it; and may Almighty God, of His infinite mercy, sanctify unto him all his sorrows! I frequently think how often he used (before he was fourteen years of age) to say, " My own dear mother, how happy I am ! nobody can be happier than I." Alas, alas ! Look over the six years which have passed since that period, and we find a whole life of woe, such as is rarely experienced by the generality of men, huddled into it. From his works and his woes he has already experienced a long life, and when he dies he will not die without some dignity, and have his name perpetuated.'

The choice of Christchurch as burial-place holds an additional pathos; for in the ' whole life of woe ' which Pugin experienced before he came of age it was associated both with happiness and with ambitions. When he was thirteen years old, and thought that nobody could be happier than himself, he made a drawing of the Priory Church and the ruins of the Castellan's house; and in 1828, after a severe illness, he stayed there with his mother while convalescing, and ' was truly delighted with the magnificent Priory church, the ruins of the castle and the castellan's house, as well as the beautiful marine scenery of the town and neighbourhood.' [1] Christchurch, in fact, gave him both Christian Architecture and boats, and it ' struck him as being particularly well calculated for his retreat when desiring to study apart from

[1] *Ferrey;* p. 70.

the turmoil of business in London.'[1] He decided, therefore, to make it his home, and began negotiating for ' the site for a house in a retired situation near the town of Christchurch, called Holfleet,[2] commanding a view of all the objects he admired.'[3]

It was not to be. He was under age, and his father, ' remembering and disapproving his conduct in connection with the theatrical world,'[3] refused to become guarantor or to give his consent to the transaction.

He could not live at Christchurch, though for some time the ambition remained. But he could choose as his wife's resting-place the Priory that he loved, near the spot that might have been their home.

She was buried in the north chancel aisle of the church,[4] opposite the Berkeley chantry, and the year after his conversion to Catholicism he covered her grave with a black marble slab, inlaid with a brass plate [5] inscribed in beautiful Gothic lettering : *Here lieth the Body of Anne, the first and beloved wife of Augustus Welby Northmore de Pugin, Architect. who departed this life at London, on the xxvii day of May in the year of our Lord, Mdcccxxxii. R.I.P. Amen.*

The use of the ' de ' in his surname is noteworthy. It is one of the few occasions in his life on which it occurs. But it was the only thing that remained to him in which he could do her honour : she had been the wife of a struggling architectural craftsman and a ruined man ; but she had been the wife of a nobleman as well.

On his watch he scratched another inscription : *This day,*

---

[1] *Ferrey ;* p. 70.
[2] *I.e.* Hoffleet Farm, parcel of the Manor of Fernhules or Fernhill Court.
[3] *Ferrey ;* p. 71.
[4] ' The funeral was remarkable. The interment did not take place till the 15th of June at 8 o'clock P.M., the remains being brought to the church on the 8th of June, and deposited during the interval in Prior Draper's Chapel. The service was read in the choir, the coffin being placed in the centre, an unusual practice.' [*Ferrey ;* p. 70.]
[5] Not a brass cross, as stated by Ferrey, who also gives the inscription incorrectly.

May 27th, 1832, *my dearest Anne died unto this world, but lived unto God.* She 'died unto this world,' but her memory remained with him to the end. Until his death, there hung in his room a miniature of a young woman. It was not a portrait of his wife; but it was like her. Until his death, also, there lay in his studio a heavily-corded packing-case. No one knew what it might contain, and it was not the most convenient object to be perpetually in the workroom of a busy man. But on one occasion it had a use. A window refused to open, or to shut; or some similar mishap occurred; and John Hardman Powell, Pugin's son in law and the husband of Anne Garnet's only child, stood upon the packing-case to rectify the matter. At that moment Pugin entered the room, and immediately, almost in a frenzy of rage, ordered Powell to step down. After Pugin's death the case was opened. It contained a rosewood work-box from which the tray had been removed and in which was a death-mask of his first wife, a cast of one of her hands, and a piece of unfinished needlework, a garment intended for her child. It appeared that she had been small and of a delicate beauty. She was eighteen when she died.[1]

---

[1] Information of Mrs. W. H. Watts.

CHAPTER V

" Of Grettir I can say nothing, for his condition seems to me like a rolling wheel. Strong though he is, I fear he will have more dealing with trouble than with kinsmen's support."

The Saga of Grettir the Strong.

THERE is a feverish atmosphere about the next three years of Pugin's life, though the facts are simple enough. On 19th December, 1832, after a long illness, the elder Pugin died, predeceasing by four months his wife, who died on 28th April, 1833 ; and Pugin, being now of age and not entirely without fortune, went to live at Salisbury, married a second time,[1] removed to the Plains of Waterloo at Ramsgate to be near his aunt, Selina Welby, whose heir he eventually became, and settled down to those architectural and theological studies which were to change the whole course of his life.

The cause of the feverish atmosphere of this period is to be found in the reason for his going to Salisbury—the Cathedral. For the Cathedral as it were sums up the contrast which was during that period tormenting him : it was both his torture and his delight. Any other place with a fine mediæval building would have suited him equally well as a residence ; but he had visited Salisbury four years before when on his way to Christchurch with his mother, and the mutilated Cathedral drew him back. It was only after his return that he realised to the full the extent of those mutilations.

Ferrey[2] gives a partial list : ' The destruction of the Hungerford and Beauchamp Chapels, and the removal of the porch of the north transept ; the demolition of the screen

---

[1] In 1833 ; to Louisa Burton.   [2] *Ferrey* ; p. 73.

which separated the Lady Chapel from the choir, and the elevation of the pavement so as to alter all the proportions of the former; the destruction of the Saints' Chapels in the western transept, and of the rood-loft before the choir; the removal of the monuments from their appropriate places transported in order to line the arcades of the Nave; and the destruction of the detached belfry tower.' The contrast between the spirit of the men who raised up such buildings and the spirit of those who hastened their decay was becoming painfully obvious; and it was becoming increasingly obvious that he himself, at any rate doctrinally, was on the side of the despoilers. The seeds of an impossible position were being sown in his mind: for he was become a lover of the beauty of God's house: and in that house God's glory no longer dwelt. There was something wrong. Whatever he studied, wherever he went, there was both beauty and something wrong. There was always this agonising contrast.

In the meantime, however, there was his own work as architectural student to which to attend, and he set about the matter with his customary intensity, though the more he worked the more painful the contrast became.

To start with, there was the Cathedral itself, mutilated but still lovely, with drawings of which he filled a quarto volume. And then there was the Cathedral library, access to which he gained through the friendship of his wife with the librarian, he Rev. John Greenly, a man who had the distinction of having served as a naval chaplain at Trafalgar. 'For many hours together,' Ferrey states,[1] ' he was in the habit of shutting himself up copying the beautiful illuminations of the ancient missals and service books. There was not a page of any interest from which he failed to glean something; and he made a surprising number of drawings in an incredibly short space of time.' And finally, since no one city could offer

[1] *Ferrey;* p. 93.

enough to satisfy his passionate ardour in search of mediæval beauty, there was all that the rest of England could offer to an enthusiastic traveller.

He set out on his tireless search for ancient beauty ; and he found the Road to Rome.

The stages of this search are given in a series of letters to a friend in Salisbury named Osmond, ' whom he found desirous of acquiring a knowledge of mediæval architecture.' [1]

The first of these, dated from Wells in Somersetshire, ' is headed by a clever sketch, contrasting a modern tablet stuck against a wall with a beautiful canopied tomb and recumbent figure.' [2]

' My dear Sir,

If you want to be delighted, if you want to be astonished, if you want to be half mad, as I at present am, for God's sake come over to Wells. The most magnificent things for detail that can be seen, splendid remains of every style, and every description of Gothic architecture. You have no conception of the magnificence of the cathedral, &c. One day would suffice. I am well acquainted with everything here, and have got introductions to all the most secret corners ; and I declare I would not leave you till you had seen every interesting object in the place. Pray come, I entreat of you. I leave here either at the end of the week—that is the beginning of next, about Tuesday or Wednesday. . . . I would not think of wishing you so much to come down here were I not certain you would be delighted. No *artists* indeed ! The figures of the west front are magnificent—splendid specimens of sculpture. Tell that to Mr. Lucas [3] ; and tell him that the *antique* fades away before the *ancient*. Gothic for ever !

---

[1] *Ferrey ;* p. 74.   [2] *Ib. ;* p. 75.
[3] Probably Richard Cockle Lucas (1800–1883), sculptor and enthusiastic student of the Elgin Marbles, who made the statue of Sir Richard Colt Hoare, second baronet, F.R.S., F.S.A., in Salisbury Cathedral.

Mr. Caunter, one of the vicars here, is most anxious to see you, so pray come down and don't be ruled by your wife, for without you make a pilgrimage to this shrine you will never obtain absolution for the number of *blisters* [1] you have been the instrument of fixing and polluting against ancient arts. Give my kind remembrances to Mrs. Osmond and all my good friends at Salisbury, and believe me your most sincere friend and fellow labourer,

A Pugin,

Freemason, though not a member
of the man-milliner's lodge.

Send a line to me by post : direct Mr. Pugin, at Mr. Hatch's, Vicar's Close, Wells.' [2]

The next letter was written from Ramsgate, and the heading was beautifully inscribed and illuminated; sketches illustrative of the works criticised were included in the text.

' Saint Laurence Octr xxvij anno domini mdcccxxxiij

Dear Osmond

I fear you will by this time have thought me neglectful in not acknowledging the receipt of a most acceptable and kind present from you in the shape of an enormous Cheddar cheese, which although not strictly Gothic in its present shape may be daily rendered more so by cutting it into 4, which will make it a quatrefoil. But I fear me much in the course of a short time its style will be scarcely perceptible, as it will have gone through such a variety of form, owing to the extreme partiality of all at home to do full justice to its merits. It is, in truth, excellent, and the only drawback on the enjoyment of it is that we have not the kind donor to partake of it with us, which was the case the last time I had the pleasure of

---

[1] The term *blisters*, ' frequently employed by Pugin, referred to the numerous tablets which Mr. Osmond was in the habit of affixing to the walls of churches as memorials.' [*Ferrey*; p. 91.]

[2] *Ferrey*; pp. 75–6.

tasting such cheese. I should have sent a letter off directly on our receiving your present, had I not been absent on a journey when it came, not in search of the beautiful but the needful, which is not so easily obtained ; from which I am only just returned. I have long had it in contemplation to send you an account of my proceedings after I left you at Exeter, and as nothing is like the present time I will proceed, with the help of my memory and memorandum book, to give you a full, particular, and true account of my adventures. After leaving you at Exeter I had a most delightful day's ride to Bristol through Taunton, where I had a *sight* of the magnificent tower whose fame you have no doubt heard of. It is without exception the finest tower of the kind in England, though I must say we are deficient in this country of those magnificent masses which are to be seen in the towns of France, Flanders, and Germany ; for beautiful as the Tower at Taunton is it still seems to want something to carry it off at the top. The towers of Boston and St. Nicholas at Newcastle are in this respect far preferable.

While at Bristol I paid particular attention to the Cathedral, where I find many things deserving most particular attention. This Cathedral has been generally overlooked as undeserving of notice, but the fact is that there are parts about it equal to anything in the country. The groining of the aisles, the carving in parts of the stalls, the vestry, the tombs in the aisles round the choir, the great west window, the Norman entrance to the Chapter House from the cloisters, all are most interesting, and to real Gothic men, like you and me, it affords a great treat. The east window is so truly beautiful that I have just marked out the tracery of it for you ; the original glass is still in it, and the effect is wonderfully rich and varied. I then steamed from Bristol to Chepstow in Monmouthshire ; here is, I may say, one of the most perfect castles I have ever seen. The parts about it are magnificent,

and the extent of mouldings immense. To give you some
idea of its preservation, the wooden gates are all remaining;
they are composed of three pieces of oak halved together
crossways, then two thicknesses of one and a-half oak plank
with a sheeting of iron, and bound with iron bars bolted
through all. It is to be remembered that the tide from the
Severn rises higher here than at any other part of the world,
the rise and fall being at spring tides upwards of seventy feet.
Leaving this interesting spot, I walked by the side of the
river Wye to Tintern Abbey, distant about eight miles.
Although I can manage to give you an idea of a Gothic
building, it is quite impossible to convey by writing any
conception of the beautiful scenery of the banks of the river
Wye. The richest foliage and loftiest trees arise up amid
overhanging masses of rock, and the terrific and beautiful are
everywhere blended. I ascended a place called the Wyndcliff,
where I had the sight of four cathedrals and fourteen counties.
The day was remarkably fine, and those views you and I saw
on the Exeter road faded to nothing before it. A heavy
thunder-storm coming on, I was glad to push on for the quiet
inn at Tintern, where I rested for the night, and next morning
proceeded to view the far-famed abbey. The situation is
beautiful; as a ruin the building is also; but dare I oppose
the torrent of popular opinion and not admire Tintern Abbey
as a building? yes I dare, and I say that, as a building, it is
anything but admirable. Were I to express this opinion to
the tourist and the general observer I should be set down
either for an ignorant brute or an opinionated upstart; but I
am sure if you and I were to go over it together you would
agree with me. The only thing really worthy of admiration
is the west window, which is very beautiful, and of which I
send you a sketch; but the rest of the building is by no
means equal, and the plan, mouldings, windows, &c., are very
common-place; I therefore mounted the Hereford coach

with four horses, and a very pleasant ride brought me to that city—an old fashioned but not ancient looking town, common brick houses, dull shops and empty streets being the features of Hereford. Maddened by the sight I rushed to the cathedral ; but horror ! dismay ! the villain Wyatt [1] had been there, the west front was his. Need I say more ? No ! All that is vile, cunning, and rascally is included in the term Wyatt, and I could hardly summon sufficient fortitude to enter and examine the interior. In this church there is much to admire, a good deal to learn, much to deplore. 1st, Much to admire :— the Saxon parts of the nave, the stalls, the bishop's throne, the tombs, the Lady Chapel, the vicar's cloisters, are all most beautiful and interesting, of which you may be sure I took complete sketches. 2nd. A great deal to learn :—there are portions of the Lady Chapel and the Bishop's throne that are perfectly unique and truly extraordinary. 3rd. Most to deplore :—what do you think of a regular Roman altar-screen, a modern window over it, with the Last Supper from West, like a great transparency ? " What do you think of it ? " said a canon, triumphantly, when he showed it to me. " Think of it ! " said I ; " why I think it is yet more execrable than the window of New College Chapel." The canon was dumb. Then, only conceive the fine Saxon ornaments imitated in plaster in the most wretched style ; a plain ceiling to the nave ; the Lady Chapel filled with bookcases, and the end towards the church plastered up ; the building ruinous in many parts, and the cloisters absolutely left to fall. All these things raise emotions in the breast of the real antiquarian not easily subdued. I next shaped my course to Malvern, to see the abbey there and the celebrated Hills. Here is a church in which the stained glass has not fallen a victim to Protestant zeal. It is truly magnificent, and the drawing of the figures is

---

[1] James Wyatt ; 1746–1813 ; the ' restorer ' of Salisbury and other cathedrals, and architect of Fonthill Abbey, Wiltshire.

correct and beautiful, the colouring rich and varied. These windows may be rated among the finest specimens of English glass of the 15th century. The paving-tiles are likewise decidedly the finest in the kingdom ; such a variety of patterns and such a quantity of tiles I never saw anywhere. A few years ago a meeting of the fashionables of Malvern was called to subscribe towards the repairs of the delapidated building, and by the help of raffles, &c., a few pounds were collected. Two hodfulls of mortar were got to repair the church, and the remainder of the money expended in putting in a window of the aisle the arms of the subscribers in stained glass, with their names in full, a monument of their folly and arrogance. The very mullions in which the glass is placed are rotten and falling. The church itself is in dreadful repair ; fall it must, and all that is to be hoped is, that in its fall it may annihilate those whose duty it was to have restored it ; but of this we may be sure, that if it falls while there is a congregation within its walls, it will clear some away that ought to be got rid of, for such a set of lounging idlers as the fashionables of Malvern are only to be matched at Brighton or Cheltenham. I must now for the present conclude, leaving the rest of my journey, which is too extensive for one letter ; and if you have the patience to permit it, I will send you soon the second part of my travels in search of the beautiful. And now, with kindest remembrances to your wife and family, believe me now and ever your most sincere friend and fellow-mason,

A. W. Pugin.' [1]

The letter describing the second part of his ' travels in search of the beautiful ' is as follows :—

' Island of Ely ! ! ! January, Thursday, 1834.
Dear Osmond,

I fear by this time you have thought that I did not mean to fulfil my promise of sending you another long letter,

[1] *Ferrey* ; pp. 76–82.

containing the second part of my travels in search of the picturesque and beautiful, but I assure you I have not forgotten it, as this epistle feebly showeth. I left off my last account at Malvern, from thence I proceeded to Worcester. Here I was much disappointed ; with the exception of Prince Arthur's Chantry the church does not contain a monument of any consequence, and the building itself was dreadfully battered about in the Civil Wars, when Worcester was a stronghold of the Cavaliers, and it has been very badly repaired in several places. The cloisters are rather curious, as they contain the ancient lavatories for the monks to wash at. The spirit of the clergy here towards the building is detestable ; but in order to give you an idea of it I will recapitulate an anecdote as I had it from the person who is *nominally* clerk of works to the Cathedral. The western gable having become ruinous, the upper part was required to be taken down. The gable terminates in a rich cross, part of which remained and was very similar to some at Sarum. Accordingly the mason having received orders to restore the gable, caused a rich cross to be cut, together with a base for it, forming the top stone of the gable. All was complete, the cross was finished, attached to the tackle ready for hoisting. A canon appears, and the following conversation ensues. Persons : Canon, a Mason. The scene the west end of the Cathedral.

Canon. Hollo, mason ! what is all this ? what d'ye call it ? what is it for ?

Mason. It is the stone cross, sir, to terminate the western gable.

Canon. Who ordered it ? who is to pay for it ? who gave directions for such a thing ?

Mason. The Chapter, sir, directed me to restore the gable, and as the cross was there——

Canon. Don't talk about the cross being there ; it is

impossible the Chapter intended going to this expense. Why
it is perfectly useless ; the funds will not permit of such things.
(The Dean appears.) Mr. Dean, I was saying it was impossible
you could sanction such a useless expenditure as the cross for
the west end.

Dean. Cross ! what cross ? I ordered the gable to be
plainly restored ; I had no idea of all this.

Mason. The expense of the cross is inconsiderable, and
the effect——

Dean. Don't talk to me of effect, sir. I will not suffer the
cross to be erected ; things must not be done in this manner,
or we shall never know where we are.

The result is plain. The cross I saw lying in his stone-
yard, and the gable ends thus, Λ. As it was the preparation
for the music meeting, the church was turned into a carpenter's
shop for seven weeks previous and three after. Divine service
is suspended during the week. If there were no other, is not
this a decided objection to allowing such a performance ?
You know my opinion well on this subject, and the more I
have an opportunity of judging, the more I am strengthened
in it. Excepting the Cathedral, Worcester does not contain
anything of interest. Disgusted, I was glad to turn my way
to Lichfield, where I duly arrived, but late in the evening and
dripping with wet. . . . [Ferrey at this point gives an
irritating footnote : ' He here relates an amusing incident
somewhat of a Pickwickian character, through a mistake in
entering the wrong bed-room, but it is hardly worth
recording.']

On proceeding to the Cathedral, which from its distant
appearance promised great things, what was my horror and
astonishment on perceiving the west front to have been
restored with brown cement, cracked in every direction, with
heads worked with the trowel, devoid of all expression or
feeling, crockets as bad, and a mixture of all styles. My

surprise, however, ceased on the verger's informing me that the whole church was improved and beautified about thirty years ago by the late Mr. Wyatt. Yes, this monster of architectural depravity—this pest of cathedral architecture—has been here ; need I say more ? I wound myself up to the pitch to bear the sight of the havoc he had committed. Of course here his old trick of throwing the Lady Chapel into the choir by pulling down the altar-screen ; then he has *pewed* the choir *and walled up* the arches of the choir, making the aisles nothing but dark passages. The man, I am sorry to say, who executed the repairs of the building was a pupil of the wretch himself, and has imbibed all the vicious propensities of his accursed tutor, without one spark of even practical ability to atone for his misdeeds. The repairs of the Cathedral are conducted in a most puerile manner. What think you of replacing finials and crockets upon the pinnacles, &c. ? while flying buttresses themselves threaten to fall daily. But, notwithstanding all these defects, there are points in Lichfield Cathedral that render it extremely interesting. First, the stained glass brought from a convent in the Netherlands, and which now fills the east window of the choir, is without exception the most beautiful I have ever seen for richness of colours and beauty of design. Then the nave is truly beautiful, and the chapter house, with library over, is exceedingly interesting. Lichfield is a dull place, without anything remarkable ; and I can assure you in all my travels I have never seen a pleasanter city than Salisbury. From here I then proceeded to Oxford, through that most detestable of all detestable places—Birmingham, where Greek buildings and smoking chimneys, Radicals and Dissenters are blended together. At Oxford I was much delighted with the restoration of Magdalen College Chapel by Mr. Cottingham,[1] which

---

[1] Lewis Nockalls Cottingham, F.S.A. (1787–1847). He was among those who failed in the competition for the design of the new Houses of Parliament.

I can truly say is one of the most beautiful specimens of modern design that I have ever seen, and executed both in wood and stone, in the best manner. It is impossible for me to give you an adequate idea of the interest of the city of Oxford, where at every turning you meet a buttress and face an oriel window. With what pleasure could I walk through the place with you, and point out the various places of interest it contains ! Indeed I fondly cherish the hope of some day taking a long journey with you in pursuit of our favourite object ; for believe me there is no person existing with whom it would afford me so much pleasure to travel as yourself. I fully hope and expect to join you for a few days in the spring on my way to Havre de Grace for a nine month's journey in Normandy and the Low Countries to collect originals and sketches. What a time to look forward to !—what a treat ! I have already completed three new books, and have another in hand to be completed when I return to Ramsgate, as I am at present on another tour, and am now at Ely, where I have arrived to-night. I have as yet seen but little of the Cathedral, but shall be up with the lark to examine it to-morrow.

I have been at the Cathedral all the morning. How I am delighted ! how I am pained ![1] Here is a church, magnificent in every respect, falling into decay through gross neglect. Would you believe it possible ? there is no person appointed to attend to the repairs of the building, and the only person who has been employed during the last sixty years is a brick-layer. Not even common precautions are taken to keep the building dry. The lantern never was completed, and I fear never will be ; but its effect is truly magnificent as it is, and makes one long to see it as originally intended by its great

[1] 'It is said that when Pugin saw the ruins of its [the Lady Chapel's] arcading, once so glorious in its beauty—wherein are carved, in the spandrils above each canopy, incidents in the scriptural and legendary history of the Blessed Virgin—he burst into tears. He estimated the cost of the restoration of the Lady Chapel at £100,000, but said that no workmen could be found competent to do the work.' [*The Cathedrals of England and Wales* ; Francis Bond ; p. 105.]

architect.[1] The fine western tower is falling into great decay,
and alarming fissures have taken place and are becoming
menacing to various portions of the western end which
receive the pressure of the tower. I truly regret to say that
in my travels I am daily witnessing fresh instances of the
disgraceful conduct of the greater portion of the established
clergy. At a place in Lincolnshire called the ——, the Rev.
—— goes to perform the service in *top boots* and *white cord
breeches*. Then I have seen the —— of Lincoln Cathedral,
the Rev. Mr. ——, son of the late Bishop —— (who refused
to subscribe to the erection of his throne in —— Cathedral),
lost £7000 at the last Lincoln races. I can assure you that,
after a most close and impartial investigation, I feel perfectly
convinced the Roman Catholic Church is the only true one,
and the only one in which the grand and sublime style of
church architecture can ever be restored. A very good chapel
is now building in the North,[2] and when it is complete I
certainly think I shall recant. I know you will blame me, but
I am internally convinced that it is right. But of this subject
I beg you will make no mention in your letter to me till I see
you, for then I can more fully explain my ideas. I do most
truly long to hear from you. I shall be back at Ramsgate in
less than a couple of weeks, and must beg you to let me hear
from you before long, as it will be a great pleasure to me. I
am very happy to inform you that the fourth and last number
of my work will be shortly published,[3] and that it is meeting

[Ferrey adds a footnote to this passage :—' Were Pugin now alive what a
" Contrast " he might draw between the condition of Ely Cathedral in 1834 and its
present state !—so beautifully has it been restored by G. Scott (a *Protestant architect*),
and even the Lantern is proposed to be constructed according to its ancient form.']

[2] Probably either St. Peter's, Stonyhurst (1832–6), or St. Ignatius', Preston
(1833–6) ; both of which were designed by Joseph John Scoles (1798–1863), whose
St. John's, at Islington, was heavily (though, as was shown in an editorial article in
The Builder of 1 April 1843, not wholly justly) censured by Pugin in *The Dublin
Review* in one of the articles which were reprinted as *The Present State of Ecclesi-
astical Architecture in England*.

[3] The four books referred to in this letter appear to be the four parts of his
Ornaments of the XVth and XVIth Centuries.

with the greatest success. I shall have several new books to show you when I come down, for I work without ceasing, and trust I continue to improve. Remember me kindly to all my friends at Sarum, and last but not least to your wife; tell her I fear my wife will imitate her example, for a few weeks will, I expect, bring a little Gothic boy or girl, I don't know which yet.[1] God bless you. I trust to find you and yours well in the summer, till then I am, believe me, your most sincere friend and fellow craft, *4094*

A. W. Pugin.'[2]

The proposed expedition to Normandy took place, and in an undated letter to Osmond he wrote:

'I expect to sail next Thursday for France, and if the wind proves fair I shall soon be up to my ears in dilapidated chateaux, ruined abbeys, ancient libraries, venerable cathedrals, ancient towers, and splendid remains of every description of the middle ages. Leave your *blisters*, leave your Doric porticoes, leave all and follow me. When I return I will unfold such a tale as will seduce you from home and lethargy to continental beauties and glory; but I must tear myself from all sublime ideas, and return to common-place matters of fact.'

To this he added a postscript:—

'Please to relate the following fact to Mr. Fisher. Not long since during divine service at a small church that

---

[1] This harmless quip is probably the origin of the tale that, years later, when his mind was failing, he ordered his third wife to produce him a Gothic baby. It seems probable that this and the preceding letter are wrongly dated by Ferrey, and that the dates should be October 1834 and January 1835 :—first, ' the fourth and last number ' of the *Ornaments* was published in 1836, and so would probably not be referred to in Jan. 1834 as shortly to be published; secondly, the delay between Jan. 1835 and 1836 can easily be accounted for by a postponement till his return with fresh drawings from the Continent; thirdly, Edward Welby Pugin was born on 11 March 1835, ' a few weeks ' after Jan. 1835. This emendation fits in, too, with Edward Pugin's statement (*Art-Architect*; p. 76) that his father was received into the Catholic Church in 1835, although 1834 seems to be the commonly accepted date.

[2] *Ferrey*; pp. 83–9.

A design for a Church a design 1821 9 years old
my first design . drawing 1852

has been lately disguised by some modern repairs, a person was struck blind by a flash of lightning, which was attracted by an *iron head of tracery* placed in a wood panel immediately behind him. The electric fluid then descended to the top of the seat, where it left the following extraordinary marks ! [There follows a scrawl which might be read as *CARVE*] During the same storm the house and shops of the founder himself were struck, and 200 tons of one sort of tracery shivered to atoms.

Yours most truly,

A. W. Pugin.' [1]

In those three years Pugin travelled and saw much ; but ' in all his travels he had never seen a pleasanter city than Salisbury.' And nowhere, perhaps, is his life better illustrated than in Salisbury. For in Salisbury is that Cathedral, charged with a richness of beauty, one of the supreme works of the Catholic mind, mellowed by time and mutilated by the hand of man, which was to him both an inspiration and an agony : an inspiration, for it expresses the loveliness of adoration ; an agony, for the wonder of its glass had been shattered by reforming zeal, its tombs and figures had been mauled and scrawled in the incredible vulgarity of sightseers, and over its fabric the fell energy of Wyatt and others had been allowed full sway. And in Salisbury is that little church of St. Osmund, which was the best that Pugin was enabled to do to replace the Cathedral as a home of the Mass.

There is a pathos in the presence in one city of those two churches—the Cathedral, perfect for the purpose for which it had been built and from which purpose it had been diverted ; and, almost under its shadow, the church of St. Osmund, the meagre substitute for that magnificence, which the poverty-stricken Papists of Salisbury only received through the

---

[1] *Ferrey ;* pp. 90–1.

generosity and comparative wealth of one of their number, Mr. John Lambert,[1] a solicitor of that town.

In spite of its meagreness, St. Osmund's has a certain charm —the charm of the inexpensive miniature, of the carefully tended substitute for unattainable things. The church is small. It stands on a minor street, and it is built inexpensively of flint with cut stone at angles and for the tracery of windows. There is no spire—a spire would have cost more than the 'thirty shillings' which Pugin himself was later to make famous. Inside, the roof is plainly timbered, and the wood-work is of an inexpensive kind. Yet the whole effect, though meagre, is not shoddy. The arches are pleasing of pro-portion, the pillars sufficiently sturdy, the simple rood-screen stands before an unexceptionable chancel. The impression given is of dignified poverty, as of one with slender resources who should place all he has at the service of a king in exile.[2]

It is said that when the building of Westminster Cathedral was decided upon, the Gothic and Renaissance styles were vetoed, and the Byzantine chosen, because it was considered neither desirable to compete with the Abbey or St. Paul's, nor possible to excel them. That this principle was not acted upon in the case of St. Osmund's is no loss, since the result remains to symbolise the resurgence of Catholicism in England : the new-budding of a spirit which men had con-sidered dead, unchanged though weak, hopeful though poor ; and since it symbolises, too, the tragedy of Pugin as Catholic architect, as a man of intense creative energy who saw the majesty and loveliness of Gothic and never had full scope to express himself in stone.

[1] Afterwards Rt. Hon. Sir John Lambert, P.C., K.C.B., Mayor of Salisbury in 1854, 'being the first Catholic Mayor of a Cathedral city since the Reformation.' *The Downside Review ;* June 1914 ; p. 213.]

[2] A south aisle has been added to St. Osmund's in recent years, and Pugin's plain capitals have, with doubtful propriety, been carved to make them correspond with the decorated capitals of the new piers.

In Salisbury, also, is that building which is known as ' The Hall of John Halle.' This building, added to the back of his house in 1470 by a wealthy wool-merchant named John Hall for the use of the Guild of Wool Staplers, is now scheduled as an Ancient Monument and used as part of a shop for the sale of glass and china.[1] When Pugin first came to Salisbury it had long been turned into an inn with the house to which it was attached, the open-timbered roof with its fans of plaster being hidden by a flat ceiling, and the room itself being divided into two floors. Under Pugin's direction the ceiling and dividing floor were removed and the building restored as nearly as might be to its original form. It is said that Pugin himself discovered the original glass of the windows hidden away under the roof timbers. There is a tradition, too, that Pugin, who decorated the chimney-piece and other parts of the Hall, painted the coat of arms over the carved oak screen at the south end of the room at a single sitting. Concerning this, Mr. Harry Sirr states that he ' rose exceptionally early and worked for eight hours without a break until he had completed it in colour with his own hand.' [2] This may well be the case : Pugin's powers of concentration and rapid execution were terrific ; and in the presence of the mutilated Cathedral, which he was unable to touch, he may well have turned with passionate energy to the task of preserving and restoring whatsoever he might of Salisbury's mediæval beauty.

It was at Salisbury, too, that Pugin was first to carry out his old ambition and build himself a house.

Only a short time elapsed between his letter to Osmond in which he described a Canon of Worcester stating that a cross

---

[1] Those who may fear for the safety of such a building when used for mercantile purposes, may be at rest : the interest which the occupiers take in the æsthetic and historic qualities of their house is only equalled by the courtesy with which they display it to the enquirer. Would that all ' scheduled ' monuments were in such hands.

[2] *Sirr, F.R.I.B.A.*

was ' perfectly useless ' on a Cathedral, and the commencement of his own building; and when that building was
completed it upheld a cross; for his house contained a chapel;
and in the course of that time he had been received into the
Catholic Church.

CHAPTER VI

CONVERSION

The night passed and the clear dawn appeared.
The Song of Roland.

As was only to be expected—since at that time Catholicity and sincerity were commonly held to be contradictory—Pugin was accused of having become a Catholic on purely æsthetic grounds ; or, as Ruskin was later amiably to express it, of having allowed himself ' to be blown into a change of religion by the whine of an organ-pipe ; stitched into a new creed by the gold threads on priests' petticoats.'

Pugin's character, record, and writings prove that the charge was false.

Men such as Pugin or Huysmans do not become Catholics because of the attractiveness of Catholic art. They become Catholics *through* their love of art. For Catholicism is Universal, and, as such, as it were ' has many mansions,' and each mansion has a different door. That a man should enter through the door named Beauty is to his credit rather than otherwise.

In Pugin's case, to say that he joined the Catholic Church because of his love for Catholic art was particularly absurd ; for in the Catholic England of his day there was no art for him to admire. The Liturgy was robbed of its external magnificence, and the Catholic clergy showed little or no desire for its restoration. The Mass, except for the private chapels of rare wealthy Catholics and a few other places, was said in garrets, in tawdry assembly-rooms, in lofts over stables. Even the private chapels of the wealthy, such as at

Lulworth and Wardour, were nearly all in the Italian style
that he loathed. To a man of Pugin's temperament, in fact,
Rome was not seductive. Even if he had joined the Catholic
Church because of love of her art, it could not have kept him
there.

The charge of insincerity, however, could be pressed one
step further. It could be said that Pugin became a Catholic
not because of the immediate seductive power of Catholic art,
but because he saw that Catholicism was the only means by
which the glories of mediæval art could be restored, and that
he intended by means of Catholicism to be the restorer of
that art. The charge is more subtle, but equally false. One
glance at the state of Catholicism in England at the time will
show this. There was no flood tide of Catholicism in sight
on which Pugin could hope to swim to glory. The Emancipation Act had only recently and grudgingly been passed.
The Oxford Movement was still in its infancy. Newman had
only just produced the first of the Tracts for the Times. In
any case, such personal ambition is entirely contrary to the
whole tenor of Pugin's life. If he joined the Catholic Church
for the sake of glory, it was God's glory he sought, not his
own. Personal ambition is unthinkable in connection with
one whom Mr. Clark justly calls ' this uncouth renegade,
this lob who did ten men's work while they slept, and allowed
them to claim it as their own.' [1]

The fact that Pugin could give it as his opinion in his
letter to Osmond that the Catholic Church was ' the only one
in which the grand and sublime style of architecture can ever
be restored,' does not affect the case. It was merely, so to
say, an additional point, though an extremely uncertain one,
in the Church's favour. The real reason was given in the
same letter to Osmond : that he was ' perfectly convinced
that the Roman Catholic Church is the only true one.'

[1] *Clark;* p. 166.

'I learned the truths of the Catholic religion,' he afterwards said[1], 'in the crypts of the old cathedrals of Europe. I sought for these truths in the modern church of England, and found that since her separation from the centre of Catholic unity she had little truth, and no life; so, without being acquainted with a single Priest, through God's mercy, I resolved to enter His Church.'

In reply to an article in *Fraser's Magazine*, in which his sincerity was questioned, Pugin wrote a letter, justifying his action in detail, which the Editor, whose Protestantism was stronger than his sense of justice, refused to print. Pugin then published it in pamphlet form as *A Reply to Observations which appeared in* Fraser's Magazine *for March* 1837. This pamphlet does not occur in the British Museum Catalogues; but it appears to be the source of the following extract given by Ferrey[2]:—

'My education certainly was not of a description to bias me towards Catholicism; I had been taught to view it through the same distorted medium as the generality of persons in this country; and by the time I was at all capable of thinking on the subject, I was thoroughly imbued with all the popular notions of racks, faggots, and fires, idolatry, sin-purchase, &c., with all the usual tissue of falsehoods so industriously propagated throughout the land, that by such means men may be led to detest and fear what they would receive with joy and reverence, could they but behold its simple truth.

It was, I say, with such perverted feelings I first became a student in ancient art. Soon, however, I found it necessary to begin a new and different course of study to what I had hitherto pursued. The origin, intention, and use of all I beheld around was then perfectly unintelligible to me; but,

---

[1] *The Tablet;* 25 Sep. 1852, p. 617.
[2] Quoted in *Ferrey;* pp. 103–5; wherein, however, mention is made neither of the source, nor of *Fraser's Magazine,* nor of the reason for publication in pamphlet form. But see *The Edinburgh Catholic Magazine;* May 1837; p. 227.

applying myself to liturgical knowledge, what a new field was open to me ! with what delight did I trace the fitness of each portion of those glorious edifices to the rites for whose celebration they had been erected ! Then did I discover that the service I had been accustomed to attend and admire was but a cold and heartless remnant of past glories, and that those prayers which in my ignorance I had ascribed to reforming piety, were in reality only scraps plucked from the solemn and perfect offices of the ancient Church. Pursuing my researches among the faithful pages of the old chronicles, I discovered the tyranny, apostasy, and bloodshed by which the new religion had been established, the endless strifes, dissensions, and discords that existed among its propagators, and the devastation and ruin that attended its progress : opposed to all this, I considered the Catholic Church ; existing with uninterrupted apostolical succession, handing down the same faith, sacraments, and ceremonies unchanged, unaltered through every clime, language and nation.

For upwards of three years did I earnestly pursue the study of this all-important subject; and the irresistible force of truth penetrating my heart, I gladly surrendered my own fallible judgment to the unerring decisions of the Church, and embracing with heart and soul its faith and discipline, became an humble, but I trust faithful member.

I therefore hope that in Christian charity my conversion will not any longer be attributed solely to my admiration of architectural excellence : for although I have freely acknow-ledged that my attention was first directed through it to the subject, yet I must distinctly state, that so important a change was not effected in me, but by the most powerful reasons, and that after long and earnest examination.'

Actually, Pugin's change of faith not only caused him to forgo the æsthetic pleasure of services in the Cathedral for attendance in the miserable room which served as chapel for the Catholics of Salisbury, but, far from being likely to bring him increased opportunities, took from him one chance of an employment after his own heart. He sacrificed the possibility of being one of the principal agents in the restoration of England's ancient churches.

It did more. It sunk him at once to a lower stratum of society. True, that George III had been to Lulworth [1] and to Thorndon [2]; that England's premier earl was Catholic, together with a notable sprinkling of the gentry. But such were exceptions. Catholicism in England was the religion of small shopkeepers in the towns and peasants in the country who congregated round the chapels of their scattered manorial lords. It was a relic, and as such sometimes had a certain respectability. But it was poor and sadly tarnished by time and oppression. Worse, it was horribly tainted by foreign influences : by Jesuitry, by the unthinkable celibacy of monasticism, by all that was implied by the misunderstood word 'Inquisition,' by the mysterious and terrible power of Rome. That certain members of the ruling class belonged by heredity to such a creed was unfortunate—it was as though a man while still an infant should have been made a life member of a bad club by his father—but that a man should deliberately join such an organisation was in the nature of a betrayal.

We, who belong to an age when the splenetic outpourings of the Kensitites and their kin are commonly considered rather ridiculous, find it hard to envisage a time when the spirit of Kensitism was a serious menace both to truth and to personal safety. But men were still living in 1834 who could remember the Gordon Riots, and the time was yet to come when a Lancashire squire should have to arm his men with

---

[1] Thomas Weld, Esqr. ; 1750–1810.
[2] Robert Edward, 9th Lord Petre ; 1742–1801.

bludgeons to defend a church designed by Pugin's eldest son
—though not attacked on architectural grounds—from the
fury of the Anglo-religious mob.[1]

There was a worse thing, however, than mob violence.
There was the contempt and ignorance and bigotry of the
normal Englishman. ' And if Braybrook House,' an upholder
of the Establishment had written while Pugin was still a child,
' for want of due support should cease to be an asylum for
English ladies, educated in the pure principles of the gospel,
and employed in training up others in the same principles,
which are the foundation of our public prosperity and our
private happiness, it will immediately pass into the hands of
the papists and be converted into a regular nunnery. We have
already many such establishments in England—" black, white
and grey with all their trumpery." The premises have been
offered for sale, an abbess from Yorkshire has inspected them
in company with a Catholic priest, and the nuns are ready to
remove and set up a Catholic school connected with the
nunnery, the work of proselytism will go on in the neighbourhood (as it does in the vicinity of all Catholic establishments), and young women will be perverted and inveigled
from their parents, to become tenants of the Bedlam which is
designed for them. Woe be to that Protestant family wherein
a Romish priest finds admittance, for these men are indeed
wise in their generation ! the first lesson of monachism is to
disregard your parents. St. Benedict, when he repeats the
substance of the commandments in his Rule, *changes the fifth*,
and instead of saying Honour thy father and thy mother,
makes it Honour all men, as if, says Calmet, to denote that
his disciples must consider themselves as having no longer
father or mother or relation upon earth. This principle the
Romish priest inculcates in its utmost extent when he has
obtained the ear of a young woman, and perplexed her with

---

[1] Private information.

his sophistries. And when he has turned her brain, and separated her for ever from her parents, he congratulates himself upon having one good work more added to his account in the next world, and shuts up the poor victim of delusion for the remainder of her days, to say prayers by the score which she cannot construe, to rise at midnight and attend a service which she cannot understand, to address her supplications not to her Creator and Redeemer, but to Saints, of whom some were madmen and some knaves, and many are nonentities; to put her trust in crosses and in relics; to practise the grossest idolatry; to believe that the food which is innocent on Thursdays, becomes sinful on Fridays, and, if her devotion aspires to the higher honours of her profession, to torment herself with whipcord, and a horse-hair shift!'

Such was the opinion of Catholicism held by *The Quarterly Review* in November 1819. Reading it, one might almost suppose that that remarkable work, the *Awful Disclosures* extorted by who knows what pressure from that insane prostitute *Maria Monk*, had already become a part of the English Protestant mind. But one would be in error. It did not appear, even in Canada, the country of its origin, till 1835, about the time of Pugin's conversion.

Had Pugin joined the Church during the anti-Catholic violence of the 'fifties, his action would not have been so remarkable: it would have been in keeping with his reckless courage. What he did required a higher courage, and a more inviolable sincerity. He joined a Church which was despised, an institution on which the foul-minded were engaged in spewing their filth; but he had joined, too, a Church which would 'suffer the cross to be erected.'

CHAPTER VII

ST. MARIE'S GRANGE

" What reward shall we give you for all that you have done, Grettir ? "
Grettir replied : " I don't expect any reward for my services at present. But
. . . I will not be a hindrance in any doughty undertaking."
The Saga of Grettir the Strong.

IN 1835 Pugin bought half an acre of land about two miles
out of Salisbury, and fulfilled his ambition of building for
himself a suitable house. The site chosen was on the narrow
stretch of sloping ground between the river Avon and the
Southampton Road about the point where the road to Alder-
bury House forks off to the right. The ground rises from a
meadow almost level with the river to a terraced garden, at
the north-east edge of which, close to the road and below it,
the house stands, facing south-west across the water towards
Longford Park and the low, wooded hills beyond. Externally,
the house, which is built of brick with stone features, is
strongly marked by the influence of Pugin's continental
travels, and shows high-pitched roofs, towers, ornamental
weather-vanes, tall chimney-stacks, monograms formed in
dark bricks, and a belfry surmounted by a cross.[1] Internally,
it seems to have fulfilled those ' conditions ' of ' Commoditie,
Firmenes, and Delight ' which Sir Henry Wotton [2] laid down
as desirable in a building.

It may be presumed that to Pugin at any rate the house
fulfilled the condition of ' Delight.' Certainly to its ' Firmenes ' no exception can be taken ; for Pugin gave to his
own house all that mediæval solidity which irking financial

---

[1] The drawing in *Ferrey* (p. 72) bears only the slightest resemblance to the actual
building.
[2] *Elements of Architecture ;* 1624 ; quoted in *Eastlake ;* p. 13.

restrictions seldom allowed him to give to his other buildings. In consequence, ' several humorous disputes arose with the builder during its progress,' for the builder was not used to working for people who insisted on having ' enormously thick walls and deep splays to the windows, strong oak bars for fastenings, and not a scrap of plaster or battening where such materials were usually put.' [1]

The ' Commoditie' of the house was another matter, for Pugin had very definite ideas as to what a fifteenth-century house should be like, and he carried them out to the letter. For one thing, the rooms all communicated without any common passage. For another, there was no proper staircase, only a winding stair in a narrow turret.

On the principal floor there was a chapel, correctly orientated, fourteen feet by ten, opening out of the library, which little exceeded it in size. It is no longer used as a chapel, and its open-timbered roof has been ceiled. In addition, two of the rooms have been destroyed to make space for a staircase, and passages have been inserted between the rooms. The result, now that the chief eccentricities of Pugin's early ardour have been removed, shows plainly the beginnings of that genius as a domestic architect which he was later to display. In getting much into a little space, in making rooms look larger than their measurements warrant, and in making full use of every available foot, Pugin was a master.[2]

He called his house St. Marie's Grange,[3] a name which it still bears, and, in addition to the obvious Catholic implications of the cross, the belfry, the mural monograms, and the chapel,

---

[1] *Ferrey*; p. 96.
[2] For the privilege of seeing St. Marie's Grange, I am indebted to the courtesy of Mrs. Ord, its present occupier.
[3] The spelling ' Marie' as used here and in other of Pugin's buildings, was part of the general mediæval movement, and has since been dropped. Pugin's use of it has been unfortunate, as it has tended to associate him with the purely ' romantic' mediævalists.

he added a large tablet, on the side of the house nearest the road, on which was written in mediæval characters : *Hanc Domum cum capella edificavit Augustus de Pugin + sub invoc[atione] beatae Mariae + anno christ[i]* 1835 + *laus deo +*

Into this building, mediæval, Catholic, and strange, he retired to continue making his collection of old books, prints, manuscripts, pictures, and other ancient works of art, and to the arduous work of laying the foundations of his position as leading mediævalist and Catholic architect.

Legend gathered round his secluded life. It was said[1] that ' he used an upper room in a tower having a movable stair, which he drew up,' his habit being to work there in seclusion for days together, his simple meals being brought to the foot of the stair. This tale, though true as to his habits of solitary industry, probably had its origin in a confusion over the drawbridge which used to extend from the principal floor of the house to the road. For Pugin was afraid of fire, and the drawbridge was there as a means of possible escape.[2]

The building of this strange house, and the remarkable character of its builder, soon attracted attention in the neighbourhood, and led to two anecdotes of a more certain accuracy. Among others, William, third Earl of Radnor, called to see the uncompleted building and to meet its architect, and, finding the house unfinished with the exception of the room which Pugin used as his study, omitted to remove his hat before entering into conversation. ' The only reply he met with was a look of astonishment. Pugin rang the bell and ordered his hat ; placing it on his head, he said, " Now, my lord, I am ready." ' [3] Like his father, he was ' very susceptible of affront.' Equally characteristic was his reply

[1] *Sirr, F.R.I.B.A.*

[2] Pugin also (like Grettir the Strong) had a dislike of the dark, and in consequence inserted a window in the vault which he was later to build for his burial at Ramsgate. [Inf. of Mr. S. P. Powell.]

[3] *Ferrey ;* p. 94.

when the same Lord Radnor, 'who was well known for his simple habits and encouragement of agricultural pursuits, observed, with perhaps generous feeling, that he would as soon live in one of the smallest cottages on his estate as in his large and magnificent mansion '[1] : 'The devil you would— the devil you would, my Lord ; then what is to become of me and all other artists ? '

What was to become of Pugin himself was at the time equally uncertain, for there was not much work for an obscure Catholic architect in the neighbourhood of Salisbury, though it is possible that plans, which were never carried out, for additions and alterations to Longford Castle, Lord Radnor's house, and for a bridge near by over the Avon, belong to this period, together with a lodge built for Sir Frederick Hutchinson Hervey-Bathurst at Clarendon Park. But most of his energies seem to have been expended on architectural study, on the building of St. Marie's Grange, and on the production of his first books.

These were the separate parts of his *Ornaments of the XVth and XVIth Centuries*,[2] and *Contrasts ; or, a Parallel between the Noble Edifices of the Middle Ages and Corresponding Buildings of the Present Day*.

Of these, the part of his *Ornaments* entitled *Designs for gold and silver smiths* brought him the friendship of the learned Doctor Daniel Rock ; and *Contrasts* brought him notoriety.

On 19th August 1836, dating his letter from Alton Towers, Ashbourne, Derby—the home of John, sixteenth Earl of Shrewsbury, a man who was later to become Pugin's principal patron, and a house which Pugin himself was afterwards to adorn—Doctor Rock wrote as follows :—

' Dear Sir,

Though, as yet, I have not had the good fortune of making your personal acquaintance, but know you only by

---

[1] *Ferrey ;* pp. 99–100.   [2] See Appendix III.

your admirable and very valuable works on the architecture of our country, still I cannot resist the pleasure of addressing a line to you, to offer you my most cordial congratulations and sincere thanks for the manner in which you have contributed to honour our holy religion, by the way in which you have executed the screen part more particularly, of your Book of Designs for silversmiths. The work is a most elegant and correct one : the designs are really beautiful. In the second part I was quite at home, amid chalices, monstrances, cruets, &c. : and I cannot tell you how much I feel indebted to you, not only for the delight you afforded me as an individual who is enthusiastically attached to the study of the architecture and church antiquities of Catholic England, but for the assurance which I felt that your designs of Catholic church-plate would, on many occasions, propitiate the good-will of the man of taste towards the olden faith, and, perhaps, induce some to enquire into, and adopt its tenets. The first moving cause of several of our countrymen returning to the faith of their forefathers has, more than once, originated in similar trivial incidents. Truth is, very often, at first, like the grain of mustard-seed.

Having written a work entitled " Hierurgia," in which I attempted to trace the origin, and note the accidental changes in the vestments of the priest and his attendant ministers at mass, and to explain to our Protestant fellow-countrymen the meaning of our church ceremonies, I feel very interested in everything which can illustrate the subject. May I, therefore, request you to inform me where you found the originals or models of the second part of your Designs ? I have an ancient chalice and a very old bronze processional cross, much in the style of the one you gave, but without the figures of the blessed Virgin and St. John. I should be most happy to show them to you. I should very much like to know if there be still existing, in England, any Catholic church-plate, and the places where they may be seen. I know that much may be detected figured in illuminated MSS., in painted glass, in the sculptures of our beautiful old churches, and in collegiate and monastic seals. When you favour me with a line, direct " The Rev. Dr. Rock," and send your letter under cover to Lord Shrewsbury. Thus you will be conferring a kindness on one of the numerous admirers of that correct and refined taste and accurate knowledge which you have displayed in the illustration of our splendid and venerable national ecclesiastical antiquities. While I take this opportunity to offer you my many thanks for the instruction and delight which I have derived from the sight of your works, allow me to congratulate with you on having discovered the pearl of great price—the knowledge of the true faith—while exploring those monuments of ancient piety which were erected by the generous zeal and religious feelings of our ancient Catholic predecessors. Believe me, dear sir, with sincere esteem and regard, yours most truly,

Daniel Rock.' [1]

The friendship and support of Dr. Rock was a valuable acquisition for one who, in later years, ' might be said to have placed a stormy petrel instead of a barnyard cock on the top of every church he built.' [2] For Dr. Rock was probably the most learned Catholic ecclesiologist of his time.

But even more valuable, at the moment, was the notoriety which ensued on the publication, which took place at his own expense and at considerable loss, of *Contrasts*. For Pugin had lately undertaken work which might easily have led to more or less prolonged obscurity. He had entered the realm of ' ghosts.' He had become ' ghost ' to Mr. (afterwards Sir Charles) Barry.

[1] *Ferrey*; pp. 122–4.
[2] *Times Lit. Supp.*; 17 Oct. 1929; review of Gwynn's *Wiseman*.

CHAPTER VIII

CONTRASTS

Grettir then drew his sword Jokulsnaut . . .
The Saga of Grettir the Strong.

PUGIN was not one of those who, in the immortal words of Father Ronald Knox, correct ' I believe ' to ' One does feel.' On the contrary, his views were exceptionally definite and clear cut—so much so that to a reader bewildered by the obscurities of modern æsthetics their very definiteness seems to enshrine the simplicity of error—and he expressed them with all the vehemence and clarity of which he was capable.

To him might almost be applied some lines from *Hudibras :*

> ' For his Religion, it was fit
> To match his learning and his wit ;
> 'Twas Presbyterian, true blue ;
> For he was of that stubborn crew
> Of errant saints, whom all men grant
> To be the true Church Militant ;
> Such as do build their faith upon
> The holy text of pike and gun ;
> Decide all controversies by
> Infallible artillery ;
> And prove their doctrine orthodox
> By apostolic blows and knocks . . . '

Substitute ' earnest Christian ' for ' Presbyterian,' and one has a fair picture of the young Pugin advancing to do battle against the Philistine.

His first ' apostolic blow and knock ' appeared in 1836,

being ' printed for the author, and published by him at St. Marie's Grange, near Salisbury, Wilts,' and he lost heavily over the venture. Its title was *Contrasts ; or a parallel between the noble edifices of the fourteenth and fifteenth centuries and similar buildings of the present day ; shewing the present decay of taste : Accompanied by appropriate Text.*

Though the loss was heavy, he was well repaid in other ways. His reputation was made, and he was saved from all danger of sinking into ' ghostly ' obscurity under Mr. Barry. From being an obscure and struggling Catholic architect near Salisbury, he had moved at a stride into the position of Catholic champion.

The book which effected this change had long been growing in his mind. Ferrey considered[1] that its plan might be traced back to the ' suggestive imagination ' of his mother, and its method was foreshadowed in Pugin's letter to Osmond, already quoted, which was ' headed by a clever sketch, contrasting a modern tablet stuck against a wall with a beautiful canopied tomb and recumbent figure.' The main thesis of the book, as summed up later by Pugin himself in his *Apology for a work entitled ' Contrasts,'* was as follows :

' 1. That everything grand, edifying, and noble in art is the result of feelings produced by the Catholic religion on the human mind.

2. That destruction of art, irreverence towards religion, contempt of ecclesiastical persons and authority, and a complete loss of all the nobler perceptions of mankind have been the result of Protestantism, wherever it has been established.

3. That the degraded state of the arts in this country is purely owing to the absence of Catholic feeling among its professors, the loss of ecclesiastical patronage, and the apathy

---

[1] *Ferrey ;* p. 92.

with which a Protestant Nation must necessarily treat the higher branches of Art.'

Pugin was fully aware that this thesis was bound to meet with strong opposition.

'When I determined on publishing my work of " Contrasts ",' he wrote at the beginning of his *Apology* for that book, 'I was fully prepared for all the censure that has been, or may be, passed upon me for venturing on so bold an attempt. To carry defiance into the midst of an enemy's camp,—to put forth a theory which is in utter opposition to the prejudices and temporal interests of the great majority of the nation, will be considered as a mark of great temerity on my part. It certainly requires much zeal, determination, and fortitude, but in none of these respects shall I be found wanting.'

In a second edition of the book, which was published five years later, deeper study made it necessary for Pugin to modify this main thesis. Protestantism no longer appeared to him as 'a primary cause' but as 'the effect of some other more powerful agency,' the effect, as also was revived Paganism, of 'the decayed state of faith throughout Europe in the fifteenth century.' But of the book as first published Mgr. Ward truly wrote [1] : 'Yet considering the time and surroundings in which he lived, surely a stranger book has never been written, and it is no wonder that he could not find a publisher to accept it. To call it an attack on Protestantism would be ridiculously understating the terms of contempt which he poured forth on the Anglican establishment.'

Catholicism in England had found a man who, while his accuracy increased in the course of time, could from the very beginning smite as hard as the rankest 'No Popery' fanatic in the country.

The method followed in this smiting was simple and

[1] *Sequel;* p. 87.

straightforward. He began with two enthusiastic chapters concerning pre-Reformation English architecture, as exemplified in college chapels and monastic buildings, passing thence to chapters entitled ' Of the Pillage and Destruction of the Churches under Henry the Eighth ' and ' On the Ravages and Destruction of the Churches suffered under Edward VI. and after the final establishment of the new Religion,' and ending with a violent and contemptuous comparison between the great cathedrals and churches in their then state and as they were in the Ages of Faith. But all this was only in explanation and justification of the principal part of the book, the ' contrasts ' themselves.

These consisted of a series of illustrations—increased to fifteen in the second edition[1]—each page containing two etchings; the one, of some building or architectural feature of the middle ages, the other, of its early nineteenth-century counterpart. Of the book thus illustrated, Mr. Wingfield-Stratford writes[2] : ' Not even Carlyle's account [in *Past and Present;* first published in 1843] was so eloquent and convincing an indictment of the present in comparison with the past as the architect Pugin's *Contrasts*, a book now strangely forgotten. For if Carlyle's method was to let you read, Pugin allowed you to see.'[3]

The illustrations are as follows :

I. ' Catholic town in 1440 ' and ' The same town in 1840.' The mediæval town, a place of romantic beauty on the curve of a river, is crowded with spires, and the chief buildings in it are numbered as follows ; 1. *St. Michaels on the Hill.* 2. *Queens Cross.* 3. *St. Thomas's Chapel.* 4. *St. Maries Abbey.* 5. *All Saints.* 6. *St. Johns.* 7. *St. Peters.* 8. *St.*

---

[1] Pugin's own copy of this edition, now in the British Museum, contained a sixteenth which was never published, entitled *Catholic Church in* 1839. ' The exterior is bastard Egyptian ; the interior very tawdry and full of inattentive and even rowdy people.' [*Clark;* p. 184.]

[2] *The Victorian Tragedy ;* p. 202.

[3] For a ' Song on Pugin's " *Contrasts* ",' see Appendix V.

Alkmunds. 9. *St. Maries.* 10. *St. Edmunds.* 11. *Grey Friars.*
12. *St. Cuthberts.* 13. *Guild hall.* 14. *Trinity.* 15. *St.
Olaves.* 16. *St. Botolphs.* In 1840 many of the spires have
disappeared, their places being taken by factory chimneys,
and the numbers now read thus : 1. *St. Michaels Tower,
rebuilt in* 1750. 2. *New Parsonage House & Pleasure Grounds.*
3. *The New Jail.* 4. *Gas Works.* 5. *Lunatic Asylum.* 6. *Iron
Works & ruins of St. Maries Abbey.* 7. *Mr. Evans Chapel.*
8. *Baptist Chapel.* 9. *Unitarian Chapel.* 10. *New Church.*
11. *New Town Hall & Concert Room.* 12. *Westleyan Centenary
Chapel.* 13. *New Christian Society.* 14. *Quakers Meeting.*
15. *Socialist Hall of Science.* The satire is, superficially, somewhat crude ; but closer examination reveals subtleties. For
instance, the crosses have been removed from the roof of St.
Michael's Church, and the tower, ' rebuilt in 1750,' now stands
at the west end of the church, blocking the west window and
making it necessary for windows to be inserted in the roof. In
addition, the graveyard (from which the cross has also been
removed) is now given over partly to a vicarage large enough
for a married man, the remainder being a garden in which the
incumbent's children are playing.

II. ' Contrasted Town Halls. Guildhall, London. George
Dance, Esqr. archt.' and ' Hotel de Ville.'

III. ' Contrasted Parochial Churches. Allsouls Church,
Langham Place. John Nash, Esqr. Archt.' and ' Redcliffe
Church Bristol.'

IV. ' Contrasted Altar Screens. Hereford Cathedral 1830,'
showing modern communion plate on a ' table ' in front of
eighteenth-century panelling, the whole below an ancient
window from which the old glass has been removed, and
' Dyrham Abbey in 1430.'

V. ' Contrasted Chapels. St. Pancras Chapel, Enwood,[1]
Esqr. Archt.' and ' Bishop Skirlaws Chapel, Yorkshire.'

[1] *Vere* Inwood.

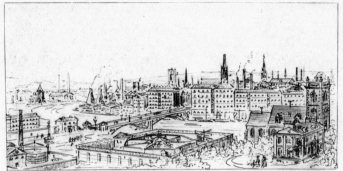

1 the new gaol 2 gas works 3 new demoli asylum 4 Hin works a Ruin of St Maries abbey 5 Prefud & Go
6 St Johns 7 St Peters 8 St Albans 9 Mr Tobbings warehouse 10 St Maries 11 the new church 12 the Town Hale 13 Mr Brown chapel
14 New wertleyan 15 seamen 16 decalint hall 17 chringer chapel 18 new passonge house 19 St Michaels repaird 1750

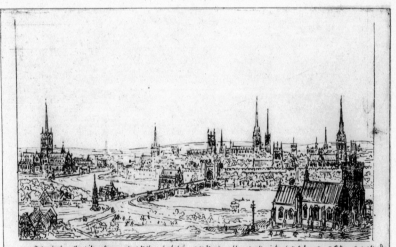

1 St Michaels on the pike 2 Bucan arch 3 St Thomas chapel 4 St Maries abbey 5 all saints 6 St Johns 7. St Peters 8 St Allands
9 St Maries 10 St Edmunds 11 gray friar 12 St Simsbury 13 guild hall 14. All hallow 15 St Olaves 16 Trinity

VI. ' Contrasted Royal Chapels. Chapel Royal Brighton,' showing a bewigged clergyman in a central pulpit preaching to the Royal Family in a gallery resembling a royal box in a theatre, and ' St. George's Chapel, Winsor.'

VII. ' Contrasted Sepulchral Monuments. Earl of Malmsbury, Salisbury Cathl. Chantrey 1823 Invt. et fecit ' and ' Admiral Gervase Alard, Winchelsea Church.'

VIII. ' Contrasted Crosses. Kings Cross, Battle Bridge, S. Geary, Archt.', showing a clock-tower, the upper part of which supports the figure of a civic dignitary and the lower part contains a police-station, and ' Chichester Cross,' a piece of beautiful mediæval work, the upper part of which terminates in a cross and the lower part serves as a shelter for passers by.

IX. ' Contrasted Public Conduits. St. Annes, Soho,' showing a police-station in front of which is a pump supporting a lamp-standard, and a policeman moving on a small boy with a jug (who in any case would not be able to draw any water since the pump is padlocked), and ' West Cheap Conduit, Thomas Ilam, 1479,' an erection in which the design is beautiful and the water free.

X. ' Contrasted College Gateways. Kings College Strand, Sir Rd. Smirke, Arct.' and ' Christs College Oxford.'

XI. ' St. Mary Overies Southwark. Old Western Doorway, destroyed in 1838 ; the destructives, the Vestry ; Agent of the Destructives, the Architect,' and the ' New Western Doorway,' a lamentable door in painted deal between sixteen-inch jambs in place of the old ones of four feet six inches.

XII. ' Contrasted Episcopal Residences. Ely House, Dover Street, 1836,' and ' Ely Palace, Holborn, 1536.' The parts of the new ' residence ' are lettered and described as follows : the three top floor windows : ' AAA The Nursery Windows '; below the central window : ' B An ill shaped Miter ' ; the three first floor windows : ' CCC The Drawing Room ';

below them : ' D The Street Door ' and ' EE The Parlour '
and ' F The way down the Area. This house has been built
with due regard to the modern style of episcopal establishments. All useless buildings such as chapel, hall, or library [1]
have been omitted, and the whole is on a scale to combine
economy with elegance ! ! ! ' With this the old ' residence '
contrasts strongly : ' a St. Etheldreda's Chapel ; b Part of the
library ; c The east cloister ; d Lodgings for guests ; e The
great hall. This venerable palace was sold to that EMINENT
surveyor C. COLE who utterly destroyed it and on its scite
erected the present HANDSOME and UNIFORM street
with its neat and appropriate iron gates in 1776.'

XIII. ' Contrasted Public Inns. Angel Inn Oxford ' and
' Angel Inn Grantham.'

XIV. ' Contrasted Residences for the Poor. Modern Poor
House,' a building on the ' panopticon ' system, which is
governed by a ' master ' with whip and irons, in which bread,
gruel, oatmeal, and potatoes is supplied to the inmates, and
from which the corpses are taken to be dissected, and an
' Antient Poor House,' a building like an Oxford College
complete with Church, of which the ' master ' is a benevolent
monk, in which ' beef, mutton, bacon, ale and cider, milk,
porridge, wheat bread, cheese ' is issued, and where the poor
receive burial with all religious rites. [2]

XV. ' Contrasted Episcopal Monuments ' : the one, a full-
length effigy of a mediæval prelate surrounded by intricate
Gothic tracery and figures of angels and saints ; the other, a
monument in the ' classic ' style, to make room for which

---

[1] An entry in Evelyn's Diary of 14 April 1669 is apposite here : ' I din'd with the
Abp. of Canterbury at Lambeth, and saw the Library, which was not very considerable.'

[2] Of this ' contrast ' Mr. Wingfield-Stratford writes [*The Victorian Tragedy*
p. 202] : ' The only unfair point in the comparison [is] that Pugin's modern poor-
house has some of the features of a prison, though this is quite unnecessary to drive
home the point that to the medieval Church the poor man had a soul to be cherished,
and to the modern Poor Law Commissioners only a carcase to be kept grudgingly
alive and then dissected.'

mediæval work has been destroyed, inscribed ' Sacred to the Memory of the Right Reverend Father in God, John Clutter-buck, D.D., ætatis suæ 73. Also of Caroline and Lydia his two wives,' the monument itself consisting of portrait busts of the said prelate and one wife, the other wife being repre-sented on a plaque upheld by a weeping cupid. Beside the monument, fixed to a mediæval pillar, is a notice : ' Persons are desired not to walk about and talk during divine service nor to deface the walls ' ; instructions which have not been obeyed, for the adjacent remains of Gothic work have been scrawled and defaced by the Protestant mob.[1]

Satire could hardly go much further.

Of course, Pugin was not entirely fair in his satire. It is hard for a man to be quite fair when he is wholly in earnest. But if the Middle Ages were not always so good as he drew them, and the early nineteenth century in some cases not so bad, yet his very exaggeration drew attention to the contrast which was really there. As in his father's architectural school, when he had seized the salient points of the situation and had expressed them in caricature, so now he expressed, hardly in caricature, the change which had passed over the art and religion of England in the course of three hundred years.

' The manner of preparing the churches for the new liturgy,' he wrote in *Contrasts*, ' consisted in blocking up the nave and aisles with dozing pens termed pews ; above this mass of partitions rose a rostrum, for the preacher, reader, and his respondent ; whilst a square table surmounted by the King's Arms, which had everywhere replaced the crucified Redeemer, conclude the list of necessary erections, which I need hardly say were as unsightly as the ancient arrangements were appropriate and beautiful.'

In an age of rampant Protestantism and artistic degradation,

[1] The ninth plate of the first edition—' Contrasted House Fronts. The professor's own house (Sir J. Soane Archt.) ' and ' Rue de l'Horloge, Rouen '—does not appear in the second edition.

he had the courage to stand forth almost alone and turn men's eyes back to their origins; he had the courage to hold up a mirror to the early nineteenth century. And it was an unusual mirror. Those who looked in it saw more than their reflections. It was as though a man, worn with years and evil living, should look in a mirror, and see beside his shameful reflection an image of what he once had been.

The fact that the mirror distorted both images a little only added to the contrast.

As it so happened, *Contrasts* appeared at a time when the public mind was prepared to receive a part of its teaching, and the lesson was made less painful by both the artistic skill and the sense of humour shown in the drawings. The Gothic Revival was steadily gaining ground, and with it a growing interest in the preservation of ancient work. *Contrasts* drew attention not only to the superiority of the old, but to the fact that the remnants of the old were still being destroyed. As Eastlake wrote[1]: 'To the circulation of this book—coloured though it may be by a strong theological bias—we may attribute the care and jealousy with which our ancient churches and cathedrals have since been protected and kept in repair. For such a result, who would not overlook many faults, which, after all, had no worse origin than in the earnest zeal of a convert?'

It was, perhaps, about this time that Pugin, rejoicing, it may be, in his new-found liberty to make use of the sign of the cross, or, more likely, merely doing so in the course of private prayer, was so rash as to cross himself in a railway carriage. An elderly lady, alone with him in the compartment, saw the action, and cried out: 'You are a Catholic, sir;— Guard, Guard, let me out—I must get into another carriage.'[2] It was another 'contrast,' and one likely both to increase 'theological bias' and to add to 'the earnest zeal of a convert.'

[1] *Eastlake;* p. 150.　　　　[2] *Ferrey;* p. 262.

CHAPTER IX

PALACE OF WESTMINSTER—PART I

"You would be very handy at many things," said Thorsteinn, "if misfortune did not follow you."
"*Men will tell of deeds that are done*," said Grettir.
The Saga of Grettir the Strong.

On the night of 16th October 1834, Mr. Charles Barry, returning to London on the Brighton coach, saw on the horizon in front of him a great red glare. It was the introduction to an opportunity such as befalls few architects. The Palace of Westminster was being destroyed by fire.

On 2nd March 1835 a Select Committee was appointed to decide what was best to be done. On 3rd June it issued its Report: that the old site be used, 'that the style of the building be either Gothic or Elizabethan,' and that ' the plans be delivered into the office of the Woods and Buildings, on or before '[1] 1st November. And on 17th July 1835 a Commission was appointed, at the suggestion of Lieutenant-Colonel Sir Edward Cust, to select in open competition not less than three nor more than five possible designs.

The choice of styles was courageous, for no secular public buildings had yet been built in the Gothic style, and the Revival itself was still in its infancy, the justification for its use and the principles of its structure being unknown, or at best only growing in the mind of Pugin and still to be expounded.

There were reasons, however, which made this choice almost inevitable. There was the fact that two important portions of the old building remained—Westminster Hall and

[1] *Illustrations of the New Palace of Westminster;* Henry T. Ryde; 1849.

the ruins of St. Stephen's Chapel—and that these, while sentiment demanded their preservation, could not be incorporated in a classical design. There was the proximity to Westminster Abbey. And there was the fact that it was commonly believed, in spite of all continental evidence to the contrary, that Gothic was an essentially English style.

In the course of the next few months, fourteen hundred drawings were made, some of which, so little was Gothic understood, had no greater claim to be called Gothic than was given them by the simple faith of their producers. On 29th February 1836 the Commissioners issued their Report; the designs sent in by Barry had been chosen.

What *The Quarterly Review* [1] termed the 'almost interminable feud' between the Greeks and the Goths had been brought to a head; and the Goths had won. The result was a flood of pamphlets which descended about the heads of the unsalaried and unpitied Commissioners. Very wisely, the Commissioners kept quiet, and the pamphleteers soon descended to livelier game, and began to rend each other. The virulence shown was such that even the dignified *Quarterly* in the architectural article already quoted saw fit to begin with what it later explained were 'humorous opening remarks.' It could hardly have done anything else, considering even the titles of the ten architectural works then reviewed: *Letter from W. R. Hamilton, Esq., to the Earl of Elgin, on the New Houses of Parliament*, Lond. 1836; *A Second Letter from the same to the same*, Ibid. 1837; *A Letter to Sir Robert Peel, Bart., M.P., on the Expediency of a better System of Control over Buildings erected at the Public Expense*, by Lieutenant-Colonel Sir Edward Cust, 1835; *Strictures on Architectural Monstrosities, &c.*, by T. Juvara, 1835; *An Apology for the Architectural Monstrosities of London, &c.*, by an Architect, 1835; *Thoughts on rebuilding the Houses of*

[1] *Q. R.;* Feb. 1837; p. 62.

Parliament, by Arthur William Hakewill, Architect, 1835 ; *Answer to Thoughts on rebuilding*, *&c.*, by Benjamin Ferrey, Architect, 1835 ; *A Letter to A. W. Hakewill*, by A. Welby Pugin, Architect, 1835 [1] ; *Prospects of the Nation in regard to its National Gallery*, by Charles Purser, Architect, 1833 ; *An Apology for the Designs of the Houses of Parliament marked ' Phil-Archimedes,' &c.*, Second edition, with a Supplement, by W. Wilkins, 1836.

Barry seems wisely to have kept himself out of the controversy. He had won the competition, and besides, he had too much to do. But Pugin was not bound by any such scruple, and however much he had to do his unconquerable energy would always find time for more, and he took a particular and personal interest in the new Houses. Pugin had sold his collaboration in the winning design to Barry, whom he had recently helped with the interior fittings and detail of King Edward's Grammar School, Birmingham, for four hundred guineas, and he had sold an unsuccessful design to his old friend Gillespie Graham for three hundred.[2] As he himself remarked to his old Covent Garden friend Thomas Grieve : ' Is not this a regular joke ? Here are these two rivals competing for one prize, and I am making the designs for both.' [3]

---

[1] *The Quarterly* mildly remarks : ' We need no stronger proof of the narrow feeling which now animates our professors of architecture than that Mr. Hakewill (p. 15) can see nothing in Westminster Hall, the Abbey, or Henry the Seventh's Chapel, but a collection of ' *noxious weeds*,' the produce of misplaced ingenuity, distortion, and grimace, which prevent the expansion of his Grecian Flora ; while that preterpluperfect Goth, Mr. S. [*sic*] Pugin (p. 71), regrets the mistake of Sir Christopher Wren in the construction of St. Paul's, and on grounds which would still more severely criminate Bramante and Michael Angelo for the still more hideous enormity of St. Peter's.'

[2] *Art-Architect ;* p. xiii.

[3] *Art-Architect ;* p. 9 ; quoting letter from Thomas Grieve to Edward Pugin, 20 Aug. 1867.

Ferrey (p. 242) gives a critique from *The Morning Post* of the Gillespie Graham design : ' Gillespie Graham has given a plan, in the genuine spirit of Gothic architecture, defying symmetry and order, but presenting combinations of convenience and picturesque grouping in perfect keeping with the character of the style, and most delightful to contemplate. The designs evince the author's intimate acquaintance with the style. The drawings by the same hand which appears to have assisted No. 64,

According to Ferrey,[1] when the Commissioners announced their preference for a mediæval building, ' no one doubted that Pugin would in any competition be at the head of the list.' And he adds that, ' had he but applied himself to the consideration of this national work with his full power and energy, and entered the competition ; who can doubt but that he would have gained one of the premiums (which were large [2]) even if he failed to obtain the execution of the design.'

Pugin did apply himself ' with his full power and energy,' and he did gain a premium. But it was a smaller one, and paid by Charles Barry.

The reasons why he did not enter for the competition himself were three : he had become a Catholic ; he doubted his own capability for such an undertaking ; and he was in urgent need of money.

With regard to the bearing of his conversion on the matter, Pugin's own opinion was definite : ' With that my chance for the Houses vanished, and I made the best of the situation.' [3]

The other two reasons are given in a letter from J. R. Herbert to Edward Pugin, dated 29th October 1867 [4]:

' These drawings were based upon that plan, which, your father always told me, was furnished by Sir C. Barry ; and when I often joked and laughed at him for this, he would reply—" I was not sure, my dear fellow, how the Judges would decide, but I was sure of the payment for these drawings.

are masterly, and *entirely* peculiar.' But Ferrey omits mention of the fact that 64 was the number of Mr. Charles Barry's entry. The exact extent of Pugin's share in the design is uncertain, but the elevations were certainly his. The plan and general design were Barry's, though even in these he owed much to Pugin's drawings of an imaginary ' St. Marie's College ' made before the Houses were burned down. For a full discussion of the question, see an article, *Who was the Architect of the Houses of Parliament ? New Light on an old Controversy*, by Robert Dell, in *The Burlington Magazine* of March 1906. Barry's share in the work was such as to reduce his sleep to four or five hours a night and to cause ' a short and sharp attack of illness ' [*Barry ; p. 147.*] Pugin's labours must have been appalling ; for in addition to Gothicising Barry's plan, he was working out his own ideas of a Parliament House for Gillespie Graham.

[1] *Ferrey ;* p. 240.   [2] They were of £500.
[3] *Art-Architect ;* p. 76.   [4] *Ib. ;* p. 100.

Besides, I could not have made that plan ; it was Barry's own ;
he was good at such work—excellent ; but the various requirements conveyed by the plan, which were not of art, and above
all the Fine Art Commissioners, would have been too much
for me."

' I may here tell you, that although his mediæval carving
works ended in his being unable to meet his engagements, he
most nobly refused the benefit of the Act.   He gave notes of
hand to all creditors and *paid them in full*.   Rolt, the timber
merchant, was so delighted with his just conduct that he
returned him half his debt.   I state this to you, that you may
know how very urgent it was that your father should be *sure*
of what was, at that time and under such circumstances, an
important sum.'

Four hundred guineas was an important sum, and Barry,
who received £8500 as premium apart from later architectural
fees, got his money's worth.   That Pugin was no niggard in
the value he gave for that and later payments is shown by
extracts from his Diaries later published by his son [1] :—

1835.

Aug.   4.—Arrived in London.   Saw Mr. Graham.

     5.—Began drawings for Mr. G.

     6.—Saw Mr. Barry.   *Working drawings.*

   10.—Mr. Barry.

   11.—Ditto.

   12.—Began large drawings.

   16.—Left London for Sarum.

   24.—Began Mr. Barry's drawings.

   25.—On ditto.

   26.—Ditto.

   27.—Ditto, all day.

Sep.   1.—Mr. Barry all day, *composition.*

    2.—Sent off drawings of Dining Room to Mr. Barry.

[1] *Art-Architect ;* pp. 11 *seq.*

1835.

Sep. 11.—Sent drawings to Mr. Barry.

First drew at St. Marie's Grange. Mr. Bury began.[1]

12.—Mr. Barry. Mr. Bury on G. G. (Gillespie Graham).

16.—On *composition* for Mr. Barry.

17.—Ditto.

18.—Ditto.

19.—Sent off Mr. Barry's drawings.

20.—Mr. Barry.

23.—Ditto.

24.—Mr. Barry came.

25.—Sent off five drawings to Mr. Barry.

26.—Worked all night.

27.—Parliament House.

29.—Sent to Mr. Barry 14 drawings.

30.—*Central portion.*

Oct.   2.—Sent to Mr. Barry 12 drawings.

3.—Paid Bury and he left.

The rest of the Diary for 1835 is in the same tenor. That for 1836 is more detailed :—

1836.

Sep. 12.—Sent fireplaces to Mr. Barry.   44.

14.—Sent working drawings of lamp to Mr. B.

On 23rd September 1836, Barry wrote a long letter to Pugin in which, after a lengthy list of drawings required, he said :

' I shall be able very soon to send you the data for the grand approach through the " Noble Hall of Rufus," by St. Stephen's Porch, St. Stephen's Hall, Central Hall, Committee Room, Staircase to the great waiting hall for witnesses, but I think you will now have enough to do for some little time to come, notwithstanding your 50-*horse power of creation.*'[2]

---

[1] Mr. Talbot Bury helped Pugin with some of the drawings for Gillespie Graham.
[2] *Art-Architect ;* pp. 23–4.

The 1836 Diary continues :—

Sep. 24.—Sent box with 24 drawings to Mr. Graham.

27.—Sent Mr. Barry's doors and framings.

Oct. 20.—Sent 5 drawings to Mr. B. K. staircase, robing room, lords, 2. Lobbies.

On 22nd October 1836, Barry again wrote to Pugin. Of this letter Ferrey remarks [1] that ' strange to say, [it] is the only one now to be obtained, most of the others being destroyed prior to Pugin's death, and what remain have been unfortunately mislaid ' :

' Dear Sir,

Being from home yesterday I could not acknowledge by return of post the receipt of the drawings of the House of Lords, King's Stairs, &c., which came safely to hand last night, and afforded me a rich treat. They will in all respects answer the purpose most admirably. I can easily imagine the great labour they must have cost you, and knowing all the difficulties, I cannot but wonder that you have been able to accomplish so much in the time. I am not much surprised to hear that your health suffers from excess of application. Do not, however, I beseech you, carry too great a press of sail, but take in a reef or two if you find it necessary in due time. I send by this morning's mail a packet containing tracings of the Grand Public Entrance, and approach to the Houses and Committee Rooms. They are most wretchedly made by a youngster, who is as dull and destitute of feeling as the board upon which he draws : they will nevertheless, I doubt not, afford you all the data you require. The groining and interior generally of the King's or Record Tower entrance you may make of any design you think proper : you need not be shackled as to height, but the groin should, I think, be concentric with the arch of the opening to the vestibule at the

[1] *Ferrey ;* pp. 244-5.

foot of the King's Stairs, which you already have. The design of this part of the building should, I think, be of a simple and massive character, and a pillar in the centre of the tower must be avoided. I am much flattered by your hearty commendation of the plan, and shall know where to look for a champion if I should hereafter require one. Truly it has cost me many an anxious thought, and an extraordinary degree of perseverance. With many thanks for your glorious efforts in the great cause, and best wishes for Mrs. Pugin's early recovery, believe me, dear sir,

Yours most truly,

Charles Barry.'

The 1836 Diary continues :—

Oct. 26.—6 drawings of North door. 22 drawings of West front. 5 drawings of interior West-end. A large drawing of West front.

Nov. 19.—Sent 8 drawings. Stained glass. 6 drawings stalls. 7 throne.

26.—Left for London. 11 drawings for Mr. Barry of ceilings. *Compartments, land front. Ditto water front.* Upper part of ditto turrets. Upper part of section of tower. Commons entrance. Speaker's Court entrance.

Drawings done at Mr. Barry's.

1 & 2. Interior of library, 3. *compartments.* 3. River front, second time. 4. *Compartments, land front,* second time. 5. Upper part of centres, second time. 6. Great oriels. 7. Upper part above ditto. 8. End Towers. 11. Lanterns of ditto. 12. Angle turrets. 13. Gable. Westminster Hall. 14. Lower part of great tower. 15. Middle story of ditto. 16. Upper part of ditto. Drawing on vellum of King's tower. 17. Entrance hall from water. 18. Throne end of House of Lords. 19. End of Speaker's chair, House of Commons. 20. Peers' entrance, hall, and dining room.

The method of work seems to have been that Barry drew out the plan and sent it to Pugin with the measurements required in the elevation : i.e. width and height of doorways, depth of mouldings, size of friezes, etc. Pugin then made rough drawings at St. Marie's Grange and sent them to Barry in London, afterwards going there himself and working them out in detail in Barry's office, ' ostensibly from Sir C. Barry's sketches,' as Edward Pugin wrote,[1] ' but in reality from my father's general designs, which he had sent to Sir Charles a few days before arriving in town himself,' a plan which ' effectually blinded all but the principals.'

The trouble was that Barry had hired a ' ghost ' and had found a collaborator. The position was embarrassing. He had been willing to employ a ' ghost,' and to pay him handsomely. But his ' ghost ' had become disturbingly real. It was not desirable to get rid, as it were, of the goose which was laying the golden eggs ; but it was desirable to keep it hidden. As to Pugin, he did not mind. He had received his four hundred guineas, and was being paid for later work. The glory did not matter. Barry could have that. He was not working for Barry. He was working primarily for the advancement of Gothic architecture ; and he was prepared to go on doing so, and to give full value, pressed down and shaken together and running over—provided things did not get any worse.

But things were bound to get worse. A clash was bound to come between two men of might labouring with heroic intensity on the same undertaking on the understanding that ' all but the principals ' should be ' effectually blinded ' to the existence of one of them. The bargain was too obviously one-sided for even Pugin's altruistic ardour to stand the strain. Barry was an established architect, and he was gaining both in money and in reputation. Pugin was not established ; he

[1] *Art-Architect ;* p. 22.

was twenty-five years old; time was slipping past; he had his way to make in the world.

In 1837 the breach came.

The exact date is not known, for the extracts from the Diary which Ferrey [1] gives as that of 1837 (with its entries for January: 11th.—On composition of centre and wings, drawing centre tower; also 16th.—Upper part of same. Taken ill. 17th.—Ill all day. Wind N. NE. [2] 18th.—Better. W. N. NE.; stormy. Ackerman's bill. Finished timber-houses. Dined at Mr. Stodeim's. 19th.—Much better. Returned Barry 10d. 31st.—Finished all Barry's drawings), actually belong, as is shown by various entries, to 1836, and the entry about finishing 'all Barry's drawings' refers only to a particular batch.

The details of the rupture are not clear; but sometime in 1837 something occurred which caused Pugin to cease work for Barry and refuse all intercourse with him for seven years —'a fact quite contrary to the oft-repeated assertion that "their mutual friendship was continuous and uninterrupted." ' [3] It seems that there was dissension over a man named John Thomas, whom Pugin had trained and whom Barry employed on Pugin's designs in preference to Pugin himself. Edward Pugin refers to 'ungenerous treatment' [3] in the matter, and implies that Barry, thinking that he had obtained enough designs from Pugin, precipitated the breach. It is possible : Pugin's mind was already moving towards a truer Gothic, and he did not like the Houses of Parliament. On one occasion, on the river, when passing the Houses, which were 'at that time without their corona of towers' [4], he exclaimed to a

---

[1] *Ferrey*; p. 243.

[2] As was the case with 'Davies' in *The Riddle of the Sands*, it would seem that 'it was always torture' to Pugin 'to feel a good breeze running to waste while he was inactive at anchor or on shore.'

[3] *Art-Architect*; p. 76. It is stated in *Barry*, pp. 132, 195, 198.

[4] *Ferrey*; p. 248.

friend : " All Grecian, Sir ; Tudor details on a classic body."
Much as he admired Barry's plan, that 'preterpluperfect
Goth' must inevitably have let it be seen that he considered
Barry's work merely clever while his own was more like
genuine stuff. The position must have been extremely galling
for a man in Barry's position, and it is quite understandable
that, thinking he had procured a sufficiency of 'Tudor
details' he should wish to 'cut the cable by which he rode
so long.' [1]

If this was the case, Barry was wrong. He had not obtained
nearly enough.

And Pugin was wrong, too. Even in 1837 he had not
'finished all Barry's drawings.'

Barry soon found out his error ; but for seven years Pugin
refused to accede to his appeals for further help. He had had
enough of 'ghosting.' He had work of his own to do.

[1] *Art-Architect ;* p. 76.

CHAPTER X

A very haughty copartner you will have in him.
The Song of Roland.

IT is not known when or by what means Pugin became acquainted with Charles Scarisbrick of Scarisbrick and Wrightington in the county of Lancaster, but designs now at Scarisbrick show that he was working on vanes and other ornamental details for the house at Scarisbrick in 1836, and it may well be that Charles Scarisbrick's decision to commence building on a large scale in 1837, by offering the certainty of prolonged and remunerative employment, helped Pugin to take the step of casting off his ' ghostly ' shackles. The opportunity offered was such as does not often befall an architect barely twenty-five years of age ; for Pugin had behind him a man who was not only the possessor of compatible taste, but also was probably the richest commoner in Lancashire and the owner of property rapidly increasing in value. Pugin did not waste the opportunity. Yet his achievement was not complete. How much finer it might have been we can only surmise, for that perversity of fate which so often dogged Pugin's steps here also placed obstacles in his way. The first of these was the character of his employer.

There are two portraits of Charles Scarisbrick preserved at Scarisbrick. They show a long, thin face, sallow beneath dark hair, sensitive, refined and melancholy, capable of irony, strong to endure. The expression of the eyes is almost haunted. It is said that he was the victim of some abiding fear. Certainly he lived at Scarisbrick a life of strange seclusion. But the secret of his character is elusive. Even at Stonyhurst, whither he was sent in 1811 at the age of ten, he was a source of puzzlement to those plain blunt Englishmen, his pedagogues—who were themselves a source of anxiety to the neighbourhood as being Jesuits.[1] With increase of years his eccentricity grew greater. 'Nathaniel Hawthorne,' we are told,[2] 'who lived in Southport' [about five miles from Scarisbrick] 'in 1856-7, was attracted by the stories he heard of the strange personality of Charles Scarisbrick. "He is a very eccentric man," wrote the author of *The Scarlet Letter*, "and spends all his time at the secluded hall, which stands in the midst of mosses and marshes,[3] and sees nobody, not even his steward. He might be an interesting person to know; but, after all, his character turns out to be one of the commonplaces of novels and romances."' It may have been. In real life it is less common. At any rate, so far as Pugin was concerned it led to grave difficulties; for Charles Scarisbrick, in addition to his other strange qualities, had a form of family pride which prevented him from rebuilding his ancestral home except on the original foundations. It is not hard to imagine the difficulties which will ensue when a man of great wealth is prepared to pour out money on the erection of architectural magnificence on the foundations of a medium-sized manor house.

Of the original house at Scarisbrick, a sixteenth-century timbered or half-timbered building, little remained when Pugin began the work of reconstruction. During the eighteenth century, the house became so dilapidated as to make rebuilding desirable. Designs for doing this on a new site were supplied to Charles Scarisbrick's father in 1802-3 by H. & J. A. Repton, whose proposal to change a flat park into

---

[1] *Stonyhurst MSS.*   [2] *Cheetham;* p. 100.
[3] This would seem to be a romantic exaggeration: Charles Scarisbrick's father had received the gold medal of the Society of Arts on completing the draining of Martin Mere in 1783. [*Cheetham;* p. 99.]

an undulating one and to place the new hall on a non-existent eminence was more creditable to their imaginative powers than to their capacity for looking facts in the face. Charles Scarisbrick's father seems to have been of the same opinion, and the suggested house, a fair example of the kind of Gothic which Pugin was to supersede, remained unbuilt. The old house, however, was crumbling and inadequate, and twelve years later, during the tenure of Charles Scarisbrick's brother, extensive restoration was necessary. The work was probably entrusted to John Foster,[1] architect of the Custom House at Liverpool. As Mr. W. A. Abram put it [2] : 'Admirable taste has been displayed in the restoration of the several parts of this ancient mansion, particularly in the old dining-hall . . . One wing, containing a large dining-hall, is modern. This noble apartment, [now the drawing-room], which is after the design of Foster, is in the Tudor style, and has an arched ceiling divided by moulded ribs springing from the elaborately ornamented corbels, the spaces between the arches being filled with panels of rich tracery.' Taking into consideration the state of 'Tudor' architecture in 1814, it is not difficult to imagine the specimen of 'admirable taste' which Pugin had to transform into a home suitable for a Catholic gentleman to live in, as a Catholic gentleman in an age of unbelief and industrial devastation might well surmise that he should live, in secluded splendour, withdrawn from the world.

The house, then, which Pugin had to raise to magnificence, consisted of a central portion, 'recased in stone and modernised in 1814,' [3] a western wing running forward from it, built 'in a rather thin style of revivalist Gothic which it would not be difficult to believe to be the work of a predecessor of Pugin,' [4]

---

[1] There is also good reason to suppose that Thomas Rickman was the architect. [Inf. of Mr. F. H. Cheetham.]
[2] Quoted in *Cheetham* ; p. 81.
[3] *History of Lancashire* ; Edward Baines ; V., p. 269.
[4] *Cheetham* ; p. 84 ; quoting letter from Mr. Sebastian Pugin Powell.

possibly a corresponding eastern wing of the original house, and, further to the east, a range of crumbling stables and similar buildings. The material was not promising; but ' the result was one of the finest buildings of the Gothic revival in all England.' [1] Some idea of what it would have been if Pugin had lived may be gathered from two painted panels over the fireplace in the west-wing drawing-room and two carved wooden panels on the west staircase. They show the ' thin ' west wing ' touched up with a window or buttress or panel here and there,' [2] the central portion and great hall rebuilt in solid and decorated beauty, an eastern wing balancing though differing from the western, a clock tower,[3] all in stone, and, further to the east, a great courtyard of stable-buildings in mellow brick. But only the western wing, the central portion, and the stables are as Pugin designed them. For Pugin died; and Charles Scarisbrick died; and when his sister, a woman of unconquerable energy, inherited at the age of seventy-two, she employed Edward Welby Pugin to complete the work, and gave him a free hand in vicarious reparation, it is suggested, for the treatment of Pugin by Barry.

[1] *Cheetham ;* p. 83.
[2] Letter from Mr. S. P. Powell, already quoted.
[3] ' To make the clock-story [of the Clock Tower of the Houses of Parliament] duly prominent all sorts of devices were thought of, till at last an example was remembered in which the whole clock-story was made to project beyond the body of the tower. The suggestion was eagerly caught at ; the example quoted differed in almost every respect from the character of the tower to be designed, and endless modifications were needed ; but the general principle was preserved, and the result is one of the most striking features of the building.' [*Barry ;* pp. 255–6.] The ' example ' was probably this at Scarisbrick : (a) There is a marked resemblance between the designs ; (b) The solution cannot have been a usual one, or there would have been no need to think of ' all sorts of devices ' before finding the right one ; (c) If the ' example ' had not been Pugin's, there appears to be no reason why Alfred Barry should have wished to suppress the source. Even if this should not be the case, it is notable that Pugin had solved the problem several years before it puzzled Barry. Pugin's rough sketch of his tower is dated 1837, his detail drawings 1839. The tower at Westminster was not begun till 1843 [*Barry ;* p. 174], and Barry expressed anxiety to Pugin over working drawings for it as late as 1852. [*Art-Architect ;* p. 56.] It seems probable that Pugin's clock tower was built, and was afterwards remodelled and increased enormously in height by Edward Pugin, retaining no resemblance to the original design. [Inf. of Mr. F. H. Cheetham.]

Edward Pugin, of whom it has been said,[1] and with little
exaggeration, that he ' had all the creative recklessness without
the genius of his Father,' naturally took full advantage of the
opportunity offered to him.   It was delightful for a young
architect to be employed by a rich widow who would let him
do what he liked, and pay royally for it ; it was delightful to
have his father's drawings to improve out of all recognition
and to his heart's content ; ' it was delightful,' in Eastlake's
words,[2] ' to invent new mouldings, to revel in fresh whims of
fenestration.'   To revel in fresh whims . . . He did so to the
full.

The result is that while the western wing remains a
simplicity of Gothic, and the centre portion is a magnificence
of Gothic, the eastern wing and tower is fantasy ; if the
western wing is as the bud, the centre is as the flower, and the
eastern portion displays the floridity of decadence.   In
consequence, anyone approaching Scarisbrick for the first
time, noticing first, as he inevitably must, that fantastic tower,
will merely think : ' So that is Gothic, a wild extravagance, a
millionaire's whim.'   But that is unjust : closer approach
shows that the centre is different, that it has a quality of
certitude, that it is ' a thing intended, wrought out, completed
and established.' [3]

This achievement is worthy of consideration in some detail in
two of its aspects: first, in the matter of architectural skill, employing the words in the sense of ability to make the utmost use of
materials ; and secondly, as an example of decorative art.

In addition to the touching up of the insipid west wing and
the bringing it into harmony with his own great hall, two
further examples of Pugin's skill are shown on the outside of
the building.   First, there is the south porch.   This was an

---

[1] *Phillipps ;* II., p. 287.
[2] *Eastlake ;* p. 357.
[3] H. Belloc : Preface to *Kai Lung's Golden Hours.*

afterthought; the doorway was originally intended to open directly into the building. But it shows no signs of being an afterthought. It is solid, with that solidity which funds seldom allowed Pugin to put into his work; and it is in harmony. Porches frequently look like an excrescence: this one looks like part of the building to which it is attached. Secondly, there is the north porch; an even greater feat of harmonisation for the north front was part of that ' recasing in stone ' which was carried out in 1814.

Inside, the first thing that one notices about the great hall is its size. When under that impression of magnitude, it comes as a surprise to learn the actual measurements. For the great hall is only thirty-two feet long (forty-three if the space beyond the screen and over the entrance lobby is included), and twenty-five feet wide exclusive of the two nine-foot bays. Its height, to the top of the lantern, externally, is eighty feet. The art of getting a seemingly large building into a limited space could hardly be better exemplified. But it is an art that has no rules: it cannot be taught; only sometimes can it be achieved.

There remained another problem for whose solution more than ordinary architectural skill was required: the adequate lighting of the house. For the plan of Scarisbrick entails that the internal communication of the house should be along the line of two corridors crossing in the centre of the building: one, the entrance lobby and its continuation, joining the north and south porches and lit through the entrance doors and the window over the south porch; the other, joining the east and west wings, capable of being lit only from above. Pugin solved it by placing a glass roof over the full length of the corridor running east and west, and letting the light get to the ground floor by making the first-floor corridor only half the width of the available space. The surprising thing about it is that, not only is the object adequately achieved, but that the means taken become a decoration. Architectural skill can hardly be more clearly shown than by turning an obstacle to achievement into an additional ornament.

Internally, the house at Scarisbrick is an adequate answer to those who would say that Gothic is 'suitable for some purposes,—melancholy, and therefore fit for religious buildings.'[1] For 'Pugin saw the Middle Ages as a period of pageantry and colour; and, . . . at Scarisbrick, we get colour everywhere : on walls, on ceilings and on floors, on doors, on shutters, and on the furniture generally.'[2] Truly, 'the interior is full of colour, and has little or nothing of the sombreness which in some minds is so often associated with Gothic buildings.'[3] Even now, though much of the colour is somewhat dimmed with age, the effect is one of splendour, and is a refutation of those who weakly fear colour through associating it with gaudiness and with vulgarity. There is nothing gaudy about the decoration at Scarisbrick : it is all sound stuff, well designed and well carried out, down to the door-knobs and wall-papers. In its production Pugin enlisted the help of those who were carrying out his designs for the Palace of Westminster, John Hardman and J. G. Crace, and there is nothing tawdry or flimsy in the work of Pugin and his assistants. The great doors, of enormous thickness, weight, and strength, still swing at a touch : the statement that Pugin was later to make,[4] that 'in matters of ordinary use, a man must go out of his way to make a bad thing,' could hardly be better exemplified ; nor that beauty follows upon good craftsmanship.

It may be thought, and with justice, that in certain particulars Scarisbrick suffers from excess of ornament. Wherever this excess appears, however, it is the hand of Edward Pugin at work. There is, for instance, the ground-floor room at the

---

[1] *Apology ;* p. 2.
[3] *Cheetham ;* p. 87.
[2] *Cheetham ;* p. 88.
[4] *Apology ;* p. 15.

southern end of the east wing. Pugin had intended this to be a 'business room' for Charles Scarisbrick: Edward Pugin turned it into a fantastic drawing-room for his sister. And there is the matter of the letters 'P' and 'A.S.' repeated with distressing frequency as a wall decoration in the great hall. But this diapering was not Pugin's work. 'Ann Lady of Scarisbrick,' as she styled herself in an inscription on the east wing, seems to have disapproved strongly of that 'man of strange and eccentric habits,'[1] her brother, and, as though to obliterate his memory wherever convenient, to have had her own name or initials neatly inscribed in Old English lettering on his building. So much for the 'A.S.' The 'P' is not so easy to account for. It is not customary for architects to plaster their initial over the buildings of their patrons, or to be given opportunity to do so. Yet there it is, large, boldly executed, oft-repeated. The explanation might be sought in the relations between that aged and dominating woman and the vivid young architect who seems only too successfully to have dominated her.[2] However, assuming that the tradition of the cause of Lady Scarisbrick's employment of Edward Pugin is true, there is a simpler explanation: Pugin had received grudged and wholly inadequate recognition for his work on the Houses of Parliament: his signature, as it were, should be placed for him on one of his works as a perpetual memorial.

After the pervasion of colour, one of the most noticeable things in the decorative scheme at Scarisbrick is the use of inscriptions and texts. Round the arch of the south porch is written: 'This Hall was built by me, Charles Scarisbrick, MDCCCXLII. Laus Deo'; round the arch of the doorway into the entrance lobby: 'Ye will show kindness to my Father's house'; along the front of the house: 'I have

[1] *Cheetham*; p. 100.
[2] It is noteworthy, though not 'scandalous' in the accepted modern sense, that the stained glass window on the east staircase should contain, on either side of its central mullion, portraits of Lady Scarisbrick and Edward Pugin.

raised up the ruins, and I have builded it as in the days of old,' and ' Every house is builded by some man, but he that builded all is God '; below the open timbers of the great hall : ' Except the Lord build the house, they labour in vain that build it ; except the Lord keep the city, the watchman waketh but in vain,' and ' It is vain for you to rise up early, to sit up late, to eat the bread of sorrows, for so He giveth His beloved sleep '; and round the inside of the central lantern in the corridor : ' For He that is mighty hath done great things for me and holy is His name. Alleluia.'

' Ye will show kindness to my Father's house ' ? The kindness shown by Lady Scarisbrick and Edward Pugin was excessive.

In nothing is Pugin's decorative genius better shown at Scarisbrick than in those doors and panels in which he combined his own work with pieces of ancient carving. These pieces of ancient carving, chiefly fifteenth-century Belgian work collected on the Continent by Charles Scarisbrick, though partly, it is said, work recovered from the stables and lumber-rooms of the old house, give no impression of being old ' pieces ' framed for preservation. They are part of a whole. In Pugin's hands, the old and the new were one.

In that unfinished house, then, and in those surroundings,[1] on 7th May 1860, seated in his chair in front of the dining-room (now west drawing-room) fire, Charles Scarisbrick died, a man ' who found . . . in the egoism of secluded splendour the true gentility.' [2] In the house were five huge volumes of drawings and plans fated never to be carried out in their entirety, with two painted stone panels, and two wooden, showing his house as it should have been. By that time Pugin had been dead eight years.

---

[1] After his death pictures and ' objects of *virtu* ' from Scarisbrick were sold at Christie's for £23,876. [*Cheetham* ; p. 91.]

[2] Dedication of *Privilege* ; Michael Sadleir.

CHAPTER XI

LORD SHREWSBURY

Neither was Oliver slow in striking.

The Song of Roland.

'How can I forbear to notice,' wrote the Rev. Henry Weedall,[1] 'that extraordinary Genius, the Architect of all his works :—that unrivalled man, just shown to the world, and then withdrawn ;—Pugin, whose name, like his own *twisted Monogram*, embodies a principle, and best stands alone ; Pugin, that Bezaleel of art, who seemed raised to detect the Pagan tendencies of our Architecture, and who first awakened that startling inquiry into the exclusive claims of Paganism to the domain of Literature and the Arts. Pugin and his noble Patron are inseparably united, mutually indebted, the one to the other. The Patron drawing out the Artist, the Artist ennobling the Patron. Pugin divides his fame, and without diminution to himself, lends a lustre to the " Good Earl of Shrewsbury." '

This 'noble Patron'—John Talbot, sixteenth Earl of Shrewsbury and Waterford, Premier Earl of England and Ireland, and Hereditary High Steward of Ireland—was an outstanding figure among the Catholics of his time, and he early showed signs of those qualities with which he was later to be distinguished : at Stonyhurst, where he had been sent at the age of eleven in 1802, he was known for his quiet demeanour, and 'was extremely diligent and had a high reputation for ability' [2]; and at St. Edmund's, whither he was later transferred, he led a rebellion and was in consequence

---

[1] *Weedall;* p. 20.
[2] *Sketches Legal and Political;* R. L. Sheil; 1855   II., p. 304.

expelled. To these qualities of meekness, ability, and willingness to fight when he considered it necessary, two more were to be added : holiness of life, and, on the death of his uncle, Charles, fifteenth Earl of Shrewsbury, in 1827, the possession of enormous wealth. Of him, his friend Ambrose Lisle March-Phillipps wrote [1] :

' God had placed him amongst the princes of his people, but he walked through the gorgeous Halls of his glorious Palace as few poor men would pace the lowliest cabin. No one ever saw a haughty look or a disdainful smile on his placid face. No one ever heard a discourteous word from his lips. He was all sweetness and gentleness, and in the midst of boundless wealth and magnificence he was poor in spirit, and loved holy poverty. His own apartment was always the plainest in the house, and the simplest in its furniture ; and no one could see it, who was initiated in the teachings of Christ's Catholic Church, without feeling his heart moved, and his soul stirred to its veriest depths.'

With this man, millionaire and saint, Pugin became acquainted in the summer of 1832. The meeting was purely accidental, and occurred at a furniture-dealer's in Wardour Street, where Lord Shrewsbury asked to be introduced to the artist responsible for some drawings which he saw there.[2] About four or five years later, when Lord Shrewsbury wished to make ' the gorgeous Halls of his glorious Palace ' still more gorgeous, and the Palace itself still more glorious, he remembered the man, now become a Catholic, whose drawings he had admired, and employed him as architect.

It was a formidable combination which assembled in what Cardinal Wiseman [3] called ' the princely towers and enchanted gardens of Alton.' For it included that learned Doctor Rock

---

[1] Quoted in *Weedall;* pp. 13–4.
[2] According to Mr. Talbot Bury (*The Builder*, 25 Sept. 1852), it was this introduction which brought Pugin his first commissions.
[3] *Wiseman;* I., p. 215.

with whom Pugin had already corresponded concerning his
Designs for gold and silver smiths, who was both Chaplain to
Lord Shrewsbury and the foremost Catholic ecclesiologist of
his time. A zealous millionaire, a zealous architect, a wise
and zealous priest, a consuming mutual ambition for the
restoration of the glory of a Church that was despised : it
was like a promise of sunrise to a shadowed world.

As to Pugin's work at Alton Towers—' so called because
of its towers, which are Gothic,' as le Chevalier Zeloni, in his
Life of the Princess Borghese, was careful to point out—it is
difficult in all cases to distinguish his work from that of his
predecessors : for the additions and restorations at Alton
were spread over a considerable period ; an architect named
Fradgley worked there for twenty-two years, and was himself
preceded by two others named Allanson and Abraham.
While, therefore, ' it is only justice to this local architect
[Fradgley] to state that much of the beautiful architectural
decorations of Alton Towers (which by the casual observer
are believed to be by Pugin), especially many of the Gothic
ceilings, a good portion of the building itself, and many of
the best features of the gardens—except those designed by
Mr. Abraham—are his designing and carrying out,' [1] Francis
Redfern, in his *History of the Town of Uttoxeter*, was going to
the opposite extreme when he did not mention Pugin at all.
Whether this was due to a desire to magnify the achievement
of a local man at the expense of an outsider, or to a dislike of
so much as mentioning the name of a Papist in connection
with the by then (after a considerable lawsuit) Protestant
property of Alton, it does not now appear possible to determine. But Pugin's work at Alton was worthy of mention,
for it is known that it included the entrance lodge, the fittings
and decoration of the chapel, ' the balustrade at the great

---

[1] *Guide to Alton Towers and the surrounding district*, &c. ; Llewellyn Jewitt ;
1869 ; pp. 39–40.

entrance, the parapet round the south side, the Doria apartments over Lady Shrewsbury's rooms, on the south-east side of the house, called sometimes the " plate-glass drawing-room," the apartments over the west end of the great gallery,' [1] the conservatory, the magnificent dining-hall, which is comparable to that at Scarisbrick and on a larger scale, decorative work in other rooms and galleries, and the ' Pugin Staircase ' which is a fine example of his ability for making the utmost use of a confined space.

The glory has departed from Alton's ' princely towers.' For Alton has been turned into public tea-rooms. The figures in armour, the trophies of arms, and the emblazoned banners are no longer in the hundred-feet-long armoury which forms the entrance hall ; nor are the gold-embroidered armigerous crimson curtains in the anteroom, nor the collection of Italian, Spanish, and Dutch pictures in the gallery ; and that part of the building once known romantically as Poets' Corner is now [2] piled high with cases of William Stretch's Dry Ginger Ale.

But the glory which came out from Alton has not departed. Lord Shrewsbury was calculated to have spent twenty thousand pounds a year on churches [3] ; and he employed Pugin as his architect ; and churches tend to remain.

The list can be prolonged almost indefinitely of ecclesiastical buildings which were largely or entirely erected at Lord Shrewsbury's expense : St. Marie's, Uttoxeter ; St. Marie's, Derby ; St. Marie's College, Oscott [4] ; St. Barnabas's, Nottingham ; St. Chad's, Birmingham ; St. George's, Southwark ; the Convent of Mercy, Handsworth ; St. Giles's, Cheadle ; St. Wilfrid's, Manchester ; Mount St. Bernard's

---

[1] *Art Journal ;* 1869 ; p. 23.   [2] Or was in May 1930.
[3] The exact extent and period of Lord Shrewsbury's munificence is not known ; but his total expenditure in charity and ecclesiastical building was calculated to have exceeded £500,000.   [*Gillow ;* V., p. 504.]
[4] See note 3, p. 63.

Abbey, Charnwood Forest; these are names taken almost at random.

Of these, St. Marie's, Uttoxeter, and St. Marie's, Derby, were the two first churches which were entirely Pugin's work, and as such deserve independent mention. The church at Uttoxeter was quite small, and of it Pugin wrote [1] that it was ' the first Catholic structure erected in this country, in strict accordance with the rules of ancient ecclesiastical architecture, since the days of the pretended Reformation.' As such, it differed in many ways from the then accepted practice. There were ' sedilia ' for the sacred ministers at High Mass, there was a Gothic holy-water stoup near the door, and a stone ' sacrarium ' and shelf for the cruets; and in place of the usual railing, there was an arch supporting the rood, though without anything in the nature of a screen. More remarkable, however, than these was the change in the arrangements for reserving the Blessed Sacrament. ' There is not a tabernacle on the altar,' he wrote, ' which is left entirely free for sacrifice, but the Blessed Sacrament, according to an ancient and formerly general practice, will be suspended over the altar in a pyx, enclosed within a silver dove, surrounded by rays of glory.' That may have been the most remarkable thing about the church; but it is also notable for the curious fact that the Right Reverend Peter Augustine Baines, Bishop of Siga, Vicar Apostolic of the Western District, and a Benedictine, refused to attend the opening ceremony when he heard that vestments of the Gothic form were to be used.

The best that a visitor to St. Mary's, Derby, in February 1926, could find to say was : ' That there had once been an ensemble of beauty and dignity in St. Mary's Sanctuary and its flanking chapels was evident; but the general effect of the interior was dismal and shabby.' [2] In addition, the tower was

[1] *Sequel*; I., p. 114; quoting *Orthodox Journal*, 20 July 1839, p. 33.
[2] *The Tablet*; 29 March 1930.

threatening collapse ; for the builders had not only used too
soft a stone but had accepted many blocks cut the wrong way
of the grain. St. Mary's, in fact, was suffering the doom of all
buildings which, ' like nearly all of Pugin's churches had to
go up too cheaply and too quickly.' [1]

All that has now been rectified. The tower has been saved,
and the interior has been completely redecorated, much of the
new work being an actual restoration of the old, so that,
though Pugin would not see his own handiwork in the
decoration of St. Mary's, he would recognise the fruit of his
genius ; his own decoration has gone, but he would find
there much of his own work restored and the remainder what
he would like to see.[2] The whole building bears his stamp
upon it. He could have prayed at ease in the new St. Mary's ;
for he was among those who could truly say : ' Lord, I have
loved the beauty of Thy house, and the place where Thy
glory dwells.' [3]

St. Mary's, Derby, then, is important for several reasons :
it is the first building to be entirely Pugin's work ; it is that
rare thing, a Perpendicular church from his designs ; it is
that still rarer thing, a church of his not only unmutilated but
restored to a state at least equal to its original condition ; its
proximity to Gibbs's Protestant cathedral offers a contrast
which shows more plainly than pages of description the service
which Pugin rendered to English ecclesiastical art.

But St. Mary's has another claim to distinction, and one
which illustrates an important aspect of Pugin's life. It was
from St. Mary's that Pugin, and Lord Shrewsbury, and that

[1] *The Tablet ;* 29 March 1930

[2] It is pleasant to learn that the work of restoration is being carried out by Pugin's
old firm of John Hardman & Company.

[3] This quotation, from the Douai Version of the 25th Psalm—*Domine, dilexi
decorem domus tuae, et locum habitationis gloriae tuae . . . Pes meus stetit in directo ;
in ecclesiis benedicam te, Domine*—was a favourite one of Pugin's, and he makes use
of it on the fifth page of his *Contrasts*, in the drawing entitled ' Church Furniture '
at the end of his *Apology*, and again in the first of his illustrations in *The Missal for
the use of the laity.*

' perfect Mediæval man,' [1] Ambrose Lisle March-Phillipps,
' drove away in high dudgeon, and took no part in the opening
ceremony.' [2]

The causes which led up to this surprising episode were as
follows : After the passing of the Catholic Emancipation Act,
Catholics became divided into three clearly distinguished
parties, which for convenience may be named the ' Old
Catholics,' the ' New Catholics,' and the ' English Catholics.'
The ' Old Catholics ' were such by heredity, and, remembering
penal days, wished for no more than to have the benefits of
the Act and to go their ways in peace ; the fact that those
ways included a mutilated ritual and shoddy accessories did
not affect the matter, such things, in fact, being hallowed by
survival of persecution. The ' New Catholics,' on the other
hand, were chiefly converts, and had all the new arrivals' lack
of diffidence in managing the affairs of an old firm. They had
seen the Church of England from the inside. They were
disgusted with the Church of England. They wanted Rome.
The ' English Catholics ' were few in number, and they consisted both of hereditary Catholics and converts. They had
seen the beauty of a day that was dead, and they wished that
beauty to be restored. The mottoes of the three parties might
have been : ' Peace for the Old,' ' Rome for Roman Catholics,'
and ' Old England for the New English.' All three parties
had one earnest aspiration in common : they all wished and
worked for the conversion of England. They differed only
in their method of approach to that undertaking. And they
quarrelled as only earnest people can quarrel who, with
entirely different mentalities, have the welfare of the same
undertaking at heart.

Pugin, from his childhood, had loathed the shoddiness of
the externals of Catholic worship. ' He had then no leaning

---

[1] *Phillipps ;* II., p. 248 ; quoting letter from Comte de Montalembert.
[2] *Sequel ;* I., p. 116.

whatever towards the Roman Catholic creed,' Ferrey wrote
of him,[1] ' and was loud in his denunciations of the men who,
wanting in appreciation of the exquisite beauty of mediæval
art, could mutilate their buildings by interpolations of
incongruous character, fill their churches with altars and
decorations of debased Italian design, and permit the very
precincts of their sacred buildings to be defiled. Nor was he
less severe upon the vestments and all modern ecclesiastical
ornaments connected with their ritual.' More, this loathing
was a grave obstacle to his conversion.

' From the period that the doctrines of the old religion were
developed in my mind,' he was later to write,[2] ' from the
circumstances above mentioned ' [i.e. historical and architectural study] ' I never entertained the least doubt of their
truth, but I had a hard struggle to convince myself that it was
a duty to leave the spots I held so sacred, and to worship in a
room inferior to many Wesleyan meeting-houses, and with
vestments and altar-furniture that would hardly have been
admitted among the properties of a travelling manager. I
had seen little or nothing of the Catholic body in England.
I once had a peep into Moorfields chapel, and came out
exceedingly distressed before the service, of which I had not
a very clear idea, was concluded. I saw nothing that reminded
me of the ancient religion, from the fabric down to the vestments of the celebrants. Everything seemed strange and
new : the singing, after the solemn chants of Westminster,
sounded execrable, and I returned perplexed and disappointed.'

The perplexity and disappointment remained, and closer
acquaintance with the Catholic body only served to increase
the loudness of his denunciations. The existing English
stuff was shoddy. The imported Italian and French was not
only debased but was also pagan in origin. The contrast
between Catholic art and Protestant art was no greater than

---

[1] *Ferrey;* pp. 40–1.   [2] *Some Remarks;* pp. 18–9.

that between good Catholic art and bad Catholic art. The one required to be crushed as much as the other. In Lord Shrewsbury, and March-Phillipps, and Doctor Rock, Pugin found men who thought as he did. They, and their supporters, formed the party of the ' English Catholics.'

It was Pugin's custom not only to collect pieces of mediæval ecclesiastical needlework and have them made up into old-style vestments, but also to design vestments himself on the mediæval pattern, though making them less full than the originals as a concession to modern ideas of convenience. As he remarked sadly when he saw Dr. Cox wearing an old French cope at St. Edmund's College : " What is the use my dear sir, of praying for the conversion of England in that cope ? "[1]

Fired with similar ideas, Lord Shrewsbury, whose generosity extended to smaller things as well as great, had a magnificent set of cloth-of-gold vestments made to Pugin's design. These, which are now kept at Oscott[2] and used on great occasions, he gave to the Vicar Apostolic of the Midland District, intending them to be used at the opening of all new churches.

On the night before the opening of St. Mary's, Pugin, who was wont to say that ' it was little use building Catholic churches if they were to be used as fiddling rooms,'[3] was disgusted to see a man with a fiddle-case making his way to the organ-loft. Pugin just managed to forbear ' knocking him down with his own fiddle,'[4] and left the church.

The next day, in spite of this, Pugin still ' understood that the Mass was to be sung to the Gregorian chant by a surpliced

---

[1] He is also stated [*Rambler* ; p. 397] to have asked a similar question of ' Father Ignatius ' (The Rev. the Hon. George Spencer, C.P.). In neither case has an answer been recorded.

[2] Lord Shrewsbury's benefactions to Oscott were so extensive that a special cart-house ' was built to accomodate [his] stage coach,' as he was a frequent visitor there. [*Oscotian*, 19 ; pp. 126–7.]

[3] *Wiseman* ; I., p. 355.   [4] *Ib.* ; p. 356.

choir,'[1] and he, and Lord Shrewsbury, and March-Phillipps arrived 'looking forward to seeing for the first time in England a real mediæval High Mass, which was to show some of his friends from Oxford the full Catholic ritual in the surroundings of Gothic architecture and vestments.'[2] Bishop Walsh,[3] however, had allowed other arrangements to be made, and when they arrived they found the Bishop in the sacristy in the cloth-of-gold vestments, and in the church, 'in accordance with the custom of the day,'[2] a full orchestra and a large choir which, crowning unritual horror, contained females. Pugin protested; but the Bishop said it was too late to alter arrangements. Lord Shrewsbury protested; and got the same answer. But on this occasion Lord Shrewsbury's meekness was conquered by that spirit which had enabled him to lead a successful rebellion in his school-days. He had learned something, too, from the enthusiastic but not always judicious Bishop Baines. He said in effect that fiddlers and female singers were not going to appear in the same church with his new vestments. The Bishop changed into a dingy set of the French pattern.

'*L'ignorance du clergé*,' Huysmans was later to write in *En Route*, '*son manque d'éducation, son inintelligence des milieux, son mépris de la mystique, son incompréhension de l'Art, lui ont enlevé toute influence sur le patriciat des âmes*.' In this case, the '*patriciat des âmes*' went off in something approaching a huff. But it had struck a gallant blow for what Pugin was accustomed to call 'the real thing.' As to Pugin himself, as he was later to write to March-Phillipps,[4] he was 'resolved to live or die, stand or fall, for the *real thing* and nobly act for the real thing.' And later in the same letter he wrote: 'The service as performed in the Catholic chapels in general is a

---

[1] *Sequel;* I., pp. 115–6.   [2] *Ib.;* p. 116.
[3] The Right Rev. Thomas Walsh, Bishop of Cambysopolis, Vicar Apostolic of the Midland District; later, in succession V. A. of the Central and London Districts.
[4] *Phillipps;* II., p. 214.

perfect mockery of the real thing, and you have no idea of the mischief all this does among men of devout minds who come to our churches expecting solemnity and finding a mere theatrical exhibition.' But Alton was like an oasis in a waste of frippery; for at Alton ' the real thing' was allowed to flourish, and in Lord Shrewsbury Pugin had a patron who could act on behalf of it as nobly as Pugin himself.

Lord Shrewsbury had early started on the right lines. Shortly after succeeding to Alton he ' removed from his Gardens and Halls whatever objectionable figures might seem to deform them; and . . . collected around him objects of tasteful art, and furnished a noble Gallery and Museum where, amidst an "instructive splendour," genius might study with improvement, and modesty might range without a blush ' [1]; a fact which must have further endeared him to Pugin who later wrote concerning Pagan and Christian sculpture [2] that : ' The principal object of the former was to display the human figure, which the latter, from the Christian principle of modesty, rather concealed. *The pagans wished to perpetuate human feelings,—the Christian, the divine.*'

From this introductory effort on behalf of ' the real thing,' there developed the spirit which studded England with churches, and which made of Alton a worthy centre for the outpouring of that munificence. For at Alton, ' to carry out the requirements of the palace, he built the beautiful model Church of St. Giles at Cheadle, a perfect gem of Ecclesiastical Architecture; and added, in the immediate vicinity of his mansion, an entire group of Ecclesiastical buildings, forming a complete *Tivoli* of Christian Art.' [3] These buildings, which make up the Hospital of St. John, were intended to be ' a perfect revival of a Catholic hospital of the old time, of which so many were seized, demolished, and perverted by the sacrilegious tyrant Henry and his successors in church

[1] *Weedall;* p. 19.   [2] *Apology;* p. 43.   [3] *Weedall;* p. 19.

plunder,' [1] and were to house ' a warden and confrater, both
in priest's orders ; six chaplains or decayed priests, a sacrist,
twelve poor brethren, a schoolmaster, and an unlimited
number of poor scholars.' [2]

The plan was never carried out completely, either in
buildings or in occupants. Yet enough was built of its three-
sided quadrangle, on its site at the edge of a hundred-foot
cliff just outside the village of Alton, to show how fine and
simple the Gothic Revival might have become, and to show
how the support of Lord Shrewsbury must sometimes have
made it appear to Pugin, in spite of the hostility of the
Romanisers, that it was to be given to him to restore in
England both the spirit and the practice of mediæval men.

It was at Alton, too, in the gorgeous private chapel which
Pugin himself had decorated, [3] that, by permission of Lord
Shrewsbury, on 8th May 1839, Pugin's second wife was
received into the Catholic Church in a ceremony some
aspects of which perhaps exceeded what might have been
expected of the Middle Ages. [4]

To a place thus hallowed by fervent labour and by an
event which gave him the most intimate domestic joy, and to
the man who made these things possible, Pugin's mind
constantly returned, and to Lord Shrewsbury he was accustomed to write frequent letters giving accounts of his activities,
his hopes, his antipathies, and the sometimes seemingly
insuperable obstacles in his way.

Some of these letters, mostly without their dates, are given
by Ferrey, the first of them after Pugin had discovered that
he had been hoaxed by a letter which informed him that the

---

[1] *Present State ;* p. 90.   [2] *Ib. ;* p. 87.

[3] In 1869, this chapel, ' although ruthlessly shorn of its relics, its paintings, altars,
shrines, and all its more interesting objects,' was ' still gorgeous and beautiful,' and
was ' held to be one of Pugin's masterpieces.' [*Art Journal ;* 1869 ; p. 49.] It is no
longer gorgeous, nor even recognisable as having been a masterpiece.

[4] For this surprising ceremony, see *Sequel ;* I., pp. 119 *seq.*, where a curious contemporary account is quoted in full.

monks of Mount St. Bernard's were themselves going to hold
stalls at a bazaar in aid of the monastery :

' I have found out at last that the alarm about the monks
at the bazaar was all a hoax ; and rumour mentions some
ladies not far distant from the Towers as the authors. I
must own it was capitally done, and put me into a perfect
fever for some days. I only read the letter late in the day,
and sent a person all the way to the General Post Office to
save the post. I never gave the day of the month a moment's
consideration. I shall be better prepared for the next first of
April.' [1]

However, there were plenty of real annoyances to be
poured out for Lord Shrewsbury's placid contemplation.
There were the Irish clergy :

' I regret to say that there seems little or no appreciation of
ecclesiastical architecture among the clergy. The cathedral
I built, at Enniscorthy, has been completely ruined. The
new bishop has blocked up the choir, stuck the altars under
the tower ! ! and the whole building is in a most painful
state of filth ; the sacrarium is full of rubbish, and it could
hardly have been worse treated if it had fallen into the hands
of the Hottentots. I see no progress of ecclesiastical ideas in
Ireland. I think if possible they get worse. It is quite useless
to attempt to build true churches, for the clergy have not the
least idea of using them properly.' [2]

There was *The Tablet*, with its habit of printing remarks
about the Oxford Movement, which Pugin, with March-
Phillipps and others, who looked on that Movement as a first
step towards reunion, considered worse than tactless. There
was the English clergy :

' Has your lordship heard that the Oratorians have opened
the Lowther Rooms [3] as a chapel ! !—a place for the vilest

[1] *Ferrey ;* p. 122. [2] *Ib. ;* p. 125.
[3] Off King William Street, Strand. Opened 31 May, 1849.

debauchery, masquerades, &c.—one night a MASQUED
BALL, next BENEDICTUS. This appears to me perfectly
monstrous, and I give the whole order up for ever. What a
degradation for religion ! Why, it is worse than the Socialists.
What a place to celebrate the mysteries of religion in ! I
cannot conceive how it is allowed. It cannot even be licensed
or protected by law, since they only have it for a time. It is
the greatest blow we have had for a long time ; no men have
been so disappointing as these. Conceive the poet Faber
come down to the Lowther Rooms ! The man who wrote
" Thoughts and Sights in Foreign Churches ! ! ! " hiring
the Lowther Rooms ! Well may they cry out against screens
or anything else. I always said they wanted rooms, not
churches, and now they have got them. Sad times ! I
cannot imagine what the world will come to, if it goes on much
longer.' [1]

There was the hydra-like quality of bad art :

' I was horrified on arriving at Manchester to-day, to find
that some pious persons had bought those horrid figures that
came out of your lordship's chapel, cast-iron brackets and all,
and given them to be fixed in the church I have built at
Manchester, St. Wilfrid's, with that French image of the
blessed Virgin for the lady chapel : it is dreadful. I will
never advise sending anything to bazaars again. Good
gracious ! the horrid things to come back again : they pursue
me like the Flying Dutchman. I thought I had seen the last
of them, and they actually go into a church that should be
perfect in its way. What to do, I know not.' [2]

There was the difficulty of dealing with the fickleness of a
Government Committee :

' There are great difficulties about Maynooth ; the grant
is quite insufficient for the building, and it appears that the
Government will neither give any more, nor consent to

[1] *Ferrey;* pp. 127-8.   [2] *Ib.;* p. 132.

Dr. Crolley's proposition to take a sum from the yearly grant for its completion, so I am quite at a stand and have no idea how it will end.' [1]

There was the work of the plagiarist :

' I have latterly nothing but Protestant business, but that pays, and by erecting my church [2] I turn it to Catholic purposes. There are so many Catholic architects now, that there is not a chance of any new buildings. I believe I design for all of them, for I see actually my own casts and figures used, and then they abuse me afterwards. These men can afford to sell cheap, for they *steal* their *brooms ready made* [3]; however, the movement progresses, and the right sort of thing becomes general, and that is the great point.' [4]

There was the architecture of Rome. Pugin was appalled by what he considered the artistic degradation of Rome. ' Happily,' he was later to write of the early days of his conversion,[5] ' at that time I did not cross the Alps, so I escaped the severest of all trials for the faith of the neophyte—the Eternal City.' Even in 1847, after he had been about twelve years a Catholic and had seen and inveighed against much Catholic work, the extent to which Rome had yielded to the Renaissance came as a shock. In this he differed markedly from Lady Gwendaline Talbot, the saintly daughter of Lord Shrewsbury, who wrote in her diary : ' I returned to Rome, after an absence of four years, on 25th November, 1834. How dear to me was the first sight of its domes, its verdure, and its hills, but, above all, the glorious cupola of St. Peter's ! ' And she added : ' Unlike all other cities, Rome is a dwelling

---

[1] *Ferrey ;* p. 132. Pugin had been commissioned by the Government to prepare plans for additions to Maynooth College, co. Kildare, and after his designs had been approved, the proposed grant was reduced from £30,000 to £18,000. Pugin, in the circumstances, considered it impossible to produce a creditable work, and resigned his position as architect.

[2] St. Augustine's, Ramsgate.   [3] See Appendix VI.
[4] *Ferrey ;* p. 133.   [5] *Some Remarks ;* p. 21.

for the soul.' Pugin, on the contrary, ' was so annoyed with Rome, that he contemplated leaving it without seeing the Pope.' [1] And as to ' the glorious cupola of St. Peter's,' he considered that it was even worse than St. Peter's itself, which he called ' the upas-tree of Christendom ' [2] : it was ' a humbug, a failure, an abortion, a mass of imposition, and a sham constructed even more vilely than it was designed.' [3] He is said [4] to have gone ' round St. Peter's in a state of rage, exclaiming, " Why they can't even carry out decently their own miserable style " ' ; and being found there absorbed in prayer, he explained that he was thanking God because he thought that he had discerned a crack in the dome. [5] The Renaissance statuary he found particularly distressing : " I attempted to say my prayers in the Gesù," he told Dr. North-cote ; " I looked up, hoping to see something which would stimulate my devotion. But I saw only *legs* sprawling over me. I expected them to begin to kick me next, and rushed out." [6]

However, he did not leave Rome in disgust immediately, although, as he afterwards stated, ' every hour he was there he felt endangered his faith,' [7] for there was still much ancient work left in Rome. On 1st May 1847, he wrote to a friend at Ushaw : [8]

' I have now seen Rome and what Italian architecture can do, and I do not hesitate to say that it is an imperative duty on every Catholic to defend true and Christian architecture with his whole energy. The modern churches here are frightful ; St. Peter's is far more ugly than I expected, and vilely con-structed—a mass of imposition—bad taste of every kind seems to have run riot in this place ; one good effect however results from these abortions : I feel doubly grateful for living

---

[1] *Rambler ;* p. 399.   [2] *Ib. ;* p. 395.
[3] *Ib. ;* p. 396.   [4] *Ferrey ;* p. 151.
[5] Inf. of Rev. P. H. Watts, S.J.   [6] *Wiseman ;* I., p. 356.
[7] *Ferrey ;* p. 151.   [8] *Ib. ;* pp. 225–7.

in a country where the real glories of Catholic art are being revived and appreciated. In Rome it is hopeless, unless by miracle. I assure you I have felt quite depressed and miserable here; I shall be quite glad to get away. Were it not for the old Basilicas and the associations connected with early Christian antiquities, it would be unbearable—the Sistine Chapel is a melancholy room, the Last Judgment is a painfully muscular delineation of a glorious subject, the Scala Regia a humbug, the Vatican a hideous mass, and St. Peter's is the greatest failure of all.[1] It is quite painful to walk about; Italian architecture is a mere system of veneering marble slabs; it is enough to make one frantic to think, that these churches with their *plaster pilasters* and bad windows, have not only been the model for all larger churches erected during the last two centuries, but have been the means of spoiling half the fine old buildings through the efforts that have been made to assimilate them to this wretched model. They must have had some fine things at one time, for there are several tombs and incised stones of the right character, and the subterranean church of St. Peter's contains several bishops and popes in fine chasubles, &c. I hope you will tell everybody that this is the place to confirm people in the true style, and I can now speak of all their matters from personal observation. I leave here on Tuesday (the 1st of May); as soon as, D.V., I return to England I will come down to Ushaw.

' My legs are still very weak, but otherwise I am stronger, and I shall feel better when I can get sight of a mullioned window again. The old Basilicas are very interesting, and if they had not given such a miserable modern dress to all the holy places, one might realize all the wonderful events connected with the early ages of Christianity within the City;

---

[1] It is clear that Pugin would not have taken Wiseman's remark about St. Mary's, Derby, [*Wiseman;* I., p. 310]—that ' on the whole it would not have done dishonour to Rome '—as a compliment.

but how is it possible to realize an idea of the residence of St. Peter, when we see a thing like a side chapel of Versailles ? or the relics of a saint in a flower-pot ? we must nail our colours to the cross, not to the mast. I never surrender; if my health will permit me, I shall publish this journey and my impressions of Rome; it will have novelty, at any rate, to recommend it.'

However, Pugin was not to leave Rome entirely without hope; for Pope Pius IX had permitted a Gothic chapel to be fitted up in the Vatican, and had caused the only Gothic church in Rome, the Minerva, to be restored in its original style. In addition, he granted an audience to Pugin, and gave him a handsome gold medal in recognition of his services to Catholic art, a token of approbation which ' gratified Pugin more than any other event in his life,' [1] and gave him the totally erroneous impression that his opponents stood condemned and that Gothic was going to return to Italy.

This audience, with its gratifying though misleading result, very nearly did not take place, for Pugin had arrived in Rome with no clothes other than the rough sailor's dress in which he travelled, and he had difficulty in borrowing a suitable costume, the man who lent it to him writing [2] : ' I have never ceased to wonder how he thrust his brawny arms through the sleeves of my coat, or drew it round his broad shoulders without bursting the seams.'

However, the feat was achieved, the coat stood the strain, and Pugin was able to write a comparatively cheerful letter to Lord Shrewsbury :

[1] *Ferrey* ; p. 228.

[2] *Rambler* ; p. 399. He states also that Pugin ' had arrived in Rome with the very minimum of luggage, and his artistic implements filled so much of his hand-bag that there was no room for a change even of his linen. His manner on his journey had been to wear whatever he had on as perseveringly as a Capuchin wears his habit till he judged it to be unfit for further use, when, without troubling the washer-woman, he would buy a new garment, and leave the old one as a legacy to the chambermaid.'

'Florence, Ascension of our Lord,
May, 1847.

My dear Lord Shrewsbury,

Ever since I left Rome I have been delighted with
Italy. By good luck, instead of coming here by sea, I took a
veturrino from Rome, and saw Assisi, Perugia, Arezzo,
Cortona, &c. I am certain that your lordship never could
have seen those places, for they contain the most magnificent
things in the world. I have seen three of the finest Gothic
altars in Christendom, and one of silver about 12 feet long.
As for the stained glass there is nothing so good on our side
of the Alps; and the sacristies are full of Gothic shrines,
reliquaries, chalices, &c. I am in a perfect mine of mediæval
art. I used to imagine that there was nothing of the kind in
this country, and I find more than in any other part of the
world. Florence is enchanting. The glass at Santa Croce is
perfectly beautiful, and the frescoes of Angelica da Fiesoli
enchanting. Rome is certainly a miserable place, quite disgusting and depressing; but Italy is yet the richest country
for true Christian art, and I do not despair of St. Peter's being
rebuilt in a better style. I saw two prelates at Rome in
immediate attendance on the Pope, who quite agreed with me.
What absurdities people have talked and written about the
pointed style not being adapted for Italy! Why, it is full of
it; there is not a little town that does not contain some fine
specimens, to my astonishment. When I was at Pistoia one
of the Canons, seeing I was an Englishman, asked me if I
knew a Mr. Pugin, a Catholic architect, and when I told him
I was the man, he embraced me, &c.' [1]

The reactions of Lord Shrewsbury to these outpourings
have not been recorded; but a man to whom March-Phillipps [2]
could write without sense of ridicule, 'Meanwhile you must
watch it from the Gothick loop-holes of your venerable

[1] *Ferrey;* pp. 126–7.   [2] *Phillipps;* II., p. 333.

Towers, and amid the noble valleys of Alton with Religion and peace and plenty around you, you can well afford to pardon and pity the follies of those who are so vainly fighting and struggling in the distance,' probably did not allow them to disturb his placidity. Pugin, however, was quite prepared to try to do so if he considered that Lord Shrewsbury was allowing himself to fall short of ' the real thing.'

'Hornby Castle.

My dear Lord Shrewsbury,

I cannot admit that I am to blame respecting the design of the dining-room. Of course I intended to make a fine thing, suitable to the purposes for which it is destined, and not a common room, fit only for a hotel. This is the very first room at the Towers that I was called upon to design, and it was quite natural that I should wish to produce something that would have a striking effect, especially when so many persons were loud in condemning the alterations, and declaring that the present room was far better than anything that could be done : yes, indeed, on the plan proposed by your lordship, at present, I do think the present room *far better* as regards design ; for the new room would be the most common-place apartment that can well be imagined. If I am not enabled to exercise any judgment, and make use of my knowledge and experience, I am reduced to the condition of a mere drawing clerk to work out what I am ordered, and this I cannot bear ; and, so far from knocking under, I really must decline undertaking the alterations, unless your lordship will consent to its being made worthy of your dignity and residence. It shall never be said that I have spoilt the dining-room at Alton : I would not do it for a thousand pounds. I always opposed the window, and at one time your lordship suggested it would do for the east window of a church, to which I quite agreed, for it is a church window in design.

From the first moment I spoke of a screen, and it is indispensable to break the current of air into the room. I never proposed anything for *mere effect*. I know my design was quite right, and again I entreat of your lordship to carry it out, or to leave the present building unaltered. . . . Nothing can be more dangerous than looking at prints of buildings, or trying to imitate bits of them : these architectural books are as bad as the Scriptures in the hands of the Protestants. I am very unhappy about it ; and as regards the hall, I have nailed my colours to the mast,—a bay window, high open roof, lantern, two good fire-places, a great sideboard, screen, minstrel-gallery—*all or none*. I will not sell myself to do a wretched thing. Lady Shrewsbury told me, when I was last at Alton, that she would rather see the present room left, unless the new one was a truly fine work : and I am sure her ladyship is right.

Ever, dear Lord Shrewsbury, &c.,

A. Welby Pugin.' [1]

Pugin had his way, and the hall at least was built as he wished ; King Edward VII said that it was the finest room he had ever dined in. [2]

Over St. Giles's, Cheadle, a building of which he wrote [3] that it would be a ' perfect revival of an English parish church of the time of Edward I. ; decidedly the best period of pointed architecture,' his difficulties with Lord Shrewsbury were of a different character. The £5000 which Lord Shrewsbury originally proposed for the building of a plain parish church was suddenly, when the building was well on its way towards completion, enormously increased.

' Hence there is a great anomaly,' Pugin was afterwards to write, [4] ' between the simplicity of its walls and mouldings and

---

[1] *Ferrey* ; pp. 119–20.   [2] Inf. of Mr. S. P. Powell.
[3] *Present State* ; p. 34.   [4] *Some Remarks* ; p. 9.

the intricacy of its detail, but all this is the result of a chain of circumstances over which I had no control, yet I have no doubt that many people imagine it is the ne plus ultra of my ideas on church decoration, and that I designed it on carte blanche, when in truth it was originally planned to meet a very limited outlay. Had we commenced on the same scale as we ended, a truly fine building might have been produced.'

But at the time the decorative artist in Pugin triumphed over the architect, and he was delighted with his handiwork. To a friend who asked him if there was any among his buildings which he considered free from defect, he replied : ' Yes, St. Giles's, Cheadle; I don't think there is any fault there.' [1] He was wrong. That a simple parochial church should contain the decoration of an elaborate cathedral, is a grievous fault, and one that Pugin himself afterwards realised. When, some years later, Pugin's approval of St. Giles's was quoted to Lord Shrewsbury, he smiled and said : ' He won't say that now though ; he abuses it as much as everything else that he has done.'

But yet St. Giles's is of a curious beauty : heavily decorated, overladen with choice richness, sombre and gorgeous, close compact, it is similar in effect to a piece of old brocaded stuff, or to one of the more intricately woven passages of Huysmans' prose. ' There is no excellent beauty,' Lord Verulam wrote in the forty-third of his *Essays or Counsels Civil and Moral*, ' but hath not some strangeness in the proportion.' There is strangeness in full measure in the proportions of St. Giles's ; and there is beauty, too, though a beauty which can best be appreciated by those who realize the circumstances which caused that disproportion ; ' for no youth can be comely but by pardon,' Lord Verulam went on to write, ' and considering the youth, as to make up the comeliness.'

That ' youth ' must be considered. St. Giles's was begun

[1] *Ferrey ;* p. 184.

in the same year in which Pugin published his *True Principles*
—principles which he himself had discovered. It is little
wonder that, in the circumstances, he did not succeed in
applying them to his own later satisfaction. Pugin was a
pioneer both in theory and in practice. As such, it was only
natural that his practice should lag behind his theory. The
wonder at Cheadle is that the disproportion between
decoration and fabric is not greater. Pugin judged his own
work by his own increasing standards. We, in order to do
him justice, must consider also the circumstances in which
his buildings were produced.

In almost all his buildings Pugin was hampered by having
to build too cheaply, too quickly, and under vexatious interference. Lord Shrewsbury's munificence was enormous ; but
it was so widespread that each individual building could
receive a bare sufficiency. At Cheadle, none of these obstacles
was in Pugin's way ; but the opportunity was vitiated by the
moment of its bestowal. The church stands, strange monument of the religious ardour of two whole-hearted men who
never attained to perfection in achievement.

CHAPTER XII

MARCH-PHILLIPPS

Then Illugi said : " I will go with you, brother. I know not whether I shall be a support to you, but I will be faithful to you and will not run from you so long as you stand upright. . . . "
Grettir answered : " You are such an one amongst men as I most rejoice in."
The Saga of Grettir the Strong.

IF in Lord Shrewsbury Pugin found a patron more friendly and munificent than he could ever have hoped, in Ambrose Lisle March-Phillipps he found a friend after his own heart.

This man, later to Gothicise his double patronymic by the mellifluous addition of ' de Lisle,' was the eldest son of a Leicestershire squire, and, to the distress of his relations, had become a Catholic when seventeen years of age. Three years older than Pugin, whom he outlived by twenty-six years, he was, like Pugin, ' inspired by two leading passions —in his case it is not too much to call them so—love for the Church, with an absorbing desire for the return of England to Catholic unity, and an intense reverence for Christian art and Gothic architecture.' [1]

This combination of enthusiasms was no mere combination of unrelated accidentals—as a man might be keen on cricket and philately. It was, rather, an interfusion of fundamentals : the enthusiasms were not so much objects on which energies were expended as passions fused into a single node from which energies sprang. At the present time, when this fusion no longer exists and its existence has almost been forgotten, it requires an effort of the imagination to understand the mental background to the activities of such men as Pugin and Ambrose March-Phillipps. The fusion came about in this

[1] *Phillipps ;* I., p. 72.

way : In the first place, these men were Catholics and they were Englishmen ; Catholicism, at its most triumphant, had produced Gothic art ; Gothic art, therefore, was Catholic art ; Catholicism and Catholic art were therefore in a sense one, and anything which affected the one would affect the other (as witness the Reformation, which, aimed at Catholicism, reduced Catholic art also to its lowest state). Secondly, Catholicism in England had produced English Catholic art ; since anything which affected Catholic art affected Catholicism, any improvement in the state of Catholic art would bring about a corresponding improvement in the state of Catholicism ; a complete restoration of Catholic art in England would be very largely instrumental, therefore, in bringing about a complete restoration of Catholicism.

Of course, the foregoing statement must not be taken as implying that March-Phillipps and his friends reasoned about the matter in this syllogistic manner. It is merely an attempt to show, in the briefest possible form, the origins of a state of mind. The fact that it was a state of mind and not an argument is shown by its obvious fallacy when put in that form— for instance, the fact that Catholicism produced Gothic does not imply that Gothic is the only form of art suitable for Catholics to produce ; and the fact that English Catholic art ceased to exist after the Reformation does not imply that the other effects of the Reformation would cease to exist on the restoration of English Catholic art.

The first manifestation of this state of mind in the case of March-Phillipps occurred at Grace-Dieu, a Leicestershire manor which his father had made over to him on his marriage. There, in 1833–4, he built himself a manor-house and small chapel in the Tudor style.

This chapel, built by William Railton, afterwards architect of Nelson's Column, was then in many respects unique. ' The chancel arch was of rather debased Tudor design, but it was furnished with a Rood-screen, the first which had been erected in England since the general destruction of Roods ordered by Parliament and Convocation in Queen Elizabeth's unholy reign.'[1]   In consequence, when Pugin first came to Grace-Dieu ' he fell upon De Lisle's [2] neck with delight at the sight of a Screen and Rood, and exclaimed with enthusiasm, " Now at last I have found a Christian after my own heart ! " ' [3]

March-Phillipps did not limit his work to the attainment of architectural and decorative correctness, and in one respect he led where Pugin followed : ' in the early days ' Pugin ' had not advocated the Gregorian chant to the exclusion of other music.' [4]   But that was soon corrected by March-Phillipps's severer taste :

' The services too at Grace-Dieu were not of the then stereotyped, meagre, or fashionable character.   During the 45 years that the chapel was open to Catholic worship . . . no figured or operatic music was heard within its walls.   No books were ever used by the surpliced choir except the Gradual, Vesperal, Processional, or Antiphonal, with their square notes and four leger lines ; and no High Mass of a maimed character without Introit, Gradual, proper Offertory, or Communion was ever sung, although Mass was frequently sung on week-days as well as on Sundays. . . . The cantors wore copes of cloth-of-gold with crimson hoods richly foliated from Pugin's best designs ; the women, mediæval hoods or cloaks like as were worn in the city guilds and else-where, whilst the acolytes were clothed in scarlet cassocks with scarlet sashes and skull-caps like as they still wear in Normandy and Provence.   The short-clipped cotta and cut-away chasuble were never seen at Grace-Dieu ; neither was there heard the tom-tomming of drums, the braying of brass

---

[1] *Phillipps ;* II., pp. 288–9.
[2] Actually the third surname was not adopted until 1863.
[3] *Phillipps ;* II., p. 289.
[4] *Wiseman ;* I., p. 354.

instruments, the twanging of fiddles, or the piping of the flute, whilst " the dreadful mysteries," as St. Chrysostom calls the holy sacrifice of the Mass, were being celebrated at the altar.' [1]

Grace-Dieu, in fact, like Alton, was a home of ' the real thing,' and, like Alton, it was to Pugin a spiritual home.

However, ' life at Grace-Dieu was not all service and plain song.' [2] There was a great work to be done, and there were battles to be fought.

The great work was one which had been exercising March-Phillipps's mind for a considerable time. As early as 9th June 1830, when he had only recently come of age, Lady Arundell of Wardour had made the remarkable prophecy [3] : " You will be the first founder or rather restorer of monastic institutions in this wretched country." After much labour, disappointment, and expense, the prophecy was fulfilled. Two hundred acres of largely waste land were bought in Charnwood Forest, and March-Phillipps, who believed ' that if Catholics could revive the monastic spirit, such a revival would promote in a wonderful manner the return of England to Catholic unity,' [4] was able to establish a small colony of Cistercians in a temporary monastery. For a time matters progressed but slowly, for March-Phillipps, though ' he managed to spend the income of three generations instead of that of one life-tenant,' [5] never had enough money for all his projects. However, in the end Lord Shrewsbury, who had previously opposed the scheme on the grounds that a teaching institution would be more valuable, came to the rescue.

' What I feel towards you,' March-Phillipps wrote,[6] ' for the glorious manner in which you have come forward to

[1] *Phillipps ;* II., pp. 292–3. [2] *Ib. ;* p. 293.
[3] *Ib. ;* I., p. 53. [4] *Ib. ;* p. 71.
[5] *Ib. ;* II., p. 320. [6] 26 Sept. 1839 ; *Ib. ;* I., p. 76.

complete the holy undertaking of the Monastery, which for
five years I have had so much at heart, I can find no words to
express—all I can do is in silence to adore the goodness of God
and to admire and venerate these sublime marks of His divine
grace which I witness in your soul, whilst I unceasingly pray
for your welfare and that of your family. . . . As for the poor
Monks, their joy and gratitude is so great that they know not
how to contain themselves.'

To his father he wrote a week later [1] :

' Lord Shrewsbury is going to build a new Monastery for
the Monks at Mount St. Bernard under Pugin's direction. He
has given three thousand pounds for this object, and will give
more later. Their present monastery, which you remember
an ugly unfinished building, is to be converted into farm
buildings for their use, and their present church is to be made
into a great barn. Lord Shrewsbury is giving away great
sums now to the Church in different parts of England, but his
giving this princely donation to Mount St. Bernard he told
me he did chiefly from affection for me, and to please me.
Pugin gives all his time, drawings, etc., gratis, and charges no
percentage on the outlay ; he says that with the materials so
close at hand he shall be able to astonish everyone with what
he will build with the money. The monks will do all the
carriage of materials themselves, and a part of the carpenters'
work, all the plane work. They desire me to thank you very
much for the strawberry plants you sent them, and which
they said had flourished exceedingly.'

The buildings which thus rose up in a desolate tract in
Leicestershire are notable for another reason besides being
the first of their kind in post-Reformation England. They
are an answer to the charge that ' the true bent of Pugin's mind
was towards the theatre . . . and throughout his life the
theatrical was the only branch of his art which he perfectly

[1] *Phillipps ;* I., p. 78.

understood.'[1] For St. Bernard's, ' as it stands to-day in its
solid simplicity, with thick walls and lancet windows, is a
striking memorial of the aims and ideas of Pugin's mind,
and of the solid work accomplished in those early days.'[2]
It might have been added : ' and of the solid work which
Pugin always desired, and which he invariably accomplished
when given the opportunity.'

Pugin's own description of the monastery[3] emphasises
this aspect :

' The whole of the buildings are erected in the greatest
severity of the lancet style, with massive walls and buttresses,
long and narrow windows, high gables and roofs, with
deeply arched doorways. Solemnity and simplicity are the
characteristics of the monastery, and every portion of the
architecture and fittings corresponds to the austerity of the
order for whom it has been raised. The space inclosed by
the cloisters is appointed for the cemetery ; a stone cross,
similar to those which were formerly erected in every churchyard, will be set up in the centre, and the memorials of
departed brethren will be inserted on plain wooden crosses
at the head of the graves. The view from this inclosure is
particularly striking. From the nature of the material used (a
sort of rubble granite) and the massiveness of the architecture,
the building already possesses the appearance of antiquity ;
and this being combined with the stillness of the place and
the presence of the religious, clad in the venerable habits of
the order, the mind is most forcibly carried back to the days
of England's faith.'

Mount St. Bernard's Abbey was probably not the only
work which Pugin did about that time without prospect of
pecuniary reward ; for it seems most unlikely that the

---

[1] Footnote to Fergusson's *History of Modern Architecture ;* quoted in *Clark ;*
p. 174.
[2] *Sequel ;* I., p. 109.
[3] *Present State ;* p. 98.

following appeal remained unanswered. It is in a letter to March-Phillipps, written at Stowe (the home of her brother, the first Duke of Buckingham and Chandos) by the Dowager Lady Arundell of Wardour: 'August 26th 1838'... Do you think that Mr. Pugin would, as it is for charity and the "Church," draw me a little sketch for an altar to be made of oak? The poor little church at Hethe, which I attend while here, is a structure of tolerable Gothic, though much too wide for its length and out of proportion, and the altar is horrible. I want to give them a decent plain cheap altar and tabernacle, such as a country carpenter could execute, but very correct and plain Gothic. The windows are plain lancet.'[1]

Pugin, in fact, like all those who work for a religion which is dependent on charity, had on occasion to give his professional services free of charge, or to withhold them. The chapel at Hethe cost £800, including the 'horrible' altar, though probably not including the house and school. But there were no funds at all for a burial-ground, which had to be acquired later.

Pugin's design for the chapel at Radford, in Oxfordshire, opened by Dr. Wiseman on 20th January 1841, can have been little, if any, more remunerative. It was 'in the early pointed style, extremely simple, but sufficient for the congregation, and truly Catholic,' and 'the whole building, including the altar, tabernacle, and vestry,'[2] cost just over £600.

For a man whose architectural ambitions were of abbeys, and cathedrals, and great collegiate establishments, and the restoration of the glories of mediæval work, there is a hint of tragedy in that he should have been required to produce £600 chapels and 'altars such as a country carpenter could execute.' But all of the work was not of that class, there was

[1] *A History of the Post-Reformation Catholic Missions in Oxfordshire;* Mrs. Bryan Stapleton; p. 86.
[2] *Ib.;* pp. 137-8.

plenty of it, and it was well done. The Gothic Revival was growing rapidly; on it had been superimposed a Catholic Gothic Revival, and Pugin was at the head of that secondary movement.

' Mr. Pugin is now actively engaged amidst a press of other business,' wrote the Editor of the *Catholic Magazine*,[1] ' in preparing drawings for several Catholic chapels, to be commenced forthwith, or early in the ensuing Spring. . . . Some of the plans we have seen, and we express ourselves very inadequately when we say that they delight us very much. The pictures give features of the designs ; their chasteness, their simplicity, but above all, their *Catholicity*, make us long to see some of our present chapels replaced by others of his erection. The style of the new edifice at Reading will be Norman, as best suiting the situation, being contiguous to the ruins of an ancient abbey ; the others are to be built, we believe, in the early pointed style of Germany, which is used in preference to the corresponding style of our own country, because it may be made to produce a much richer effect with a great deal less money.'

One result of this pressure of work was that St. Marie's Grange became impossible as a dwelling-place. In addition, it seems probable that the second Mrs. Pugin did not consider his ideas of domestic convenience compatible with married comfort. In June 1839 he wrote from Alton Towers to a friend in Salisbury :

' I am full of business, and long to talk over my operations with you. My church at Birmingham [2] will be a truly grand affair, filled with rich carving and decoration. I have several large churches to do in Ireland, and five near Birmingham, so that I am almost worked to death, and all my business, excepting Downside Priory, lies quite wide of Salisbury. I do not

---

[1] Jan. 1838 ; p. 709 ; quoted in *Sequel ;* I., p. 119.
[2] St. Chad's Cathedral.

see the probability of my being able to reside there for years. I must do something regarding my house; it cannot go on in this manner, and I am most anxious to have your advice about it. My whole prospects are entirely changed since I built it. I was then almost without architectural business, and I have now more than I can well do; indeed every moment of my time is occupied. I wish to let my house at a moderate rent. I do not like the idea of selling it, because I have no occasion for so doing, but I do not like so much money sunk without any return whatever.'[1]

In another letter, he wrote[1]:

'I have now an immense deal of business, and if I live on two or three years shall have done something worth looking at. Some of my buildings in Derby, Wexford, &c., will be completed early this summer. I have got the great church at Liverpool, with a crypt 150 feet long by 60 wide, well vaulted.'

Again[1]:

'I have twice as much as I can do, though I work early and late. Were I not driven at this moment beyond my strength, you should not wait a moment.'

Later still he wrote[2]:

'I shall come down to Salisbury, when I shall want the deeds of my house, as it is most improbable I shall ever be able to live there, and I have quite determined on disposing of it.'

Eventually, in 1841, the house was sold to a Mr. Staples, from whom he had originally bought its site. The price was £500. On the building alone he had spent £2000. In the meantime, he had gone to live in Cheyne Walk, Chelsea, and had bought a plot of ground on the West Cliff, Ramsgate, where he was later to build himself a house and church.

Pugin's architectural labours, however, were not at that time, or at any other, his only occupation. The 'real thing'

---

[1] *Ferrey*; p. 95.   [2] *Ib.*; pp. 95–6.

had to be fought for as well as designed. The Editor of the *Catholic Magazine* might find that his designs 'delight us very much'; but there were others whom they did not delight at all. The 'New Catholics' objected to the whole 'English Catholic' movement; and they chose as the immediate object of attack the new vestments which Pugin had designed on the old model.[1] The skirmishes at St. Mary's, Uttoxeter, and St. Mary's, Derby, had been inconclusive. The 'New Catholics' wanted a general engagement. They brought one about by the method, unattractive and perhaps not wholly free from mendacity, of reporting Pugin's work to the Roman authorities as 'innovations.'

The names of the complainants are not known. Bishop Baines was probably one of them. Even if he did not actually put his name to the 'complaint,' he was of the party of the complainants, and his later remarks on the subject [2] show plainly the kind of opposition with which Pugin had to deal :

'Under the pretext of diminishing the objections which Protestants have to a connection with Rome, it was proposed to re-establish the ceremonial of the ancient Church of England. For this purpose the form of the sacred vestments was altered to what it was supposed to have been four or five centuries ago, and so entirely did these new vestments differ from those in use throughout the whole Latin Church as to be no longer recognisable as of the same genus. The Chasuble, being nearly six feet in width, hung in ample folds before and behind, and nearly resembled a large shawl. The Communion rail was omitted in the new churches, even at the Communion altar ; the Tabernacle was to be removed from the altar, and

---

[1] And perhaps not wholly without reason. As Pugin himself remarked when talking with some friends in Oxford : " But after all, my dear sir, what's the use of decent vestments with such priests as we have got ? a lot of blessed fellows ! Why, sir, when they wear my chasubles, they don't look like priests, and what's worse, the chasubles don't look like chasubles." [*Ferrey*; p. 112.]

[2] *Sequel*; I., pp. 116–7.

the Blessed Sacrament suspended from the ceiling by a chain
or cord in a silver dove.'

The verbal ingenuity of this attack is worthy of examination.
In the first place, no ' pretext ' was required to justify restora-
tion of the ancient ceremonial : the lamentable state of the
English ceremonial then in vogue was enough to make it
meritorious even apart from the words of Pope Gregory the
Great [1] :

' Thou knowest, my brother, the usage of the Roman
Church in which you were brought up. But it pleaseth me
that if you have found anything, whether in the Roman, or the
Gallican, or in any other Church, that will give more honour
to Almighty God, you shall diligently adopt it ; and make a
rule taken from the many Churches for the benefit of the
English Church, which is still new to the Faith. For things
are not to be loved for the sake of places, but places for the
sake of their good things.' Secondly, the form of the vestments was not altered to what it was ' supposed ' to have been :
it was altered to what it actually had been, as Bishop Baines
might have seen for himself by looking at any ancient
ecclesiastical monument, though with modifications to make
the transition to ' the real thing ' from the shoddy less abrupt.
Thirdly, the fact that ' a large shawl ' might resemble a
chasuble was a possible justification for large shawls : it was
no argument against the use of proper chasubles.

Whether the ' complaint ' to Rome was in those terms or
not does not appear. The result of it, in 1839, was a letter ' to
Dr. Walsh deprecating the new form of vestments,' [2] and
referring to Pugin as ' an architect converted from heresy.' [3]
Mr. Denis Gwynn [4] calls the letter ' a formal discouragement.'
Pugin, who, though a convert, had a mind as simple and direct

[1] *Reply to Augustin's second question*, Bede, *Hist. Eccles.* c. xxvii. § 60 ; quoted in
Phillipps ; II., p. 218.
[2] *Sequel* ; I., p. 116.   [3] *Phillipps* ; II., p. 220.   [4] *Gwynn* ; p. 92.

as the oldest of ' Old Catholics,' was horrified. He did not appreciate the difference between ' a formal discouragement ' and a censure. Thinking that a censure had been promulgated, he turned immediately to the ' perfect Mediæval man ' :—

' Ramsgate, 1st Sunday in Advent,
Dec. 1st, 1839.

Dear Mr. Phillipps—I suppose you have heard of the Censure passed by the Propaganda on the proceedgs. of our good Bishop. If you have not, keep the intelligence closely to yourself; but it is of great importance that you should be acquainted with all that is going on against us. The Bishop showed me the other day a Letter he had just recvd. from the Propaganda, censuring his proceedgs. and denouncing me in no very measured terms. This is the result of some diabolical falsehoods and misrepresentations made at Rome by our adversaries, and the Propaganda have actually given credit at once to this exparte statement and have condemned the proceedgs. of the only Bishop in England who has really advanced the dignity of religion. Dr. Walsh found the churches in his district worse than Barns ; he will leave them sumptuous erections. The greater part of the vestments were filthy rags, and he has replaced them with silk and gold. For this he has been censured ! ! ! Is this to be believed ? can it be possible ? It is, and a blow has been struck at us, which if persisted in will be far more fatal to religion than all the attacks of the hereticks. I am filled with dismay and indignation ; but in this matter I blame those who caused these misrepresentations to Rome more than the Propaganda who are utterly ignorant of the whole business and are only in fault in giving credit to the Lies and ignorance of these informers. I am disgusted beyond measure. It is madness in the present state of things to check the restoration of the dignity of religion. We have a detestable crew to deal with

—ignorance, prejudice, timidity, tepidity. All combined—
My dear frd., we have a sorry soil to plant in, and that not
from protestm.; actually protestants in many cases are far
better inclined to Catholicism than half the soi-disant Catholics
of our days. Every attempt to restore religion to its antient
dignity and glory is met with sneers, insult, and opposition
from those who ought to be foremost in aiding the great work.

This censure has been procured by the influce. of some
English Catholic, and I fear ecclesiastick. In this censure the
bishop is accused of having at *my* instigation introduced
various *innovations* in the Liturgy and vestments. Intolerable
ignorance, these innovations as they are called are the mere
restoration of the glorious ornaments which the ascendency
of heretics has deprived us of, and because those who ought
to *delight in the study of these things are utterly ignorant of them*
we are to be denounced as *innovators*. Mark my words. Your
chapel service, which is perhaps the most devotional in
England, will be shortly put down because it is different from
what has been lately seen in the scrubby rooms called chapels
where *one urchin* is frequently the only assistant at the holy
sacrifice, which is offered up in a place and at an altar far more
calculated to excite ridicule than devotion. I am sick at heart.
The apathy of the Catholic body on these things is alarming.
I had formed dreams of returning glory; but if this censure
of the Propaganda is persisted in after the remonstrance which
has been sent, I shall abandon all my hopes. I see everything
that we had hoped dashed to pieces. Do not deceive yourself,
My dear friend, do not deceive yourself: the Catholics will
cut their own throats, the clergy will put down religion.
These are hard sayings, but they are twice mad fools; straining
at gnats and swallowing camels, the very men who do not
hesitate to violate rubrics every day to suit their convenience
or their pockets, now swelling with indignation and horror at
the idea of an ample surplice or flowing chasuble such as

almost every saint in the Calendar wore. Administer baptism
out of an old physick phial ; reserve the blessed Sacrament in
dirty cupboard ; say mass in vestment made out of an old
gown ; burn gas on the altar ; have everything as *mean,* as
pitiful, as *shabby* as you please ; hire protestant performers to
sing, *Leave out every ceremony in the ritual ;* do all this and
you will be right. But if you venture to speak of antient glory
and ecclesiastical dignity, oh, you are a man of extravagant
opinions, an enthusiast, a visionary—and *ecclesiastical censure*
awaits you. Again I say I am disgusted. *Rubrick* indeed !
Innovators ! I wonder those who have been doing all these
things venture to name Rubrick and innovations. If their
censure is acted upon and all our splendid vestments cut to
pieces, I shall try no more. Our good Bishop has given in
too soon. The censure was based on a *wrong position.* He
was accused of *innovation ;* he has not been guilty of the
Least innovation. He should therefore have stood firm ; but
he has suspended the use of the vestments everywhere. Thus
the wretched old thgs. are actually used in the new Derby
Church while Lord Shrewsbury's splendid donations are
shelved. This is tacitly acknowledging the charge. I feel cut
up beyond measure, but I do not mean to let this business
drop. I will set forth the antient glories of Catholicism and
leave people to judge why the service now performed in the
modern Catholic chapels is not a ghost of the antient rite.
There is nothing out of Oscott so good as the service in your
chapel, and that will be *put down.* I know it will. You are a
marked man for the vengeance of those who do not like *to be
put out of the way.* Pray let me hear speedily from you on
this business, and believe me ever your devd. friend,

                                        A. Welby Pugin.

Everything in modern chapels is bad—vestments, music,
altars,—and the present Race of Catholics are so used to the

miserable expedients which have been resorted to, through necessity, that they will not avail themselves of better things now that they are offered them. I feel completely upset and dejected by this business.

Pray write to Lord Shrewsbury on this business—the Propaganda have been shamefully deceived in their information. They little know what might be done in England if proper measures were resorted to. If the English Catholics were zealous and *really set forth* their religion England might be regained ; but under the present system never. Pray give my kindest respects to Mrs. Phillipps and Miss Clifford.'[1]

Pugin was not disappointed in his friend. What Purcell called ' the machinations of some narrow-minded ultra-romanisers '[2] stirred March-Phillipps as much as they had stirred Pugin. He wrote to Lord Shrewsbury :—

' Grace-Dieu Manor,
St. Ambrose's Day,' [i.e. 7th Dec.], ' 1839.

My dear Lord Shrewsbury—Though I have countless number of things to say, this letter I must reserve almost entirely to one single topick, deferring the rest to another occasion. It was with deep concern that I learnt fm. our good Bishop as well as fm. Pugin that Propaganda have judged it proper to send a letter to Dr. Walsh condemnatory of the restoration of *our old English vestments* taking the same occasion to speak in terms not only of censure, but I might even say of reprobation of our zealous Bishop for having adopted Pugin's advice relative to the vestments. That Propaganda has been grossly and fraudulently deceived as to the real facts of the case, no one can doubt who looks at the terms in wh. its censure to the Bishop has been conveyed : and that Propaganda will not hesitate to retract that censure, as soon as it has received a true statement of facts, my con-

---

[1] *Phillipps ;* II., pp. 222–4.   [2] *Ib. ;* p. 218.

viction of the rectitude, justice, and prudence of the court of
Rome clearly convinces me—but it is of the utmost importance that this statement should be made as soon as possible,
and that we should discover the *quarter* from wh. the calum-
nious charge against Pugin and our Bishop has proceeded to
Propaganda. I suspect either the English Jesuits or else
Bishop Baines, but the former more than the latter, and this
for solid reasons ; let us ascertain this point, it is of importance. In the letter wh. I received fm. Pugin on the subject
only the day before yesterday, he expressed himself as quite
broken-hearted and as determined to abandon any further
attempts for the Catholic cause, in case this deplorable determination of Propaganda be persisted in : he entreated me to
write to you strongly on the subject, for he sees clearly as I
do that we have no hope but in you and in Dr. Wiseman,
who I trust has more English feeling than to abandon us now.'

The letter is too long for complete transcription, the part
quoted being only about a quarter of the whole. But it is a
masterly and much needed defence of local rights in minor
liturgical matters, and contains some stout thrusts at the
ultra-romanisers, ' men who have no scruple themselves of
violating rubricks every day of their lives, who hesitate not
to wear Chasubles of worsted in defiance of the Church, and
who only cry out against the restorers of the ancient glories
of Religion because they know they do nothing themselves
to restore her long-lost influence, and because they hate those
who devote themselves zealously to the blessed work of
reconverting England.' It ends : ' Once more, my dear L.
Shrewsbury I conjure you to speak out as the premier Earle
of *England*, and as the restorer of the Church of God in this
kingdom : you have a right to speak and your voice will not
be contemned.'[1]

Lord Shrewsbury's action has not been recorded. But no

[1] *Phillipps ;* II., pp. 218–22.

censure was promulgated, and the Gothic vestments were restored to use. Yet it was not a victory for the 'English': the 'narrow-minded ultra-romanisers' were too strong for that. At best it was only a temporary repulse—little more than a year later in another letter to March-Phillipps Pugin was to write[1] :

'You will be grieved to hear that all the altar fittings that were made for Birgham.[2] have been condemned by Dr. Wiseman because they are all in strict conformity with the antient solemn practices. I have just given up now all hope of that church coming to anything *really good :* It will Look very well, *but it will not be the thing*. Poor Hardman is quite disheartened since the attempt on the screen, and Mr. Moore[3] is thwarted in every way by the endeavour to thrust Italian novelties and arrangements into the churches we were raising in the true old style. The bishop is cutting his most energetic assistants from under him. I have mourned so much that I have grown indifferent to what happens, and turn all my attention to publications on these important subjects, by which true principles may be inculcated and become generally understood. But really half my time goes in writing answers to annoying letters on these subjects. I greatly fear that it is the intention to *pull down the great screen after it is finished*,[4] and that it is suffered to remain at present. My immediate resignation, *I have every reason to believe this is contemplated*. There is much bitterness in store for me from that quarter. I shall continue to act in a firm, respectful, and catholic manner— truth till death. Down with the Pagan Monster. St. George and St. Edward for England.'

In Catholic internal affairs the support of March-Phillipps

---

[1] *Phillipps ;* II., pp. 225–6.
[2] *I.e.* St. Chad's Cathedral, Birmingham.
[3] The Rev. John Moore, D.D. (1807–56) ; appointed in 1840 to superintend the building of St. Chad's.
[4] The screen survives, but has been modified and made more open, as well as being advanced some distance into the nave, in order to increase the size of the choir.

and Lord Shrewsbury could only lead to a semblance of victory and a prolongation of the struggle. In anything outside that narrow circle, the battle was a losing one and fought alone. Pugin had the temerity to try to plant ' the real thing ' in Oxford after antagonising its inhabitants by a furious onslaught on the proposed Martyr's Memorial, a building of which perhaps the best that can be said is that it was put up ' on a site where these worthies did not happen to have been burnt,' the object of its erection being ' to work up a case against the Tractarians by their certain refusal to subscribe.' [1] Pugin's onslaught was in pamphlet form, and was delivered under the title of *A Letter on the Proposed Protestant Memorial to Cranmer, Ridley, and Latymer; addressed to the Subscribers to and Promoters of that Undertaking.*

It was not a work likely to endear him to the University, for the Memorial, being ' used as a sieve in whose meshes the Camdenians stuck,' [2] was already a source of controversy, and Pugin joined in the fray with a zeal wholly untempered with discretion. The matter and tone of the pamphlet may be gauged from the fact that the Reformers were described as ' vile, blasphemous imposters pretending inspiration while setting forth false doctrines,' and the subscribers as ' foul revilers, tyrants, usurpers, extortioners and liars.' That was bad enough ; but what made matters worse was the fact that under the torrent of savage invective there lay a substratum of solid historical research. From the point of view of Oxford, Pugin was not only a man who said much too much and said it much too violently : he was a man who knew a little too much as well. As to the Memorial itself, those who wished ' to work up a case against the Tractarians ' won the day. In 1841 an ' Eleanor ' Cross was put up and ' was

---

[1] *The Victorian Tragedy;* E. Wingfield-Stratford; p. 174.
[2] *Clark;* p. 234.

greatly admired and attracted much notice at the time of its erection.' [1]   When considering the reason for its existence, a touch of not unpleasing irony is given by Eastlake's next statement : ' It is generally admitted to be a most creditable work for its date.'   The irony is deepened by a remark of its architect, Mr. (afterwards Sir) George Gilbert Scott, one of Pugin's most enthusiastic admirers : ' I fancy that the cross was better than anyone but Pugin could have produced.' [2]

In the year following that in which he had thus put Cranmer, Ridley, and Latymer in their heretical places, Pugin went to stay in Oxford with the Rev. John Rouse Bloxam, who was then a Fellow of Magdalen and had become a friend of March-Phillipps through a carriage accident in a Leicestershire lane. This man, an ardent antiquarian, Tractarian, ritualist, and Gothicist, introduced him to William George Ward, then a Fellow of Balliol.   Pugin was delighted with Ward.   He found huge folio volumes of St. Thomas Aquinas and St. Bonaventure on Ward's table, and recognised the true mediæval spirit.   ' What an extraordinary thing,' he remarked to Bloxam, ' that so glorious a man as Ward should be living in a room without mullions to the windows.' [3]   Later he taxed Ward with this deficiency, who replied : ' What are mullions ?   I never heard of them ' ; adding, when Pugin expressed incredulity : ' I haven't the most distant idea what they are like.'   Pugin was horrified.   Yet Ward was ' a glorious man ' : there was the evidence of St. Thomas and St. Bonaventure and the conversations they had had on those and kindred subjects.   Ward must be joking.   Further instances of incredible architectural ignorance only deepened the impression.   ' I see how it is, my dear sir,' he said, ' you conceal your graces.'   Pugin was wrong.   Ward was not joking, and he had no Gothic graces to conceal.   However,

---

[1] *Eastlake ;* p. 377.   [2] Quoted in *Clark ;* p. 234.
[3] *Ward (Oxford) ;* p. 154.

that did not prevent his seeing who was the best man to do work in that style, and, the need arising for a considerable amount of rebuilding in Balliol, he got his new friend appointed architect.

Pugin was delighted. He had very definite ideas as to what form a College on a Catholic foundation should take. He had delved deeply into the Middle Ages for his knowledge. He knew what such a building should be. He knew that he could produce it. Balliol was a mediæval foundation. It was not so much a matter of trade as of justice that Balliol should be given buildings at least as good as those which had to be superseded.

Back in Cheyne Walk, Chelsea, he set to work with whole-hearted energy, and two clergymen, calling on him a fortnight later, ' found not merely the usual architectural drawings for a new chapel, master's house, gateway and rooms, but large perspective drawings of all these in water colours—interiors as well as exteriors—lining the entire walls of his room.' The clergymen were amazed, both at the quantity and the quality of the work, and, seeing him working single-handed, asked him why he did not give the mere mechanical part of his working drawings to a clerk. Pugin's reply was as startling as his productivity : ' Clerk, my dear sir, clerk, I never employ one ; I should kill him in a week.'[1]

In addition, he was working on a volume of smaller drawings of the proposed buildings. This book, bound in red velvet and brass, and carefully illuminated, has something of the appearance of a mediæval Missal or Book of Hours, and it was intended as a present for Ward. The pictures in it, obviously drawn with loving care, show the Balliol that he considered ought to be. It was to be a Balliol in which its Founder might have walked without unease. There was to be a great square kitchen with a fine octagonal roof ; and he

[1] *Ferrey ;* p. 187.

added a drawing showing the interior, open to the roof-timbers, with cooks at their work before huge fires. There were to be rooms suitable for the earnest labour of Christian undergraduates; he showed them plainly furnished with solid mediæval furniture, including praying-desks and one or two pictures, lightly touched in but giving the impression of being of sacred subjects.[1]

The majority of the Balliol Fellows, it appears, were suitably impressed; and well they might be; for the designs, though they show the common Gothic error of giving inadequate window area, were in that respect no worse than those ultimately chosen, and in others were very much finer.

The Master of Balliol, however, the Rev. Richard Jenkyns, was made of sterner Protestant stuff.

The tale is told of a mid-nineteenth-century nobleman, a Peelite, that when present at Disraeli's speeches on the proposed repeal of the Corn Laws, in order to prevent himself from being persuaded, he had to keep muttering: " Damned Jew ! Damned Jew ! " The state of mind of the Master of Balliol seems to have been somewhat similar. At any rate, the discussion of the matter waxed so furious that the page concerning it was later removed from the Minute Book.[2]

Pugin's designs were not accepted. One is tempted to wonder if the designs submitted by Mr. Basevi were also rejected on conscientious grounds.[3]

A touch of irony is added to the affair by the fact that the Protestant architect whose designs were eventually chosen, Mr. Anthony Salvin, had been less successful in an earlier endeavour—that competition which had been won by designs sold by Pugin to Charles Barry.

The loss of the Oxford business, however, was more

[1] This book, and some of the other drawings, are now at Balliol.
[2] Information of the present Master of Balliol and Mr. F. F. Urquhart.
[3] The President of Magdalen was less conscientious, and Pugin was employed to build a new gateway on Longwall for that College. It was his only architectural work in the University, and has since been pulled down.

Oxford's loss than Pugin's. For outside Oxford he had more work on hand than even he could well deal with, and in addition to his architectural work, he had found other occupation at a place where ' the real thing ' was allowed to flourish. Introduced by Lord Shrewsbury in 1837, in which year *Contrasts* was read in the refectory during dinner, he had become Professor of Ecclesiastical Antiquities at St. Mary's College, Oscott.

CHAPTER XIII

OSCOTT

Grettir . . . asked whether they did not want a man to work for them and said he would much like to go with them. So much he got from his talk that they let him join them.

The Saga of Grettir the Strong.

THIRTY-NINE years after its first foundation, St. Mary's College, Oscott, near Birmingham, under the able Presidency of the Rev. Henry Weedall, had grown greater in numbers than the original building, though considerably enlarged, could contain. Land for a new building was bought in the neighbourhood, and a Mr. Potter from Lichfield, who seems to have been builder as well as architect, was placed in charge of the work in collaboration with the Rev. John Kirk, of Lichfield, then aged seventy-five, 'to whom indeed is attributed the greater part of the design of the interior arrangements.'[1] Fears might reasonably have been entertained as to the results of collaboration between a professional architect and an elderly clergyman whose chief claim to fame is as the laborious collector of materials for an unwritten Catholic history; but in this case they would have proved groundless. The result, though not entirely in accordance with Pugin's *True Principles* in that elevation was not always kept subservient to plan, was generally speaking successful. Pugin himself was employed on decorative work, and was responsible for ' much of the interior decoration, and especially of the Church.'[2] The result of their combined labours was that ' the lofty halls, the spacious corridors, the numerous and well-appointed class-rooms, combine with the stately library

[1] *Oscotian*, 88; p. 68.　　　　　　　[2] *Ib.*

and the devotional and chastely-decorated chapel, to form a group worthy of a Catholic College, while the long line of terrace, with the commanding tower surmounted by the flag of St. George, looks down upon the neighbour town of Birmingham with a picturesque dignity hardly surpassed in England.'[1]

Making due allowance for possible excess of enthusiasm in the writer of a Jubilee appreciation, the fact remains that the architecture of Oscott was much better than might have been expected from the period and the circumstances of its building. How far this success was due to Dr. Weedall—to ' his untiring industry, his love of order, and his unceasing care for the good of the College '[2]—to Mr. Potter,[3] or to Mr. Kirk, it would now seem impossible to determine ; but there can be no doubt as to Pugin's share in the success.[4] At any rate, when Dr. Weedall, after being superseded in the presidency in circumstances of doubtful propriety in 1840,[5] returned to Oscott in 1853 to resume the post of President and reorganise a disordered institution, he found at least buildings in which he could take a justifiable pride.

The work itself progressed rapidly. The date 1835 is carved on the lintel of a doorway opening out of the cloister into the quadrangle. In 1836 the first stone of the chapel was laid by Dr. Walsh, ' on which occasion the Rev. Thos. McDonnell, of St. Peter's, Birmingham, delivered an extemporaneous and powerful discourse.'[6] Before the end of 1837

---

[1] *Oscotian*, 88 ; p. 17. [2] *Ib. ;* p. 46.

[3] Probably not very much to Mr. Potter, who, on Pugin's arrival, ' retired in dudgeon, and never came to the College again till 1856.' [*Oscotian*, 19 ; p. 121.] He is elsewhere [*Sequel ;* I., p. 111] said to have been ' somewhat unceremoniously dismissed.'

[4] In addition to his work in the College itself, Pugin built the North Lodge (or Gate). This is one of the buildings illustrated in the frontispiece to the *Apology*, and another drawing of it by Pugin was published in *Oscotian*, 88, opposite p. 117.

[5] He had gone to Rome to appeal against his proposed elevation to the episcopate, and on his return, after a successful appeal, he found ' the College in other hands, and all prospect of regaining his position . . . denied.' The ' other hands ' were those of the Right Rev. Nicholas Wiseman, D.D.

[6] *Oscotian*, 88 ; p. 69.

the chapel was completed, ' and the Sanctuary with its beautiful groined roof admirably decorated by Mr. Pugin.' [1]   In addition to this decoration, which included the designs for the stained glass, Pugin was responsible for a considerable part of the building itself, for, on his arrival and Mr. Potter's departure, the chapel, then nearly finished, was placed in his hands. Potter's chapel ' was a plain oblong building, and the altar was to have been placed against the flat wall at the east end.' [2]   Pugin ' knocked out the east end wall and inserted the present chancel arch,' and also ' added the apsidal sanctuary, with its beautiful groined roof,' and ' designed the reredos and inserted those ten pieces of very valuable Limoges enamel in the Gradus.' [2]

A year later occurred one of those moments which must have been for Pugin an oasis in a waste of bitterness and disappointment.   On Tuesday, 29th May, the high altar was consecrated by Dr. Walsh, and on the following Thursday ' the church was solemnly dedicated to Our Lady and opened for public worship.' [3]   There were two factors which made this opening different from other similar events.   For one thing, ' the magnificence of the ceremony was especially striking in those days, for the Pontifical High Mass was in all probability the grandest that had ever been witnessed in England since the overthrow of religion in the sixteenth century ' [3] ; and for another, Pugin himself, in conjunction with the Rev. James Brown, conducted the ceremonies.

' I also assisted at the opening of the chapel at New Oscott,' wrote Bishop Ullathorne, ' at which all the bishops were present, as well as a hundred priests.   On that occasion the more ample form of vestments was first introduced in place of the old form derived from France.   Pugin, with his dark eyes flashing and tears on his cheeks, superintended the pro-

---

[1] *Oscotian*, 88; p. 69.   [2] *Ib.*, 19; p. 134.
[3] *Ib.*, 88; p. 70.

cession of the clergy, and declared that it was the greatest day for the Church in England since the Reformation.' [1]

In the Jubilee Number of *The Oscotian*, 1888, there is reproduced a drawing by Pugin of the ' Chapel of the New College of St. Marie's, Oscott.' In the foreground is the heavily ornamented rail dividing the choir from the remainder of the building. The floor of the choir is slightly raised, and over it is spread a panelled ceiling supported on massive beams. Beyond it, the floor-level rises again to the apsidal Sanctuary, where High Mass is in progress at a tall and minutely decorated altar. Behind and on either side of the altar, tall perpendicular-traceried windows fill the spaces between the piers which support the groined roof. The whole thing is grey and dim. Light strikes obliquely on the backs of the priests and servers at the altar. The clergy in the choir-stalls on the epistle side are almost invisible in shadow ; those on the gospel side are pallid against the light. But in reality the whole scene was gorgeous with colour. Polychrome decoration had been revived and had been applied by a master. There was ' something of eastern splendour, mingled with simplicity, at once rich and quiet, in the exuberant mixture of gold and colour which this great artist reintroduced into England after a century and a half of whitewash and false marbling,' [2] and the roof and apse of the Oscott chapel were among the finest examples of his work. [3] Pugin has been accused of having ' starved his roof-tree to gild his altar,' [4] but at Oscott he had no roof-tree to starve, and all the resources of his passionate enthusiasm could be lavished on the decoration of the choir and sanctuary. But

---

[1] *The Life and Times of Bishop Ullathorne ;* Dom Cuthbert Butler ; p. 60 ; quoting Bishop Ullathorne's *Autobiography*, p. 142.

[2] *Oscotian*, 88 ; p. 112.

[3] ' Were among the finest.' The chapel has been restored more than once, and ' the soft tone of the indigo blue, which used to sooth ' the soul of Edwin de Lisle, the seventh son of Ambrose March-Phillipps, ' during the long hours of devotion in schoolboy days,' is to be seen no longer. [*Oscotian*, 88 ; p. 112.]

[4] *Eastlake ;* p. 162.

the colour of Oscott chapel did not end with painted stone and wood. Over all, the windows shed their variegated light. Immediately behind the altar, ' Our Lady is represented crowned and bearing in her arms the Sacred Infant, and attended on her right by St. Gregory the Great and St. Catherine, and by St. Thomas of Canterbury and St. Cecilia on her left. . . . The side windows, of three lights each, contain on the gospel side the figures of SS. John, Bartholomew, Peter, Matthew, Philip and Thaddeus; and on the epistle side those of SS. James, Paul, Simon, Thomas, James and Andrew.'[1] In addition, heraldry added its colour from the lower portion of the central lights of the side windows : on the epistle side, the arms of Gandolfi (argent, a base vert, thereon a poplar tree supported by two lions rampant, proper, crowned or) ; on the gospel side, the arms of Hornyold (azure, on a bend embattled counter-embattled argent, a wolf passant between two escallops sable).

On that May morning the paintwork was untouched by time, and the light passed enriched with colour through windows as yet unclouded by the blown grime of Birmingham. The flames of the candles on the altar were palely aspirant in that glowing light. Jewels and points of metal glinted like spurts of flame. Incense rose in whorls of grey and palest blue; the air was heavy with it. Before the altar, the splendour of ritual proceeded like a slow dance of exquisite restraint. The light touched to more glowing colours the robes of the celebrant and his assistants—the Bishop of Cambysopolis and Vicar Apostolic of the Midland District, his assistant priest, the deacon and subdeacon, the two assistant deacons at the throne—moving slowly about their sacrifice ; lay like a wash of colour over the white cottas of the servers, and dimmed the candle-flames of the two acolytes ; shone on the magnificence of two attending prelates ; glinted on the

[1] *Oscotian*, 88 ; p. 69.

ambient incense motes. And enriching it all was the fact that Catholicism was displayed in its glory for the first time in England for two hundred years. Long night had chastened the Church in England ; there had been the wan grey twilight of approaching dawn : the commencement of the Pontifical High Mass at Oscott was as the first appearance of the sun's rim above the horizon. Or so it must have seemed to Pugin, who loved the splendour and panoply of worship. And he, Pugin, since the previous year Professor of Ecclesiastical Antiquities in St. Marie's College, as it were a Catholic born in exile but now exiled no longer, was in a sense one with all these things. For his was the passionate love which had made much of that beauty possible ; his was the decoration of God's sanctuary ; his the windows which shed their added colour upon the Mass ; his the reredos of the altar ; his [1] the organisation of the ceremonies . . .

Dr. Weedall preached, and ' though Dr. Weedall excelled in almost everything that he undertook, preaching was evidently his grand distinguishing talent.' [2] He based his sermon on the sixth chapter of *Esdras*. His actual text does not seem to be recorded ; but the whole chapter must have seemed to Pugin like a trumpet-call :

' Cyrus the king decreed, that the house of God should be built, which is in Jerusalem, in the place where they may offer sacrifices ; and that they lay the foundations that may support the height of threescore cubits, and the breadth of threescore cubits, three rows of unpolished stones, and so rows of new timber. . . . And also let the golden and silver vessels of the temple of God, which Nabuchodonosor took out of the temple of Jerusalem, and brought to Babylon, be restored, and carried back to the temple of Jerusalem to their place, which also were placed in the temple of God. . . . And the

---

[1] Together with the Rev. James Brown, afterwards Bishop of Shrewsbury.
[2] *Oscotian*, 88 ; p. 45 ; quoting Dr. Husenbeth.

ancients of the Jews built, and prospered according to the prophecy of Aggeus the prophet, and of Zacharias the son of Addo. And they built and finished, by the commandment of the God of Israel. . . . And the children of Israel, the priests and the Levites, and the rest of the children of the captivity kept the dedication of the house of God with joy.'[1]

They kept the dedication of the house of God with joy; and as believer, as worshipper, as organiser, as artist, he, Pugin, Professor of Ecclesiastical Antiquities in St. Marie's College, was one with all those things. It was as it were a communion of sacramentals.

To a man of Pugin's temperament, such episodes are of the kind that make marks upon the soul.

More—a less common phenomenon—they inspired him with gratitude. In the spring of 1842, three years after leaving Oscott, he designed and gave a new altar for a side chapel. It was dedicated to St. George and St. Patrick, and the relics of SS. Betalion, Bonianus, and Severus were deposited within the altar-stone.[2]

---

[1] From the Douai Version of *I. Esdras*, vi., 3–16. 'The discourse was well adapted to the occasion, and was very eloquent.' [*The Catholic Magazine;* July 1838.]

[2] *Oscotian*, 88 ; p. 75.

CHAPTER XIV

TRUE PRINCIPLES

Roland planted the flag on the top of a hill, straight against the heaven.
The Song of Roland.

PUGIN'S services to Catholic art at Oscott did not end with those enumerated in the last chapter. He lived there at intervals for two or three years, in No. 9, St. Bede's passage, and the impress of his personality may be seen throughout the College, from the professor's gowns down to the iron ink-pots in the Study Place. His bill there for furniture alone, including ' the simple furniture which he had made for his room,'[1] and which is still in the College, came to £3,576 13s. 10d.

The list of Pugin's works at Oscott goes far to justify the description which Dr. Weedall was later to give of him as ' that Bezaleel of art '[2]:

' See, the Lord hath called by name Bezaleel . . . and he hath filled him with the spirit of God, in wisdom, in under-standing, and in knowledge, and in all manner of workman-ship ; and to devise cunning works, to work in gold, and in silver, and in brass, and in the cutting of stones, to set them, and in carving of wood, to make any manner of cunning work. And he hath put in his heart that he may teach, both he, and Aholiab. . . . Them hath he filled with wisdom of heart, to work all manner of work, of the engraver, and of the cunning workman, and of the embroiderer, in blue, and in purple, in scarlet, and in fine linen, and of the weaver, even of them that do any work, and of those that devise cunning work.'[3]

[1] *Oscotian,* 19 ; p. 122.   [2] *Weedall ;* p. 20.   [3] *Exodus ;* xxxv., 30–5.

There was the museum, which he started, and for which he
designed two showcases. The oak shelves, chairs, and tables,
in what is now the theological library, were made in London
from his designs. He designed the paschal candlestick,
which, eleven feet high, made of carved wood, gilded, and
formerly having ornamental branches on three sides, was stated
by Bishop Amherst, 'who had travelled a great deal,' to be
'the finest Paschal candlestick in Europe.'[1] He designed
'the carved stone image of the Madonna on the Upper
Terrace, under its stone canopy, supporting four large Gothic
lamps,' a statue for which he had a great affection, often
causing it to be copied, for 'it is an exact copy of the Madonna
in St. Chad's Cathedral, which is said to be the first image of
the Blessed Virgin set up for public veneration in England
since the Reformation.'[2] He designed a silver gilt and
enamelled Gothic pax, which was afterwards pictured and
described in his *Glossary*. The fifteenth-century pulpit
intended for the chapel being sent to St. Chad's, he 'designed
the present pulpit over the stalls, and inserted the door in the
wall to get into it, by the belfry stairs.'[3] He designed a
screen, 'a high and massive wooden structure,' which
'stretched across, from the chapel door to St. George's
chapel.'[4] He made designs for a 'Milner Chauntry,' which,
'had they been carried out, would have surpassed anything
about the College.'[5] He designed the silver church plate
that was made 'out of the extra silver forks and spoons, which
students were obliged to bring to school with them in olden
times.'[6] He designed the leaden cap or steeple on the top of
the Bell Tower, a work which in consequence 'was always
spoken of by the boys as "Pugin's night cap." '[7] Artifex as
well as artist, when a silver-gilt chalice—the first to be made

---

[1] *Oscotian*, 19; p. 138.
[2] *Ib.*; pp. 125–6.
[3] *Ib.*; p. 135.
[4] *Ib.*; p. 135.
[5] *Ib.*; p. 136.
[6] *Ib.*; p. 136.
[7] *Ib.*; p. 137.

to his design, and ordered for the opening of the chapel—
arrived in an unfinished state the night before the opening, he
'took a sharp instrument and himself carved the figure of a
crucifix upon it.' [1] He designed and gave a brass crucifix and
four brass altar candlesticks as a votive offering for having
escaped a dangerous storm when at sea. Engraved on them
is a flash of lightning and the inscription : '*Beatae Mariae
Virgini sospes ex turbidine et diris fulminibus Augustus Welby
Pugin, ex voto.*' [2] He designed two sets of vestments, and,
sidelight on the lack of good craftsmanship of the day, had to
have them 'made in London, by the costume makers of the
Italian Opera,' the only people at that time capable of working
from his designs. [3] In addition to all these works, 'tradition
points out a room at Oscott where on Saturday afternoons he
instructed craftsmen from Hardman's, of Birmingham.' [4]
More, he made the designs which he was teaching them how
to carry out. In *The Laity's Directory* for 1839, there appears
an illustrated two-and-a-half-page advertisement of 'Ecclesiastical Ornaments, Designed from Ancient Authorities and
Examples, by A. W. Pugin, *Architect and Professor of Ecclesiastical Antiquities at St. Mary's College, Oscott;* Executed in
a very superior style, and with scrupulous regard to Canonical
Laws, by John Hardman, Jun.,[5] *of Birmingham.* Consisting
of Crucifixes of various dimensions, Altar and Processional
Candlesticks, Processional Crosses, Portable Vats for Holy
Water, with Sprinklers, Sacrying Bells, Morses for Copes,
Sanctuary Lamps, Altar-bread Boxes, Stoups for Holy Water
in Chambers or Churches, Bindings for large Altar-Missals,
Thuribles, Chalices, Ciboriums, Monstrances, Cruets, Taber-

---

[1] *Oscotian,* 19; p. 137. [2] *Ib.;* p. 137.
[3] *Ib.;* p. 123. [4] *Sirr, F.R.I.B.A.*
[5] 1811–67. The producer of nearly all Pugin's work in glass and metal. Founded
the Ecclesiastical Metal Works (John Hardman & Co.) in Birmingham, in 1838, to
which he added the Stained Glass Works in 1845. Dr. Weedall might with justice
have mentioned him as Aholiab when he described Pugin as Bezaleel. His nephew
and partner, John Hardman Powell (1827–95), was Pugin's only pupil, and afterwards married Anne, Pugin's only daughter by his first wife.

nacles, Antependiums, Branches for Lights, and every other description of Church Furniture.'

It was a busy life, and a happy one; for he had a large amount of work on hand, and all his energies were turned towards the production of ' the real thing.' It is no wonder that he ' always spoke of his " Oscott days " with enthusiasm and even affection.' [1] On all sides in Oscott his work was appreciated. He was idolised by the students of the College —and ' they warmly expressed their feelings in an address, which upon one occasion they presented to him.' [1] He was approved by Bishop Walsh, who, on the formal transfer, on 18th October 1839, of the Marini Library to Oscott, ' made the first speech, and, after alluding to the recent opening of the New College, went on to remark :—" I feel deeply indebted to the talents and zeal of the celebrated Mr. Pugin for the beauty of our Chapel, the solemnity added to the religious ceremonies, for many valuable presents to the Museum, and for various other acts of kindness." ' [2]

In one sense, however, all these works at Oscott, many and satisfying as they are, were subsidiary to his work there as lecturer. His actual works gave as it were a taste of ' the real thing.' His lectures showed why ' the real thing ' was worthy of its name, by what principles it could be applied to modern needs, and by what methods that application could be carried out. They were lectures on craftsmanship, in an age when craftsmanship hardly existed, by a craftsman and trainer of craftsmen. They were lectures on Christian art by one who was himself a Christian artist. They were a devastating attack on shoddy workmanship and shams, and a trumpet-call to better things, by one who was himself a partial fulfilment of

---

[1] *Oscotian*, 19; p. 123.

[2] *Oscotian*, 19; p. 153. It seems to have been a thoroughly cheerful and friendly occasion; for, later in the proceedings, ' Mr. Hugh Cholmeley spoke a sonnet in Italian in praise of Bishop Walsh,' and was followed by Herr Benz, the professor of German and Music, who made ' a humorous speech in German.'

his own prophecy that ' God will yet raise up some glorious men, who will restore his sanctuary.' [1]

In 1837, at the ' Old College ' at Oscott, the lectures began, and they continued in the ' New College ' in a room which is still inscribed ' Architectura.' Four of them were printed in *The Catholic Magazine* in 1838 and 1839. The first of these lectures ends with a passage in which he expounds his theory of the service of art to religion :

' The Mass, whether offered up in a garret, or a cathedral, is essentially the same sacrifice ; yet, who will not allow that, when surrounded by all the holy splendour of Catholic worship, these august mysteries appear ten times more overpowering and majestic ? St. Augustine declares that, whilst hearing the solemn chaunt of praise, as melody was poured into his ears, truth flowed to his heart ; may we not then confidently hope, in the like manner, that, whilst the senses are rapt in extasy, by the outward beauty of holiness, the divine truths will penetrate the soul thus prepared for their reception.'

The third lecture, on glasswork, amplifies his remark that West's window in Hereford Cathedral was ' yet more execrable than the window of New College Chapel,' [2] and is an admirable piece of critical straight-hitting. Of Sir Joshua Reynold's window he writes :

' It is in this manner [i.e. using rectangular panes] that the miserable attempt in the west window of New College, Oxford, was executed. To admit the insertion of this trans-parency, the whole of the ancient tracery of this once beautiful window was cut and destroyed ; while, at an enormous expense, a subject was introduced, two thirds of which con-sists of dirty brown clouds, under which are the representations of some women, having the appearance of third-rate actresses,

[1] Letter to *The Tablet*, 15 March 1851.   [2] See p. 43.

but who are dignified with the designation of the Cardinal
Virtues. The wretched man who lives by showing people the
horrible window through the hole in the organ, impudently
points it out as an object for special admiration.'

In two other lectures, which were published in book form
in 1841 as *The True Principles of Pointed or Christian Architecture*—those printed in *The Catholic Magazine* were largely
but amplifications of some aspects of these—Pugin stated
definitely those rules by which he considered that all construction should be guided.

With commendable straightforwardness, the book enters
immediately upon its thesis :

' The object of the present Lecture is to set forth and explain
the true principles of Pointed or Christian Architecture, by
the knowledge of which you may be enabled to test architectural excellence. The two great rules for design are these :
1st, *that there should be no features about a building which are
not necessary for convenience, construction, or propriety ; 2nd,
that all ornament should consist of enrichment of the essential
construction of the building.*'

As a corollary he adds :

' The neglect of these two rules is the cause of all the bad
architecture of the present time. Architectural features are
continually tacked on buildings with which they have no
connection, merely for the sake of what is termed effect.'

It was not only in this particular that Pugin was in advance
of his time, and of some of the architects of ours :

' In pure architecture the smallest detail should *have a
meaning or serve a purpose ;* and even the construction itself
should vary with the material employed, and the designs should
be adapted to the material in which they are executed.' [1]
With his next statement, however, he comes on to more
controversial ground :

[1] *True Principles ;* p. 1.

'Strange as it may appear at first sight, it is in *pointed architecture alone that these great principles have been carried out*. . . . Moreover, the architects of the middle ages were the first who *turned the natural properties of the various materials to their full account*, and made *their mechanism a vehicle for their art.*'

Nevertheless, he makes out a good case for his position, and incidentally shows that he had a true comprehension of Gothic :

'A pointed church is the masterpiece of masonry. It is essentially a stone building ; its pillars, its arches, its vaults, its intricate intersections, its ramified tracery, are all peculiar to stone, and could not be consistently executed in any other material. Moreover, the ancient masons obtained great altitude and great extent with a surprising economy of wall and substance ; the wonderful strength and solidity of their buildings are the result not of the *quantity or size of the stones employed*, but of the *art of their disposition.*' [1]

The argument then continues : stone is the right material for Gothic ; Greek architecture was founded on construction with wood ; therefore Greek Architecture consists as it were merely in building a wooden shed with stone.—'The finest temple of the Greeks is constructed on the *same principle* as a large wooden cabin ' [2]—therefore, for a stone building, Gothic, being more suited to the material, is superior to Greek.

In detail, too, the superiority remains : buttresses of some sort are necessary to the strength and appearance of a building ; the Gothic buttress, as it rises, diminishes with the lessening pressure ; the classic buttress has to take the form of an engaged column, which, first, is designed for a superincumbent weight, secondly, gives the impression of having once been detached, the wall being built afterwards, and thirdly, does not diminish with the lessening pressure.

[1] *True Principles ;* p. 2.   [2] *Ib. ;* p. 3.

Classic—or as Pugin would have it, ' Pagan '—architecture
leads, in fact, inevitably to shams. And what of Gothic ?
The following extract gives an example of the application of
both Pugin's ' principles,' and is a good specimen both of his
prose and of his style in disputation :

' I have yet to speak of flying buttresses, those bold arches,
as their name implies, by which the lateral thrust of the nave
groining is thrown over the aisles and transferred to the
massive lower buttresses. Here again we see the true principles of Christian architecture, by the conversion of an
essential support of the building into a light and elegant
decoration. Who can stand among the airy arches of Amiens,
Cologne, Chartres, Beauvais, or Westminster, and not be
filled with admiration at the mechanical skill and beautiful
combination of form which are united in their construction ?
But, say the modern critics, they are only props, and a
bungling contrivance. Let us examine this. Are the revived
pagan buildings constructed with such superior skill as to
dispense with these supports ? By no means ; the clumsy
vaults of St. Paul's, London, mere coffered semi-arches,
without ribs or intersections, *have their flying buttresses ; but
as this style of architecture does not admit of the great principle of decorating utility*, these buttresses, instead of being
made *ornamental, are concealed by an enormous screen*, going
entirely round *the building. So that in fact one half of the
edifice is built to conceal the other*. Miserable expedient !
worthy only of the debased style in which it has been
resorted to.' [1]

For the rest, the lecture goes on in a style of dogmatic
pugnacity. Henry the Seventh's Chapel at Westminster
receives its meed of praise, but is condemned as a whole
because of the stone pendants in the ceiling, which are an
example of ' *constructing the ornament instead of confining it to*

[1] *True Principles ;* p. 4.

the enrichment of its construction.[1] St. Paul's Cathedral is given an additional thrust on the score of its ' fictitious dome . . . a mere construction for effect.'[2] The suitable pitch of roofs is laid down as that ' which is formed by two sides on an equilateral triangle.'[3] The best forms for base moulds and weatherings are carefully illustrated and their use justified by the necessity for avoiding ' feather-edged joints.'[4] He states that in pointed buildings the window-jambs must be built in courses and that the stones composing them should not be either large or regular, as otherwise ' the effect of the window is spoiled ; the eye, owing to the regularity of these projections, *is carried from the lines of the jamb to them,* while in the old masonry the irregular outline of the stones does not interfere with the mouldings of the window.'[5] This first section, too, on stonework, contains another important assertion :

' The severity of Christian architecture requires a *reasonable purpose for the introduction of the smallest detail,* and daily experience proves that those who attempt this glorious style without any fixed ideas of its unalterable rules, are certain to end in miserable failures.'[6]

Though Pugin may not have ' treated his subject very philosophically,' as a reviewer in *The Quarterly* seems to have expected, this section contains a valuable mixture of solid theory and sound application.

The second section deals with metal-work :

' And I shall be able to show that the same principles of suiting the design to the material and decorating construction were strictly adhered to by the artists of the middle ages

---

[1] *True Principles ;* p. 6. Pugin's strictures on the Chapel are considerably milder than those of the son of Sir Christopher Wren, who wrote of ' its sharp angles, jetties, narrow lights, lame statues, lace, and other cutwork and crinkle-crankle.' (*Life of Sir C. Wren ;* p. 308.)

[2] *True Principles ;* p. 8.   [3] *Ib. ;* p. 11.

[4] *Ib. ;* p. 15.   [5] *Ib. ;* p. 17.

[6] *Ib. ;* p. 17.

in all their productions in metal, whether precious or common.'[1]

He proceeds to do so:

'In the first place, hinges, locks, bolts, nails, &c., which are always *concealed in modern designs*, were rendered in pointed architecture, *rich and beautiful decorations*.'[1]

These points, together with others, are soundly exemplified. But then there comes a change. There was a wealth of horrible stuff to be cleared away before there should be room for tolerable ironwork. Pugin advances like one attacking a bed of nettles with a stick, his prose gathering momentum for the onslaught:

'The fender is a sort of embattled parapet, with a lodge-gate at each end; the end of the poker is a sharp pointed finial; and at the summit of the tongs is a saint.[2] It is impossible to enumerate all the absurdities of modern metal-workers; but all these proceed from the false notion of *disguising* instead of *beautifying* articles of utility. How many articles of ordinary use are rendered monstrous and ridiculous simply because the artist, instead of making the *most convenient form*, and *then decorating it*, has embodied some extravagance *to conceal the real purpose for which the article has been made!* If a clock is required, it is not unusual to cast a Roman warrior in a flying chariot, round one of the wheels of which, on close inspection, the hours may be descried; or the whole front of a cathedral church reduced to a few inches in height, with the clock-face occupying the position of a magnificent rose window. . . . But this is nothing when compared to what we see continually produced from those inexhaustible mines of bad taste, Birmingham and Sheffield;

---

[1] *True Principles;* p. 19.

[2] There is a noteworthy resemblance between the ironwork here described and that illustrated in *Pugin's Gothic Furniture*, a volume of drawings made in the late 'twenties by Pugin's father, though one of the drawings therein (a 'Gothic Sofa'; dated Nov. 1826) seems to have been by Pugin himself. The poker in *Pugin's Gothic Furniture* has an angel for handle, and the tongs a bishop, while the hearth-brush is reminiscent of the nave of a church!

staircase turrets for inkstands, monumental crosses for light-shades, gable ends hung on handles for door-porters, and four doorways and a cluster of pillars to support a French lamp; while a pair of *pinnacles* supporting an arch is called a Gothic-pattern scraper, and a wiry compound of quatrefoils and fan tracery an abbey garden-seat. Neither relative scale, form, purpose, nor unity of style, is ever considered by those who design these abominations; if they only introduced a quatrefoil or an acute arch, be the outline and style of the article ever so modern and debased, it is at once denominated and sold as Gothic.' [1]

So much for the horrors of early nineteenth-century metal-work. But there were other horrors which required attention. Contemporary wall-papers, upholstery, and curtains are contemptuously condemned, and suggestions made for their improvement. But that is a mere parenthesis. He returns to metal:

'Cast-iron is a deception; it is seldom or never left as iron. It is disguised by paint, either as stone, wood, or marble. This is a mere trick, and the severity of Christian or Pointed Architecture is utterly opposed to all deception.' [2]

Honesty has received its meed of consideration. Now for beauty; for the beauty which adorned the metal-work of the past, which should never have been allowed to lapse. The extract is curious as illustrating both Pugin's ardour in his search for ancient beauty and for his passionate love even for the names of sacred things:

'In the sacristy at Aix-la-Chapelle is a treasury of inestimable value, consisting of shrines, reliquaries, crosses, crowns, ampuls, chalices, pyxes, books of the Holy Gospels, paxes, and enamelled images of silver, all executed during the finest periods of Christian art, the richness of their material being only surpassed by that of their design. . . . Their

[1] *True Principles;* pp. 21–2.   [2] *Ib.;* p. 27.

construction and execution is decidedly of a *metallic character*. The ornament is produced by *piercing, chasing, engraving, and enamel;* many of the parts were first formed in thin plates of metal, and then shaped by the pliers. Engraving is a style of ornament peculiar to metal. The old goldsmiths were undoubtedly the inventors of our present engraved plates for printing. They increased the effect of the ornamental engravings by hollowing out the ground in certain parts, and filling it in with coloured enamels. . . . There are some exquisite examples of chalice feet enamelled with sacred subjects in the sacristy of Mayence Cathedral, and a circular reliquary at Aix, which Dr. Rock considers to have been used as a pax, which is a transcendent specimen of the art of enamel. The covers of the great books of the Holy Gospels were enriched with chasing, enamels, and even jewels; the crucifixion of our Lord in the centre, and the emblems of the Evangelists at the corners of an elaborate border. Precious stones of every description were studded on these ornaments, which presented a wonderful combination of richness and beauty, produced by gold enamel of various hues and sparkling gems, arranged with the purest design and most harmonious effect.'[1]

A final and not undeserved thrust is then given at the metalworkers of his time, and then, loving the beauties of the past, despairing of the tasteless extravagance or incompetence of contemporary work, he turns to that institution which brought about the beauty that he loved :

'Mechanics' institutes are a mere device of the day; the Church is the true mechanics' institute, the oldest and the best. *She was the great and never failing school in which all the great artists of the days of faith were formed.* Under her guidance they directed the most wonderful efforts of her skill to the glory of God; and let our fervent prayer ever be, that the

[1] *True Principles;* pp. 27–8.

Church may again, as in days of old, cultivate the talents of her children to the advancement of religion and the welfare of their own souls ; for without such results talents are vain, and the greatest efforts of art sink to the level of an abomination.' [1]

So ends the first of these two lectures.

The second deals in a similar manner with various other architectural matters, beginning with a consideration of woodwork, and dealing particularly with open timber roofs and the use and misuse of barge-boards on gables. It then passes on to the damage inflicted on the cause of Gothic by incompetent revivalists :

' The modern admirers of the pointed style have done much injury to its revival by the erroneous and costly system they have pursued : the interiors of their houses are one mass of elaborate work ; there is no repose, no solidity, no space left for hangings or simple panels : the whole is covered with trifling details, enormously expensive, and at the same time subversive of good effect. These observations apply equally to furniture : upholsterers seem to think that nothing can be Gothic unless it is found in some church. Hence your modern man designs a sofa or occasional table from details culled out of Britton's Cathedrals, and all the ordinary articles of furniture, which require to be simple and convenient, are made not only very expensive but very uneasy. We find diminutive flying buttresses about an arm-chair ; everything is crocketed with angular projections, innumerable mitres, sharp ornaments, and turreted extremities.[2] A man who remains for any length of time in a modern Gothic room, and escapes without being wounded by some of its minutiæ, may

---

[1] *True Principles ;* p. 30.
[2] The drawing which Pugin gives of the interior of a modern Gothic room, to show how such things should not be done, shows specimens in no wise more fantastic than some in *Pugin's Gothic Furniture* already mentioned. In fact, he might have made his example even more ridiculous by including his father's Gothic *Horizontal Grand Piano Forte.*

consider himself extremely fortunate. There are often as many pinnacles and gablets about a pier-glass frame as are to be found in an ordinary church, and not unfrequently the whole canopy of a tomb has been transferred for the purpose, as at Strawberry Hill. I have perpetrated many of these enormities in the furniture I designed some years ago for Windsor Castle. At that time I had not the least idea of the principles I am now explaining; all my knowledge of Pointed Architecture was confined to a tolerably good notion of details in the abstract; but these I employed with so little judgment or propriety, that, although the parts were correct and exceedingly well executed, collectively they appeared a complete burlesque of pointed design.'[1]

He could hardly say fairer than that.

However, other matters remained before the true principles could be said to be adequately expounded:

' I now come, in the last place, to consider decoration with reference to propriety; what I mean by propriety is this, *that the external and internal appearance of an edifice should be illustrative of, and in accordance with, the purpose for which it is destined.*'[2]

In other words, to take the three principal examples which Pugin himself gives, a church should be built and decorated like a church, not like a pagan temple or ' a very meeting-house '[3] with a sham ecclesiastical façade; and a college should be built and decorated like a college, not like the London University, ' with its useless dome and portico '[4]; and the dwelling-place of an English Christian gentleman should be built and decorated as such, not like an Italian palace, or defenceless castle, or fantastic abbey. In fact, ' the

---

[1] *True Principles;* p. 35.   [2] *Ib;* pp. 35–6.   [3] *Ib.;* p. 38.
[4] *True Principles;* p. 45. He adds: ' It may, however, be urged in its defence [i.e., of the London University building] that anything *ecclesiastical or Christian* would be very inappropriate, and that the *Pagan* exterior is much more in character with the intentions and principles of the institution.'

severity of Christian architecture is opposed to all deception.' [1]
It might be argued that the severity of all architecture which
aspires to be an art is opposed to all deception, and many
benefits might accrue if that argument were more frequently
applied.   But there remain certain practical difficulties.[2]

For a few more pages the book pursues its turbulent way,
rhapsodising over mediæval beauties :

'. . . the great altar, rich in hangings, placed far from
irreverent gaze, and with the brilliant eastern window terminating this long perspective ; while the chantry and guild
chapels, pious foundations of families and confraternities,
contributed greatly to increase the solemnity of the glorious
pile.' (p. 42.)

Lashing out at shams :

' All plaster, cast-iron, and composition ornaments, painted
like stone or oak, are mere impositions, and, although very
suitable to a tea-garden, are utterly unworthy of a sacred
edifice.' (p. 38.)

Striking renewed blows at paganism in all its forms :

' And how can we (who surround the biers of our departed
brethren with blazing tapers, denoting our hope and faith in
the glorious light of the Resurrection), carve the *inverted
torch of Pagan despair* on the very tomb to which we conduct
their remains with such sparkling light ? ' (pp. 39–40.)

Then it closes [3] on a note of humility and hope :

' In conclusion, Christian verity compels me to acknowledge that there are hardly any defects which I have pointed
out to you in the course of this Lecture which could not with

---

[1] *True Principles ;* p. 38
[2] Mr. H. Robertson, F.R.I.B.A., remarks in his *Architecture Explained* (pp. 152–3)
that : ' The question of honesty in a building or in any work of art is undoubtedly a
complex one, and special circumstances may attenuate or even justify a fraud.   A
convenience in a public park may masquerade as a Greek temple, when the setting
and surroundings practically dictate it.   But in the Art of Design, as in the Art of
Life, honesty is generally the best policy.'   It does not appear that Pugin ever
designed ' a convenience in a public park.'   But if he had been called upon to do so,
one may surmise that it would have been somewhat monastic in character.
[3] *True Principles ;* pp. 55–6.

propriety be illustrated by my own productions at some period of my professional career. Truth is only gradually developed in the mind, and is the result of long experience and deep investigation. Having, as I conceive, discovered the true principles of pointed architecture, I am anxious to explain to others the errors and misconceptions into which I have fallen, that they, profiting by my experience, may henceforward strive to revive the glorious works of Christian art in all the ancient and *consistent* principles. Let then the Beautiful and the True be our watchword for future exertions in the overthrow of modern paltry taste and paganism, and the revival of Catholic art and dignity.

✚

𝕷𝖆𝖚𝖘 𝕯𝖊𝖔!'

The Quarterly Review for December 1841, in a review of various architectural works, including Pugin's *True Principles*, pays Pugin the compliment of practically making his ' principles ' its own. But there the compliment ends ; Popery had crept into Pugin's work, and Popery had to be put in its place :

' Mr. Pugin has made a mistake in calling it [Gothic] Catholic architecture—in the sense which he gives to the word—meaning by it *Papal*. St. Peter's and the Jesuits' churches at Rome are the proper types and representatives of Papal art : vast, brilliant, gaudy, full of pretension, appealing directly and servilely to the imagination, frittered into incongruous details, which it is vainly endeavoured to hold together by a composition rationalistic in reality, while it aspires to an assumption of religion : in fact a republication of heathen architecture without its simplicity, and emblematic of a heathen mind, veiled under the garb of Christianity.' [1]

The article then rises to more direct criticism [2] :

[1] Q. R. ; Dec. 1841 ; p. 140.   [2] Ib. ; pp. 144-5.

' Mr. Pugin has not treated his subject very philosophically, or with much insight into the deeper principles of architecture. But the point which he has illustrated is of great importance, and though, as we venture to repeat, he labours under the singular misconception that the beauties of Gothic owed their origin to the Papal and not to the Catholic spirit of the times in which it sprung up, there is much in his little work which is ingenious and interesting. The falsity of such a notion ought to be exposed and insisted on at a time when there seems to be too great a disposition to interest the imagination in matters of religion, and so in young and uninstructed minds to palliate the corruptions of the popish system. And, as before remarked, it might be shown at once by pointing out not only the natural connection and analogy between true Catholic principles and true taste in art; but the similar analogy between the pretensions, exaggerated fancies, appeals to human nature in its corrupt forms, and mixed incongruities of greatness and meanness, truth and falsehood, in Popery, with the same characteristic defects, in the architecture which grew up in Italy more immediately under the papal influence, and which are found less and less prevalent in each country in the same proportion as it was free from the worst tendencies of that fearful usurpation.'

It seems almost a pity that the reviewer did not apparently know of the word ' Nordic.' However, he goes on to quote Pugin's two chief ' principles,' and kindly adds, sugaring the anti-papal pill : ' These principles, so far as they go, are sound and just.'

They are. More : he had discovered them.

But yet, taking it as a whole, the book is plainly the work of a tormented mind. It is in a sense a muddle ; but not the muddle of incompetence ; rather, the turmoil of one who is fighting for what he values more than life itself, assailed on all sides by enemies. For in Pugin's mind lay the image of an

England jewelled with architectural magnificence. Before his eyes lay its scattered fragments, mutilated by time, by religious violence, by the hand of the faithless philistine. The old order had been broken, its relics were being destroyed, the faith and knowledge which had made that beauty possible had been lost. That faith he had ; that knowledge he had rediscovered. But the representatives of that faith, except in isolated instances, were not with him. St. Peter's stood as a mockery, a denial, of everything that he admired. For every beauty that he longed to see restored, there was the destruction of a hundred beauties to be lamented. For every truth that he held, there were hydra-headed falsities to be destroyed. For every genuine piece of work that he could point out for emulation, or that he himself could produce, there was an ever-growing mass of meretricious shams, and shoddy work-manship, and squalor. He was like one swimming for his life across a rushing current, under the necessity of fending off, while he swam, the assaults of flood-borne timber. Little wonder that the work is not marked by orderly arrangement, that he ' has not treated his subject very philosophically,' that he expresses himself with violence.

It may be difficult in this age of artistic dilettantism to appreciate the point of view of one who could take archi-tecture passionately. But if a man should try to imagine an artist and fervent admirer of Rembrandt living in an age when the few remaining works of Rembrandt were being destroyed or mutilated or restored in the style of Angelica Kauffmann, and the one form of art appreciated or produced was that of Benjamin West, he might get some idea of Pugin's point of view. But he would have to add a conception of art as inextricably connected with the worship of God.

The True Principles achieved a second edition in 1853. Its exquisite drawings alone are sufficient to make it worth procuring from its dusty resting-place in the least used shelves

of some library ; and those who may wish to lay the foundations of some reasonable critical standard by which to judge
the works both of the past and of the present time could do
worse than turn to its yellowing pages. They need have no
fear of being turned into 'preterpluperfect goths': ferro-
concrete and skyscrapers and thousand-roomed hotels require
a difference in application.

CHAPTER XV

APOLOGY

He could not count the battalions, they were so many. Astonished within himself, he descended the hill as quickly as he could and told them all : " I have seen pagans —no man upon earth ever saw so many ! There are before us fully a hundred thousand. We shall have battle, such as never has been."

The Song of Roland.

The True Principles, with its analytical power, its violence, and its passionate enthusiasm, was not enough. In that work Pugin had, as it were, justified the cause for which the Gothic army was to fight, he had freed that army from its most troublesome allies, the pseudo-Goths, and he had delivered many shrewd thrusts at the weak points in the array of the enemy. It now remained to strengthen his own forces, to justify yet more definitely their position, to point out the many places in which the forces of the Pagan had attained a footing, and to show that where the Pagan stood the Christian could yet more firmly stand. After that, the battle could become general, and God would (or perhaps would not) defend the right. In any case, once more : *Laus Deo !* This he proceeded to do, in *An Apology for The Revival of Christian Architecture in England*, published in 1843, and fittingly dedicated to the man who, as it were, played Oliver to Pugin's Roland : ' To the Right Honourable The Earl of Shrewsbury, Waterford, and Wexford.'[1]

This dedication deserves remark, both for its manner and its matter. In the first place, it commences with a cross, and another cross appears, as was his custom in correspondence,

---

[1] ' Since the patent of creation to the Earldom of Waterford, 1446, the Earls of Shrewsbury have constantly been styled . . . "Earls of Wexford," though no instrument of creation is extant, nor does it appear that any such instrument ever existed.' [*Complete Peerage ;* G. E. C., 1896 ; VII., p. 137 n.]

before Pugin's name. In the second place, it is printed in mediæval characters. In addition, the initial letter M takes the form of a charming drawing, in which a kneeling figure representative of Pugin himself, dressed, apparently, in a mediæval architect's robe, presents a book to a Lord Shrewsbury, who is dressed in the robes of a mediæval nobleman. Behind Lord Shrewsbury is a shield of the arms of Talbot, and behind Pugin is a shield of his own arms. The relations between the two, as Christians, as mediævalists, as gentlemen, and as architect and patron, could hardly have been more fittingly expressed in typography and illustration.

' My very good Lord,

It would be most unnatural and ungrateful in me, when putting forth a Treatise relating to the Revival of Christian Architecture in England, were I not to dedicate the same in an especial manner to your Lordship, who has been the main support in the furtherance of that good work, and to whom I am so greatly bounden.

May God in his mercy grant, that as your Lordship's noble ancestor, the Talbot of famous memory, extended the temporal glory of England by deeds of arms, so may your Lordship continue to increase the spiritual welfare of these realms by reviving the ancient glories of the English Church, of whose faith your noble house has furnished so many witnesses.

That your Lordship may long be blessed with health and strength to carry out to a happy conclusion the many good designs you have in hand, is the constant prayer of

Your Lordship's devoted and faithful Bedesman,

+ A. Welby Pugin.' [1]

The book opens with a general attack on contemporary architecture.

---

[1] Lord Shrewsbury died on 9th November 1852, two months after his ' devoted and faithful Bedesman.'

'Private judgment runs riot; every architect has a theory of his own, a beau ideal he has himself created; a disguise with which to invest the building he erects. This is generally the result of his latest travels. One breathes nothing but the Alhambra,—another the Parthenon,—a third is full of lotus cups and pyramids from the banks of the Nile,—a fourth, from Rome, is all dome and basilica; whilst another works Stuart and Revett on a modified plan, and builds lodges, centenary chapels, reading-rooms, and fish-markets, with small Doric work and white brick facings. Styles are now *adopted* instead of *generated*, and ornament and design *adapted to*, instead of *originated by*, the edifices themselves.'[1]

That the complaint was largely justified in fact is shown by an article in *The Quarterly Review* in 1837[2]:

'In our suburban streets we have seen salmon and mackrel lying in stately funeral under Doric pillars, and tripe surmounted with metopes, triglyphs, and guttæ of the most classical proportions. In some of our fashionable club-houses, after every interior accommodation has been provided for the members, a portico is superadded, apparently commensurate, not so much with the building itself, as with the unexpended residue of the subscription, and adorned, like the family picture of Dr. Primrose, with as many columns as the artist could afford for the money. While the undecorated windows are left, like Tilburina's maid, in primitive simplicity, a portico, the indispensable necessary of our architectural life, is patched on to every visible wall of our rising *pseudo-palaces*.' Pugin continues[3]:

'This may, indeed, be appropriately termed the *carnival* of architecture: its professors appear tricked out in the guises of all centuries and all nations; the Turk and the Christian, the Egyptian and the Greek, the Swiss and the Hindoo, march

---

[1] *Apology;* pp. 1–2.   [2] *Q. R.;* Feb. 1837; p. 76.
[3] *Apology;* pp. 2–3.

side by side, and mingle together ; and some of these gentlemen, not satisfied with perpetrating one character, appear in
two or three costumes in the same evening.

Amid this motley group (oh ! miserable degradation !) the
venerable form and sacred detail of our national and Catholic
architecture may be discerned ; but *how* adopted ? Not on
consistent principles, not on authority, not as the expression
of our faith, our government, or country, but as one of the
disguises of the day, to be put on and off at pleasure, and
used occasionally as circumstances or private caprice may
suggest.

It is considered suitable for some purposes,—MELAN-
CHOLY, and *therefore fit for religious* buildings ! ! ! a style
that an architect of the day should be acquainted with, in order
to please those who admire old things,[1]—a style in which
there are many beauties : such is the heartless advocacy which
our national architecture frequently receives from its professed admirers ; while others are not wanting, even in the
most influential positions, who venture to sneer at and insult
its principles, either because they are far beyond their comprehension, or that they are so besotted in their mongrel compositions, that they tremble at the ascendency of truth.'

To this passage there is a long and notable footnote :

' It is a perfect disgrace to the Royal Academy, that its
Professor of Architecture [2] should be permitted to poison the
minds of the students of that establishment by propagating

---

[1] 'If a pointed design is sent, it is generally in accordance with the whim of the
architect's employer ; and then a symmetrical front regular, to the utter incon-
venience of the internal arrangements, is dressed up with tracery, battlements, and
pinnacles ; and these sit as uneasy on the modern block, as the chimney stacks and
attics on an Albert Terrace Parthenon.'

[2] Charles Robert Cockerell, R.A., Professor of Architecture in the Royal Academy,
1840–57 ; one of the unsuccessful competitors for the new Houses of Parliament.
After being introduced to each other by Clarkson Stanfield, Pugin said of Cockerell :
" The man is a great artist, though I do not believe in the style he works in " ; and
Cockerell of Pugin : " The most earnest and enthusiastic man in his profession, and
has the greatest belief in it of anyone I ever met." [*Sirr, F.R.I.B.A.*] Cockerell was
one of the subscribers to the Pugin Memorial Fund.

his erroneous opinions of Christian architecture. The influence which his position naturally gives him over their minds is doubtless considerable, and the effect of his instruction proportionately pernicious. Not content, however, with the disparagement of ancient excellence, which he introduces in his official lectures, he is *practically* carrying out his contempt of pointed design in both Universities, and in a manner that must cause anguish of soul to any man of Catholic mind and feeling.

The ancient buildings of King's College, models of perfection in their way, are actually being demolished, to make room for a monstrous erection of mongrel Italian, a heavy, vulgar, unsightly mass, which already obscures from some points the lateral elevation of King's Chapel, and which it is impossible to pass without a depression of spirits and feelings of disgust. A man who paganizes *in the Universities* deserves no quarter; and it becomes a question whether the greater share of blame attaching to such transactions is due to the architect who could so wed himself to the bastard compositions generated in his studio, as to intrude his huge deformity not only in the vicinity but on the site of ancient excellence; or to the authorities of the University, who, in the very teeth of the present revival, have sanctioned so gross a violation of propriety. But their madness is paralleled at Oxford, where the same architect is erecting another unsightly pile of pagan details, stuck together to make up a show, for the university galleries immediately facing the venerable front of St. John's, and utterly destroying this beautiful entrance to the most Catholic-looking city in England. The pagan character of this edifice has, however, awakened the disgust of some of the most learned members of the University; and if it pleases the admirers of gin-palace design, it will draw down the indignation of every true disciple of Catholic and consistent architecture.

But, although some men, by dint of name, fortune, and station, may rule for a brief space, and mock that excellence to which they can never attain, yet their day is fast drawing to a close ;—several of the junta who have disfigured the face of the country are already gone ; and, like Bunyan's giants in the Pilgrim's Progress, the others are so enfeebled that they can only snarl at the revival of excellence. Their works will hardly be endured for the time they have to run, and the remembrance of them will be the laughing-stock of posterity ; and when the ancient glories of our native land are restored, and this generation of pretenders have passed away, men will be amazed that a period could have existed when they were permitted to disfigure and destroy, unchecked and un-reproved.'

The last sentence has a powerful quality of rhythm, an oratorical turn and return, a certain magnificence of invective. ' A man who paganizes *in the Universities* deserves no quarter ' ; ' the admirers of gin-palace design ' : there are several ways of beginning an argument : a cudgel-blow is one of them ; and not necessarily the worst, when the enemy is multitudinous and hated. At any rate, it makes the situation clear : no quarter is to be given, or expected. Pugin was never one to try to win a match on points : he wanted victory. The battle joined, he expounds what he is fighting for :

' The object of this tract is, therefore, to place Christian architecture in its true position,—to exhibit the claims it possesses on our veneration and obedience, as the only correct expression of the faith, wants, and climate of our country.' [1]

It was no mean design. But carrying it out was another matter.

' To advocate Christian architecture merely on the score of its beauty, can never prevail with those, who profess to think

[1] *Apology;* pp. 3–4.

that all art and majesty is concentrated in a Grecian temple. We must turn to the principles from which all styles have originated. The history of architecture is the history of the world : as we inspect the edifices of antiquity, its nations, its dynasties, its religions, are all brought before us.'[1]

In other words, the architecture of past epochs sprang from the religion and social state of its creators, and was expressive of them. But what of contemporary architecture ?

' Will the architecture of our times, even supposing it solid enough to last, hand down to posterity any certain clue or guide to the system under which it was erected ? Surely not ; it is not the expression of existing opinions and circumstances, but a confused jumble of styles and symbols borrowed from all nations and periods.'[2]

As to the perpetrators of these ' thrice-cooked hashes of pagan fragments,' their case was clear enough :

' These uncompromising advocates of classic styles would be utterly repudiated by the humblest architect of pagan antiquity, were he now to return to earth. Vitruvius would spew if he beheld the works of those who glory in calling him master.'[2]

So much for the neo-pagans. They were merely as the ' carrion a man shoots before the fight begins.'[3] The works of the real pagans were worthy of a more dignified approach :

' I believe them to be the *perfect expressions* of *imperfect systems ;* the summit of human skill, expended on human inventions : but I claim for Christian art a merit and perfection, which it was impossible to attain even in the Mosaic dispensation, much less in the errors of polytheism. The former was but a type of the great blessings we enjoy,—the latter, the very antipodes to truth, and the worship of demons. I can readily understand how the pyramid, the obelisk, the

---

[1] *Apology ;* p. 4. [2] *Ib. ;* p. 5.
[3] *The Ballad of the White Horse ;* G. K. Chesterton.

temple, and pagoda have arisen ; whence the arrangement of their plan, and the symbols which decorate them have been generated. I am prepared to join in admiration at the skill which piled such gigantic masses on each other, which fashioned so exquisitely each limb and countenance ; but I cannot acknowledge them to be appropriate types for the architecture of a Christian country.

If we worshipped Jupiter, or were votaries of Juggernaut, we should raise a temple, or erect a pagoda. If we believed in Mahomet, we should mount the crescent, and raise a mosque. If we burnt our dead, and offered animals to gods, we should use cinerary urns, and carve sacrificial friezes of bulls and goats. If we denied Christ, we should reject his Cross. For all these would be natural consequences : but, in the name of common sense, whilst we profess the creed of Christians, whilst we glory in being Englishmen, let us have an architecture, the arrangement and details of which will alike remind us of our faith and our country,—an architecture whose beauties we may claim as our own, whose symbols have originated in our religion and our customs.' [1]

That might seem a good enough opening to a justification for the use of Gothic on railways and the entrances to urban cemeteries. But a nasty flank-attack had to be repulsed first : there were those who ' objected . . . that the pointed style, especially Christian, was not developed till several centuries after the crucifixion of our Lord.' [2] However, attack was, as usual, the best means of defence :

' Like protestants who rail at ecclesiastical solemnity, because it is not to be found in the persecuted church of the apostles, they urge the non-existence of spires under Roman emperors as a proof, that they were not generated by the Christian principles. But modern men are constantly referring to the church in her suffering state, described by our Lord

[1] *Apology;* pp. 5–6.   [2] *Ib.;* p. 6.

under the similitude of a grain of mustard-seed, while they refuse to recognise her, when, as the greatest of all trees, she extended triumphant in beauty and luxuriant foliage over the earth.' [1]

Gothic, then, was the highest development of architecture as representative of Christianity. But, alas, in the sixteenth century there was ' a great contention between Christian and pagan ideas in which the latter triumphed and for the first time *inconsistency* in architectural design was developed.[1] And inconsistency in architecture, when it once creeps in, increases and multiplies and fills the land, so that three hundred years after he could write :

' Never, in the annals of architecture, have so many glorious opportunities offered, in a short space of time, for the accomplishment of noble buildings. Within my own recollection, three royal palaces, half the metropolis, churches without number, vast restorations, entire colleges in both universities, galleries, civic buildings, bridges, hospitals, houses, public monuments, in every possible variety ; and with the exception of the New Houses of Parliament, we have not one edifice of the whole number that it is not painful to contemplate as a monument of national art. [2]

Architecture, in fact, had become a jumble of bungling adaptations.

' In no one instance has the purpose or destination of the building formed the ground-work of the composition : Grecian or Gothic, Ecclesiastical or Civil, it has been a mere system of *adaptation*. One man has adapted a temple, another a castle, a third an abbey ; but temples, castles, and abbeys owed their existence to other wants and systems, foreign to those for which they have been employed, and utter failure is the natural result. Had the various buildings been allowed to tell their own tale, to appear in their natural garb, were it

[1] *Apology ;* p. 7.   [2] *Ib. ;* p. 9.

rich or simple, what variety and interest would our architectural monuments present !—but no, public buildings, it
was said, could not be Gothic, and therefore must be Grecian,
that is, with pediments and porticos. The reasons assigned
were,—1st, That Gothic was so very expensive, which is a
positive falsehood; and, 2ndly, That they would not be in
character. Now, how an edifice that is to consist of doors,
windows, walls, roofs, and chimneys, when consistently
treated, and these various features made parts of the design,
can be *less in character*, than a building where they are bun-
glingly concealed and disguised, it is impossible to imagine.' [1]

In other words, a building should as it were grow out from
its own inner necessities, and should not have those necessities
cramped by the imposition of a façade which had sprung from
other needs. Similarly, to take a classic example, a needlecase
should be a needlecase, not something 'in the Form of a
Harp.' And similarly with Railway Stations :

' The Railways, had they been naturally treated, afforded a
fine scope for grand massive architecture. . . . I do not
hesitate to say, that, by merely following out the work that
was required to its natural conclusion, building exactly what
was wanted in the simplest and most substantial manner,—
mere construction, as the old men weathered the flanking walls
of their defences,—tens of thousands of pounds could have
been saved on every line, and grand and durable masses of
building been produced; but from inconsistency, whenever
anything sublime has been attempted at the stations, the result
is perfectly ridiculous.

In every instance the architects have plainly considered it
an opportunity for *showing off what they could do*, instead of
carrying out what was required. Hence the colossal Grecian
portico or gateway, 100 feet high, for the cabs to drive through,
and set down a few feet further, at the 14-inch brick wall and

[1] *Apology;* p. 9.

sash-window booking-office.[1] This piece of Brobdignagian absurdity must have cost the company a sum which would have built a first-rate station, replete with convenience, and which would have been really grand from its simplicity. . . . At Rugby, because Rugby School, as rebuilt lately, has bad battlements and turrets, the old station had four half-turrets with the best side turned out, and a few sham loop-holes; a little further on, Gothic is dispensed with, and the barrack style prevails; at either end, two modern Greek buildings of colossal dimensions, both of which are utterly useless. The London gateway could not shelter a porter; while the Birmingham entrance [2] was so unsuitable for its purpose, that the company have been obliged to erect various sheds right up to the large columns, and tack on a brick house, to make it at all available for its intended purpose.

These two gigantic piles of unmeaning masonry, raised at an enormous cost, are a striking proof of the utter disregard paid by architects to the *purposes* of the building, they are called upon to design; and many thousands have been fairly thrown away on every line in the erection of show fronts, and inconsistent and useless decoration.' [3]

The lesson, plain enough already, is driven home by a plate. If men wish for convenience, economy, and beauty, they must leave aside all fripperies, and shams, and fictitious grandeurs, and concentrate instead on building whatever it may be as well as they can. In fact, as another convert, Mr. G. K. Chesterton, has pointed out in his *Ballad of the White Horse*, they must ' cast their hearts out of their ken to get their hearts' desire.' For convenience and economy go hand in hand with sincerity, and beauty follows upon sincerity like a good gift come unaware.

---

[1] At Euston; Philip Hardwick (1792–1870), architect; one of the subscribers to the Pugin Memorial Fund.
[2] Philip Hardwick, architect.   [3] *Apology;* pp. 10–11.

It is an austere doctrine, and requires more from those who would practise it than perhaps most men are able to give. For Pugin himself the matter was simpler than it is for us. He had two beliefs which we have been denied : the first, that England was a Christian country ; the second, that Christian sincerity must lead inevitably to ' pointed ' architecture ; and in consequence could ' feel quite satisfied that when this principle [of sincerity] becomes generally understood, good, consistent, and picturesque masses of building will arise, with all the variety and beauty of olden times.' [1]

That was for the future. In the meantime there were stout blows to be struck at the existing enemy. There were the new Cemetery Companies, for instance, which ' have perpetrated the grossest absurdities in the buildings they have erected,' among them ' a superabundance of inverted torches, cinerary urns, and pagan emblems, tastefully disposed by the side of neat gravel walks, among cypress trees and weeping willows.'

The actual buildings were even worse :

' The central chapel is generally built on such a comprehensive plan as to be adapted (in the modern sense) for each sect and denomination in turn, as they may require its temporary use ; but the entrance gateway is usually selected for the grand display of the company's enterprise and taste, as being well calculated from its position to induce persons to patronize the undertaking by the purchase of shares or graves. This is generally Egyptian, probably from some association between the word catacombs, which occurs in the prospectus of the company, and the discoveries of Belzoni on the banks of the Nile ; and nearly opposite the Green Man and Dog public-house, in the centre of a dead wall (which serves as a cheap medium of advertisement for blacking and shaving-

[1] *Apology* ; p. 16.

strop manufacturers), a cement caricature of the entrance to an Egyptian temple, 2½ inches to the foot, is erected, with convenient lodges for the policeman and his wife, and a neat pair of cast iron hieroglyphical gates, which would puzzle the most learned to decypher ; while, to prevent any mistake, some such words as " New Economical Compressed Grave Cemetery Company " are inscribed in *Grecian* capitals along the frieze, interspersed with hawk-headed divinities, and surmounted by a huge representation of the winged Osiris bearing a gas lamp.' [1]

Then again, there was the new building of St. Paul's School,[2] ' another flagrant instance of the inconsistency of modern design. No sooner had the architect received the commission of erecting a building for this ancient foundation, than he turned to his stale collection of pagan authors for the authorities and details of an edifice, that was instituted by one of the most pious churchmen of England for the education of Christian youths ; and nothing better suggested itself to his narrow mind, than an unmeaning portico raised on stilts, serving only to darken the apartments over which it projects, an incipient dome, and a pagan frieze ; . . . Within the ancient school-room was an image of our Lord in the temple, teaching the doctors, before which the poor scholars sung a daily hymn and litany : but of all this not a vestige remains ; and in lieu of holy Name or deed, we have fifty bulls' heads decorated for pagan sacrifice, *copied from the temple of the Sibyls,* with not so much as an image of the pious founder in a niche, to awaken the remembrance of departed worth in the hearts and minds of those, who daily benefit by Colet's bounty.' [3]

The new buildings of Christ's Hospital also call forth severe strictures :

---

[1] *Apology ;* p. 12.   [2] 1823–4 ; George Smith, archt.
              [3] *Apology ;* pp. 12–3

' The opening towards Newgate Street might be mistaken
for the back way to the Compter, or a place where relatives
might hold intercourse with the inmates of that prison. . . .
The edifice is, moreover, only *Gothic on one side :* for, if by
chance the spectator turns the corner, he perceives an elevation
not at all dissimilar to that of the Fleet Prison towards Farring-
don Street.' [1]

However, there was something to be said for these buildings :

' Altogether, the works of Christ's Hospital are sad failures,
owing to their not being conceived in the ancient spirit ; but
still it must be owned, in justice, that when they were commenced, so little were the real principles of Christian architecture understood or recognised, that it would have been
difficult to have found any one, who could have done much
better than the architect employed. It is a positive duty to
point out all these defects, to prevent others from falling into
similar errors ; but, at the same time, we cannot but feel a
personal respect for a man, who endeavoured to revive the
old thing, at a time when there were few to sympathise or
encourage.' [2]

In addition, they call forth two long footnotes which are of
interest as further expounding Pugin's principles of true
construction, and as showing that he was capable of seeing
weaknesses in his own work as well as in the work of others.
The pertinent passages are as follows :

' Now, although it would be most absurd and inconsistent
to employ the same detail and enrichments on all sides of a
building placed in an enclosed position,[3] yet the spirit of
construction should remain unchanged, even in the meanest
offices. By simple chamfers and weatherings, the mere

---

[1] *Apology ;* pp. 13–4. [2] *Ib. ;* pp. 15–6.
[3] He is referring to the new buildings of Lambeth Palace, which contain ' a kitchen
court that might have been in the rear of the Euston Hotel.'

essentials of good masonry, the character is perfectly maintained in every portion of the old buildings; and, what is
most important, *naturally maintained;* that is, it would be
impossible to do them better in any other way. *Details of
this kind* do not require *designing*, but only *constructing*. For
instance, the best gate must be the *strongest framed;* the sharp
edges must be taken off the stiles and rails without weakening
the joints and shoulders; they are chamfered and stinted,
and the gate must and will look admirably well, and, of course,
be in character with a pointed building, because a pointed
building is a *natural building. In matters of ordinary use, a
man must go out of his way to make a bad thing* . . . '[1]

'In my own case I can truly state, that in buildings which
I erected but a short time since, I can perceive numerous
defects and errors, which I should not now commit; and,
but a few years ago, I perpetrated abominations. Indeed, till
I discovered those laws of pointed design, which I set forth in
my "True Principles," I had no fixed rules to work upon, and
frequently fell into error and extravagance. I designed and
drew from a sort of intuitive feeling for Christian architecture,
in consequence of the numerous examples I had seen. I
entered into all the beauties of the style, *but I did not apply
them with the feelings and on the principles of the old architects.*
I was *only an adapter*, and often guilty of gross inconsistency.
But, from the moment I understood that the beauty of
architectural design depended on its being the expression of
what the building required, and that for Christians that
expression could only be correctly given by the medium of
pointed architecture, all difficulties vanished . . . '[2]

All difficulties vanished? Only the fundamental ones.
There still remained the difficulty of building masterpieces
without money and in the face of ignorant interference; and
there remained the difficulty of time: when those words were

---

[1] *Apology;* pp. 14-5.   [2] *Ib.;* pp. 15-6.

written he had but nine more years to live, and eight of those years were to be spent in doing three men's work in embellishing with a wealth of mediæval detail the work of another architect.

However, his seven years of freedom from the intolerable exactions of Charles Barry had not yet come to an end. The *Apology* continues on its turbulent way. It reviews the Bank of England, whose ' street elevations . . . are certainly the most costly masses of absurdities that have ever been erected '[1]; the Halls of the various Companies, which ' have been rebuilt at such an enormous cost,' and ' are really distressing to look upon '[2]; the roof of the Guildhall, which ' is an abomination, and disgraceful to the civic authorities '[3]; the New Royal Exchange, which is ' another stale dish of ill-adapted classicisms.'[4]

Assuredly Pugin had ' seen pagans—no man upon earth ever saw so many ! ' But what was to be done ?

' Can we ever hope to see a Christian architect come forth from the Royal Academy itself, where deadly errors are instilled into the mind of the student, with the very rudiments of instruction ? Pagan lectures, pagan designs, pagan casts and models, pagan medals, and, as a reward for proficiency in these matters, a pagan journey ! When the mind of a youth is well infused with contempt for every association connected with his religion and country, he is sent forth to measure temples, and, in due time, he returns to form the nucleus of a

---

[1] *Apology ;* p. 16. The Bank of England was enlarged and practically rebuilt by Sir John Soane (1753–1837), F.R.S., R.A., Professor of Architecture in the Royal Academy, who was succeeded as architect to the Bank by C. R. Cockerell in 1833.

[2] *Ib. ;* p. 17.

[3] *Ib. ;* p. 18. In 1789 the Guildhall was rebuilt, though the greater part of the original walls were retained, by George Dance (1741–1825), R.A., predecessor of Sir John Soane as Professor of Architecture in the Royal Academy. *Dict. Nat. Biog.* (XIV., p. 11) admits that his front to the Guildhall was not ' creditable to his taste.' It was restored in Gothic in 1867.

[4] *Ib. ;* p. 18. Built in 1840–4 by Sir William Tite (1798–1873), later President of the Royal Institute of British Architects, and one of the subscribers to the Pugin Memorial Fund.

fresh set of small Doric men, and to infest the country with classical adaptations in Roman cement.'[1]

However, there was a solution.

' I would also have travelling students, but I would circumscribe their limits. Durham the destination of some,—Lincolnshire's steepled fens for others,—Northampton spires and Yorkshire's venerable piles, Suffolk and Norfolk's coasts, Oxford, Devonshire, and Warwick, each county should be indeed a school,—for each *is* a school,—where those who run may read, and where volumes of ancient art lie open for all inquirers.[2]

Then would they learn that the same perfection of design is to be found in the simplicity of the village steeple, as in the towering central spire,—in the rubble walls of a sea-coast chancel, as in the hewn ashlar and fair mouldings of the large churches,—that consistency of architectural proportion has stunted the pillars of the simple nave, and roofed it with massive beams, while it has lifted the shafts of the cathedral to a prodigious height, and vaulted the vast space with stone, —that architectural skill consists in embodying and expressing the structure required, and not in disguising it with borrowed features. The peasant's hut, the yeoman's cottage, the farmer's house, the baronial hall, may be each perfect in its kind : the student should visit village and town, hamlet and city ; he should be a minute observer of the animal and vegetable creation, of the grand effects of nature . . . so well did the ancient builders adapt their edifices to localities, that

---

[1] *Apology ;* p. 20

[2] A ' Pugin Travelling Fund ' was founded in his memory, to enable students to travel as he suggested. ' The Committee hope to raise at least £1,500.' By 1861, £1,074 had been raised. (*Ferrey ;* Appendix.) In 1865, £969 11s. 6d. of this sum was funded by the Royal Institute of British Architects to provide ' The Pugin Studentship,' which is still offered for competition. It has been held by such well-known men as Sir John Sulman, of Sydney ; Sir Aston Webb, President R.A. and R.I.B.A. ; Sir George Washington Browne, President of the Royal Scottish Academy ; Mr. Leonard Stokes, President and Royal Gold Medallist of the R.I.B.A. ; Professor W. R. Lethaby ; Mr. Charles Mallowes ; and Mr. J. J. Joass. [Inf. of Mr. Ian MacAlister, Secretary, R.I.B.A.]

they seemed as if they formed a portion of nature itself, grappling and growing from the sites in which they are placed. . . .

The student of Christian architecture should also imbue his mind with the mysteries of his Faith, the history of the Church, the lives of those glorious Saints and Martyrs that it has produced in all ages, especially those who, by birth or mission, are connected with the remains of ancient piety in this land. He should also be well acquainted with the annals of his country,—its constitutions, laws, privileges, and dignities,—the liturgy and rubrics of the Church,—customs and ceremonies,—topographical antiquities, local peculiarities, and natural resources. The face of the country would be then no longer disfigured by incongruous and eccentric erections, compounds of all styles and countries; but we should have structures whose arrangement and detail would be in accordance with our Faith, customs, and natural traditions. Climate would again regulate forms of covering, and positions of buildings. Local interest would be restored, and English architecture assume a distinct and dignified position in the history of art; *for we do not wish to produce mere servile imitators of former excellence of any kind, but men imbued with the consistent spirit of the ancient architects, who would work on their principles, and carry them out as the old men would have done, had they been placed in similar circumstances, and with similar wants to ourselves.*[1]

What a hope! But Pugin had it. The remainder of the book is an attempt to show in particular cases how that hope might be brought to fulfilment.

He begins with a discussion of the pointed style in relation to ecclesiastical buildings:

'With that portion of the English clergy who have the happiness of being in communion with the Holy See, there

[1] *Apology;* pp. 20–2.

cannot arise any doubt whatever. They hold precisely the same faith, and in essentials retain the same ritual, as the ancient English Church. They, consequently, require precisely the same arrangement of church, the same symbols and ornaments, as were general in this country previous to the schism . . . any departure from Catholic architecture is utterly inexcusable.'[1]

However, it was among his fellow Catholics that he met with the most exacerbating opposition, and they had to be dealt with in passing, Ireland, incidentally,—than which ' there is no country in Europe where the externals of religion present so distressing an aspect '—receiving a long footnote to itself :

' Men of devout minds are scandalized with the foreign trumpery that is introduced on the most solemn occasions, and the noisy theatrical effects that are substituted for the solemn chants and hymns of the Church. . . . It is painful to see these wretched practices puffed off in Catholic journals, and described much in the same strain as is used in the Theatrical Observer,—a list of performers,—criticisms on the execution of solos and quartets during that Holy Sacrifice which fills even the angels with awe and reverence. Since Christ himself hung abandoned and bleeding on the Cross of Calvary, never has so sad a spectacle been exhibited to the afflicted Christian as is presented in many modern Catholic chapels, where the adorable Victim is offered up by the Priests of God's Church, disguised in miserable dresses intended for the sacred vestments, surrounded by a scoffing auditory of protestant sight-seekers who have paid a few shillings a head to grin at mysteries which they do not understand, and to hear the performances of an infidel troop of mercenary musicians, hired to sing symbols of faith they disbelieve, and salutations to that Holy Sacrament they mock and deny.'[2]

[1] *Apology* ; pp. 22–3.   [2] *Ib.* ; pp. 24–5.

That passage alone is sufficient to rebut the charge that Pugin's Catholicism was purely æsthetic. Incidentally, it was hardly the best way to endear himself either to the ancestral Catholics, to whom the squalor of persecution had come in the course of time to seem normal, or to the new converts, to whom ' foreign trumpery ' was a welcome change from the sordid dulness of pre-Tractarian Protestantism. However, Pugin was among those who believed that it was ' natural, and therefore right for man to approach his Maker as he would approach an earthly sovereign, with nothing of sordidness or neglect, with more than decency, with much of splendour ' [1]; and being such, for him there could be no compromise.

' With respect to the present Anglican Church the case is, of course, by no means so clear and positive. Still, if she acted on her present acknowledged doctrines and discipline, without even taking into consideration any probable change in her position, she must turn to Catholic antiquity for the types of her architecture and ornament.

This argument is based on *principles and formularies ;* for abuses cannot be either advanced or received in support of any position. I am not taking into account the various grades of opinion and practice that are unhappily to be found among those who act in the capacity of Anglican clergymen. I deal only with canons and rubrics ; and if these were properly and universally carried out, a vast move would be made in the right direction.' [2]

Perhaps. The question was an awkward one to tackle in 1843 ; and maybe to-day the question is even more difficult. But Pugin did not shirk the matter. He dealt with it in nine separate aspects, and summed it up as follows :

' If, as I have shown, the Anglican Church requires bell towers, spires, naves, chancels, screens, fonts, altars, sacred

---

[1] *Q. R. ;* Feb. 1837; p. 234.   [2] *Apology ;* p. 25.

symbols and ornaments, I will ask whether the types of these various features are to be found in the ancient pointed churches of England, or in the classic temples of antiquity ? Surely no one can hesitate to admit at once that, in the former, we have perfect models for imitation ; while, in the latter, we cannot find one corresponding arrangement or detail : and therefore, even in its present position, by its own existing canons and rubrics, the Anglican Church is bound, consistently, to work exclusively on the principles of Christian architecture, and to renounce all pagan adaptations whatsoever.' [1]

There follows a short section on collegiate establishments, which are dealt with in a similar direct manner :

'Any departure from Catholic antiquity in a college is unpardonable. . . . Are Queen's, Worcester, or the new quadrangle of Christ Church, to be compared for one instant with Merton, New College, or Magdalene ? They rather resemble sick hospitals or barracks of the last century, than the abodes of piety and learning . . . it is, indeed, monstrous, now that the ancient detail is so much better understood, and the facilities of execution far greater, to see vile compounds of Italian details rising amid the glories of Catholic antiquity in both Oxford and Cambridge.' [2]

Then, after touching briefly on 'hospitals for the poor,' which 'ought, undoubtedly, to be erected in a style at once simple and religious,' [3] he passes on to consideration of 'Sepulchral Memorials,' which 'are so intimately connected with ecclesiastical architecture, that it seems necessary to enter upon some details on the subject before proceeding to other matters.' [4]

To the assertion that the use of classic costume in memorial effigies was necessary owing to ' the unsightly form of modern habits, which would render the effigy of the deceased ludicrous

---

[1] *Apology* ; p. 31.   [2] *Ib.* ; pp. 31–3.
[3] *Ib.* ; p. 33.   [4] *Ib.*

in appearance, if represented with them,'[1] he replies that
'this would be perfectly true if it were necessary, or even
correct, to adopt the ordinary costume of domestic life in
such cases; but it is scarcely possible to find any person
sufficiently dignified in station to warrant an effigy, who does
not hold some official situation, either ecclesiastical, civil, or
military; the robes and insignia of which, if properly and
severely represented, would produce effigies little inferior in
solemn effect to the ancient ones.'[2]

A footnote points out that 'the ancient monumental
effigies invariably represent the deceased persons in their robes
of state'; and then he adds :

'To represent persons of the present century in the costume
of the fourteenth, is little less inconsistent than to envelop
them in the Roman toga. As I have before said, architecture
and art should be a consistent expression of the period, and it
will not be difficult to show, that, adhering strictly to these
principles, we can in the present age revive the most solemn
and Christian memorials of the dead.'[3]

The passage is of importance, as showing both Pugin's
philosophy of art, and the strength and weakness of his
position. 'Architecture and art should be a consistent
expression of the period.' The artist, in fact, product of his
time and country, should be the perfect craftsman, neither
imitating the past because it was past, nor striving after a new
thing because it was new, but giving of the best that was in
him; a man, in effect, able to say : 'By the grace of God I
am what I am, and this work is *my* work.' But it might be
argued that in an '*époque de la ribaudaille utilitaire*' a man
acting on this principle would best perform his artistic function
by producing '*des monuments qui symbolisent son activité et sa
ristesse, son astuce et son lucre, en des œuvres moroses et dures.*'[4]

[1] *Apology*; pp. 33–4.   [2] *Ib.*; p. 34.   [3] *Ib.*
[4] *Certains*; J. K. Huysmans; p. 170 (*Le Fer*

But Pugin did not think so. He would seem to have had a strangely simple faith in human nature ; to have believed in spite of all evidence to the contrary that men were as their fathers were, that their immeasurable offensiveness was but the aberration of the fundamentally sound—the fundamentally sound being the truly Christian and therefore the truly 'pointed.' Hence his fury, the fury of one who loves greatly, for a man must love a thing before he wishes to reform it. Hence the fury of his already quoted attack on the externals of contemporary Catholic worship ; hence the fierceness of his disapproval both of incompetent Gothic Revivalists and of ardent Romanisers like William George Ward, as well as of the innumerable 'pagans.' They were really so sound ; they only needed freedom from evil teachings ; they only needed direction and encouragement ; they only needed *Contrasts*, or *The True Principles*, or *The Apology* ; they only needed to look into their own perfectly sound and 'pointed' hearts. . . . That was the difference between Pugin and that other great mediævalist dreamer, Huysmans, who had no such illusions and who loathed the age in which he lived and all its works. Huysmans, in consequence, was able to take a certain perverse pleasure in its ' œuvres moroses et dures,' to look on at its works with acquiescent disgust, to find a painful gratification in the sight of habitual vagaries, to take a bitter defensive pleasure in the vagaries themselves. But Pugin was as one heart-stricken, perpetually in the position of seeing one highly esteemed and beloved falling lamentably into error for the first time. That was what hurt so much. That was what gave to his pen a pungency which might have been popular if it had not been papist.

In the meantime, English Christians were entitled to have Christian memorials. 'For the English clergy, there is not the slightest difficulty ; those in communion with the Holy See using the same number and character of sacred vestments

as of old.'[1] The position of the Anglican clergy was similar,
though less ornate. For instance, while the Catholic Deacon
should be vested in 'Amice, albe, and dalmatic, stole and
maniple, holding the book of the Holy Gospels,'[2] the
Anglican Deacon should be solely 'in an albe.' Memorials
could be provided for 'Civil Personages' with equal ease :
'The Sovereign should be represented in the Royal robes
which are still used in the coronation, and which are precisely
the same in number and description as those used in the days
of St. Edward,'[2] while suitable costumes could be found for
others in the social scale down to 'private gentlemen,' for
whom 'a long cloak, disposed in severe folds, would produce
a solemn effect.'[3] Below the rank of gentleman, memorial
portraiture was difficult. However, 'for the humbler classes,
a cross, with the instruments of their trades or crafts, with
marks and devices, would be sufficient and appropriate ; and,
in a rural district, a mere wooden or stone cross, with the
name of the deceased'[3] ; and 'surely the Cross must be the
most appropriate emblem on the tombs of those who profess
to believe in God crucified for the redemption of man ; and
it is almost incredible, that . . . the types of all modern
sepulchral monuments should be essentially pagan ; and urns,
broken pillars, extinguished lamps, inverted torches, and
sarcophagi, should have been substituted for recumbent
effigies, angels, and emblems of mercy and redemption.'[4]

The Apology then passes on to a short section justifying the
use of pointed architecture in civil buildings. The argument
may be summarised : 'We are such men as our fathers were,
and therefore should build as they built.' Two passages,
however, are of importance as exemplifying still further
Pugin's position : the first :

'Any modern invention which conduces to comfort, cleanli-

---

[1] *Apology*; p. 34.   [2] *Ib.*; p. 35.
[3] *Ib.*; p. 36.   [4] *Ib.*; p. 37.

ness, or durability, should be adopted by the consistent architect; *to copy a thing merely because it is old, is just as absurd as the imitations of the modern pagans.* Our domestic architecture should have a peculiar expression illustrative of our manners and habits : *as the castle merged into the baronial mansion, so it may be modified to suit actual necessities ;* and the smaller detached houses which the present state of society has generated, should possess a peculiar character '[1]; the second :

'There is no reason in the world why noble cities, combining all possible convenience of drainage, water-courses, and conveyance of gas, may not be erected in the most consistent and yet Christian character. *Every building that is treated naturally, without disguise or concealment, cannot fail to look well.'* [2] To this second passage there is a footnote :

'A gas lamp, if designed simply with reference to its use, would be an inoffensive object ; but when it is composed of a Roman altar, surmounted by the fasces, and terminated by an incense tripod, it becomes perfectly ridiculous.'

The man who wrote those words was neither a dry-as-dust antiquarian, nor a romantic mediævalist : they are the words of a man who has realised to the full the austerity of art. That he fell short of this ideal in his works is no wonder, quite apart from the many accidental difficulties in his way. For he was a pioneer. As well could one blame a man who hacks a path through a jungle for falling short of the perfection of tarmacadam. And in either case, to point out the shortcomings is but another way of emphasising the magnificence of the achievement.

The last eleven pages of the book consist of a section entitled ' Modern Inventions and Mechanical Improvements.' The title is misleading : after a couple of pages it passes on to a consideration of sculpture and then to a ' conclusion '

---

[1] *Apology;* p. 38.   [2] *Ib.;* p. 39.

which is in the nature of a crescendo of enthusiasm of which the climax, as in *The True Principles*, is the words 'Laus Deo.' A few extracts will serve to show the general trend.

'In matters purely mechanical, the Christian architect should gladly avail himself of those improvements and increased facilities that are suggested from time to time. . . . The readier and cheaper the *mechanical* part of building can be rendered, the greater will be the effect for the funds . . . '[1]

'Had this point [the provision of ties] been considered in the original structures, the pressure might have been effectually counteracted, by inserting iron shafts in the centre of the great piers, and chains from them in the thickness of the triforium and clerestory, reaching to the four extremities of the building. . . . *We do not want to arrest the course of inventions, but to confine these inventions to their legitimate uses,* and *to prevent their substitution for nobler arts.*'[2]

'Another great mistake of modern times is the supposition that Christian architecture will not afford sufficient scope for the art of sculpture. So far from this, while a Greek temple admits only of such decoration in the pediment and round the frieze, every portion of a Christian church may and should be covered with sculpture of the most varied kind. . . . There is in fact no difference of *principle* between the fine draperied works of the classic sculptors and those of the middle ages ; the difference is in the *objects represented* and the motives of the artists. The principal object of the former was to display the human figure, which the latter, from the Christian

---

[1] *Apology ;* pp. 39–40.
[2] *Ib. ;* p. 41. In this matter also Pugin was in advance of contemporary thought : ' Now iron is not only in itself an objectionable material to employ, from its tendency to expand and contract with atmospheric changes, but its force depends on cohesion ; and that cohesion is not infinite, like that of gravitation, to which we can imagine no limit, but it is capable only of a certain resistance, beyond which it gives way. And therefore a building which depends on it always carries within it the seeds of its own destruction, and the suggestion of its own fall, howsoever distant the event.' [*Q. R. ;* Dec. 1841 ; p. 147.]

principle of modesty, rather concealed. *The pagans wished to
perpetuate human feelings,—the Christians, the divine.'* [1]

' The albe of purity and chaste girdle were exchanged for
light and often indecent costume, to exhibit the human figure
after the manner of an opera dancer. . . . We do not want to
revive a facsimile of the works or style of any particular
individual, or even period ; *but it is the devotion, majesty, and
repose of Christian art, for which we are contending ;*—it is not
a *style,* but a *principle.* Surely all the improvements that are
consequent on the study of anatomy and the proportions of
the human figure can be engrafted on ancient excellence ; and
an image, in correct costume, and treated in accordance with
Catholic traditions, would afford equal scope for the display
of the sculptor's art as a half-naked figure in a distorted
attitude, more resembling a maniac who had hastily snatched
a blanket for a covering than a canonized saint.' [2]

' In conclusion, it must appear evident that the present
revival of ancient architecture in this country is based on the
soundest and most consistent principles. It is warranted by
religion, government, climate, and the wants of society. It
is a perfect expression of all we should hold sacred, honourable
and national, and connected with the holiest and dearest
associations.' [3]

' The spirit of Dunstan, of Anselm, and St. Thomas, were
extinct ere that of Cranmer could have prevailed. We must
not forget that this country was separated from the Holy See
by the consent of the canonically instituted clergy of this
realm, with a few noble but rare exceptions. The people
were actually betrayed by their own lawful pastors. . . . I

---

[1] *Apology ;* pp. 42–3.
[2] *Ib. ;* 44. To one who remarked, ' not without the intention of provoking
him,' that perhaps ' as Adam and Eve were naked before they fell, nudity might
be a good symbol of the state of paradisiac innocence regained by the saints,'
Pugin replied with a shout : " Why, my dear sir, you are a preadamite heretic."
[*Rambler ;* p. 400.]
[3] *Ib. ;* p. 45.

mention these things, because it is a common error, into which I was formerly led, to cast the whole odium of the loss of the ancient faith in England on the king and nobles, whereas the Catholic hierarchy of this land, who basely surrendered the sacred charge they should have defended even to death, essentially contributed to the sad change.'[1]

'An Englishman needs not controversial writings to lead him to the faith of his fathers; it is written on the wall, on the window, on the pavement, by the highway. Let him but look on the tombs of those who occupy the most honourable position in the history of his country,—the devout, the noble, the valiant, and the wise,—and he will behold them with clasped hands invoking the saints of Holy Church, whilst the legend round the slabs begs the prayers of the passers-by for their souls' repose.'[2]

'In short, Catholicism is so interwoven with everything sacred, honourable, or glorious in England, that three centuries of puritanism, indifference, and infidelity, have not been able effectually to separate it. It clings to this land, and develops itself from time to time, as the better feelings of a naturally honourable man who had been betrayed into sin. What! an Englishman and a protestant! Oh, worse than parricide...'[3]

'Can a man of soul look on the cross-crowned spire, and listen to the chime of distant bells, or stand beneath the lofty vault of cathedral choir, or gaze on long and lessening aisles, or kneel by ancient tomb, and yet *protest* against aught but that monstrous and unnatural system that has mutilated their beauty and marred their fair design? Surely not. And truly such feelings of reverence for long-despised excellence has been awakened among so many of our learned and devout countrymen, that we may begin to hope, indeed, that our redemption draws nigh. We have already lived to hear the

---

[1] *Apology;* pp. 46–7.   [2] *Ib.;* p. 49.
[3] *Ib.;* p. 50.

name of Canterbury's blessed martyr pronounced with accents of veneration ;—a hundred pens, most ably wielded, are writing in defence of ancient piety and practice ;—a thousand voices are raised against the abominations of modern innovation. England is, indeed, awakening to a sense of her ancient dignity ; she begins to appreciate the just merits of the past, and to work eagerly for the future. The last few years must, or ought to have, worked a great change in the feelings of English Catholics towards the Anglican church-men ; and it is evident that, if it be God's will that departed glories are to be restored, it will be effected rather by rebuilding the ruined walls of Zion than by demolishing the poor remains that are left. The tide of popular innovation that so lately threatened us with a common destruction seems providentially stayed. God forbid that we should endeavour to obtain a transept in a scramble with dissenters, but rather prove our-selves to possess the feelings of the true mother in Solomon's judgment, and freely give up all, than see what we hold so dear divided ; and by perfecting ourselves, and carrying out true Catholic principles in charity, devotion, and zeal, hasten forward that union to which, in the words of an ecclesiastical periodical, we may even begin to look forward, and which is rather to be obtained through the sacrifice of the altar and midnight supplication, than by the clamours of an election platform or the tumult of popular commotion.

✛

Laus Deo ! '[1]

In other words, the conversion of England to Catholicism and the restoration of true art were corollaries one of the other, and both were more likely to be attained by prayer than by Daniel O'Connell.

[1] *Apology;* pp. 50–1.

The Apology has been treated thus at so great length for three reasons : first, because some at least of the ideas which it contains are still of value ; secondly, because it holds, as it were, the cream of Pugin's thought and writings ; and thirdly, because of the insight it gives into Pugin's own mind, his theories, his ardour, and his aspirations ; for of none of his works could Pugin more truly have stated, paraphrasing the fine words of Mrs. Catherine Jacson in the Preface to her *Desultory Retracings*, that in this book his real life spirit was laid open ; that it was not carelessly written, but in earnest truth from the heart ; that if anything he had ever said was true and real, this was so, there being in it no word that was not genuine ; that he had written it because it was true, and because he had deemed it to be a tribute due from him to those influences of the past which he recognised increasingly as claiming more than a silent tribute of gratitude and just honour, as claiming, so far as in him lay, a rescue from oblivion.

CHAPTER XVI

THREE CHURCHES

" Great lady ! what deed that is wrought by a man
shall be sung of as worthy if this be deemed small ? "
She answered : " Certainly you are very unlike any other man now living."
The Saga of Grettir the Strong.

HITHERTO, Pugin's life and works have been considered
principally in relation to his own religious aspirations and to
the Catholic resurgence in England. In order to gain a just
idea of Pugin as executant as well as theoriser, it is now
necessary to examine in greater detail, first, the state of Gothic
architecture before his principles were propounded ; secondly,
the superiority of his work over that which preceded it ;
thirdly, the obstacles which prevented fuller achievement ;
and fourthly, lest judgment be warped by present appearances,
the mutilation which much of his work suffered after passing
out of his hands.

Throughout the eighteenth century, while country districts
were well supplied with churches, towns had not nearly
enough. This need increased with the enormous growth of
the urban population which resulted from the Industrial
Revolution. In addition, the social unrest which followed
upon the Napoleonic wars caused the Church of England to
be looked upon as an important buttress against disruptive
social forces. The need for new churches was seen simul-
taneously to be religiously advisable and socially imperative.
In 1818 the Church Building Society was formed, and its
efforts were quickly supported by an Act of Parliament, by
which a million pounds was supplied for building churches in
populous districts. As a result of this Act, two hundred and

fourteen churches were built, one hundred and seventy-four
of which were in a style then confidently believed to be
Gothic. The reason for this high proportion was that it was
discovered that Gothic was cheaper. Classic churches
required a large amount of stone for porticoes and pediments;
Gothic churches could be built, to a great extent, of brick and
cast iron. In this way Gothic, which in the previous century
had been a freakish form of house-building for the rich,
suddenly became a way of building churches economically
for the poor. The result, in general, was lamentable, and, if
no other Gothic buildings had existed, would have gone far
to justify George Moore's sneer at Gothic [1] as ' a style arising
out of ignorance of the Parthenon.' But the style of these
buildings was worse: it arose out of ignorance of Gothic.
In addition to this ignorance, the builders of the Commissioners' churches were sadly hampered by the fact that
the amount of money allowed per head of congregation was
wholly inadequate. In consequence, the largest possible
roof-area had to be obtained at any cost to appearance.
Further, since Protestant churches at that time required that
the largest possible number of people should be able to see
and hear the preacher, they tended to a square and box-like
form and to the possession of galleries. And finally, to these
flimsy boxes was added uncomprehended and meanly executed
Gothic detail.

Some of these churches, of course, in cases where funds
were not so restricted, rose above this dead level of incompetence. For instance, St. Luke's, Chelsea, of which Mr.
Clark writes [2] that ' even now there is something distinguished
in its slim tower, something almost exciting in its perverse
flying buttresses. But,' he adds, ' the building suffers from
that meagreness of construction which we noticed at Tetbury,
and which gives a cardboard look to almost all the Gothic

[1] *Avowals*; p. 278.   [2] *Clark*; pp. 118–9.

churches of the time; nor is the detail any less mean than usual.'

Whatever the Commissioners' churches might be, in fact, and however much perverse pleasure they may give to those who have a taste for such curiosities, they were not 'the real thing': they bore the same relation to mediæval work as a cheap 'transfer' does to Oriental china. As such, they are only an episode in the development of the Gothic Revival, and their chief importance 'lies in the reaction they provoked, in the wild sparks they shook from Pugin's burning brain, and in the Camden Society's grave call to rubrical exactness.' [1]

In his *Contrasts* Pugin wrote [2] :

' Of the feelings with which the old churchmen undertook the erection of their churches we can easily be acquainted, by referring to the solemn office of the dedication :—*Domus quam aedificavi volo Domino, talis esse debet, ut in cunctis regionibus nominetur ; praeparabo, ergo, ei necessaria.*

Magnus est Deus noster super omnes deos ; quis, ergo, poterit praevalere ut aedificet dignam Deo domum. Domine Deus noster, omnis haec copia, quam paravimus ut aedificaretur domus nomini sancto tuo, de manu tua est. Quis prior Domino dedit, et retribuetur ei ?

The Church commissioners' instructions are the very reverse of these noble sentiments. They require a structure as plain as possible, which can be built for a trifling sum, and of small dimensions, both for economy and facilities of hearing the preacher, the sermon being the only part of the service considered ; and I hesitate not to say, that a more meagre, miserable display of architectural skill never was made, nor more improprieties and absurdities committed, than in the mass of paltry churches erected under the auspices of the commissioners, and which are to be found scattered over every modern portion of the metropolis and its neighbourhood

---

[1] *Clark* ; p. 132. [2] P. 49.

—a disgrace to the age, both on the score of their composition, and the miserable sums that have been allotted for their construction.'

Three years after the first publication of *Contrasts* Pugin was to have an opportunity to substitute his own idea of Gothic for a building projected by one of the Commissioners' architects.

On 19th January 1834, Bishop Walsh presided over a meeting of the Catholics of Birmingham, at which the Reverend Thomas Michael McDonnell moved the resolution, seconded by John Hardman, ' That it appears to this meeting highly desirable that a commodious and splendid Catholic Church . . . be erected in the town of Birmingham.'[1] An architect was engaged, and plans drawn out ; and then, owing to strong differences of opinion over the site, in which Mr. McDonnell, ' a man of considerably more than average ability, but . . . a curiously difficult disposition,'[2] too vigorously joined, the scheme was dropped after only £138 had been collected towards its fulfilment.

This was fortunate ; for the architect was Thomas Rickman,[3] a man whose buildings were notable ' for their want of character and originality, and as displaying " more knowledge of the outward form of the medieval style than any real acquaintance with its spirit ".'[4] In other words, his work was typical ' Commissioners' Gothic.' The presence in Birmingham of St. George's Church, designed by him for the Commissioners in 1819, might now be considered reason for employing another architect. But at the time, ' Commis-

[1] *A History of St. Chad's Cathedral, Birmingham*, 1841–1904; compiled by the Cathedral Clergy; p. 10.
[2] *Sequel ; II.*, p. 110.
[3] 1776–1841. One of his first works was the enriching of a shop-front ' with a design taken from the choragic monument of Thrasyllus.' (*Dict. Nat. Biog.* ; XLVIII., p. 267.) His theoretical work was far superior to his practical, and he was the author of a praiseworthy book entitled *An Attempt to discriminate the Styles of Architecture in England from the Conquest to the Reformation.*
[4] *Dict. Nat. Biog.* ; XLVIII., p. 267.

sioners' Gothic ' was the only Gothic ; and the Catholics of
Birmingham wanted a Gothic cathedral.

In 1839, Bishop Walsh revived the scheme for the new
church, and the majority of the Catholics of Birmingham again
rallied to his support. This time, Mr. McDonnell's opposition
was quickly, and violently, overborne ; and Pugin, whose
work was becoming known, was called in to advise about the
building.

The plans for Rickman's St. Chad's are still preserved by
Pugin's grandson, Mr. Sebastian Pugin Powell, in Oxford.
On the back of one of them there is a hurried pencil sketch of
a church. There is nothing very remarkable about the building thus illustrated. No detail appears. It is just a plain,
solid church. What is remarkable is that it should appear on
the back of one of Rickman's plans. It is as though a rough
sketch of a modern express railway engine should be found on
the back of plans for Stephenson's ' Comet,' and less than ten
years have passed between the drawings. Rickman's plans
are of a flimsy hall with Gothic ornamentation ; Pugin's
sketch is of a mediæval church.

It is not difficult to imagine the scene when that rough
sketch was made :—The Bishop and his advisers waiting in
rather uneasy dignity for what the author of *Contrasts* might
have to say of plans which they had once approved ; the
thought perhaps in their minds that, if it could be reconciled
with their artistic consciences, it might be as well to make
some use of this eccentric protégé of the rich Lord Shrewsbury
who otherwise might not help as much as they hoped ; the
sudden entrance of a burly figure dressed like a deck-hand on
a trawler ; a momentary glance at the meticulously executed
plans spread out before him ; a gust of vehement speech :
' My dear sirs, that thing is not a church ; it is a plaster
conventicle. *This*'—a treasured plan slapped down on its
face and a pencil skidding over it under stubby fingers between

a jest and a laugh—' *This* is what a Catholic church should be '; heads bowed over the sudden drawing; a realisation that they had seen churches something like that—old churches —churches that had once been Catholic . . .

No time was wasted. The original church of St. Chad was pulled down after Easter. On 29th October 1839, the foundation-stone of Pugin's church was laid.

It must be admitted that St. Chad's is not so finely mediæval as Pugin's rough sketch on the back of Rickman's plan. For one thing—a notable failure on Pugin's part to carry out his belief in the functional basis of architecture—its choir and sanctuary are much too small for their purpose. For the rest, probably the worst that can reasonably be said of it is contained in Eastlake's criticism [1] :

' Indeed, a glance at the details reveals at once the period of its erection—that period in which after long disuse the traditions of Mediæval art were revived in the letter rather than in the spirit. Its slate-roofed spires are " broached " at an abrupt and ungraceful angle. Its buttresses are long and lean, with " set-offs " at rare intervals, and coarsely accentuated. Its walls of brick—once red, but now toned down by time and the noxious smoke of Birmingham to dingy brown— have a mean impoverished look about them, which is scarcely redeemed by the freestone tracery of its windows, or the canopied and really cleverly carved figures which adorn its western portal.

Internally the building displays evidence of Pugin's strength and weakness in an eminent degree. The chancel fittings, the rood screen with its sacred burden, the altar tombs—in a word, the *furniture* of the church—are, if we accept the motive of the style in which they are designed, as correct in form as any antiquary could wish, and are wrought with marvellous refinement. But in general effect the interior is

[1] *Eastlake;* pp. 156–7

far from satisfactory. The attenuated and lanky nave piers rise to such a disproportionate height as scarcely to leave room for the arches which surmount them. The walls are thin and poor, the roof timbers slight and weak looking. There is no clerestory, and the aisle roofs follow that of the nave in one continuous slope. The aisles are moreover extraordinarily high in proportion to their width. An English poet has described to us the beauties of " the long-drawn aisle," but here the aisles appear to have been drawn out the wrong way. The chancel is of far better proportions, and with its elaborate rood screen richly gilt and painted, its oak fittings and bishop's throne, its canopied reredos and mural decoration, is decidedly *the* feature *par excellence* of this church.'

The criticism is harsh. But Eastlake was judging the building by the highest standards, as Pugin would have liked it judged. It was by those standards, the finest works of the Middle Ages, that Pugin judged his own work. But that is not enough. To say that Pugin's work was not so good as mediæval work is, by the very fact that comparison is called for, praise of his work. The extent to which that praise is merited can only be realised by comparison with the earlier works of the Revival, and by consideration of the difficulties which he had to overcome. To show the greatness of the superiority of Pugin's work over that of his predecessors, it is only necessary to add that no one would think of comparing one of the Commissioners' churches with a genuine mediæval building.

The obstacles which Pugin had to overcome before he could produce a work worthy of that comparison were considerable. In the first place, even granting that St. Chad's has more of the letter than the spirit of Gothic, it must be remembered that Pugin, then aged twenty-seven, had played a considerable part in the rediscovery of that ' letter,' that he had had to train workmen capable of producing even the

' letter,' and that at the same time he was attaining to a knowledge of the ' spirit ' and was infusing it into both workmen and work. He was, in fact, both in theory and in practice, a pioneer.

In addition, there were two other chief obstacles to be overcome : shortage of money, and the opposition of the Romanisers.

Money shortage was felt early in the building of St. Chad's, for the hilly nature of the site made elaborate foundations necessary. These, though they made possible the building of a fine crypt, cost so much that if Lord Shrewsbury had not come to the rescue with £2,000 the church could not have been finished. As it was, the greatest economy had to be exercised, and the outside kept as plain as possible. The ' mean impoverished look ' of which Eastlake complained was the result of actual poverty, not of architectural meanness. In addition to this, the opposition of the Romanisers was a source of incessant worry.

' An affair has happened at Birmingham,' Pugin wrote to March-Phillipps,[1] ' which has gone through me like a stab. We have had a tremendous blow aimed at us. Dr. Wiseman has at last shown his real sentiments by attempting to abolish the great Rood-Screen after good Mr. Hardman has given £600 for its execution. I say attempted, because I immediately wrote to John Hardman to this effect, that if the screen was suppressed I should not remain architect to the church *one day* longer. You know how decidedly I act on these occasions, and you know how I can sacrifice anything to the advancement of Catholic principle.'

Wiseman was large-minded enough to yield, and Pugin won his point. The irking opposition of the Romanisers, however, continued : even in answering his invitation to the opening ceremony, Bishop Baines, whose opposition both to

[1] 18 Dec. 1840; *Phillipps;* II., p. 213—4.

Gothic and the regular clergy seems to have been spiced with a certain venom, wrote to protest against the use of Gothic vestments. On this occasion, however, Lord Shrewsbury's money and Pugin's cloth-of-gold had the support of Dr. Wiseman's acquiescence, and won the day. On 23rd June 1841, St. Chad's was solemnly opened in the most splendid manner, the only compromise with popular feeling being the substitution of parts of an unpublished Mass by Haydn for Gregorian Chant,[1] which, however, had been used exclusively at the consecration two days earlier. After the opening there was a dinner, lasting from six o'clock till nine, in the course of which Dr. Wiseman expressed the thanks of Catholic England for Pugin's exertions, and the whole company rose to drink his health. It is not surprising in the circumstances, that ' in replying, after a few broken sentences thanking the assembly, and asking their prayers for him, his voice refused to utter more, and sinking down on his chair he burst into tears.' [2] It is not surprising, for Pugin's one ambition was the increase of God's glory through the Catholic Church, and in St. Chad's, overcoming the obstacles inherent in the revival of a forgotten art, and in the face of shortage of money and the opposition of those among whom he had hoped to find his supporters, he had achieved it. He had made a new thing for the glory of God, and into it he had poured something of the spirit of the old. It was both an achievement and a promise.

In St. George's, Southwark, which was opened with great splendour and the help of Mario and Tamburini of the Italian Opera [3] on 4th July 1848, both the achievement and the

---

[1] Marked progress is shown by the possibility of Gregorian Chant even being considered. Eighteen years before, at the opening of the new Chapel at Downside, ' Count Mazzinghi composed a Mass for the occasion, a special feature whereof were the seventy-two Amens at the end of the *Credo*.' Incidentally, Bishop Baines was then the celebrant. [*The Downside Review*; June 1914; p. 27.]

[2] *Sequel*; II., p. 15.

[3] Doubtless to Pugin's distress. However, females were excluded from the choir;

promise were less. But the obstacles were correspondingly greater. There is a touch of irony in the fact that in this, one of the buildings in which Pugin was least enabled to do himself justice, Pope Pius IX. should have taken the keenest interest, desiring ' a long account of it to be compiled from the English journals, and inserted in the Roman official *Gazette*,' [1] and giving a gold chalice and paten worth 1,000 scudi.

But for the enthusiasm and capacity for collecting money of the Rev. Thomas Doyle, and the active support of some Catholic laymen, in particular of the Hon. Edward Petre, sufficient funds could never have been raised. By 1838 it was deemed that there was enough money in hand, and Pugin was called upon to offer plans. Whether the committee's instructions were not clear, or Pugin was carried away by his enthusiasm at the greatness of the opportunity which seemed to be offered, is not known. At any rate, he produced designs which were far beyond the committee's means. They showed a large cruciform cathedral ' with a central tower and pinnacles recalling St. Hugh's or the Rood Tower of Lincoln Cathedral,' and with ' a clerestoried nave of six bays with separately gabled aisles, transepts, and a choir, also aisled, terminating in an apse with very tall windows such as we see in the great " hall churches " of Münster, Soëst, Erfurt and other North German cities.' [2] In addition, there were to be a chapter-house, cloisters, convent, and presbytery. The committee, very reasonably, tempered their enthusiasm with discretion, and asked the cost of the projected work and the length of time it would be in building. To these questions, Pugin vouchsafed no direct reply. Instead, he quietly gathered

---

a step in the right direction which even now has not become universal. *The Times* complained that the clergy lacked good looks, a new aspect of the æsthetics of divine worship. [*Sequel;* II., p. 185.] The 'Protestant Association' celebrated the occasion by distributing upwards of ten thousand violently anti-Catholic tracts.

[1] *The Rambler;* Sep. 1848, p. 17. [2] *Bumpus;* p. 175.

together the plans, 'took up his hat, wished the gentlemen good day, and walked out of the house.'[1]

The following day, some members of the astonished committee called on him for an explanation, and received one which was as reasonable as their questions, though much more vehement :

'You asked me to furnish designs for a cathedral, chapter-house, cloisters, and conventual buildings, upon a grand scale. I complied with the request, and supposed that I was dealing with people who knew what they wanted. The absurd questions, however, put to me soon showed my mistake. Who ever heard of a complete cathedral being built in the life of one man ? Those structures have been the gradual work of centuries, begun by one founder, and carried to completion by his successors. How could I possibly frame an estimate for a building, a small portion of which might possibly only be raised during my lifetime ? That which would cost little one year, might, by the increased price of materials, be doubly expensive in future years. Everybody acquainted with building operations knows the fluctuating nature of these things. Common sense should have taught the Committee not to put such absurd questions to me. If you approve my design, adopt it, and carry out all or part, in its integrity, as the means may be forthcoming.'[2]

Few things show better the gulf which lay between Pugin's burning mediævalism and the nineteenth century. The points of view were irreconcilable, and, to Pugin's lasting regret, his fine designs were shelved. Instead, he was told how much money the committee had at its disposal—information which the most elementary common sense on either side would have procured him in the first place—and was persuaded to make another set of drawings, this time for a building which, while it was to cover 'a space of ground sufficient in extent for a

<hr>

[1] *Ferrey*; p. 169.   [2] *Ib.*; pp. 169-70.

real cathedral,' owing to financial stringency could not be given 'that indispensable cathedral feature—the clerestory.'[1]

'In process of Canonisation,' Pugin was later to write in his *Remarks on articles in the 'Rambler,'* 'there is always a devil's advocate, and I am satisfied there is the same personage in the erection of every church, who contrives to mar the result. Sometimes he appears in the character of a furious Committee-man, sometimes as a prejudiced ecclesiastic, sometimes in the form of a liberal benefactor, sometimes as a screw; but there he is in some character or other, thrusting in his claw, and spoiling the job. St. George's was spoilt by the very instructions laid down by the Committee that it was to hold 3,000 people on the floor space at a limited price; in consequence height, proportion, everything was sacrificed to meet these conditions.'

Pugin, in fact, had the same problem to solve as the architects of the Commissioners' Churches.

The site chosen for this, the largest of Pugin's experiments in cheap building, was that on which Lord George Gordon had harangued his religious mob on 2nd June 1780. On 8th September 1840 the foundations were begun; and on the 28th of the following May, secretly, for fear of the descendants of the Gordon mob, at seven o'clock in the morning, the foundation-stone was formally laid.[2]

St. George's has greater merits than might have been expected in the circumstances. The high expanse of the western tower opening into the church was grandly conceived. 'The double chancel-screen, with its graceful arches and light tracery, though suggestive of wood-work rather

[1] *Bumpus;* p. 169.
[2] This fear of the mob remained. Edward Petre died before the church was finished; and his widow thought it wise to arrange that the Petre Chantry Chapel, also designed by Pugin, should be placed as 'remote as might be from the most public of the thoroughfares.' [*Sister Mary of St. Francis, S.N.D.;* edited by Dom Bede Camm, O.S.B.; p. 116.]

than stone in design,'[1] and apparently 'modelled on that exquisite Late Decorated stone structure in the retrochoir of Beverley Minster,'[2] was 'effectively relieved against the dimly-lighted chancel behind.'[3] The chancel, though small, is a thoroughly sound piece of work, and although ' architects of the present day may smile at the simplicity of its reredos, a row of ten narrow niches be-pinnacled, and canopied, and crocketed, each containing a small figure, flanked by two broader and higher niches of the same design, each containing a larger figure . . . one must bear in mind that these details were designed and executed at a time when such design and such execution rose to the level of high artistic excellence beside contemporary work.'[4] In at least one respect, too, the nave is superior to that of its model, Austin Friars in Broad Street, where the window tracery is all of one pattern ; and it is adorned by some fine stained glass made by Wailes of Newcastle from Pugin's designs, that in the great west window being the gift of Lord Shrewsbury.

The faults of the building are considerable. ' In the first place,' Eastlake wrote,[5] ' the common yellow brick used for the walls is the meanest and most uninteresting of building materials, and in London, where it is chiefly used, speedily acquires a dingy appearance.' Even worse, some of the stone used on the outside of the building was so inferior in quality that it was ' already in a rapid state of decay '[6] eight years after the building had been started.

' But,' Eastlake continues, ' independently of this draw-back, there is a want of vitality about the building. The pinnacles which crown the buttresses are cold and heavy. The carved work, though executed with care and even delicacy here and there, is spiritless, except in the treatment of animal form. Crockets and ball-flower ornaments are needlessly

---

[1] *Eastlake* ; p. 155.
[2] *Bumpus* ; p. 173.
[3] *Eastlake* ; pp. 155–6.
[4] *Ib.* ; p. 156.
[5] *Ib.* ; p. 155.
[6] *The Builder* ; 9 Sep. 1848.

multiplied. The tracery of the windows is correct and aims at variety; and the doorways are arched with orthodox mouldings, but there is scarcely a single feature in the exterior which arrests attention by the beauty of its form or the aptness of its place.'

Concerning the interior, Eastlake was no less severe:

'Internally the nave is divided into eight bays, with an aisle on either side, carried to nearly the same height as the nave. There is, consequently, no clerestory. The nave arches reach at their apex to within a few feet of the roof, and the great height thus given to the thinly moulded piers (unintersected as they are by any horizontal string courses, which at once lend scale and apparent strength to a shaft) is a defect which becomes apparent at first sight. The aisle walls are singularly slight for so large a church, and one looks in vain for the bold splay and deep reveal which are characteristic of old fenestration.'

He might have added that the small size of the gorgeous side chapels still further damages the general effect.

But yet, in spite of the severity of Eastlake's strictures, and the venomous malignity of Ruskin,[1] who, as Ferrey pointed out,[2] was determined that nothing should be right if it emanated from a Catholic, St. George's, far from being a failure, is a triumph over crushing difficulties.

The first of these was the disproportion between funds and size of building. For the rest, Pugin can be heard in his own defence:

'In most cases,' he wrote,[3] 'churches are commenced on a cheap principle, and when carried up and too late, some persons are anxious to improve the effect, and then gold leaf and colours are introduced to supply that richness which would have been far better produced in carved stone, and if

[1] Appendix 12 ('Romanist Modern Art') to *The Stones of Venice*.
[2] *Ferrey*; p. 168.　　　　[3] *Some Remarks*; p. 9.

originally designed, at much the same cost. This was the case in the side chapels of St. George's. Had the pious benefactors who paid for the coloured decorations contributed the same sum to have improved the fabric, when first designed, they could have been groined with stone, and lined with imperishable ornament.'

Passing from the particular to the general, he goes on :

' I am quite willing to admit that many of the new churches that have been erected on the old principle, are full of defects, but in reviving a long-lost art this was unavoidable. It should be remembered that the whole restoration has been a series of experiments, everything had to be created from the employer to the artizan. After three centuries of neglect, and the loss of the ancient traditions, and of the very means employed by the old artists, it was no easy matter to reproduce their skilful works, in all their variety. A few years ago it was impossible to have procured the commonest articles of church furniture in any but the most debased style—not a carver in wood or stone, and in metal work such was the difficulty of procuring operatives, that I was compelled, for the first altar lamp I ever produced, to employ an old German, who made jelly moulds for pastry cooks, as the only person who understood beating up copper to the old forms.' [1]

These points, combined with Eastlake's comparison with contemporary work, are enough to discount many of the faults in St. George's. But there is more yet to be said before a visitor to the church can get a just idea of Pugin's work. In the first place, St. George's was intended to be a parish church, not a cathedral, and so should not be judged in accordance with this later dignity. In the second place, it was never finished. Its great squat tower is only the base of the tower which was designed, and which was to be crowned

[1] *Some Remarks* ; p. 15.

with a singularly graceful spire.[1] In the third place, the
completed end of the church is hidden by buildings which
were not intended in the original plan, so that it is quite
impossible to get a just impression of the exterior. And
finally, St. George's passed into the hands of people who
were quite incapable of appreciating such good work as Pugin
had been enabled to do. No sooner was it finished than one
of its finest features, the opening of the tower into the church,
' was obliterated by the erection of a lumbering organ loft.' [2]
Mr. Bumpus refers to this as a ' ridiculous blunder.' The
phrase is too mild to describe the action of people who, when
something approaching a fine church has been built with
inadequate funds, immediately destroy the best architectural
feature which shortage of money has allowed the architect to
introduce. What Pugin himself would have thought of a later
' blunder ' may be gauged from his letter to *The Tablet* of
2nd September 1848 :

' For all these things the powers of darkness wrestle with
us, and each succeeding triumph of the cross adds to their
fury ; and when the glorious Rood was again erected in the
metropolis of England [at St. George's], surrounded with
burning tapers and flowering branches, and surpliced
choristers, after its demolition by Act of Parliament, and three
centuries of prostration, it was hardly to be expected that
such a triumph, such a theme for exultation, could have
passed over without some oppressing voice. No ; but the
reproach came not from the Calvinistic rabble, it was not
raised by Protestant Commissioners and with Parliamentary
powers. It was declared *intolerable* by a son of the Church,
and the last yell of Protestant exultation which accompanied

[1] The drawings for this masterly piece of work are still preserved by Mr. S. Pugin
Powell. It is to be hoped that the Southwark Diocese may eventually make some
reparation for its predecessor's mutilation of Pugin's work by having his tower and
spire completed.
[2] *Bumpus ;* p. 172.

the fall of the Rood in the Elizabethan era has been faintly
echoed by a Catholic writer [in *The Rambler*] on its restoration
in the nineteenth century.'

The echo may have been faint; but it grew in power;
and a later generation pulled down the rood-screen—' the
only really *cathedral* feature the church possessed '[1]—and
added it, after alteration, to the lamentable organ-loft at the
other end of the church.[2]   And later still, as though to add
the last artistic insult, the fine lectern, the only object left to
break the monotonous vista of 240 feet, was ' removed from
its proper place in the choir into an obscure corner at the east
end of the north aisle.' [3]

In November 1842, at the invitation of Dr. Cox, President
of the College, and Bishop Griffith, a former President, Pugin
visited St. Edmund's College, at Old Hall, near Ware, in
Hertfordshire.

The students were delighted at this visit, for there was talk
of rebuilding the Chapel, and they presented him with an
address which was somewhat marred by the fact that the paper
was headed by a drawing of the barrack-like buildings of the
College, buildings which caused Pugin to refer to the place
as the " Priest Factory." [4]

' Dear and respected Sir,
    Feeling ourselves highly honoured by your presence
amongst us, long anxiously expected, we hasten to present
you with a testimonial of our sentiments. While others more
favoured have lived in the very circle of your actions, we, in
our retirement, have communed with you solely in your
writings. But think not that, therefore, our esteem has been

---

[1] *Bumpus*; p. 172.
[2] It is gratifying that the Rood itself has been replaced, and now hangs at the
chancel arch. Pugin's original design (published in *Ferrey*), which had no screen
but showed the Rood on a slender arch across the entrance to the chancel, remains
as an ironic prophecy.
[3] *Bumpus*; p. 174.   [4] *St. Edmund's College*; p. 148.

less enthusiastic. We have watched your constant exertions in the revival of the real glory of art, we have witnessed your successful labours for the beautifying of the House of God, and great has been our respect, heartfelt our gratitude. A time has at length arrived when these feelings, so long secret, may be made manifest, and we rejoice in the hope that this small manifestation will give some passing satisfaction to you as highly deserving. The approving voice of many truly learned has already gone forth to cheer you in your career of utility and fame. And amongst these may we not number several of our own body, several amongst the anointed of God? They have been happy in their appointment to raise the broken altars of Israel—they have been further happy in having one who might render the beauty of these altars a fitting throne for the Eternal. In this twofold honour may a share be reserved for us. May we be one day their successors, and may we too have the advantage of your co-operation. That for many years your mind may be guided by the Framer of all beauty, that you may long continue the worthy embellisher of His temples is the united earnest prayer of

The Students of St. Edmund's.' [1]

It was an encouraging beginning, and Pugin replied in fitting, though less turgid, language :

' London, Feast of St. Francis Xavier, 1842.

My dear friends,—The shortness of my stay at St. Edmund's College having prevented me from making a suitable acknowledgement to the kind address you presented to me, I take an early opportunity of expressing the great satisfaction which I have received from this unexpected testimony of your kind feelings towards me, not so much on personal grounds, but as the evidence of your views respecting the great revival of

---

[1] *Ferrey ;* pp. 137–8.

Catholic art. You may be assured, my dear friends, that it is
the bounden duty of all Catholics throughout the world, but
especially in our native land, to forward with all possible
energy the restoration of Christian architecture. It is not a
mere question of taste, or of abstract beauty and proportion,
but it has far higher claims on our veneration as the symbolism
of the ancient faith. Viewed in this, its true light, ecclesiastical
architecture cannot fail to receive from those who are destined
to the sacred function of the priesthood that consideration
which it deserves. From you, therefore, who will at some
future period minister at these very altars which are now
erecting under the sanction of your respected bishops (at St.
George's and other churches), this testimony of the feelings
you entertain on this important subject is most gratifying
to me.

There is but one sentence in the whole address which did
not afford me sincere pleasure. I allude to the epithet of fame
referring to my labours. This savours of paganism. Architectural fame belongs rather to the Colosseum than the
Cathedral. It would be a fearful and presumptuous attempt
in any man to exalt himself by means of the temples of God.
It is a privilege and a blessing to work in the sanctuary. The
majesty of the vast churches of antiquity is owing to the
sublime mysteries of the Christian faith and the solemnity of
its rites.

The ancient builders felt this. They knew the small share
they could claim in the glories they produced, and their
humility exceeded their skill. How unbecoming then would
it be for any man at the present time to exult where works are
after all but faint copies of ancient excellence. God has
certainly permitted me to become an instrument in drawing
attention to long-forgotten principles, but the merit of these
belongs to older and better days. I still enter even the
humblest erections of Catholic antiquity as a disciple to the

school of his master,[1] and for all that is produced, we must cry in most bounden duty, ' Non nobis, Domine, non nobis, sed nomini tuo da gloriam.'

Recommending myself to your prayers and exhorting you to take every opportunity of informing yourselves in Catholic art,

I remain, your devoted friend,
+ A. Welby Pugin.' [2]

Truly ' no man ever saw so many pagans ' as Pugin, who could find their influence even in the verbose enthusiasm of the students of St. Edmund's. But his reply is of deeper interest than that. It shows both his purpose and his approach. His purpose was selfless : the giving of glory to God. His approach was humble : the following of ancient excellence. The result might be only faint copies. But by ever turning with humility and ardour to the past, the copies would become less faint, and God's would be the glory.

On 17th September 1845 the work started, and the ' great chapel ' of St. Edmund's began to rise incongruously beside the ' Priest Factory '.

For a time all went well. The work, entrusted, like almost all Pugin's buildings, to Mr. George Myers, progressed rapidly, and in a little over a year the roof was on. But in 1847 Dr. Griffith died, and Pugin lost the support of a man whose capacity for raising money was only equalled by his enthusiasm for Gothic. For a time work practically ceased, and the great screen was not begun until after October 1848, when, by the terms of the contract, it should have been finished.

Even in the lifetime of Dr. Griffith, funds were barely

---

[1] ' In March 1840, he was at work gathering fresh inspiration from a tour through some of the old parish churches of England. He visited Stamford, Newark, Grantham, Crowland, the Norfolk coast, Norwich, Milford, Bury St. Edmund's, Laversham, and Ipswich.' [*Wiseman*; I., p. 358.]

[2] *St. Edmund's College*; pp. 249-51.

sufficient. The walls had to be made so thin that the fact
that Pugin gave them adequate strength can be adduced as
evidence of his genius.[1] In the roof this evidence is even
stronger ; for, though of necessity so slight that it creaks in
windy weather, it is still pronounced to be safe. The contract
for the whole outer fabric was for less than £6,500.

Dr. Cox exerted himself to raise more money, but funds
came in slowly.

' I do hope to live to see this chapel carried out,' Pugin
wrote[2] ; ' it will be a very grand job. Above all, [secure] all
stained glass for the side windows, move everything for this, to
subdue the light and throw the true effect over the building.'

Even in 1851 he could still write of St. Edmund's[3] that
' one great chapel, very nearly completed, yet lingers on in an
unfinished state, when a little effort might render it available
for divine service, and, in the meantime, many students must
quit the college without that true love of ecclesiastical art that
is only imparted to the soul by a devout assistance at the
functions of religion in these solemn edifices. The mere
inspection of them is nothing, it is when they become associated with the life of divine worship that they produce the
full power and lift the soul in ecstasy.'

However, the necessary efforts were made, and on 16th
May 1853 the chapel was opened and consecrated. By that
time Pugin was dead, and the carrying out of his already much
modified plans had been entrusted to his son.

Externally, the chapel is notable for its fine simplicity,
which is emphasised on the south side by Edward Pugin's
ornate ' Scholefield Chantry.' It consists of a chancel crossed
by north and south transepts, and a sacristy. Its length is
116 feet, width 32 feet, greatest height 56 feet. The width of
the transepts is 26 feet, their combined length 68 feet.

---

[1] *St. Edmund's Chapel* ; p. 33.   [2] *Ib.* ; pp. 37–8.
[3] *Rood Screens* ; pp. 117–8.

Internally, the outstanding feature of the chapel is the graceful, seven-arched, double rood-screen, probably modelled on that at Oberwesel, of which Pugin wrote lovingly[1] as ' one of the most perfect, as well as the most beautiful screens in Germany '. Built of Caen stone, with shafts, capitals, and bases of Bolsover stone, the St. Edmund's screen was the object of Pugin's particular care, and he considered it one of his most successful efforts. Beyond it lies the magnificent choir, wherein Pugin, free from the sudden glut of money for decorative purposes which so often gave point to the sneer ' that he starved his roof-tree to gild his altar ',[2] was enabled to give his best in fine simplicity. At St. Edmund's both ' roof-tree ' and ' altar ' were equally starved. Its beauty ' lies in the lofty grace of the outlines, the delicate tracery of the slender windows, and the perfect harmony of the proportions.' The range of Pugin's powers as architect could hardly be better exemplified than in St. Giles's, Cheadle, and St. Edmund's, the one showing that, when necessary, he could go to extremes of over-decoration without vulgarity, the other justifying the statement that ' Pugin knew how to make even a bare wall look attractive.' [3]

Fine as it is, St. Edmund's is not as Pugin had intended. Many of his designs had to be modified to save expense. His graceful spire had to be left out entirely, and also the continuation of the stone carving of the reredos round the sanctuary walls as far as the stalls, and the *sedilia*. The pinnacles between each set of stalls—according to tradition, the last drawings that he made—which would have relieved the monotony of the long, straight line of canopy, had to be omitted ; and the return stalls which he had planned were vetoed, it is said by Cardinal Wiseman on erroneous rubrical grounds, but also possibly because they were considered

---

[1] *Rood Screens* ; p. 37.   [2] *Eastlake* ; p. 162.
[3] *St. Edmund's Chapel* ; p. 83.

inconvenient at the time. The Griffith Chantry in the south transept was to have been separated from the antechapel by a stone screen. This proved too costly, and an oak screen was substituted, and the design of the tomb, altar, and reredos simplified and the tomb itself placed to one side instead of in the middle. Before the altar and reredos were put up, their design was still further modified by Edward Pugin to save expense.

In addition to these modifications, various alterations and additions have been made. The Lady Chapel and Shrine of St. Edmund in the angle between the north transept and the chancel, made strong enough to support Pugin's still unbuilt spire, are Edward Pugin's work, as also is the Scholefield Chantry outside the south side of the chancel. Half the east window in the north transept had to be blocked up when the Lady Chapel was built, giving it a curious shape. The floor of the sanctuary has been lowered and retiled, and a third row of stalls added. The polychrome decoration of parts of the sanctuary dates from 1870.[1] The pictures between the windows in the chancel, and the Stations of the Cross in the antechapel, are additions. An organ, given by that ' glorious man ', William George Ward, was added to the Rood Loft.[2]

The history of these three buildings, St. Chad's, St. George's, and St. Edmund's, might be paralleled in almost all Pugin's buildings. They are fair examples of the difficulties he had to overcome, and of the alterations and mutilations which his work has almost invariably received. To attain a clear idea of Pugin's ability as architect, two things are therefore necessary : to consider the history of whatever work is being examined ; to compare it with its forerunners in the Revival.

---

[1] It included red and gold curtains painted on the stonework on either side of the altar. Happily, they were obliterated in 1893, just over fifty years after Pugin had written [*True Principles* ; p. 27] that ' the severity of Christian or Pointed Architecture is utterly opposed to all deception.'

[2] A fortunate accident has recently made its removal advisable, and it is now on a loft on the east side of the north transept where it hides the already mutilated east window.

CHAPTER XVII

ROOD SCREENS

Great was the heat and the dust rose.
The Song of Roland.

It is related [1] that, at the opening of St. Edmund's College chapel, Edward Pugin remarked of the organ then recently placed upon the rood screen : " Had my father been here, every note of that organ would have been a dagger in his heart."

The surprising thing about Edward Pugin's words is that they were, metaphorically, quite true.

The reason for this is to be found in that, while Pugin held all his opinions passionately, two subjects about which his opinions were particularly passionate were church music and rood screens. 'A man', he wrote to March-Phillipps,[2] 'may be judged by his feelings on Plain Chaunt. If he like Mozart he is no chancel and screen man.' That a chancel should have its screen and rood became to him an axiom of Christian art, and the substitution for the rood of an organ, which as likely as not would be used for Mozart, on top of a screen was little short of sacrilege. For the screen was that which divided the congregation from the Holy of Holies ; and the screen upheld the rood.

To-day it seems a little ridiculous that anyone should feel violent emotion over the need for a piece of church furniture which is absent from the great majority of churches. That Pugin felt this emotion he made plain enough. For instance, when Pugin's ideas of architecture and William George Ward's ideas of comfort clashed in the house that he built for

---

[1] *St. Edmund's Chapel ;* p. 43.   [2] *Phillipps ;* II., p. 218.

Ward near St. Edmund's College, he wrote[1] : 'I assure you
if I had known Mr. Ward would have turned out so badly, I
would never have designed a respectable house for him. He
ought not to be allowed to reside in the vicinity of so fine a
screen. I would assign him a first floor opposite Warwick
Street Chapel. Who could have thought that the glorious
man whom I knew at Oxford could have fallen so miserably
low? it is very sad.' Again,[2] when showing an Anglican
friend his rood screen in St. Barnabas's, Nottingham, he said:
" Within is the holy of holies. The people remain outside.
Never is the sanctuary entered by any save those in sacred
orders." And then, to his horror, a priest appeared in the
sanctuary, showing the screen to two ladies. Pugin turned
to the sacristan : " Turn those people out at once. How dare
they enter ? " But the sacristan replied : " Sir, it is Bishop
Wiseman." And Pugin, powerless, retired to the nearest
bench, and burst into tears.

This idea of the sacrosanct quality of rood screens had
developed in Pugin's mind in the course of his studies of
ancient examples. They do not appear in his earlier churches.
As soon as he started to build them, opposition arose. For
the Romanisers were nearly as violently against screens as
Pugin was for them. In *The Rambler* of 29 July 1848, there
appeared the first part of a long article against the use of
screens, over the initial ' X '. The editorial introduction to
it ended : ' we shall be happy to give a place in our pages to
any communications with which we may be favoured on
either side of the question, being convinced that a calm and
temperate discussion of its merits will both bring to light
many facts and reasonings both for and against their revival,
which are not sufficiently known, and which will prove
extremely interesting to those who wish to consider the subject
in all its bearings.'

[1] *Ward (Oxford);* p. 155.   [2] *W. G. Ward;* p. 386.

The invitation was accepted with alacrity, and 'many facts and reasonings both for and against' were brought to light. On 5th August, the second part of 'X.'s' article appeared. On 12th August, 'Q' had a long letter against screens, and 'Y' a short one in favour. On 19th August, 'X' returned to the charge, and 'Z' and 'BB' joined in. *The Rambler* then became a monthly: in the September number there were three letters on the subject; in November only one, but lengthy: in December, after a long letter in favour of screens, the editors sensibly wrote that since they saw 'no prospect of any advantage by prolonging a discussion already carried to a more than sufficient length,' the correspondence was closed. Before the month was out, however, they changed their minds, for 'H' had thought of some further points against the use of screens, and in January 1849 he was allowed to close the discussion.

Those who supported screens had hardly, as it were, had a fair deal. But so far as Pugin was concerned, it did not matter. He could always write a book. In 1851 he published his views on the subject in *A Treatise on Chancel Screens and Rood Lofts, Their Antiquity, Use, and Symbolic Signification.*

The details of the discussion in *The Rambler* are of little importance at the present day; for the Rood Screen Controversy has long since, for all practical purposes, been settled. The main lines, however, may be summarised as follows: The opponents of screens considered that they interfered both with that clear view of the altar and in particular of the Elevation which had become normal, and with the proper performance of various Italian devotions, such as Exposition[1] to which they were attracted. The 'chancel and screen men,' on the other hand, considered that there was no need for the

---

[1] Incidentally, the *Quarant' Ore*, or Forty Hours' Exposition, first took place in England in Pugin's heavily screened church of St. George, in Southwark, the building which had given rise to the controversy, in October 1848, when the controversy was in progress. [*Sequel;* II., pp. 268–9.]

people to have an uninterrupted view of the altar, and held
that screens were not incompatible with any devotions which
could suitably be performed in England. It was not so much
a struggle, in fact, between opposing arguments as between
irreconcilable points of view. In consequence, as a sort of
cockpit of English Catholicism, it went far to justify a remark
in *The Saturday Review* of 16th August 1862,[1] concerning
Catholic periodicals of the previous twenty years, that ' It is
clear . . . that an amount of pugnacity exists among Roman
Catholics, which by no means finds a [sufficient] vent in
onslaughts on Protestantism.'

The Oratorians, being the leaders of the Italianate element
in the revival of Catholicism in England, were drawn into the
fray. ' The Oxford men with some few exceptions ', Pugin
wrote,[2] ' have turned out the most disappointing people in
the world. They were three times as Catholic in their ideas
before they were reconciled to the Church. It is really quite
lamentable. They have got the most disgusting place possible
for the Oratory in London, and fitted up in a horrible manner,
with a sort of Anglo-Roman altar. Those things are very
sad, and the mischief they do is inconceivable. What a
glorious man Formby [3] is. He is about the only man who has
stuck to the true thing, and never bowed the knee to Baal. A
man may be judged by his feelings on Plain Chaunt. If he
likes Mozart he is no chancel and screen man. By their music
you shall know them, and I lost all faith in the Oratorians
when I found they were opposed to the old song.'

But epistolary disapproval was not enough. The converts
could be bearded in their lair. An interview took place, and
resulted in what seems to have been little better than a childish
' scene ' on the subject of architectural orthodoxy, between

---

[1] Quoted in *Lord Acton and his Circle ;* Abbot Gasquet, O.S.B. ; p. xliij.
[2] *Phillipps ;* II., p. 218.
[3] The Rev. Henry Formby (1816–84) ; formerly Vicar of Ruardean, co.
Gloucester.

'Father Wilfrid,'[1] Pugin, and March-Phillipps. Newman, drawn in as mediator, showed his unfailing discernment and tact from Maryvale near Oscott. His letter, dated 3rd June 1848, ended[2]: 'If I had any right to criticize the conduct of many excellent men, men far more useful in their generation and holy than I am, I could say much about the grief I feel at the neglect I see, of that so good and true maxim, In necessariis Unitas, in *dubiis libertas*. How is it, my dear Mr. Phillipps, that you understand this so clearly in doctrinal questions, yet are slow to admit it in ritual? I do not say you, but are there not persons, who would be more distressed at a man's disliking a chancel skreen than at his being a Gallican? This I I am sure of, that, from the infirmity of human nature, a reaction is the necessary consequence in the minds of hearers, when able and eloquent men state truths in an extravagant or a peremptory way. If Mr. Pugin persists, as I cannot hope he will not, in loading with bad names the admirers of Italian architecture, he is going the very way to increase their number. Men will not be put down without authority which is infallible. And if we go to authority, I suppose Popes have given a greater sanction to Italian than to Gothic.'

It was no good. Newman succeeded in his first purpose, of restoring Faber and March-Phillipps to their former affectionate terms. But beyond that he could do nothing. The controversy was not one which could be settled by any 'calm and temperate discussion' such as that of which the Editor of *The Rambler* had expressed his hopes. The opposing parties did not, as it were, speak the same language: they were 'Romans' and 'Goths': the controversy was the whole difference between them.

This matter of screens, which had started as but an incident, took on a wholly exaggerated importance. The antagonists

---

[1] The Rev. Frederick William Faber (1814-63); formerly Rector of Elton, co. Huntingdon.
[2] *Phillipps*; II., p. 204.

argued vehemently as to the necessity, advisability, or possibility of screens, as though screens were the main object in view. But the point at issue was whether Renaissance Italian or Mediæval English ideas were to prevail in Catholicism in England. Screens were, so to say, a strong-point the possession of which would give the final victory. If the screens party won the day, the 'all seeing' principle in church architecture, as exemplified by the Oratorians, would remain as but an occasional alien extravagance. If the anti-screens party won, the 'all-seeing' principle would become the normal, and Gothic would be tolerated only in so far as it could be made to fit in with Roman ideas. For the leaders on either side there could be neither weakening nor compromise.

Pugin's difference with Ward on the subject makes this clear. Ward, having attacked rood screens in *The Rambler*, over the initial 'H', on the grounds that they were undevotional, and not wishing to assail an old friend under cover of anonymity, wrote to Pugin acknowledging the authorship, and received a reply to this effect : ' Sir, it needed not your note to convince me that you were the perpetrator of the scandalous letter. I can only say that the less we have to do with each other in future the better, for I must plainly tell you that I consider you a greater enemy to true Christianity than the most rabid Exeter Hall fanatic.' Ward clinched the matter with a sturdy pun : 'I knew Pugin was strong in rood screens ; I didn't know he was so good a hand at rude letters.'[1] And he later summed up their difference succinctly[2] : " I have great sympathy with Pugin. He was very like me. He was a man of one idea, and so am I. His idea was Gothic Architecture, mine is devotion to Rome."

In the circumstances, no compromise was possible, and the simple common sense of Lord Arundel and Surrey,[3] as

[1] *Ward (Oxford)*; p. 155. [2] *W. G. Ward*; p. 386.
[3] Henry Granville Fitzalan-Howard, afterwards fourteenth Duke of Norfolk (1815–60) ; described by Montalembert as ' the most pious layman of our times '

expressed in a letter to March-Phillipps dated 11th May 1850, could do nothing to still the storm :—

'Why do you call one particular branch of Art, however beautiful, Christian Art? It appears to me to be at least strange in a Catholic to forget that, under the much abused Churches of Roman and Greek form, so many Saints have received their inspirations; and that at this moment the spread of Religion in France is conducted entirely without reference to the external form of the building. There is nothing Gothick in the Church of Notre Dame des Victoires, so favoured by the Blessed Virgin as the Mother Church of the Archconfrerie of the Heart of Mary. Neither does it appear essential anywhere that the return to Christianity should be accompanied by a return to the architectural tastes of our ancestors. God bestows His graces and favours without reference to these considerations. This is not matter of theory but of fact. It was under shelter of these very Gothick Churches that wicked men in England suffered the Reformation to take place. And assuredly the Piety and Zeal of the Oratorians themselves should be a proof that a return to Catholicity does not necessarily imply a return to mediæval art. You will be astonished when I tell you that I really have thought much of the enthusiasm on either side was in joke. I could not seriously believe that Catholics could speak with so much bitterness towards each other on account of such differences. I do feel, whatever may be reserved for us, that if we quarrel upon such matters as these we shall deserve the effects of disunion which we shall undoubtedly feel. I do not think you often find Saints greatly occupied with these matters, or that it is conductive to Sanctity to think too much about them. I think variety pleasing, always within the limits that the Church willingly sanctions, and I confess

[*Dict. Nat. Biog.*; XXVIII., p. 39] ; and by *Burke* as ' an amiable, excellent, and highly respected nobleman.'

in travelling I like to find in one place a Gothick, in another a Grecian, and in a third a Byzantine Church. But to feel a repugnance to any one form in which it appeared due attention had been intended to the suitable display of treasure in the ornament of the temple dedicated to God would appear to me actually wrong. I am quite aware that you will pity and despise me for all this, and I will not bore you with more of it. But the simple fact is that there are men of piety on both sides of the question, and I am sure I should be glad enough to let each do what he will and only suffer me to worship God in either the Gothick or the Roman edifice, as may be most convenient at the moment. I cannot help thinking there must be many who hold this opinion, and are heartily tired of unnecessary disputes.' [1]

This might not unreasonably have been considered the last word on the subject. But it was not a point of view that appealed to Pugin. Nine years before he had written [2]: 'Milk-and-water men never effect anything; they deserve drowning in their own insipid compositions.' Time had only strengthened that opinion. Even if Lord Arundel and Surrey had been right in admitting the tolerability of a Grecian church anywhere (a thing which Pugin would have violently denied), he had missed the whole point. The point was not whether St. Peter's might be tolerable in Rome, and Notre Dame des Victoires in Paris; it was whether the Church in England was to be English or Italianate. In Rome, the Church had allowed herself to be bedaubed with the horrors of Pagan Renaissance decoration. In England, the Church was rising again from its foundations. There was no need for it to bear up a Pagan carapace. It could look straight back to the glorious past and rise up again as it once had been. As for feeble compromisers like Lord Arundel and Surrey, they were as bad as the Oratorians. There was no possible

---

[1] *Phillipps;* I., p. 315.   [2] *Present State;* p. 91.

compromise. ' If a man liked Mozart he was no chancel and screen man.' Those who were not for screens were against them. Those who were against them were as dangerous to true Christianity as ' the most rabid Exeter Hall fanatic.' More so : they were an enemy within the gates. It was time to show them up for what they were : it was time that the truth about rood screens should be known.

The *Treatise on Chancel Screens and Rood Lofts* goes to the heart of the matter in the opening paragraph : ' The subject on which I am about to treat is one of far more importance than the generality of men will be willing to admit ; it is not a mere question of architectural detail, respecting a few mullions and a transverse beam, but it involves great principles connected with discipline, and even faith, and it is a question in which all those who either wish for a revival of ancient solemnity and reverence, or even the preservation of what yet remains, are most deeply interested.' He then goes on to show that in the sixteenth century, though ' pagan ' details were adopted, the general arrangement of churches, including the presence of screens, remained unchanged. ' But gradually, from the adoption of the details of classic antiquity, the buildings themselves became objects of imitation, till revived paganism displayed its full absurdity in the huge *room* called the Madeleine. Designed by infidels, built by infidels, and suited only for infidel purposes, and then turned over, for want of another use, to become a church ! ' A building of which ' the very decorations are an insult to Christianity.'

As such, it was a good weapon with which to attack his opponents : ' I have been induced to speak particularly of this edifice, as it is the beau ideal of a modern church in the minds of those who are opposed to screens ; for the principles of these men, worked out to their legitimate ends, are subversive of every tradition and the whole system of ecclesiastical architecture. Screens are, in truth, the very least part of the cause of their animosity to the churches of their Fathers, for if any man says he loves pointed architecture and hates screens, I do not hesitate to denounce him as a liar, for one is inseparable from the other, and *more*, inseparable from *Catholic arrangement in any style*, Byzantine, Norman, Pointed, or debased. We have now to contend for the great principles of Catholic antiquity,—tradition and reverence against modern development and display. It is not a struggle for taste or ornament, but a contention for *vital principles*. There is a most intimate connection between the externals of religion and the faith itself; and it is scarcely possible to preserve the interior faith in the doctrine of the holy eucharist if all exterior reverence and respect is to be abolished.'

He then goes on to point out that, the Mass being the focal point of Catholic worship, ' it is but natural that the place where this most holy sacrifice is to be offered up, should be set apart and railed off from the less sacred portions of the church, and we find this to have been the case in all ages, in all styles, and in all countries professing the Catholic faith down to a comparatively very recent period, when in many places all feelings of sanctity, tradition, and reverence, seemed to have been superseded by ignorant innovation and love of change.'

The purpose of the book is then given in greater detail: ' It will be shown in this work that the idea of room-worship, and the all-seeing principles, is a perfect novelty ', as much a novelty as the Protestant arrangement of churches so that the congregation should hear all that the minister said. There follows a two-page parenthesis on Protestant architecture, which includes in a footnote the statement that he had been compelled ' to adopt the conclusion, that the most fearful acts of destruction and spoliation were committed by men who had not only been educated in the ancient faith, but who were contented externally to profess its doctrines.'[1]

'But to return, I cannot too strongly impress on the minds of my readers that the very *vitals* of Catholic architecture are assailed by the opponents of screens.'

The argument then jerks back to the practice in the early Christian basilicas, in which, such was the atmosphere of awe about the sacred mysteries, with the help of the general plan of the building and the presence of solid screens, curtains, and veils, nothing of the celebrant ' could be discerned by the congregation except an occasional glimpse of his head '; and truly, ' so sacred, so awful, so mysterious is the sacrifice of the mass, that if men were seriously to reflect on what it really consists, so far from advocating mere rooms for its celebration, they would hasten to restore the reverential arrangements of Catholic antiquity, and instead of striving for front seats and first places, they would hardly feel worthy to occupy the remotest corner of the temple.' Even in St. Peter's, ' the modern all-seeing principle ' was not fully admitted; for, ' when the Pope celebrates, there is a living screen of Swiss troops and noble guards that effectually shuts out the sight of what is going on, except to those taking part in the functions, or a favoured few, who by means of gold or interest are seated in raised loggia.' If, in spite of this, the all-seeing principle is still advocated, the only logical conclusion is a church with a sloping floor, as otherwise ' the *spectators* . . . form a far greater barrier than any screen-work.' Therefore, ' if religious

---

[1] In the footnote he expresses a hope that he might ' be able before long to put forth an impartial statement relative to the destruction of Catholic edifices and ornaments consequent on the change of religion in England.' This may refer to a part of his *A New View of an Old Subject : or, the English Schism impartially considered*, the incomplete manuscript of which was found and edited by Edward Pugin who announced it as in preparation in 1875. Pugin himself, in an advertisement in his *Earnest Address*, had announced it as ' preparing for press ' in 1851. Or it may refer to his projected *Apology for the separated Church of England, etc.*, which is discussed by Edmund Sheridan Purcell in his ' Appendix ' to Ferrey's *Recollections*. Neither work was ever published, and it seems probable that, if not identical, the one may have been a part of the other. See Appendix III., and p. 303 *sq.*

ceremonies are to be regarded as spectacles they should be celebrated in regular theatres, which have been expressly invented for the purpose of accomodating great assemblages of persons to hear and see well. It has been most justly said, that there is no legitimate halting-place between Catholic doctrine and positive infidelity, and I am quite certain that there is none between a church built on Christian tradition and symbolism and Covent Garden theatre with its pit, boxes, and gallery.'

As for screens, they arose 'from a natural as well as a symbolical intention,—it is a natural principle to enclose any portion of a building or space which is set apart from public use and access, and when such a boundary is erected round the place of sacrifice in a church, it teaches the faithful to reverence the seat of the holy mysteries, and to worship in humility.'

This was an ancient custom: 'the choirs of the early Christian churches, which were all frequented by the people, were enclosed by open screens, like trellis-work, usually made of brass, and this principle has descended through all ages in churches destined for *parochial worship and the use of the people*, while in cathedral, collegiate, and conventual churches, which were intended more especially for the use of ecclesiastics, the solid screens were invariable, not only across the nave but round the choir, so that the canons and religious were completely enclosed', the chief reason for this being the need for protection from draughts during the long offices, and, secondarily, the desirability of freedom from distraction from the peregrinations of layfolk.

'But, like every other object generated in necessity, the church soon turned them to a most edifying account, and while the great screen was adorned with the principal events of our Lord's life and passion, surmounted by the great rood, the lateral walls were carved with edifying sculptures and

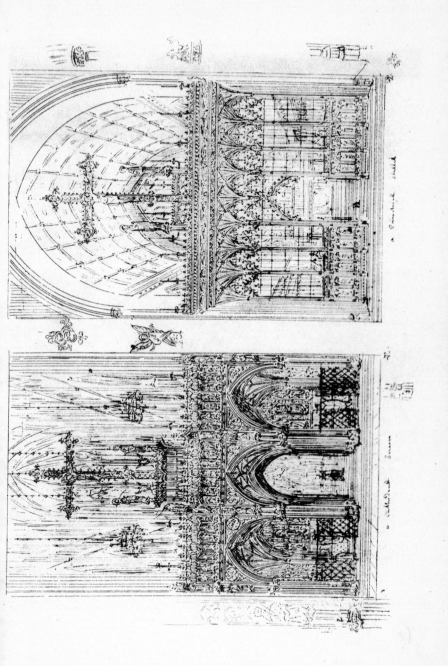

sacred histories, many of which still remain, as at Notre Dame, Paris, Amiens, Chartres, Auch, &c. I do not think that the theory, which some writers have advanced, of these *close* screens being erected to increase the mystery of the celebration, and to procure greater respect for the sacrifice, is tenable; the mass is not more holy in one church or one altar than another, and it is most certain that no parochial churches, built as such, ever had close screens, but always open ones; and, indeed, we very often find altars erected outside these close screens of cathedral and conventual churches, for the benefit of the people, as will be seen by the plates given in this work, which would involve a complete contradiction in principle, supposing the high altar to be hid on symbolical grounds. The *close* screens belong properly to the choir rather than the altar, as in many Italian churches served by religious, the clergy sat behind the screen, while the altar is partly without, so that the celebration served both the religious and the people.'

This being the case, therefore, close screens ' are certainly most unsuitable for any churches to be erected in this country under existing circumstances, where the limited extent of means and number of the clergy render it necessary for all services to be available for the faithful in general, and the bishops' churches, like the original basilicæ, to be in a manner parochial.'

But open screens were a different matter. Equally ancient, they became universal: ' they commenced many centuries *before the introduction of pointed architecture*, and *they have survived its decline;* in fact, they belong to the first principles of Catholic *reverence and order*, and *not to any particular style*, though, like everything else connected with the church, they attained their greatest beauty in the mediæval period.'

These statements are supported by appeals to San Michele, Florence, old St. Peter's, Rome, and Antwerp Cathedral.

But practical considerations were as strong as historical :
' they prevent any irreverence or intrusion in the sacred places
at those times when no celebration or office is going on ; and
symbolically, they impress on the minds of the faithful the
great sanctity of all connected with the sacrifice of the altar,
and that, like the vicinity of the " burning bush," the ground
itself is holy.' In addition, besides saving the altar from being
(as he himself had seen) ' turned into a hat-stand within a few
minutes after the holy sacrifice had been offered up upon it,
while animals defile the frontals, and lazzaroni lounge on the
steps ', open screens served ' a most edifying purpose ; while
the principal one across the chancel or choir sustains the great
rood, with its attendant imagery and ornaments, the lateral
enclosures are surmounted by ranges of metal standards for
lights, to burn on great feasts, while the mouldings and
bratishings are enriched with texts and sacred devices.'

He then sums up his thesis : ' 1st. That open screens and
enclosures of choirs and chancels have existed from the
earliest known period of Christian churches down to the
present century, that they form an essential part of Catholic
tradition and reverence, and that no church intended for
Catholic worship can be complete without them. 2nd. That
their introduction belongs to no particular period or style,
and that their partial disuse was not consequent on the decline
of pointed architecture, but to the decay of reverence for the
sacred mysteries themselves, as I have found screens of all
styles and dates. 3rd. That closed screens are only now
suited to conventual and collegiate churches in this country,
the cathedrals being required for the worship of the people,
from whom the view of the altar has never been purposely
concealed. 4th. That those who oppose the revival and
continuance of open screens are not only enemies of Catholic
traditions and practices, but the grounds of their objections militate as strongly against every symbolic form and

arrangement in ecclesiastical architecture, and, therefore, till they retract their opposition they are practically insulting the traditions of the church, impeding the restoration of reverence and solemnity, and injuring the progress of religion.'

In passages such as this recapitulation of his thesis, Pugin displays an excess of vehemence and a lack of logical coherence —for instance, those who oppose a ' revival ' cannot reasonably be called enemies of ' practices.' It must be borne in mind, however, that, when the *Treatise* was written, Pugin was disappointed in all his most ardent aspirations : the return of England to Catholic unity was as far from fulfilment as the restoration of mediæval beauty which was to be means towards that return ; those converts on whose support he had relied had nearly all deserted him in favour of all that he considered most debased in Catholic worship ; Newman's prophecy was being fulfilled, that his unrestrained ardour would swell the numbers of his opponents. The book was in the nature of a forlorn hope. In addition, overwork was bringing about that complete mental breakdown which was to kill him within the next twelve months.

The second part of the book—' On the Enclosure of Choirs '—deals in greater detail with the historical aspects of the matter, and with the origin and furniture of rood lofts.

There then follow five sections descriptive of screens in Italy and Spain, Germany and Flanders, France, Brittany, and England. The next four chapters deal with destroyers of screens, herein named ' ambonoclasts '.[1] ' The Calvinist Ambonoclast ' opens with a loving description of ' the

---

[1] Derived from ' ambones,' the name of two stone pulpits at the lower end of the choir, from which the Epistle and Gospel were read to the congregation. They were also called ' jubés,' from the ' Jube, Domine, benedicere ' said from them before the lessons of the Office. When these ' ambones ' were joined by a gallery, the rood loft came into existence.

ecclesiastical beauty of Catholic London', and in particular
of the glories of the rood loft of ' the old parish church of
S. Mary-at-Hill' which ' was inferior to none in the beautiful
partition of its chancel'. It then gives an imaginative description of the destruction of the rood at the hands of ' the New
Gospellers', and ends: ' Nearly three hundred years have
elapsed, and the rood was again raised in glory in this very
city, and the cry " Away with it ! " was again heard. Came
it from the blaspheming Jews ? No. Came it from the bitter
Calvinists ? No. Came it from the incarnate fiends ? No.
It proceeded from a *modern Catholic ambonoclast ! ! ! !* '

' The Pagan Ambonoclast ' is a sort of cautionary tale, in
which Louis de Chantal, ' last commendatory abbot of
Conques,' having travelled to Rome and been imbued with
pagan ideas, orders the destruction of the great rood and loft
of the abbey church at Conques, and is afterwards murdered
in the French Revolution, his executioner being the most active
of the workmen whom he had employed to destroy the
rood.

' The Revolutionary Ambonoclast ' is even more directly
cautionary. Jacques Frénin, the executioner of the Abbé de
Chantal, having bought the parish church of Conques as a
place to store timber, decided to burn down the rood loft to
make more room, and was accidentally trapped inside the loft
and perished in the flames.

' The Modern Ambonoclast ' deals with Pugin's opponents,
and brings a touch of pleasing humour into the controversy :
' This character is of comparatively recent creation,—none of
the species having been seen about in this country previous
to the consecration of St. George's church. About that time
two or three made their appearance, and, though not by any
means in a flourishing condition, they have somewhat
increased. It has been asserted that their first dislike of
screens arose from a desire of literary notoriety, and that,

finding several old women of both sexes [1] had taken a most unaccountable and inexplicable offence at the ancient division of the chancel, and the restoration of the crucifix, which had been so wisely destroyed in the good old days of Queen Bess, they profited by the occasion to increase the sale of a periodical. But this may be mere calumny ; and, indeed, it is very probable that it is a case of pure development, as at first they did not exhibit any repugnance to pointed churches, which they rather lauded, and only took objection to certain upright mullions and painful images ; but they speedily developed other propensities and ideas, and latterly have exhibited symptoms almost similar to hydrophobia at the sight, or even mention, of pointed arches or pillars. The principal characteristics of modern ambonoclasts may be summed up as follows :—Great irritability at vertical lines, muntans of screens, or transverse beams and crosses ; a perpetual habit of abusing the finest works of Catholic antiquity and art, and exulting in the admiration of everything debased, and modern, and trumpery ; an inordinate propensity for candles and candlesticks, which they arrange in every possible variety ; they require great excitement in the way of lively, jocular, and amatory tunes at divine service, and exhibit painful distress at the sound of solemn chanting or plain song ; at divine worship they require to sit facing the altar, and near the pulpit, and then, if the edifice be somewhat like a fish-market, with a hot-water pipe at their feet, a gas-pipe in the vicinity, and a stove in the rear, they can realize a somewhat Italian atmosphere in cold and cheerless England, and revive some sparks of that devotion that the gloomy vaulting of Westminster and the odious pillars of a new rood screen had well nigh deprived them of. It must be, however, stated, to their credit, that the modern ambonoclasts, unlike their predecessors, confine their attacks to strokes of the pen ; and we

[1] The phrase is notable as an early instance of the use of this later well-known quip.

do not believe that they have hitherto succeeded in causing the demolition of a single screen.[1] Indeed, it is probable that, if the development of their real character had not proceeded so rapidly, they might have caused some serious mischief to Catholic restoration ; but the *cloven foot* is now so visible, that men are looking out in expectation of the *tail*, and are already on their guard.'

There then follow twenty-four pages of rather disappointing 'Conclusion'. Strong, slashing stuff, parts of it are worthy of the *Apology* or the *True Principles ;* but it gives an uneasy impression that Pugin had shot his bolt, and knew it. He is like a general who, realising that the capture of a particular tactical feature in the opposing position would give him victory, yet cannot bring himself to trust everything to its assault, but must perforce disperse his attack along the whole front, and end by being weak everywhere.

This 'Conclusion' was Pugin's despairing general attack on the influence of the Renaissance, less than a quarter of it dealing directly with screens. 'Bad as was the Paganism of the fifteenth and sixteenth centuries, it was dressed out in much external majesty and richness ; but now nothing is left but the fag end of this system ; bronze and marble are replaced by calico and trimmings ; the works of the sculptor and the goldsmith are succeeded by the milliner and the toyshop ; and the rottenness of the Pagan movement is thinly concealed by gilt paper and ribands,—the nineteenth century apeings of the dazzling innovations of the Medician era. Cheap magnificence, meretricious show, is the order of the day ; something pretty, something novel, calico hangings, sparkling lustres, paper pots, wax dolls, flounces and furbelows, glass cases, ribands, and lace, are the ornaments and materials

---

[1] The boast was premature ; for, nearly seventy years later, it was to be written that ' it seems that one of the strongest arguments against erecting a screen at all is that experience shows that sooner or later someone will pull it down . . . ' [*Sirr, F.R.I.B.A.*]

usually employed to decorate, or rather disfigure, the altar of sacrifice and the holy place. It is impossible for church furniture and decoration to attain a lower depth of degradation, and it is one of the greatest impediments to the revival of Catholic truth. It is scarcely possible for men to realize the awful doctrines and the majestic ritual of the Church under such a form; and yet these wretched novelties are found on the altars of some of the most venerable temples, equally as in the abortions of modern erection.'

The charge was true. It is due to the vigorous onslaughts of Pugin that the charge is not so true to-day. He was equally accurate in the reason he adduced for this descent to frippery: ' O, spirit of ancient Catholic art, how is it that you no longer abide among its people? What curse, what blight, has deprived us of your aid? Is it not that the sons of the church have forsaken the old traditions of faith, and have gone straying after strange forms and gods, and substituted debased novelties for ancient excellence, and to these profane and irreverent representations they have given the name of Christian saints, using the mysteries of religion as a mere peg whereon to hang their abominable productions.'

On a particular kind of painting, not yet wholly extinct, he is equally sound, though it had nothing to do with the key position of the rood screen: ' heart painting', he points out, ' has a most extraordinary vogue. Without being wanting in the respect due to the authorized devotion of the sacred heart, I should be deficient in duty as a Christian artist if I did not protest most strongly and candidly against the external form in which it is usually represented. It is quite possible to embody the pure idea of the divine heart under a mystical form that should illustrate the intention without offending the sense; but when this *most spiritual idea* is depicted by an anatomical painting of a heart copied from an original plucked from the reeking carcase of a bullock, and done with sickening accuracy of fat and veins, relieved on a chrome yellow ground, it becomes a fitting subject of fierce denunciation for every true Christian artist, as a disgusting and unworthy representation for any object of devotion.'

Three quarters of the ' Conclusion ' are past before there is any direct mention of screens, and then only to give an unconvincing answer to an accusation. ' It was currently reported that the learned Père Martin declared that the old screens contributed to the loss of faith among the people. Now if the reverend father did make this statement, I have no hesitation in contradicting it, and for this reason, that in those times when the cathedrals had enclosed choirs, they were erected and used for the purpose of keeping up a great choral service, and a worship of Almighty God *irrespective of popular assistance ;* but coeval with these were multitudes of grand parochial churches, like S. Maclou, at Rouen, relatively as magnificent as cathedrals, and where there never existed any enclosed choirs at all, but open ones, as I have shown in this work ; it appears therefore that the assertion of the reverend father has been made hastily, and without sufficient grounds.' The ' assertion ' to which Pugin refers, was made to Dr. Wiseman in answer to a question as to what ' the learned Père Martin ' thought about screens : ' He answered that they were unknown in the ancient church before the XIIth century—that there is not one existing now that was not built after 1330 : and that they contributed more than anything else to the spread of the reformation, by preventing the people from being corporally present at the service.'[1] Pugin's answer is inadequate. He first understates Père Martin's charge against screens, and then brings forward in evidence ' multitudes of grand parochial churches ' which

---

[1] *Lingard ;* p. 302. Pugin's historical views, and those here expressed, are so utterly at variance, that it is only just to both parties to remark that the whole question of the ætiology of *cancelli, ambones, pulpitum,* and screens is still obscure, though Pugin was almost certainly mistaken (p. 232 above) in his belief that mediæval screens descended from the *cancelli* of the early Christian churches.

either had screens (in which case the statement is not refuted), or were without screens (in which case Pugin shows his own claim to the universality of screens to be unfounded).

The tone of the ' Conclusion ' changes after consideration of the remarks of ' the celebrated antiquary, Père Martin, the Jesuit.'[1] Pugin had been met by a counter-attack, and had failed to repel it, and the sting was taken out of his general attack in consequence. The ' general attack ' dwindled into little more than a consolidation of the position already gained, far short as it was of the original objective. And yet the ' Conclusion ' is of importance, since it expresses clearly Pugin's ideas on the Gothic Revival as a whole, and shows how far removed he was both from the dry-as-dust anti-quarian and from the sentimental mediævalist, and how near he was, but for this predilection, to the point of view to which Lingard gave early expression and which has since prevailed. For to Pugin, the Gothic Revival was no mere restoration of forms : it was to be in the true sense a revival—a renewal of life.

' Our churches should now combine all the beauty and symbolism of antiquity with every convenience that modern discovery has suggested, or altered ecclesiastical discipline requires.' In parenthesis it may be remarked that, in Lingard's eyes these two conditions were best fulfilled without the use of screens. Pugin continues : ' The revival would then become a living monument and a true expression of the restoration of religion in the land. But I grieve to say, from what I see of the majority of pointed churches now erecting, that they are calculated to inflict greater injury on the cause than even the Italian abortions, which can only excite disgust, and drive men to the opposite opinion. . . . It is now time that the movement assumed a regular principle ; in the com-mencement everything was strange and ill understood ; step

[1] *Lingard ;* p. 302.

by step we had to fathom, and works which now appear easy
of execution were then deemed almost impracticable. . . .
It is quite certain that our present race of architects, as a body,
do not yet understand the language : they transcribe words,
and even sentences, accurately, but it is a dead imitation of
something already done, and not a living creation . . . '

In his final paragraph Pugin gives the remedy : ' I therefore
most earnestly conjure all those men who profess to revive
true architecture to look to the wants and circumstances of
the time, *not to sacrifice principles, but to prove that the real
principles can combine with any legitimate requirement of religion ;*
let the bishops and clergy practically perceive that Christian
architecture fulfils perfectly all their wants : let there be light,
space, ventilation, good access, with the absence of drafts,
which destroy devotion and excite prejudice against Pointed
doorways. Avoid useless and over-busy detail, and rely on
good proportions and solemnity of effect. Above all, we must
remember that everything old is not an object of imitation—
everything new is not to be rejected. If we work on these
golden principles, the revival would be a living monument,
as it was in days of old ; and that God may grant us means to
carry it out, that he will enlighten the hearts of the obdurate,
and unite the faithful in one great bond of exertion for the
revival of the long-lost glory of his church, sanctuary, and
altar, is the earnest prayer of the writer of this book.'

The volume closes with thirteen beautifully executed
drawings of rood screens and lofts.

It must be admitted that the *Treatise* is a somewhat disappointing work. It contains much interesting information
about the history and arrangement of screens, some most
attractive drawings, and some fine passages of invective
against the revived ' Paganism.' But it does not fulfil its
object, which was to prove the necessity for screens. All it
does prove is that Pugin was passionately fond of them : and

we to-day, now that the heat of controversy has died down, can admit the attractiveness of screens without arguing their necessity.

For Pugin, this was impossible ; and a clue as to why it was so may be found in the fact that the drawings of screens are all gathered together at the end of the book. It is as though Pugin were saying : " You have read my arguments. They are sound enough. But just look at the things themselves, and you will see that I *must* be right." One is given the impression that Pugin loved screens before he understood them, and that his arguments were worked out to justify this liking ; and that it was only then that he realised that if screens could once be shown to be an essential of Catholic art the whole position of his opponents would become untenable. Screens, in fact, started as a strong predilection, developed into an argument, and ended as a principle which the argument was not strong enough to support.

The strongest argument in favour of screens—that they are very pleasant to look at—as it so happened was not one which Pugin could use ; for it went counter to his own two first principles of architecture : ' 1st, *that there should be no features about a building which are not necessary for convenience, construction, or propriety ; 2nd, that all ornament should consist of enrichment of the essential construction of the building.*' [1] Instead, he had to adduce functional reasons, whose justice his opponents vehemently denied, and historical reasons, which were partially vitiated by his own last paragraph already quoted, and in which he went against the opinions of ecclesiologists of greater weight than himself. In 1844, Dr. Lingard had written of Pugin's plans for St. Cuthbert's Chapel, Ushaw [2] : ' with respect to the inside, it was dusk when I opened the lithographs, and I could not see distinctly. The organ on the screen appeared so like one of my fowls clapping his wings,

---

[1] *True Principles ;* p. 1.   [2] *Lingard ;* p. 301.

that I unconsciously exclaimed, "What have we here? The devil crowing over the choir?" It is, in my opinion, most frightful—and the four candles most ridiculous—and the rood and images above most unsightly. Do, I beg of you, sweep all away. Why must we put up roods, when for two hundred years they have been swept away in every country in Europe?' Again, in developing his opinion that those in the ante-chapel should have a full sight of the altar [1] : 'It was so originally when the altar was placed between the clergy and the people. I suspect that it was only after the monks had contrived for their own comfort choirs between the altar and the people, that roods were introduced, and those frightful figures of the crucifixion stuck up over the entrance to the choir ; that as the people were shut out from the sacrifice, they might at least have some object to entertain their thoughts with while it was performed. . . . Do, I implore you, think well before you admit of such an incongruity.' In addition, Lingard did not give Père Martin's opinion as an isolated theory : he adduced it in support of his own ' belief that screens were in a measure responsible for the decay of religion.' [1] On general historical points, he was no less definite : ' Why because, when windows were not glazed, it was necessary to have curtains on each side of the altar, have them now? Why because, when men got up at midnight to say matins in the depth of winter, they therefore enclosed themselves as snugly as they could in the choir, have such a choir now walled round, and shut out by a screen from the public view ? ' Incidentally, on this last point Pugin was nearly in agreement with Lingard : ' In restoring the ecclesiastical architecture of the middle ages, there are certain modifications and changes which the altered position of religion renders absolutely necessary ; for instance, in erecting a cathedral or bishop's church it should be so arranged as to *be perfectly available for the public*

---

[1] *Lingard;* p. 302.

worship of the faithful, and the choir, on that account, should
not be enclosed in a solid manner, but with open screens like
the great parochial churches at Lubeck,' &c.[1] But Lingard
goes on [2] : ' Let our churches be adapted to our wants, as
those of ancient times were to the wants of those who built
them. At all events have the church built so that all who
attend may see the service.'

Pugin would very nearly have agreed. The only difference
between them was that Pugin liked screens.

But, after all, the importance of these remarks of Lingard's
in relation to Pugin's advocacy of screens lies in the fact that
Lingard was in no sense Italianate. On the contrary, he was
very definitely an Englishman, and strongly hostile to various
new devotions imported from Italy by the Romanisers who
opposed screens partly on the ground that they interfered
with their new devotions. Pugin, by mixing his advocacy
of screens with an attack on the ultramontane activities of
such men as Ward and Faber, was confusing the issue. The
battle was not only between Goths and Romans, with screens
as a tactical position necessary to both : there was a strong
body of intelligent English opinion as hostile to screens as
the most Italianate of Oratorians ; men to whom the restoration of screens was definitely a retrograde step.

It has remained for a writer of the twentieth century to
express the idea underlying the opposition of such men as
Lingard who, perhaps not with full consciousness, were
embodying a development in the Catholic mind. Concerning
an impenetrably screened church in Abyssinia, Mr. Evelyn
Waugh writes [3] : ' At Debra Lebanos I suddenly saw the
classic basilica and open altar as a great positive achievement,
a triumph of light over darkness consciously accomplished,
and I saw theology as the science of simplification by which
nebulous and elusive ideas are formalised and made intelligible

[1] *Rood Screens ;* p. 119. [2] *Lingard ;* p. 303. [3] *Remote People ;* pp. 88-9.

and exact. I saw the Church of the first century as a dark and hidden thing. . . . And I began to see how these obscure sanctuaries had grown, with the clarity of the Western reason, into the grand open altars of Catholic Europe, where Mass is said in a flood of light, high in the sight of all, while tourists can clatter round with their Baedekers, incurious of the mystery.' The disuse of screens was an advance into the open : it enabled the Church to do what no other Faith has done and has survived—to expose its mysteries to the world.

Pugin himself nearly achieved that realisation : he saw that Catholic art should be ' a living creation,' that it should ' combine with any legitimate requirement of religion.' But he could not carry on that admission to its conclusion. His mind was turned too obstinately towards the past. For the past had for him associations of a peculiar intimacy. It was become a part of him. It was holy. It had brought him to the Faith.

CHAPTER XVIII

PUGIN

His hair was black and his visage brown. He was neither too large nor too small.
The Song of Roland.

IT has been found impossible to devise any strict chronological framework in which to arrange the events of Pugin's
life after his conversion. He might have been treated primarily
as architect, and the sequence of his architectural development
traced from St. Marie's Grange at Salisbury to St. Cuthbert's
College, Ushaw. He might have been treated as author, and
the development of his ideas traced from his *Furniture* to his
Glossary. He might have been treated as controversialist in
relation to the Catholic Revival in England, and his development traced from the flail of the Protestant in *Contrasts* to the
goad of his fellow Catholics in the *Earnest Address*, taking in
on the way his position as intermediary between the Catholic
Episcopate and the Oxford Movement.

But in none of these could a chronological sequence have
been preserved. His life was too tumultuous. As the Rev.
John Rouse Bloxam said of him,[1] he " did in a few years the
work of a lifetime " ; and it was work in many fields. In
consequence, whatever framework had been chosen, it must
have been broken by consideration of his manifold activities
in other directions. It has been found necessary, therefore, to
treat of Pugin, in spite of his continuous development, not as
a progression in time, but as it were as a fixed centre from
which various energies radiated. There was an enormous
architectural output. There was an almost continuous stream

[1] *Wiseman;* I., p. 357

247

of books and pamphlets. There was an important position in the Catholic Revival and the many controversies connected therewith. There was a revival of forgotten craftsmanship. Hitherto, all these things have been treated as facets of one central activity. It is now necessary to try to penetrate more directly to that centre ; to find the man himself.

As might be expected, the first thing met with in that attempt is a church.

Before leaving St. Marie's Grange and going to Cheyne Walk, Chelsea, in 1841, Pugin had bought some land on the West Cliff at Ramsgate and begun to build there the house, named The Grange, which was to be his home for the rest of his life. The choice of site seems to have been guided primarily by his hunger for the sea, and secondarily by a wish to be near his sole remaining aunt, Selina Welby, whose heir he afterwards became. In addition, it was conveniently placed in relation to London, and so to the greater part of his architectural practice. But however many reasons may have been adduced for the choice of Ramsgate, it is clear that it was chosen chiefly because it gave him a harbour in which he could keep his boat, and contact with the health-giving traffic of the sea.

The influence of his second wife, who foresaw the needs of a growing family, may be seen in the size and general convenience of the house, a simple gabled building in brick, which shows few of the eccentricities which made of St. Marie's Grange an architectural curiosity, though to-day it might be considered too mediæval in arrangement for complete convenience. From a paved courtyard at the back, the principal entrance leads into a fine open-timbered hall of the full height of the house, two sides of which are occupied by the staircase, the other two by a wooden gallery on brackets giving access to the bedrooms. To the right of the hall, Pugin placed the drawing-rooms, which he decorated with carved stone mantelpieces and panelled mahogany ceilings. The dining-room, opposite the entrance door, was fitted with some good specimens of furniture of his own design, and the walls covered partly with panelling and partly with armorial wall-paper containing the Pugin martlet and the motto *En Avant*. It was 'a picturesque arrangement,' as Eastlake observed,[1] 'but open to objection, inasmuch as it would appear impossible for inmates to pass from one reception room to another, or to reach the rooms above, without coming within sight of the entrance door.'

The windows of the house, casement throughout, were nearly all fitted with small panes of glass in quarries ; but, notable exception, those which faced out upon the sea were filled with plate-glass.

Attached to the house, on the east, there was a chapel, wherein, from 1843, the few Catholics of the neighbourhood might be present at Mass.

But that was not enough. The time had passed when Catholicism in England should cling precariously to the private chapels of those who could afford them. A chapel might suffice for the few residents, and the rare Catholic summer visitors, and the French fishermen who sold their catches at Ramsgate. But it did not suffice for a man whose one ambition it was, by the restoration of mediæval beauty, to increase God's glory through the Catholic Church. In the year 1846, to his own design and at his own expense, Pugin began to build, at a little distance to the east of The Grange, a church which was to express to the full his ideas on the restoration of Catholic art. Free for once from the exigencies of clients and the disproportion of funds which hampered all his other work, in this church, dedicated to St. Augustine, and placed on a site within two miles of where that saint and his forty Benedictine companions had landed

---

[1] *Eastlake ;* p. 164.

in England, Pugin could build to please himself. In six years, though the church was unfinished when he died, he had spent on site, and church, and fittings, £15,000.

With characteristic generosity, so that Catholicism in the neighbourhood might be more immediately and adequately served, he began with a Chapter House which could be used as a chapel till such time as the church could be opened.

The church has not been free from adverse criticism; notably by Mr. Clark, who quotes from the *Remarks on Articles in the 'Rambler'* Pugin's statement that 'if the time does arrive that I am allowed to build a church without harassing restrictions, and a reasonable sum to carry it out, I will undertake to produce a building that, for effect, *true economy*, and convenience, will reconcile even the Rambler men to pointed architecture'; and adds that in this statement 'St. Augustine's shakes one's faith. The masonry is solid and the whole building has no obvious faults, but it has none of those qualities which may often be found in the simplest traditional parish churches, none of the repose, much less the thrill of great architecture. The exterior is undistinguished, the interior crowded; the masses are unco-ordinated, the proportions are bad. Pugin lacked the essential quality of a great builder—he did not think in volume; his wonderful dreams were wasted because he did not dream in three dimensions.'[1]

The criticism is worthy of consideration in detail in any attempt to appraise Pugin as man and architect. In the first place, the solidity of the masonry, to which attention is rightly drawn, should be more strongly emphasised, for it is a sufficient answer to any shallow critics who, misguided by the unavoidable flimsiness and over-decoration of certain of his buildings, should look on Pugin as a mere scene-painter among architects, as one who used his meagre walls merely as 'flats' on which to paint the necessary scenery.

[1] *Clark;* p. 169

To say that a building ' has no obvious faults ' is but faint
praise, and, standing alone, in this case is inadequate.   Ruskin,
in his savage hatred of Catholicism, venomously referred to
Pugin as ' one of the smallest possible or conceivable architects.' [1]   It is not necessary to go to the opposite extreme in
order to do Pugin justice : it is only necessary to point out
that he had discovered the principles by which a lost art
could be revived, and, doubly a pioneer, was engaged in
putting those principles into practice; and to ask one question :
Of what other Gothic building between 1840 and 1860 can it
be said that it ' has no obvious faults ' ?   Too much must not
be claimed for St. Augustine's ; no more than Pugin would
have claimed for it himself.   St. Augustine's was at that time
the best that he could do ; he was not yet forty years of age ;
he was still learning.   He would have demanded for himself
no higher position than that of precursor, and for his building
no more than that it was nearer ' the real thing ' than those
which had preceded it.

As to St. Augustine's having ' none of those qualities
which may often be found in the simplest traditional parish
church, none of the repose, much less the thrill of great
architecture', the criticism is too subjective to throw much
light on the building itself.

' The exterior is undistinguished, the interior crowded ;
the masses are unco-ordinated, the proportions are bad.'
Various points must here be considered.   For one thing, the
church is unfinished.   It was intended that the at present
squat tower should be raised another stage and should support
a spire.   In any case, it was not Pugin's aim to raise a ' distinguished ' church.   His aim was a building which should be
a model of simplicity, solidity, and correctness, a building
suitable to be placed on the top of a wind-swept cliff over-
looking the North Sea.   Internally, it must be admitted, the

---

[1] Appendix 12 (' Romanist Modern Art ') to *The Stones of Venice*.

church is crowded. But then St. Augustine's is a small church, and it is probably no more crowded than any mediæval church of the same size before superfluous altars, chapels, and statuary were destroyed in the sixteenth and later centuries. As to the badness of the proportions, it must be remembered that the present crowded and solid seating arrangements were probably never intended by Pugin, and that much of the height of the church is lost because the bases of the piers and columns are hidden.

' One of the greatest surprises', the Abbot of St. Augustine's writes,[1] ' is in store for one who happens to see the interior when the entire seating is removed. Not only is its greater height regained, but also the beauty of the proportion is increased.'

The final passage in the criticism is a more serious charge— that Pugin lacked the essential quality of an architect in that he did not think in volume ; an attack which is in substance but a restatement of the accusation of theatricality brought against his work. This, to which the success of the scenery in *Kenilworth* unfortunately lent excuse, is well stated by Mr. Clark [2] :

' There is a malicious footnote in Ferguson's *History of Modern Architecture* which must always distress Pugin's admirers. " The true bent of Pugin's mind was towards the theatre, and his earliest successes achieved in reforming the scenery and decorations of the stage ; and throughout his life the theatrical was the only branch of his art which he perfectly understood." I used to think this part of an elaborate protestant sneer, for the note goes on to say, " It is, no doubt, very beautiful ; but as protestants we may be permitted to ask whether all this theatrical magnificence is really an

---

[1] The Rt. Rev. Abbot Erkenwald Egan, O.S.B., to whose courtesy I am indebted for much information about St. Augustine's, in his (anonymous) *St. Augustine's, Ramsgate.*

[2] *Clark ;* pp. 173-4.

essential part of the Christian religion." But I am afraid it is shrewd criticism. Pugin's etchings, with their brilliant lighting and their well-placed figures, are primarily dramatic, and his buildings belong to the old Wyatt tradition of scene-painting.'

The charge is also made, by implication, in *The Rambler* [1]:

' He made out in reply [to a suggestion that processions might walk just as well in an undivided hall] that a procession was no good unless it played bo-peep among the pillars, appearing and reappearing in the intercolumniations, like an army marching through a wood.'

If the former was a 'protestant sneer', the latter was certainly a Roman Catholic one; and, but for Mr. Clark's unwilling support, they might be dismissed as such. As it is, the matter deserves closer examination.

If the charge of theatricality be taken merely as a sneer, as implying that Pugin enjoyed plastering flimsy walls with excessive ornament, it is rebutted by his own protests against the way much of his work was spoilt by money being given for decoration which had better been expended on the fabric. If it be taken as implying that he looked on his churches not as isolated æsthetic phenomena but as settings in which certain actions were to be performed, he would have claimed that such was the case. He was Catholic before he was architect, and he looked upon architecture as a servant of religion, as is shown by his own statement concerning churches [2] that ' the mere inspection of them is nothing, it is when they become associated with the life of divine worship that they produce the full power and lift the soul in ecstasy.'

But the criticism goes deeper than that. It implies that Pugin saw his churches not as such, but as separate decorative designs on flat surfaces, which, being brought together and arranged rectangularly, would form a church; as a scenic

---

[1] *Rambler* ; p. 397.   [2] *Rood Screens* ; p. 118.

artist, with a drop-scene and some flats, might achieve a
drawing-room. The criticism is dangerous, since it contains
one aspect of a truth. As has already been stated, Pugin was
doubly a pioneer in that he had discovered the principles on
which he was building, and was the first to try to put them
into practice. But Pugin, among other activities, was
decorative artist as well as architect, and as such, too, was
doubly pioneer : while trying to recapture the spirit of ancient
detail he was training craftsmen capable of producing it. It
could not be expected that execution in these two spheres
should keep pace with development in theory. Neither can
it be expected that complete co-ordination between these two
spheres should have been achieved. In nearly all his buildings,
generally because of circumstances outside his control, Pugin
failed to achieve it, as was the case, for different reasons, at
St. George's and St. Giles's. The surprising thing is that this
co-ordination was ever achieved, as in the great hall at Scarisbrick. Whether it was achieved in St. Augustine's is a matter
best left to individual opinion. But that Pugin was no mere
scenic artist among architects is shown by the very plan of the
church : a scenic artist turned loose upon St. Augustine's
would not have known where to begin.

Built of Whitby stone, faced internally with ashlar and
externally with knapped flint banded with stone courses, St.
Augustine's consists of a fifty-five-foot nave and thirty-five-
foot chancel, a south aisle and Lady Chapel of equal length,
a south transept, and a central tower.

The plan is doubly notable. In the first place, no architect
in the Wyatt tradition, whose ambition was for unimpeded
Gothic vistas, would have built a small church in which, owing
to the central position of the tower, huge supporting piers
were necessary where they most interfered with sight ; nor
would he have shortened the appearance of nave and aisle
and transept by placing screens before chancel and Lady Chapel

and chantry. In the second place, it shows that Pugin's belief
that a building should be fitted to its locality was no mere
theory to be cast aside in favour of some scenic idea of Gothic :

'It is evident', Eastlake wrote,[1] 'that Pugin strove to
invest the building with *local* traditions of style. This is
shown in the general arrangement, the single transept and
other peculiarities of plan being characteristic of Kent.'

The nave is separated from the aisle, which almost equals
it in breadth, by two massive piers which support the south
side of the tower, and a column. From the first pier spring
the chancel arch, the arch over the entrance to the Lady
Chapel, and the first of the two arches which separate the
Lady Chapel from the chancel. From the second pier spring
three more arches : over the entrance to the south aisle and
transept to the chancel pillar ; over the nave to a column
built out from the north wall, which, together with the
similar column at the north end of the chancel arch, supports
the north side of the tower ; and to the column before mentioned from which a similar arch springs to a column at the
west end of the church. These two slighter arches are
repeated, in the aisle over the south door into the churchyard,
and over the entrance to the Lady Chapel.

The chancel, laid with rich encaustic tiles, is enclosed by a
fine rood screen in dark-stained oak from which the crucifix,
in accordance with a mediæval practice, leans forward over the
nave. Under the great east window, the first to come from
John Hardman's workshops, is the altar, simple and massive,
on four grey marble shafts, on which stands the delicately
carven tabernacle, a crocketed and buttressed spire sixteen
feet in height. This last, with the canopy of the font at the
west end of the aisle, both considered too large for the church,
were among Pugin's works at the Exhibition of 1851, and
were presented to the church in gratitude by Mr. George

[1] *Eastlake ;* p 163.

Myers, the builder of nearly all Pugin's churches and his assistant at St. Augustine's. Jutting out from the north wall of the chancel, to the west of a two-lighted window, is a stone organ-gallery guarded by a breast-high parapet supported on seven arches. The ceiling, with those of Lady Chapel and transept, is richly panelled and decorated in oak.

The Lady Chapel, separated from the chancel by a dark oak screen similar in design to the rood screen, contains a fine altar and retable in solid stone with curtains hanging in the ancient manner from brackets on either side. The chapel is entered through a pair of wrought-iron gates, put there as a memorial to Pugin at the desire of his fellow architects. Made by John Hardman, and designed by John Hardman Powell, ' they were unanimously declared the finest specimens of iron craftsmanship of modern times '[1] at the Exhibition of 1862. The east window of the chapel was also the gift of the Pugin Memorial Committee; the two south windows were Pugin's own work.

Outside the chapel, in the space between it and the Pugin Chantry, a silver lamp in the form of a mediæval ship burns before a statue of ' Our Lady, Star of the Sea ' set in a finely decorated niche. It was the gift of shipwrecked sailors, men to whom Pugin was accustomed to give personal service as well as food and clothing.

The Pugin Chantry, or Chapel of St. Lawrence, occupies the greater part of the transept, from which it is divided by a high oak screen of peculiarly fine design and workmanship. The floor is covered with Minton tiles, displaying Pugin's coat of arms, his monogram, and ' I.H.S.', and bordered with martlets in a running scroll of foliage. Under the south window, in a deep alcove in the wall, is the effigied cenotaph of the architect, who, with several members of his family, lies in the vault beneath.

[1] *St. Augustine's.*

No one examining St. Augustine's, and realising that everything in it, from the sturdy walls to the magnificent font, from the stark piers to the most delicate tracery of screens or niche, was either the work of one man or the direct result of his influence, can fail to admit that here at any rate the greatest decorative artist and craftsman of his time was combined with his equal as an architect. In the fine words of Dom Aelred Waterhouse,[1] 'The Church is his tomb and his memorial.'

Even so, St. Augustine's is incomplete. The top part of the tower, and the spire which Pugin intended as a landmark for passing ships, have not been built; and the decorative ceiling over chancel, and Lady Chapel, and transept, has not been continued over nave and aisle and roof of tower. But these are minor matters, and of little moment (though it may be hoped that even yet the firms of Pugin & Pugin and John Hardman may return to Ramsgate to complete their founders' work) compared with the work completed. What is of importance, and in this case particularly so, is that St. Augustine's, unlike so many of his buildings, passed into worthy hands.

In 1856, 1259 years after the landing of St. Augustine, members of the same Benedictine Order returned to Thanet, and St. Augustine's, appropriately, became their headquarters. Since then, St. Augustine's has become an Abbey Church, and the Grange has become part of an Abbey, and much new building has been done. But the church has been allowed to remain unchanged.

At the Grange, in attempting what *The Catholic Magazine* of November 1838 called 'the noble, though somewhat arduous task, of re-Catholicising this once Catholic nation', Pugin practised to the full those habits of industry with the expectation of which he disturbed one of the Oxford converts whom he found placidly employed in a stream near Oscott:

[1] *The Thanet Catholic Review;* July 1931, p. 57.

" Fishing, my dear sir ! " he exclaimed disgustedly ; " life is not meant for that sort of thing. At six o'clock this morning I was at the top of St. Chad's steeple." [1]

At six o'clock, when at home, it was his custom to enter the chapel at the Grange for private prayer and the dedication of the day's work to God ; and his punctuality was such that the withdrawal of the four heavy external bolts of the chapel door would coincide with the tolling of the Angelus from the church.

Thence he retired to the library, where he worked till half-past seven, when the bell rang for morning prayers which were always said by him in a cassock and surplice. Breakfast followed, a seven-minute meal, after which, except on feast days, when he attended Mass in the church at eight o'clock, he worked till one ; he then had dinner, a meal of the simplest character which lasted a quarter of an hour and at which he drank neither wine, beer, nor spirits.

After dinner it was his custom to inspect his buildings (not always with satisfaction, if one may judge from a letter to Mr. William Leigh [2] : ' . . . the price of labour is excessive— the men have struck on my job I have in hand—this is the second time this year they have advanced '), and visit his only pupil, John Hardman Powell, who, though he lasted longer than the hypothetical clerk whom Pugin refused to employ on the grounds that he would kill him in a week, nevertheless gave way under the strain and had to retire for a prolonged rest.

The rest of the afternoon was then passed in more work, during which he was sometimes visited by friends. But that was not allowed to interfere with the tumultuous outpouring of design. ' He drew with an extraordinary rapidity ', Mr. J.

[1] *Wiseman ;* I., p. 357.
[2] May 1846. For the privilege of using this and other letters to Mr. Leigh I am indebted to the courtesy of his grand-daughter, Miss Leigh, of Scar Hill, Wood-chester Park, Gloucestershire. For Pugin's letter-writing, see Appendix V.

D. Crace wrote,[1] ' (I used to watch him with a sort of reverence); appeared to have everything clear in his mind, and simply to pour it out from the point of his pencil; and he would often carry on a lively conversation all the time', a conversation diversified with ' a continual rattle of marvellous stories, slashing criticisms, and shouts of laughter.' [2]

Tea, at which he indulged his liking for celery—another favourite food was Dutch cheese [3]—was followed by more work and letter-writing till nine o'clock, a labour which he got through in the train if he had been to London. Then, until ten, when Compline was sung in his chapel, as a relaxation he amused himself with the designs for St. Augustine's; after which he settled down to literary activity, writing, and studying historical and theological works such as those of Collier, Lingard, Dugdale, Stow, and Du Cange.

' A witty writer in a recent periodical ', he wrote,[4] ' advised me to stick to my trowel; but I reply that I am a builder up of men's minds and ideas as well as of material edifices, and there is an immense work and a moral foundation yet required before they are prepared to receive, understand, and practically realise the glories of Christian Art. Building without teaching or explaining is useless, and is fully exemplified by the greater proportion of the pointed churches that have been raised, and although erected on old symbolic principles and traditions, are used for the most part on the most modern system, with all the abominations of singing galleries, communion rails, and a due quantum of trumpery. *I shall never rest till I see the majestic architecture that was originally generated by the Catholic faith*—again a *living expression of the majesty of Catholic rites*, and not, as it often is at present, a mediæval disguise for modern debasement. (Le bon temps viendra.) God will yet raise up some glorious men, who will restore his sanc-

---

[1] *Crace.*
[2] *Barry;* p. 196, n.
[3] Inf. of Mr. S. Pugin Powell.
[4] Letter to *The Tablet;* 15 March 1851.

tuary, and obtain a great and final triumph for Christian Art.'

Mr. Clark states [1] that 'his sole recreations were the reading (and alas ! writing) of theological works and the conduct of church services.' That was the reason.

The phrase ' God will yet raise up some glorious men ' throws further light on Pugin's mind when taken in connection with his statement that ' any man who possesses the true spirit of Christian art, so far from desiring to occupy an unrivalled position, is delighted when he is equalled, and overjoyed when he is surpassed.' [2] For Pugin saw his own architectural position in an unusual perspective. His own greatness or otherwise as an architect was of no importance. The question was not one of degree but of kind. He might be a worse architect in his particular line than Rickman. It did not matter ; for he was doing something different, and what he was doing was right. But its rightness was not judged by any purely æsthetic standards. It was judged by its potentiality for giving glory to God. That others should improve on his work was therefore a matter for rejoicing. For himself, he would claim no more than that God had chosen him to start things again on the proper lines.

But he fully realised the importance of this position. He was an instrument by which God was carrying out His purposes. In all humility and reverence those purposes had to be fulfilled. His own enormous output as architect and decorative artist was but a hint of what would follow when God should ' raise up some glorious men '. His own importance lay in the fact that he had been chosen to make straight the path for those who were to follow.

There approaches the curious paradox which may be noticed in the letters of saints to those who need direction : an impression of certitude where one of the utmost diffidence

[1] *Clark ;* p. 160.   [2] Quoted in *The Tablet ;* 15 September 1852.

might be expected. The matter can only be expressed in a
seeming contradiction : out of the height of their humility,
they speak as the instruments of God.

In a similar way, Pugin, who believed himself to be God's
instrument in the beginning of a glorious revival, spoke with
a dogmatism which would be intolerable in one who was
purely an artist. He was an inspired teacher and as such
entitled to speak ; though, not being a saint in the ordinary
sense of the word, he allowed his teaching to be coloured by
a very human anger at matters of which he did not approve.
His belief in the sacred character of his mission is further
shown by his habit of beginning and ending his letters with a
cross. And no one in his position, without that belief, could
have written his *Earnest Address on the Establishment of the
Hierarchy* which was published at the beginning of 1851.
Nine years before, on 12th January 1842, he had written to
March-Phillipps [1] :

' The Vicars Apostolic are the only legitimate ecclesiastical
authority at present in Engld., for I hold all the deans, canons,
Bishops, etc., at less estimation than the worst French chasuble
man amongst us. I mean with reference to real authority '.

In 1851, that authority was to be transferred from the
Vicars Apostolic on the restoration of the English Catholic
Hierarchy. It seemed to Pugin his duty to inform the new
Authority on various matters.

With pleasing irony, he adorned his title-page with a
quotation from the Lamentations of the Prophet Jeremias :
' Our Fathers have sinned and are not, and we have borne
their iniquities.' Then, justifying his writing on the grounds
that he could not ' refrain from offering some observations,
which, by the blessing of God, may be the means of infusing
great zeal and encouragement into the English Catholics, and,
at the same time, by removing some misconceptions, may

---

[1] *Phillipps ;* II., p. 227.

restore reciprocal charity between us and our separated
countrymen', he entered immediately upon a consideration of
the sins of the fathers and their unfortunate results :

'The state of Christendom,' he wrote, 'is full of matter
for the serious reflection of sincere and religious men. We
not only behold nations which were Catholic barely three
centuries ago now utterly changed, but in countries where
externally the old religion yet prevails, it is so lamentably
degraded from what we may consider the standard of Catholic
excellence, and so great is the progress of indifference and
infidelity, that it becomes a matter of the very highest importance to ascertain the primary cause to which all these sad
changes may be attributed, and to discover the roots of the
cancer that has eaten so far into a divinely constituted system
as the church Catholic, and I believe we shall not fail in tracing
it to *the common evil of state and temporal power crushing the
free action of the church, and enslaving its ministers in worse
than Egyptian bondage.* To begin with England—which we
all know was once a Catholic country, abounding in ecclesiastical foundations, possessing all the means, all the materials,
for the preservation of the faith, the instruction of the people,
and support of religion in the greatest solemnity and order—
how comes it to pass that it is no longer so ? that, without
invasion, or conquest, or change of dynasty, the whole has
been altered, transformed, the churches plundered, the
country separated from Catholic unity, and, in fine, brought
to its present lamentable religious position ? Who has done
this ? By whom has it been brought about ? Is it the work
of Protestantism or not ? *I boldly answer, No !*

'It is a fearful and terrible example of a Catholic nation
betrayed by a corrupted Catholic hierarchy. Englishmen
have been betrayed, and what is more, betrayed by the very
power from whom, under God, they had a right to expect
protection and safety. It was in a solemn convocation, when

England's churchmen were assembled, a reverend array of bishops and abbots and dignitaries . . . and yet the fear of a tyrant and the dread of losing a few remaining years of wealth and dignity so far prevailed, that they sacrificed the liberty of the English church at one blow, that church whose liberties at their several consecrations they had sworn to defend, whose freedom they were bound on oath and conscience to preserve. The deed is signed. Harry is declared the *supremum caput* of England's church: not *vox populi*, but *by the voice of the convocation*, the church is sacrificed, the people are sacrificed, and the actors in this vile surrender are the true and lawful bishops and clergy of England.'

The implication was plain: these things might recur, and the most unceasing vigilance against state interference was necessary.

There were other matters on which Pugin considered that the new hierarchy, for which he had the greatest enthusiasm, ought to be properly informed. In particular there was the state of the waverers among the High Churchmen. In his letter to March-Phillipps just quoted, he wrote:

'I never went so minutely into matters before, but the result has been that I am convinced the present Church of Engld. is 10 times more protestant than I thought it, and I would not remain one second in such a concern, even with the hope of converting the Grand Turk and the Emperor of China. My dear friend, delays in conversion are very dangerous, generally *fatal*. I really tremble for those who do not unite.'

But he trembled still more for those who might, by their untactful behaviour, interfere with the work of conversion. The Tractarians needed gentle handling. Pugin pointed out that the mistakes had not been all on one side, and that, while the original Catholic hierarchy was responsible for the loss of the Faith in England, the Reformed Church had preserved a considerable amount of Catholic doctrine throughout its three hundred years of separation.

' Catholics, as well as Protestants,' he wrote, ' have been in the habit of assigning the odium of all the ecclesiastical devastations, the plunder of treasuries, destruction of shrines, and suppression of the religious houses to Protestant outrage. Such was formerly my own notion of this matter; and I have no doubt it is the prevailing impression on the minds of nine-tenths of the people. *But it is not so.* All this ruin was brought about by the old ecclesiastical authorities before a single professed Protestant appeared on the scene.'

Again:

' The people were very much better than their clergy, and had it not been that the latter were so fettered and bound by the state power as to act like machines in the hands of the civil magistrate, the English nation never would have submitted to these alterations in divine service and articles of faith. But it is very easy to conceive what difficulties attended even a faithful people when betrayed by their own clergy, and is a most striking example of the necessity of *free action* for the ecclesiastical powers advocated in this tract, for without it a Catholic hierarchy itself offers no security to the faithful, as the sad case of England's schism fully shows.'

Although it went against his custom in controversy, Pugin saw plainly that attack could only serve to strengthen High Churchmen in their position. Sad though it was to see these men abused by members of their own church for carrying out its rubrics and ordinals, it was ' still more grievous, that the yells of Protestant ignorance raised against these men should have found an unnatural echo even among some of our own body, who, if they did but reflect that the difficulties and anomalies with which these same men are now contending, were first caused by the base compliance of the old Catholic hierarchy itself, which brought the English church under the bondage of the state, and that they should be regarded by us rather as victims of Catholic degeneracy than the consequence of Protestant error. It is not for those who have gained the ship of Peter, and ride securely in the storm, to mock the unwearied efforts of those good and earnest souls who yet man the shattered bark of England's church, brought among Protestant shoals by its old Catholic commanders, and who still, amid *mutiny* and *oppression*, yet labour to guide her to a haven of safety : and I will say that, battered as is that old hull, it is a great breakwater between the raging waves of infidelity and Catholic truth in this land ; that it has held so long together, under so many disadvantages and difficulties, must be a work of Divine Providence for some great end which remains to be developed.'

Another point to which Pugin drew the attention of the new hierarchy was the practice of the pious of making legacies for church purposes instead of setting aside a fixed annual sum. The results of 'this legacy system', as he called it, were frequently lamentable,[1] and the prospect of its being made illegal was most encouraging.

'The moment a rich old fellow dies,' he wrote, 'all the relations to the ninetieth degree turn up and assemble, and if they understand his money has been left to the church the indignation is general. . . . And now another bishop considers he has a prior claim or equal right on the residue. The first bishop cannot admit the justice of the premises. It must be referred to arbitration. Grave men travel up to London, put up at first-rate hotels, keep up good cheer, drive about in glass coaches, see sights, and occasionally sit in a back room round a green baize table. Portly and sinewy lawyers, with attendants bearing blue bags full of documents, read long extracts from interminable deeds. Rejoinder next day, all the preceding arguments demolished, time is up, but to-morrow the first party will again address on fresh grounds. Days go

---

[1] They included, incidentally, the failure to carry out Pugin's designs for the buildings at Downside ; a project which in any case would have had its difficulties, since Pugin had omitted to take into consideration the sloping nature of the site.

by, one week gone, hotel bills running on, the cost of a small parochial church in the second pointed style swallowed up already, proceedings becoming a bore, a compromise proposed, could not two mutual friends settle it? They agree, divide again, and deduct expenses. Only one-third of the whole sum reduced by subdivision to a very moderate amount. Both bishops reported to be immensely rich, and to have received an inexhaustible fortune, no subscriptions in consequence. . . . Both bishops are considerably minus at the end of the year that the great benefaction fell in.'

The remedy for this state of affairs was simple: that Catholics should ' transact most important matters in the old Anglo-Saxon fashion, over shrines and before altars, and save large sums in stamps and deeds, which are no security after all, and often made the subjects of vexatious litigation.'

The three last pages of the pamphlet contain passages which show even more clearly the sense of mission underlying Pugin's work:

' I trust that what I have brought forward will be the means of animating every Catholic, and every just and honest man, in this land with the spirit of strongest resistance of any measures that would tend in the least degree to bring our hierarchy, founded on principles of true ecclesiastical liberty, and, indeed, an *apostolic* rule, under the iron grasp of state government; from the enmity of the worldly powers we have *nothing* to fear; from their favour and protection *everything*. We neither ask for temporal aid or temporal honour: the faithful will provide the first, the second is not worth having. Nor has the Sovereign in her gift so noble a title to respect as that which the very office of a bishop, duly performed, imparts to the ecclesiastic who holds it. . . .

' It will be vain if you agree with me in denouncing the temporal evils of rich endowments and state pensions, if you do not supply the necessities of the church by renewing the apostolic system of *continual* and *successive offerings.* . . . Let us show what a free hierarchy can do without pension from the state, *without endowed property, without tithes or rates, or one coercive payment from friend or foe.* . . . What ought men not to expect *under a free system and external peace?* and if we live as we ought as Catholics *to serve God* nothing is impossible to achieve. I fear not our enemies ; I fear not our calumniators ; I fear not the tyranny of state measures. I have but one fear ; that is, *I fear ourselves.* I fear we have been so long slumbering on under our imperfect ecclesiastical rules, that now the whole is come in all its fulness, we shall not duly appreciate the blessing, and respond to our altered circumstances. We are comparatively a small body ; but we could spare many that bear our name, and yet be strengthened in our cause.

'I would we were quit of all those men, who, while retaining the name of Catholic, could betray the church to state tyranny. I would we were quit of all those men, who, retaining the name of Catholic, afflict the pastors and scandalise the faithful, by forsaking the holy sacraments of the church. I would we were quit of all those men, who, while retaining the name of Catholic, exhibit no realisation of its principles in their lives, but squander their revenues in every species of worldly vanity and folly, neglecting the church and its ministers, and abandoning the temple of God to decay. I would we were quit of all those indifferent men, bearing the name of Catholic, who are almost too apathetic to try and save their own souls, and who never aid or contribute in any good work whatever ; and I would we were quit of all men who degrade religion by dressing it up in pagan and paltry externals, and who import the worst style of the most corrupt period of continental ecclesiology into a land full of the purest Catholic traditions. For all these are only drags on the wheel of the revival of faith and Catholic art and practices ; and I believe, if we had only true zealous men left, like Gideon's three hundred lappers up of water, we should be in a better position to resist the Midianites. But this cannot be. We must trust in the arm of Almighty God to support us, and animate all with a good spirit. If ever there was a time or occasion when we might hope for unity in the Catholic body, this is one. If there could be imagined a moving cause so powerful as to break up local prejudices, party feelings and unworthy division, it is this restoration of ecclesiastical government, and gathering our shattered and separated fragments into a real church. If there ever was a magnetic power to draw gold from misers, to make niggards liberal, and sluggards active, it is now. If ever there was an event which was calculated to promote unity of action and unity of soul, to make men confess their past sins, and to make good resolutions for the future, to make them liberal to religion, and devout and thankful to God, animating them with a true spirit of the faith they profess, and lead them to discard for ever paganism and its wretched incongruities, and to labour with heart and soul for the revival of the true architecture created by the Christian religion itself, it is the foundation of this English Hierarchy which should be our delight and our glory, and which should now become one of the earnest objects of our lives and actions to support and maintain in all *freedom, honour, and integrity, in sæcula sæculorum*. Amen.'

As might have been expected, the ' milk-and-water men ' were horrified at this plain speaking, at this letting of light into shady places in past and present Catholic polity, and there was even some talk of getting the *Earnest Address* placed on the *Index* at Rome. Pugin announced his willingness to withdraw any expression which might seem to border on heresy, and the matter perforce was dropped, though one signing himself ' A Catholic Priest ' impugned Pugin's orthodoxy at some length in a letter in *The Tablet* of 8th

March 1851. In the following number, Pugin replied in a letter which was also separately printed, and which was very similar to a private letter of justification which he found it advisable to send to Cardinal Wiseman.[1] In it he made his position quite clear :

'. . . ought we not to be thankful, that in such a schism as that of the 16th century, so much of the old principle has been retained, that sincere men are continually led to embrace Catholic truth, simply by carrying out the principles in which they have been educated as Church of England men, to their legitimate conclusion ? *This was my own case*,[2] and it has been the case of hundreds, who would probably have remained utterly ignorant of Catholic principles, had their lot fallen among ordinary Protestant sects.'

These amicable feelings towards all that was good in Anglicanism he still further justified by quoting words written by Bishop Milner long before the Oxford Movement :

'*If they will not be good Catholics, I am desirous that they should remain good Church of England men, being convinced that thereby the sacred code of revelation will be much less violated, and the public peace and happiness much more effectually secured.*'

But to Pugin attack was the best means of defence, and the most natural :

' But while I submit in the most absolute manner to the dogmas of faith as proposed by the Church, I claim on the other hand a legitimate right of exercising the faculties with which I have been blessed by God, in the consideration of the temporal causes that have exercised so fatal an influence on religion, and, above all, denouncing the important element of modern Paganism, which has corrupted and debased the externals of religion to a lamentable extent. On these points

---

[1] Printed by Edward Pugin in the 1875 edition of the *Earnest Address*.

[2] ' I can truly assert that the greatest stride I made in my conversion to the Catholic faith was, in endeavouring to become a strict Church of England man, by studying its system.' [A. Welby Pugin : *Apology for ' Contrasts '* ; p. 21.]

I am not to be silenced by cowards, or bigots, or those who
work by expediency, instead of the broad basis of truth. And
while I have a pen left, and a hand to wield it, I will write,
and exhort, and denounce the destructive influence of modern
and debased taste in the externals of religion.'

This sense of a spiritual mission appeared, too, in his
dealings with clients. Normally, the wishes of the employer
tend to be sacrificed to the reputation of the architect. With
Pugin, they had to be sacrificed to the glory of mediæval art,
and he was willing to sacrifice his own employment as well.
As has already appeared, he was ready to give up his work
for Lord Shrewsbury rather than build an unworthy dining-
room. With others, he was equally firm.

To a Catholic bishop who asked for designs for a church
which was to be ' *very* large,—the neighbourhood being *very*
populous ; it must be *very* handsome,—a fine new church
had been built close by ; it must be *very cheap*,—they were
very poor, in fact had only £—— ; when could they expect
the design ? ' his reply was masterly in its brevity : ' My dear
Lord—Say *thirty shillings* more, and have *a tower and spire*
at once. A. W. P.' [1]

Work for ' a noble lord, whose seat in Lincolnshire had
been greatly injured, and partly destroyed by fire,' [2] was no
less boldly sacrificed. Being called in to advise on the reconstruction, he explained that the style of the parts that remained
was so debased that the only solution was a complete rebuilding. This did not appeal to the owner, who kept asking,
' Well, what shall I do ? what shall I do ? ' ' Do ? ' he
replied, ' Why, put a barrel of gunpowder and blow up what
remains, and when it is demolished then I'll tell you what to
do.'

Even more abrupt was his behaviour towards Lord Stuart
de Rothesay, who was building a curious castellated house,

[1] *Ferrey ;* p. 171.   [2] *Ib. ;* p. 172.

partly out of some French monastic ruin, at High Cliff, near
Christchurch in Hampshire. Becoming dissatisfied with his
weird building, he called in Pugin as consulting architect,
who, in the course of the afternoon of his arrival, made plans
for necessary alterations. These, naturally enough, entailed
considerable demolition of recently completed stonework.
Lord Stuart de Rothesay demurred when the matter was
discussed after dinner, and further consideration was postponed till the morning. But Pugin did not appear at breakfast. He had decided that he could not waste any more time
over a freak. He had more important things to attend to.
He had got up at six o'clock, and caught the London coach.

This astonishing brusqueness was not carried into private
life, and his kindly nature and thought for others is shown in
a letter inviting a friend for Christmas, at which time, and on
Twelfth Night, it was his custom to have lavish ' costume '
entertainments :

' My dear Thornton,
　　　　From what Edward says I have every reason to hope
and expect that you will act honestly, and come on Saturday.
We shall expect you by the train which gets in at ten minutes
past six. Tea ready—good fires. Why is one of your little
girls left behind ? Pray bring her. It will make me unhappy
if you don't ; for it will be a great grief to her to be left
behind, and we have plenty of room for her ; so now do
bring her with you, and let her enjoy herself at Xtmas. The
more the merrier. I am your sincere friend,
　　　　　　　　　　　　　　A. Welby Pugin.' [1]

But at the same time, his tumultuous nature must have
imposed a strain on his family and friends.

' Pugin was infinitely amusing in his peculiar way,' the Rev.
James Bowling Mozley wrote after one of Pugin's visits to

[1] *Ferrey ;* p. 182.

Oxford in 1840,[1] '. . . architecture of course, church ceremonies, liturgies, antiquities of all kinds, being the subjects.
He is the most unwearied talker for a spirited one that I ever
heard. From six o'clock to eleven on Saturday he was on the
move, never stopping, and when he left off he was quite the
same as when he began . . . everything moves his wrath,
especially in architecture. Such an one " ought to be hanged "
for building such a steeple. He is never satisfied with half
terms, but sends people to their final destination the instant
they become offensive. I said the Dean of York ought to be
suspended. " In what way, sir ? " as quick as lightning.'

Again, writing to March-Phillipps, the Rev. J. R. Bloxam
said [2] :

' Mr. Pugin has gratified me, more than I can express, by
his three days' sojourning within our College walls. His
conciliating manners and extensive knowledge of ecclesiastical
and architectural antiquities have gained him the respect and
commendation of all who have had the pleasure of meeting
him. And though I am at this moment suffering from
exhaustion produced upon a feeble frame by

" Thoughts that breathe and words that burn,"

I cannot resist acknowledging with grateful delight the
instruction imparted by his drawings, lectures, and conversation. To know such a person is indeed a privilege.'

It was also, of course, rather a strain. But to the poor and
to humble folk connected with the sea, it was solely a privilege.

In the hall at the Grange, he kept a chest filled with suits
of clothes, which he distributed to the destitute, sending them
away not only clothed but fed ; and when they died, if they
were of the Faith, he attended personally to their burial,
giving them with reverent care the full funeral rites in his own
church of St. Augustine.

His was no mere cheque-writing philanthropy. His services were personal. For instance, finding one Sunday afternoon that the captain of his lugger, who had sprained his leg, was without necessary comforts, he himself carried down to him from the Grange a mattress, blankets, and provisions. Again, when two hundred German emigrants were detained in the harbour by the weather, he supplied them with necessaries and at his own expense brought down the priest from the German chapel in London to attend to them. On their departure, thirty of them came as a deputation to offer thanks. Language proved a bar; but the extent of his services had been such that their spokesman, reduced to gesture, flung himself on the ground and placed his head beneath Pugin's foot.

In one matter at least, Pugin's generosity had a permanent result. Seeing the misery of fever-stricken sailors left destitute in Ramsgate, he hired two small houses in King Street, near the harbour, and engaged nurses to tend them. It is to the credit of the people of Ramsgate that, when their attention had thus been drawn to the state of affairs, they did not lag behind. Funds were raised. Pugin added his own handsome subscription, and the present Sailors' Infirmary came into being.

In few things is Pugin's power shown to better advantage than in his dealings with his craftsmen. With employers, in particular with committees, he was not so successful; for he lacked the ability to suffer gladly those with whom he disagreed. But with craftsmen it was different: he could choose them, and train them, and fire them with his own enthusiasm. First among these was George Myers, to whom Pugin entrusted all his buildings except when overruled by his employers.

Their first meeting was at Beverley, where Pugin was sketching in the Minster. Myers, then a mason in a small way of business in the town, found Pugin at work, became deeply interested, and helped him with ladders and scaffolding where necessary. A few years later, tenders were invited for St. Mary's, Derby, Pugin's first church, and Myers, who wished for the contract and found that it was likely to be given to a local man, sought an interview with the architect in the hopes of getting fair play. There was mutual recognition and surprise, and Pugin clasped him in his arms, exclaiming : " My good fellow, you are the very man I want, you shall execute all my buildings." [1]

The choice was wise : in Myers Pugin had found a man who was more than a contractor : he was a friend and a collaborator, and a trainer of craftsmen. It was necessary that Pugin should have such a man, as otherwise even he could not have got through the enormous amount of work. But with Myers, as time went on, detailed drawings became unnecessary. A kind of shorthand, expressive of intention, was all that was required. This was done, with lightning rapidity, in ink, the barest rough outlines being touched in in pencil first. No copies were kept : Myers could be trusted to carry out the intention : and more drawings could be made later if necessary. The method appears in a note to Myers scribbled on one of the drawings, of a canopy with Madonna, dated 1845, in the collection of the Royal Institute of British Architects :

' I don't think the sketch I sent you for the B. Virgin for Mrs. Petre's altar [2] was late enough in style. I now send you a later one. Of course the whole front will be cut in bas-relief. The carving should be strictly of the same date as the chantry.' [3]

Even so, it was only with nightmarish industry that the work could be performed. Change of labour, or change of scene while working, were his only recreations. Even when at sea he worked. While the *Apology* was in preparation, he

---

[1] *Ferrey ;* p. 187.   [2] In the Petre Chantry, St. George's, Southwark.
[3] *Sirr, F.R.I.B.A.*

disappeared for several weeks, and then, more strangely clad than ever in a pilot-coat much too big for him, he called unexpectedly on his publisher, who remarked upon his costume. "Oh, it is of no consequence," Pugin said : " I caught up the first garment that came in my way, getting into harbour after a stiff gale off Calais ; but here are the plates for my book. They are all ready for proving." The publisher, astonished, asked how and where he had finished the etchings. Pugin said he had finished them in the boat. The publisher was incredulous. " Not a bit of it," Pugin said ; " the motion of the sea makes no difference to me." [1] The performance seems to have been repeated.

But yet there are fragmentary anecdotes which show a human side to his terrible concentration. He never did architectural work on Sundays. He never learned to sharpen pencils properly, hacking at them with surprising clumsiness ; but always prepared them for the next day's work before going to bed. He had a trick of sliding a ruler over the paper with his thumb while sketching, which enabled him to produce parallel straight lines with astonishing speed and accuracy. He had never been taught the normal architectural method of making tracings by scraping the back of the paper with a knife ; when shown it by his pupil, John Hardman Powell, he said : " If I had only known that it would have saved me days of my life." [2] He tried to paint in oils, but found the process too slow, and gave it up. [3] He spent more than he could well afford on his library, and collection of old pictures and prints and metal-work and carving. It was his one indulgence ; and even that was connected with his work.

It was a strange figure that might be seen emerging from the Grange to go about his architectural business, rather below normal height, thick set, with long straight black hair and

---

[1] *Ferrey ;* pp. 143–4.   [2] Inf. of Mr. S. Pugin Powell.
[3] Bryan's *Dictionary of Painters and Engravers.*

T

flashing, penetrating eyes ; his loud voice might be heard,
giving directions, and his ringing, frequent laugh. The light-
heartedness of his manner was repeated in his costume, from
the shapeless, carelessly tied shoes to the low-crowned,
battered hat. Loose, light-coloured trousers were frequently
surmounted by a wide-skirted black dress-coat (which gave
him, incongruously, something of the appearance of a dis-
senting minister of the time), and a loosely tied neckerchief.
Over all, there was a huge dark-coloured cloak with many
and capacious pockets, which were an essential part of his
equipment.

'I never saw heavier rain,' he wrote to Lord Shrewsbury
from Basle,[1] ' and those who had any luggage got it soaked ;
thanks to my large pockets and mackintosh I escaped dry.
It is quite delightful to travel without encumbrances. I care
nothing for custom houses and baggage offices. *I have everything about me, and cannot leave anything, it is the only way to
travel with comfort.* I met two Oscott students with six large
packages, out for three weeks' tour ! ! ! '

Thus clad, and with his luggage about him, including ' a
tabular compendium, written and drawn upon vellum, in the
most minute and beautiful manner, containing a chronological
list of the kings of England and France, the anniversaries of
the saints in the English Calendar, the dates of great national
events, a chart of the British Channel (indicating the shoals),
tide tables, sectional outlines of the mouldings and forms
belonging to different dates, and many other aids to memory
connected with religion and architecture',[2] it was his
custom to take the road, whenever possible in a gig, since
that enabled him to stop and examine every old church
that he passed.

It is significant that he should travel about the country
with a chart of the Channel ; as it is that boats should appear

---

[1] *Ferrey ;* p. 131.   [2] *Ib. ;* p. 289.

among his architectural drawings made on the Continent.
" There is nothing worth living for," he said, " but Christian
Architecture and a boat." After hours of concentration on a
mass of ' pointed ' detail, there was rest and refreshment in
the clean curve of a fishing-boat's sheer, there was calm and
healing in the movement of the sea. As a boy, he had found
' some element of real power in the boats.' That element
remained. Behind him always there was the unchanging sea,
a source of power, a desire, and a reconciling.

At home, his costume was the same : semi-nautical, uncouth. Only on great occasions was it changed, as, for
instance, for important visitors. Then, since, like that other
prince of independents, Charles Waterton, the naturalist, he
refused to wear normal evening dress, he would array himself
in knee breeches and buckled shoes and a velvet cloak which
hung down to the knee.[1] Thus garbed, with two attendants
holding candlesticks, he would greet his guests.

The sea did much for Pugin ; but it could not do enough.
His life was too vehement, and he was doing too many things.
In addition to the overwhelming labours connected with his
profession, he was closely involved in the delicate negotiations
springing from the Oxford Movement. His visits to Oxford
in 1840 brought him more than abortive employment at
Balliol. It gave him the friendship of such men as Oakeley,
Faber, Dalgairns, and Bloxam. Into that atmosphere of
tortuous theology, his abrupt and rapid speech, his excitability,
his full-bodied wrath that was free from any irritability, and
his transparent honesty, came like a refreshing wind. " I have
heard Catholic doctrine ", the Rev. Bernard Smith, of Leadenham, remarked, " even in a Wesleyan church. Perhaps some
Roman priest may have assumed the *rôle* of a Wesleyan
minister without the Wesleyans being aware of it." He was

---

[1] Not to the ground, as shown on the Albert Memorial.
[2] Inf. of Mr. S. Pugin Powell.

met by a storm of anger and abuse. "How dare you say such
things?" Pugin ended; "if you knew English Catholics
personally, you could not say them."[1] In the presence of his
bluntness and fire traditionary prejudice against the 'astute-
ness' and 'Jesuitry' of Papists could not live, any more than
it could years afterwards when faced by the noisy simplicity
of Father Bernard Vaughan. They trusted him. And at the
same time, as one of the few links between the Oxford Movement and Catholicism, he was trusted by Dr. Wiseman.

It was a difficult position, for Pugin and March-Phillipps
were hoping for corporate reunion, and theirs was the
responsibility of advising Wiseman on the handling of the
unprecedented situation. Their programme was the gradual
winning of the English mind to sympathy with Catholic
ideals, devotions, and art, and, as a corollary, keeping the
Roman question in the background. But time was necessary
for this, and they were buoyed up by the hope ' that Newman
would undermine the Protestant traditions of the Church of
England before he could see his own way to submission to
Rome.'[2] At the same time, though individual conversions
could not be discouraged, they were to be deprecated since
they tended to hinder the course of corporate reunion. It was
a harassing situation for any busy man to deal with, and was
made the more difficult by the action of *The Tablet*, which
persisted in confusing Catholicism and Irish politics and in
hurling virulent abuse at the Tractarians for insincerity and
at their Catholic friends for dallying with heretics.

The situation was somewhat eased when the reaction after

---

[1] *Wiseman*; I., p. 372. Pugin had a milder controversial manner, but he seldom
managed to calm himself sufficiently to make use of it. One occasion when he did
so was with the lady who, as already noted (p. 76), demanded an instant change of
compartment on realising that she was travelling with a Catholic. The change, at
the moment, was impracticable, the train moved on, and ' Pugin reasoned gently
and quietly with her, so that on arriving at the next station the lady had no desire to
get out, and before the journey's end, she was shedding tears of sorrow and regret
for her past hatred of such good Christians.' (*Ferrey*; p. 262.)

[2] *Gwynn*; p. 103.

Tract 90 showed that the influence of Newman and his friends on English Protestantism had ended. But in its place there came a terrible disappointment. Pugin had worked and longed for corporate reunion. Catholic art was to help to bring it about, and from it was to spring further glories of Catholic art. But the hopes of reunion dwindled, and individual converts nearly all went over to the Italian side.

Bloxam was of the opinion that ' this disappointment of his confident hopes of assistance from the Oxford School in the Gothic revival, contributed materially to the illness to which Pugin eventually succumbed.' [1] It may have done so. Certainly he was in bad health in 1846, and in the winter of that year ' was suffering from a most severe illness, produced by anxiety of mind.' [2] His letters to Mr. William Leigh show how much the strain had told upon him: In May he wrote :

' I expect to be in Rugby next week & could come over to Leamington, that is if I am well enough to travel, for I am quite losing my strength ' ;

again :

' I should have sent this before, but I was taken very ill on Sunday with a violent attack of fever & was obliged to come home & go to bed. I am now much better but very weak ' ;

in September he wrote :

' I herewith forward the designs of your house. I should have sent them sooner, but I returned home immediately after the consecration of Cheadle & have been confined to the house ever since, & I fear I shall not be able to move for some time for I am suffering from an internal complaint that requires the greatest quiet & I am forbidden even to walk about the house.'

Whatever the cause of his illness, it was to lead up to one of the most miserable episodes of his life.

[1] *Ward (Oxford)*; p. 155.   [2] *A Statement of Facts*, &c.

In the summer of 1844, while staying at Alton Towers, Pugin dreamed twice in one night that his wife, Louisa Burton, whom he had married in 1833, was dangerously ill. He started for home the next day, and was met by a special messenger sent to urge his immediate return. His wife was unconscious when he arrived, and died shortly afterwards, on 23rd August 1844, leaving him, in addition to her step-daughter then aged twelve, five small children. On 10th August 1848, he married his third wife, Jane Knill,[1] who bore him two children, and who, sympathising in all her husband's projects, entered almost immediately upon the agonising task of tending him in his decline.

' By the enclosed card you will perceive that I am married, and have got a first-rate Gothic woman at last, who perfectly understands and delights in spires, chancels, screens, stained windows, brasses, vestments, etc.'

So Pugin wrote on his wedding-day to the Rev. James John Hornby, his friend and employer at Winwick.[2] But in the five intervening years he had suffered the stress of three abortive engagements.

No useful purpose would be served by recording the names of the people concerned. The important point is the accumulation of worries which beset him in the last ten years of his life. In one case, the breach seems to have been brought about by the relations of his affianced, on the grounds that he was not a good enough match for a first cousin once removed of Lord Shrewsbury's. In another case, by his own friends, on the grounds that the lady was not good enough for him. Incidentally, she afterwards married a rich man, and left money to Pugin's children other than those by his third wife.[3]

The third case was such that he found it necessary to have

[1] Daughter of Thomas Knill, and first cousin of Sir Stuart Knill, first baronet, Lord Mayor of London.
[2] *Wickham;* pp. 146—7.
[3] Inf. of Mr. S. Pugin Powell.

printed for private circulation *A Statement of Facts relative to the Engagement of marriage between Miss* [. . .], *and Augustus Welby Pugin, Esq. of S. Augustins, Isle of Thanet.*

Nearly the whole pamphlet, with the omission of names, is given by Ferrey, but there is now no need to go further into his justification; for no reply was ever issued by the lady's relations. A few extracts will serve to show the state of affairs.

' I became acquainted with Miss [. . .] nearly three years since, when she came with her parents on a visit to Ramsgate; but our intimacy did not commence till the winter of 1846: at that time I was suffering from a most severe illness, produced by anxiety of mind; and Miss [. . .], who was staying in the neighbourhood, came frequently to pass a great part of the day at my residence, and her extreme kindness and attention contributed, in no small degree, to my ultimate recovery. It was then that I had an opportunity of appreciating the many admirable qualities she possessed; and, notwithstanding all that has subsequently happened, I feel bound to say that my opinion, as regards her talents and accomplishments, remains unchanged. . . .

' Immediately after my return from the continent, Miss [. . .] came to Ramsgate, and she then told me that she was quite convinced of the truth of the Catholic religion, and that she could not bear to continue in her present position. . . . However, her resolution remained unchanged; and in a letter dated July 19, she writes: " I thought, on the whole, the best thing I could do was to let the change that had taken place in my sentiments be known at once. Oh, the courage it required to do so ! My eldest brother was furious, and declared he would quarrel with me if I did not give up reading those accursed books . . . "

' Up to this period, I had never mentioned my affection for Miss [. . .] to herself or anybody else, although I had loved

her in secret for a considerable time; and it is worthy of
remark, that her religious change was accomplished without
any knowledge of my sentiments towards her, by which she
might have been biassed. . . .

'Although at that time I had not been unfortunate enough
to come in contact with Mr. [. . .], yet, from some circumstances that had occurred, I judged him to be a man so deeply
prejudiced against the Catholic faith, that it was next to
impossible that he should consent to my union with his
daughter. . . .

' " I am full of work at the house, improving everything
before you come, so that we shall have nothing to do but
enjoy the place afterwards. I am panelling the best rooms,
putting new stained glass into the windows, redecorating the
ceilings, and the three crosslets will not be forgotten. I am
fitting out in every department, and I do trust everything will
please you. You have no idea of the work we have to get
done by Easter. I have between thirty and forty people
working different ways. There are five at your jewellery at
Birmingham; of course I cannot pretend to vie in intrinsic
value with thousands of people; but no woman, not excepting
the Queen, will have better ornaments, as regards taste, than
you will." . . . '

Miss [. . .] was shortly afterwards received into the
Church, whereupon her relations prevented her from being
present at Mass. There followed an obscure period, during
which letters were intercepted and the pressure applied can
only be guessed at, ending by Miss [. . .] breaking off the
engagement, and eventually, in 1850, marrying a Clergyman
of the Church of England. . . .

'And thus,' Pugin ends, ' this unhappy business has been
brought to a state as destructive to my peace of mind as it is
disgraceful to those concerned in it. We behold a woman of
five-and-twenty years of age overwhelming a man with

kindness, making him the depository of her most secret thoughts, corresponding with him in terms that could not admit of a doubt as to her sentiments in his regard, and even renewing that correspondence, of her own accord, after it had been broken off for months; then pledging herself to marry him in the most solemn manner, allowing him to make an entirely new settlement of his property in her favour; permitting him, with full knowledge and concurrence, to expend very large sums, not only in alterations on his own residence, but on her jewels and dresses, for which she furnished the patterns and dimensions; inducing him to take long journeys on her account; and at last, when the time had arrived for the fulfilment of her engagement, she abandons him in the most cruel manner possible, and even adds insult to injury.'

In 1851, Pugin was appointed one of the Commissioners of Fine Arts in connection with the Great Exhibition, and was given charge of the Mediæval Court. In it were shown specimens of altars, shrines, tapestries, painted glass, chalices, patens, vestments, sculpture in stone and wood, ornamental tiles, and other objects, the greater part of which was made from his own designs by Myers, Hardman, and Minton. In it, too, were the jewels which he had prepared for Miss [. . .]. But she, by that time, was safely married to her clergyman. She probably had never seen the jewelry. But it was much admired by Queen Victoria.

One of the greatest difficulties in the way of the revival of any art is that it must, in a sense, start at the wrong end. It must, that is, imitate a result, whereas the original artists initiated a method. In consequence, a revived art always tends to flatness and lack of vitality, bearing a relationship to its original comparable to that of a tracing to an original drawing. The remedy is twofold: first, to discover the principles by which the old artists were guided, and secondly, to encourage craftsmen to independence within the limits of those principles. In few things is Pugin's grasp of Gothic better shown than in that he saw both the danger and the remedy before they had been realised by others. In his *True Principles* and *Apology* he had anticipated William Morris in his demand for simple solidity of construction. In his *Floriated Ornament*, published in 1849, he anticipated Ruskin.

In Pugin's library there was an ancient botanical work, *Eicones Plantarum*, published at Frankfurt in 1590, and with its help Pugin managed to identify the original plants on which some old designs were based. In his *Floriated Ornament* he produced a volume of original designs each one of which was based on a real flower. Gothic ornament was to be freed from the trammels of imitation, and was to return to nature for its sources; for nature was inexhaustible, and an art founded upon nature must always live.

Remarkable as was this attempt to make Gothic decoration once more a living thing, it was preceded by five years by a book in some ways even more surprising. This was the *Glossary of Ecclesiastical Ornament and Costume*, in which, with the help of eighty coloured plates of beautiful designs, he set forth the glories of Catholic art. Its influence was immense, and stimulated a revival of polychromatic decoration after two hundred years of whitewash in the churches of the Establishment.

' No well-directed attempts in recent times had been made to introduce coloured embellishments into churches;' Ferrey somewhat plaintively wrote,[1] ' but a stimulus was now given to such efforts, and although Protestant prejudices were opposed to coloured decorations, yet they were depicted with such fascinating effect in the pages of the Glossary that many of his symbols, suited only for the walls of a Roman Catholic edifice, were innocently repeated in our English churches.'

[1] *Ferrey*; p. 148.

Yet its influence is not the most remarkable thing about the *Glossary*. It is chiefly notable for what it is : an anticipation of all that was best in the later development of revived mediæval decoration. Even its heraldic specimens, at a time when that art was almost at its lowest ebb, would not have been unworthy of Mr. G. W. Eve, or of Miss Helard, or of Anselm Baker, the herald monk of Mount St. Bernard's.

It is almost incredible, when one examines this bulky volume, with its multiplicity of crafts and its exquisiteness of detail, its boldness of design and exactness of execution, that it is the work of one who was already an overburdened architect. There must have been a secret behind that power ; and that secret Pugin's secret. In his buildings, and in his other books, it is elusive, as though spoken in a key to which modern ears are not quite attuned. But in the richly coloured pages of this book it lies open for anyone to read.

There is a type of successful athlete that seems to achieve victory by natural genius. It is as though 'nature were bound to their success.' How much of this aptitude for achievement is due to hidden labour, one cannot say ; nor how much to natural quickness in co-ordinating actions. But in whatever proportion these qualities may be present, there remains a necessary residue, a certain habitude of courage, an unresting, fearless exercise of will. It is a kind of courage which is better realised in its results than by definition. It is that which gives to its possessors the combination of ' a fierceness of conception with a certitude of execution upon the basis of a just appreciation of means and ends which is the highest quality of the man of action.' [1] Possessors of it are by their nature athletes in whatever they desire to undertake. They are, in the fullest possible connotation of the word, ' whole-hearted.'

Pugin was one of nature's athletes ; and, like an athlete,

[1] Joseph Conrad, in *The Mirror of the Sea*.

he 'glean'd his teeming brain'; so long as his brain lasted.

How much longer it might have stood the strain, we may only surmise. For Mr. Barry's pertinacity was, after seven years, rewarded with success. In 1844, the year in which his *Glossary* was published, Pugin consented to renew his work on the new Houses of Parliament.

CHAPTER XIX

PALACE OF WESTMINSTER—PART II

"I am not conquered; as long as a good vassal is living, he will never be vanquished."

The Song of Roland.

ON 3rd September 1844, Charles Barry wrote :

' Dear Pugin,—I am in a regular fix respecting the working drawings for the fittings and decorations of the House of Lords, which it is of vital importance to me should now be finished with the utmost possible despatch. . . . I know no one who can so thoroughly relieve me of my present troubles of mind in respect of these said drawings as yourself . . . '[1]

In other words, Barry had had to swallow his pride. Whether he found difficulty or not in so doing, does not appear ; but that he did so on several occasions is clear, for it was only after repeated appeals that Pugin consented to help. The trouble was that Barry could not get on without Pugin, while, on the other hand, Pugin could get on very well without Barry. Pugin was in a position to state his own terms. They were simple : that Barry should not be his nominal employer, however much work he might do for him in practice.

' The last time I saw your father,' an anonymous correspondent wrote to Edward Pugin on 9th September 1867,[2] ' he was at the Government works, busily designing the details for the ornaments of the House of Lords. I remember he said that, after all, they could not do without employing him *publicly*, but, said he, " I now work for the Government, and Barry shall no longer get the credit of my plans." '

---

[1] *Art-Architect ;* p. 35. [2] *Ib. ;* p. 11.

Anonymous evidence is unsatisfactory; and if Pugin did say that, he was wrong. He might work nominally for the Government; but Barry still got the credit for his plans.

The most surprising thing about the whole episode is neither that Pugin insisted on Governmental employ, nor that Barry still got the credit for his work. The surprising thing, after his previous experience, is that Pugin consented to work again for Barry at all. For he knew what to expect:

'When my father again consented to design for Sir Charles,' Edward Pugin wrote,[1] 'he did so—as he himself constantly assured me—solely on condition of having an official appointment under Government, over which Sir Charles should have no control; "for," he said, "as soon as Barry has obtained what he requires from me, he will repeat 1837."'

The reason for this consent was given, curiously enough, by the Rev. Alfred Barry, who wrote[2]: 'He held strongly certain principles, on the evolution of which he greatly disagreed with his friend: he was one whose name and genius could at all times command an independent authority. Yet for the furtherance of his art he was willing to accept a distinctly subordinate position, and to work under the superintendence and control of another. His acceptance of the post, and the spirit in which he discharged its duties, showed the generosity and unselfishness which were his well-known characteristics.'

Barry knew well how to play upon these aspects of Pugin's character. On 25th November 1845, he wrote[3]:

'Dear Pugin,—I have ordered £100 to be paid to your account at the London and Westminster Bank, according to your wishes; but verily you are a man of little faith.

'Know you not that I am well aware that your remuneration

---

[1] *Art-Architect;* p. 76.   [2] *Barry;* p. 195.
[3] *Art-Architect;* p. 36.

hitherto has been altogether inadequate to your deserts, and that the *Fat* is yet to come. You say that I am a reasonable man, and so I am, and it shall not be my fault if your remuneration ultimately is not all that you can wish; but I will not do you the injustice to believe that filthy lucre is the main spring of all your efforts on behalf of the great work, but that like myself you are prepared to make a sacrifice for the glory of making it the means of establishing for the future what you believe the one and only true style of art. When, however, we meet again, we shall talk over this matter, and I have no doubt I shall be able to appease your mind and put it in a fit state to enable it to proceed with your holy work at Ramsgate with fitting composure and christian resignation.'

It is not a pleasant letter to read; no more so than is any letter in which advantage is taken of the generosity of the chivalrous. As a reasonable man, Barry saw that Pugin could not go unrewarded; but as a sensible man he saw that, if he could put the matter to Pugin in the light of a sacrifice—more, a sacrifice that he himself was already making—then he would get those services at a cheaper rate. He succeeded. The ' Fat ' to which Barry referred was computed by Edward Pugin to have come to between £3,000 and £4,000, exclusive, of course, of his governmental salary as Superintendent of the Works.[1] If these figures are accepted—and there is no reason to dispute them—it appears that Barry paid Pugin something under £500 a year for about eight years. The figures are unfortunate. If Pugin was a mere ' ghost ' employed to do odd jobs by an overburdened architect, the payment was excessive. But if, on the other hand, Pugin was indispensable and did for Barry all the detail work, from the tracery on the Victoria Tower to the ink-pots, and from the great river façade to the umbrella-stands, an uneasy impression remains

---

[1] *Art-Architect;* p. 40.

that Barry's appeal to Pugin's generosity was more successful than is pleasant to contemplate.

No useful purpose would be served by going fully into the details of the tasteless controversy over the extent of Pugin's share in the new Houses of Parliament. Like all pamphlet wars, it was unsatisfactory : quotation and counter-quotation ; evidence and counter-evidence ; assertion and counter-assertion ; mutual implications of bad faith. The extent, and rancour, and confusion of the controversy may be gauged by the titles of some of the pamphlets : Edward Pugin entered the field with *Who was the Art Architect of the Houses of Parliament ? A Statement of Facts, founded on the letters of Sir Charles Barry and the diaries of Augustus Welby Pugin. London :* 1867 ; a pamphlet which, by its very title, confused the whole issue from the start. Who was the Art Architect ? The question first requiring answer was what an ' Art Archi-tect ' was. Edward Pugin did not answer it. However, Sir Charles Barry having died six years before, his son, as diffident as himself in admitting Pugin's activities, replied in *Sir Charles Barry and Mr. Pugin. The Architect of the New Palace at Westminster : a reply to the Statements of Mr. E. Pugin. By Alfred Barry, D.D.* ; a pamphlet which received a second edition in 1868. But Edward Pugin, whom tradition reports as having silenced the Duke of Cambridge in a swear-ing match before resigning his commission in a yeomanry regiment, was no less prompt in the case of a doctor of divinity : *Notes on the Reply of the Rev. Alfred Barry, D.D., Principal of Cheltenham College, to the " Infatuated Statements " made by E. W. Pugin, on the Houses of Parliament. By E. Welby Pugin. Second edition. Revised and enlarged. London :* 1868.

The details of this quarrel between two sons over a matter affecting their fathers' reputations are not edifying, though occasionally amusing enough. The pity of it is that the two sons did not collaborate : the Houses of Parliament are great enough to uphold the reputations of more than one man. But that was impossible. Edward Pugin wished to do justice to his dead father, and in doing so he could only make it appear that Sir Charles Barry had not done him justice while alive. Conversely, the only way in which Alfred Barry could defend his father from this charge of ungenerous behaviour was by showing that Pugin's relation to the Houses had been so 'ghostly' as to be practically non-existent.

In this, Alfred Barry did not succeed, though he might occasionally score at Edward Pugin's expense. The evidence against him was too heavy. He might boldly claim that the letters 'A.W.P.' in the drawing for the Throne Room stood, not for 'Augustus Welby Pugin,' but for 'Albertus Walliæ Princeps.' He might account for the fact that no drawings for elevations by his father could be found, by stating, first, that they had been destroyed ; secondly, that Pugin's drawings were but copies of Sir Charles Barry's ; and thirdly and alternatively, that if the Pugin drawings were originals they had never been used. He might even, joyously, catch Edward Pugin out in a definite mis-statement, pointing out that, far from an entry in Pugin's diary for April 1835 having any-thing to do with the Houses of Parliament, it could only refer to Pugin helping Barry over the Birmingham Grammar School ; for the Select Committee had not at that time issued its decision on the style of the new buildings. But for the extent of Pugin's work on the Houses of Parliament the evidence is overwhelming. In the first place, there are 'eight huge portfolios'[1] of designs in the Victoria and Albert Museum, some of them made under Pugin's direction by John Hardman Powell, who, incidentally, designed the glass.[2] In the second place, there is a mass of detail drawings in the possession of Mr. Sebastian Pugin Powell in Oxford. They

[1] *Clark ;* p. 167.   [2] Inf. of Mr. S. Pugin Powell.

include Numbers for the Umbrella Stands, Candelabra for Commons Lobby, Calendars for Inkstands, 'Railings Throne House of Lords,' 'Bell Pulls for refreshment rooms,' and 'Division Lobby Chandelier.' And finally, there are the letters.

With these, the controversy immediately rises into something very like melodrama. In 1858, when it was decided to publish Pugin's Life, Sir Charles Barry was asked for particulars concerning the Houses of Parliament. He replied: " My dear fellow, there are no particulars ; what particulars could there be ? " [1] Pugin's widow then remarked that she had recently found a large number of Sir Charles Barry's letters to her husband of the years 1835–6, whereupon Barry exclaimed : " Good heavens ! I thought he had destroyed all my letters." [1] He had reason to think so ; for it was Pugin's custom to destroy all letters at that time. The preservation of Barry's letters seems to show that in that case at any rate he considered the breach of custom might be justified. The situation required delicate handling ; and received it. Barry asked Edward Pugin, then aged twenty-three, to come to dinner and bring the letters so that they might go through them together. Edward Pugin did so ; conversation turned on other topics ; when Edward Pugin was leaving, Barry said : " Oh, by the bye, did you bring those letters with you ? " [1] Edward Pugin said that they were in his greatcoat pocket ; Barry said that it was too late to go through them that night, and asked Edward Pugin to leave them behind. He did so. There were seventy-six of them. They have not been seen since.

Of course, they may simply have been lost. On the other hand, Barry had strong motives for getting rid of them. In 1835 he had employed an obscure 'ghost' ; a perfectly legitimate proceeding, for the work was too great for one

[1] *Clark ;* p. 165.

man. The trouble was that by 1844, when the need for the renewal of the same help had become urgent, Pugin had become famous. What Barry really needed was not Pugin's help but his collaboration. But he could not admit this publicly; for if he did, the secret of the sale of the original designs might be guessed. It was necessary to be discreet, and the border-line between discretion and deception is easily passed. As to Pugin, he could be relied upon to become the ' ghost ' of his former self for the glory of Christian art. There was no real danger there. But equally, every year that passed made it increasingly impossible that the truth of their relation-ship should be made known. The sudden discovery of the letters must have been like a blow between the eyes.

But there was another reason for the suppression of the letters. The discretion of Edward Pugin could not be relied on at all. He would not be satisfied with publishing merely enough to show his father's share in the building, embarrassing as that would have been. He would almost certainly publish them entire; and that was probably unthinkable for other reasons.

When asked why he had not himself competed for the Houses of Parliament, Pugin said [1] :

' Barry's grand plan was immeasurably superior to any that I could at the time have produced,[2] and had it been otherwise, the commissioners would have killed me *in a twelve-month*. No, sir, Barry after all is " the right man in the right place " ; what more could we wish ? '

The Rev. Thomas Mozley, in his *Reminiscences*,[3] shows clearly that being ' in the right place ' at Westminster was not wholly enviable :

' Poor Barry ! What a life he led, and what a thing it is to

---

[1] *Ferrey ;* p. 247.
[2] Pugin's own idea for the Houses of Parliament was to place them on either side of Westminster Bridge, joining them by a bridge over the road, the ' houses ' them-selves being as now on the upper floors. [Inf. of Mr. S. Pugin Powell.]
[3] II., p. 155.

be a great architect ! . . . How meekly did he allude to his troubles, his difficulties, and his vain requests ! . . . Worse than all, there was that imposter Reid,[1] with his miles of ventilating tubes piercing everywhere Barry's masonry, wood, and iron, costing 100,000*l.*, and unintelligible to everybody —it was believed to Reid himself. Last of all there was the Select Committee.'

Verbally, Barry may have been meek. But it is improbable that his correspondence with Pugin was confined solely to business matters. He must have known Pugin's opinion of employers who would spoil good work. He would have been sure of a sympathetic audience there. It seems almost certain that in his letters he must have said what he thought of people who would change their minds, and put unnecessary obstacles in his way, and delay important decisions, and let themselves be fooled by the egregious Reid. Barry, in fact, *could not* allow the letters to be published. For they contained his opinion of his employers.

On the other hand, when destroying his letters to Pugin— assuming, that is, that they were destroyed and not, as Ferrey suggests,[2] ' unfortunately mislaid '—it would have been a generous action on Barry's part to have followed his usual custom [3] and destroyed also various letters of Pugin's which tended to minimise the extent of his work. But they were

[1] Dr. D. B. Reid, an ' authority ' on warming and ventilation, who had ' formed a plan, by which all chimneys were to be dispensed with, and all the smoke and vitiated air of every room in the building were to be carried into great shafts, forming towers in external design, in which large furnaces were to create sufficient upward draught.' Fresh air was to be brought into the building in a similar manner ; and ' various mechanical contrivances ' were also to be employed. In January 1840, ' without any provision whatever as to the relative subordination of the two authorities thus created ' [*Barry* ; pp. 166–7], he was appointed to arrange the warming and ventilation of the new Houses. His scheme, which entailed perpetual alteration of Barry's plan, ended by requiring about one-third of the cubic contents of the building and by destroying Barry's fire-proofing arrangements, and after some years he was dismissed. Barry's troubles may be imagined. One good thing came of them, however : the decorative central tower originated as a great ventilating shaft.

[2] *Ferrey* ; pp. 244–5.

[3] ' He does not appear to have preserved, except in a few cases, the numerous letters from eminent persons, which he must have received.' [*Barry* ; p. iv.]

not destroyed, and Alfred Barry saw their value, and printed them in his ' reply.'   One of them, dated 16th June 1844, suffices to show their trend :

' I am sure I can never do you real service except in absolute detail [1] ; you should fully make up your mind as to every arrangement and then turn the small work over to me . . . as I said before, I can do you no good except in actual detail, and in that more by ferreting out the fine things that exist than composing new ones.'

It was a useful point to be able to make.   But the fact remains that the Houses of Parliament contain an enormous amount of purely decorative work, and that Barry worked Pugin hard.   Even if one compares Pugin to a bookbinder and Barry to the author of the books, it must be admitted that Pugin was responsible for the appearance of a huge library.

How hard Barry worked his collaborator may be gauged by various later letters which, by some unrecorded chance, were not returned to Barry.   The loss of the seventy-six early letters is of little importance : they would only have served to enlarge a monument of ingratitude ; and as Edward Pugin wrote [2] :

'. . . singularly enough, of the four letters—all that are left to me, of the early correspondence,—one proves that my father designed the " *elevations* " of the Palace to Sir Charles's plans externally and internally—the second, that he designed all the " *sectional drawings* "—the third that he designed " *sets of exquisite details ;* "—and ', he concludes, ' *elevations, sections, and details, make up the entire building.*'

In this, of course, Edward Pugin was wrong : there was the plan : and the plan was indubitably Barry's.   And Barry's,

---

[1] Apart from the fact that Pugin's work extended far beyond ' absolute detail,' this was an understatement : " Whenever Mr. Barry's fire of enthusiasm began to pale, a visit from his ' Comet ' sufficed to brighten it." [*Barry ;* p. 196 n.]

[2] *Art-Architect ;* p. 29.

too, was the perhaps most difficult work of all, the struggle with the Select Committee.

But although Pugin's work may have been, for him, the less difficult, in extent it was prodigious ; for every decorative feature of the great building, inside and out, was his work. Somehow, in addition to his architectural practice, and his historical researches, and his controversies, he found time and energy to cover with a wealth of exquisite detail the greatest building of the Gothic Revival.

On 7th January 1851, Barry wrote to Pugin[1] :

' A little sketch for a hexagon pump in the cloisters will be acceptable when you have time. . . . Inkstands of proper mediæval character will undoubtedly be wanted, therefore send to me, when you can, one or two rough sketches for them.'

Three days later he wrote again[1] :

' I enclose a Diagram of the mere requirements of official inkstands and paper holders, which you can lick into shape in any way that occurs to you, and send me a sketch.'

On 11th August[2] :

' I approve of your design and arrangement of the wall tiles for the smoking room, as well as of the arrangement for the floor tiles, which must, I think be charged with decorations to avoid meanness.'

On 22nd October[2] :

' When is it likely all the rough patterns of chandeliers, &c., will be ready to be tried up *en place* ? '

On 5th November[2] :

' With the exception of the cloak stand for Committee Rooms, which being intended for corners must be upon a circular or octagonal plan, the rough sketches for the furniture will do very well.'

On 11th November[3] :

' The details for the gates will do capitally.'

[1] *Art-Architect ;* p. 47. [2] *Ib. ;* p. 49. [3] *Ib. ;* p. 50.

On 17th November [1] :

'If you should have any of the *Working Drawings of the furniture* for the official residences ready, pray send them to me ; as it is high time that the orders were given for it. The tile arrangement for the Division Corridor fireplaces will do very well.'

The pressure of work was too great. On 10th December 1851, Pugin wrote a vehement letter to the Lords of the Committee for Trade repudiating the purchase of a shield for the Exhibition, the cost of which was ' out of all character for such an object, useless and obsolete, except as a space to exhibit metal chasing ', and which was ' a positive revival of Pagan art ' and ' a most objectionable object to select '. He went on to say :

'I have been preparing a short account of our reasons (barring the shield), which has unfortunately been retarded by my late severe attack of nervous fever, from which dangerous malady I am only very lately delivered, and the state to which it has reduced me prevents my returning too quickly to anything that requires much mental exertion ; but if, by the blessing of God, my faculties are again restored to their former strength, I will send a fair copy . . . ' [2]

He might bravely call it ' nervous fever,' and continue working. But already in that year it seems that he had had a presentiment that death, which he dreaded, was near at hand ; and had gone into retreat, and prepared himself for its coming. It was the beginning of the end.

On the same day, Barry wrote again to Pugin. He was beginning to realise that he was pressing him too hard [3] :

'I am delighted to have the cheering intelligence contained in your letter of this morning respecting yourself. . . . Pray take care of yourself for the sake of your friends, and, I may

---

[1] *Art-Architect ;* p. 50. [2] *Ferrey ;* pp. 140–1.
[3] *Art-Architect ;* p. 51.

add, the country at large. No. 1 Design for the railing, which I return, will do for Westminster Hall. . . . Again, beware of tasking your energies too much . . . '

A week later, however, on 18th December, the full pressure was reapplied [1] :

' My dear Pugin,— . . . The drawings for the Court Lamp Brackets will do very well, and I have given Bayne orders to prepare patterns accordingly. With respect to the drawings sent to Quarm [2] this morning for the borderings of leather tops to tables, I propose to have the rolls made by Hardman and supplied to Gillows ready for use, and have sent orders for them to Birmingham accordingly. . . .

' Fifteen boxes for letters are required for the Committee rooms. Send to me a sketch for them, with such working details as Hardman will require for the metal work, as soon as you are able. Some small interlaced patterns for papers for small rooms are also wanted, as soon as you can conveniently send them to Crace. . . . The drawings for the Badges for the Commons Gallery front will do very well . . .

' Eighteen umbrella stands, 8 ft. long, are required for the Lower Cloisters. If anything of quaint design should occur to you for them let me have a sketch of it when you are able.'

Eighteen umbrella stands of quaint design. . . . It must have been a torment to Pugin's exacerbated brain. For the time was at hand when even he could do no more. He was breaking under the strain. The trouble was that, while Barry was hopelessly overworked in dealing with the Houses of Parliament, Pugin was already overworked with other things as well. But Barry, with the terrible cruelty of the overworked, could not let him rest. Encouragement had to be given to the all too willing workman, encouragement

---

[1] *Art-Architect ;* p. 51.   [2] Barry's clerk of the works.

which would act upon that self-sacrificing violence like a goad :

'I thank and commend you greatly,' he wrote on the 30th December,[1] ' for the trouble you have taken, and the successful result of your proposed arrangement of the Commons' shields.'

And again, two days later, for " it was no ordinary amount or quality of work which satisfied Mr. Barry " [2] :

'My dear Pugin,—I am rejoiced to find that you are all alive again. I admire the patterns for papers received this morning, and have given Crace orders to have the blocks cut immediately. Metal guards are required for the Library and Committee Room fires. . . . Let me have your notions on the subject as soon as you can, and at the same time a sketch for blotting cases, foolscap size, and simple candlesticks, not exceeding 10 inches high.'

The demands for designs became continuous. On 13th January, he wrote [3] :

'My dear Pugin,—Your idea of the Ink and Paper stands is a good one, and may be acted upon, but I should like to see the full-sized drawings before the work is put in hand. . . . The ink-holders should be of glass, on the fountain principle, cut on the exterior in a knowing manner. . . . '

Two days later [3] :

'My dear Pugin,—I give you full credit for the details and construction of the Ink and Paper Stands, which will make an excellent job. . . . A certain number of knowing rosaces, to be punched through plate iron and tinned, are required for filling a ventilation hole in the wall, in each of the bays in the Cloister. They are 14 in. in diameter. . . . '

On 17th January [4] :

'My dear Pugin,—I entirely approve of the principle of your design and details for the umbrella stands . . . Each

[1] *Art-Architect;* p. 53. [2] *Barry;* p. 196 n.
[3] *Art-Architect;* p. 54. [4] *Ib.;* pp. 54-5.

bay of the Cloister will accommodate 24 cloaks, and I propose
to have an umbrella stand in each window opposite to them,
containing accommodation in each of them for 20 cloaks,
which I have indicated in a tracing returned with your drawings enclosed.   Have the goodness, therefore, to make out
all the working details and forward them direct to Hardman,
with orders to put them in hand, and get them done with all
despatch.   The number required will be 20.   I am glad you
approve of my suggested alteration in the designs of the Ink
and Paper Stands, and agree with you as to the *modus operandi*.
. . . The rosaces will do.'

Two days later again[1] :

' My dear Pugin,— . . . I shall be glad of other varieties
of beasts or cognizances that may be appropriate.   There are
23 required.   You are right in your proposed alterations in
the arrangement of the rings for the umbrellas at the ends of
the stands.   I absolve you from all blame in preparing the
monster stand drawing, and commend you for the wonderful
arrangement contained in it. . . . '

The correspondence was not to continue much longer.
The time was running out in which Barry could offer praise
for a ' wonderful arrangement' of umbrella stands, could
demand glass ink-holders ' cut on the exterior in a knowing
manner ' of a man who had designed cathedrals, of an architect
who could probably have given him lessons in everything
connected with his art except the planning of a Parliament
House, the management of a Committee, and the use of
Renaissance architecture in London Clubs.

[1] *Art-Architect ;* p. 55.

CHAPTER XX

DEATH

By that time the day had departed and the night had come.
The Song of Roland.

THE enormous pressure of work went on, the terrible, selfless labour of those who believe, and have power to act up to their belief, that the greatest privilege possessed by man is to be allowed, while on earth, to contribute to the glory of God. For such, no day is ever long enough, no labour adequate. Had they the strength of a hundred men, it would not be enough; for their desire is infinite. Yet the very intensity of their desire gives them the strength of ten. But ten men's strength is more than one man may stand. There comes a breaking-point.

The first definite proof, in Pugin's case, that this point had been reached occurred at Ramsgate, where, returning one evening to St. Augustine's, and meeting his medical attendant, he asked him if he had heard of the disaster outside the harbour. Five merchant ships, it appeared, had been sunk while trying to reach the entrance. The doctor, impressed by Pugin's detailed knowledge of the tragedy, repeated the story at a dinner-party that evening.

The whole affair was an hallucination.

Once, in youth, Pugin himself had suffered shipwreck. In failing, it would seem that his mind returned.

But the collapse was not immediately entire. There was a period of racking ill-health, of relapse and recovery, of almost incessant torment, while the incredible labour of his life went on. Glimpses are given in his letters to Herbert Minton, of

Stoke-upon-Trent, an intimate friend and an earnest collaborator in the recovery of the art of making encaustic tiles.

In January 1852, delighted with the results achieved,
Pugin wrote [1] :

'I declare your St. Stephen's tiles are the finest done in
the tile way; vastly superior to any ancient work; in fact,
they are the best tiles in the world, and I think my patterns
and your workmanship go ahead of anything.'

But in the same month he wrote again [2] :

'I believe I have been too hurried so soon after such an
illness. I cannot get my bodily strength up at all, and I
perspire intensely, to that degree as to be obliged to put on
five or six shirts a day, &c.'

And a little later [3] :

'I have been dreadfully ill, so ill that it was at one time
doubtful if I could ever recover; but by the blessing of God
I am certainly gaining strength very fast, and I have lost
nothing of mental power, as I think you will find by the work
I send to you. There is no probability of my being in
London for the next month or two, and the medical men
recommend perfect rest till the advanced time of spring, and
then to travel in an easy and gentle way.'

Again he wrote [4] :

'I am in such a deplorably nervous state that I am at times
scarcely answerable for what I write; I am so dreadfully
afflicted in the head. You seemed to think I had cheated you
and sent you a false account (though now I don't believe you
did), and I cried like a child, and trembled all over in dreadful
perspiration, and I thought my fever had returned. Pray,
my dear Minton, don't agitate me, the doctors say I am not
to be agitated. If you saw your poor old friend so reduced as
I am—thin, trembling, hollow-eyed, changed, and yet work-

[1] *Ferrey*; pp. 251–2.   [3] *Ib.*; p. 252.
[2] *Ib.*; pp. 252–3.   [4] *Ib.*; p. 253.

ing tremendously at times—you would be very careful not to distress me.'

And later[1] :

' You have no conception of the dreadful agony which I still suffer, the least thing agitates me ; I feel trembling and my eyesight is dimmed. I am obliged to bathe my eyes with sea water, and to drink the coldest water to bring my sight again.'

It must be remembered that the man who wrote those words, in addition to a large architectural practice and many other activities, was burdened with the whole detail work of the new Palace of Westminster. More, he was goading his already failing powers in the composition of an illustrated historical work, entitled *An Apology for the separated Church of England since the reign of the Eighth Henry. Written with every feeling of Christian charity for her children, and honour of the glorious men she continued to produce in evil times. By A. Welby Pugin. Many years a Catholic-minded son of the Anglican Church, and still an affectionate and loving brother and servant of the true sons of England's Church.* Concerning it he had already in the previous year written to Minton [2] :

' I am almost distracted, for in addition to all other labours, I have a most important work on the real cause of the change of religion in the 16th century, which will place matters in a totally new light, overthrow the present opinions on both sides, and may be the means of tending to much mutual charity on both sides, and a better understanding. The present state of things in a Christian country is afflicting, and it all proceeds from men not being able to separate the temporal tyranny of Catholic States from the religion itself, which suffers all the odium of the system to which one was bound up and tied.'

In the circumstances, it is not surprising that among his

---

[1] *Ferrey* ; p. 253.   [2] *Ib.* ; p. 265.

hallucinations was one that there had come about an increase of 'mutual charity on both sides, and a better understanding,' that the object for which he and March-Phillipps had so long and earnestly laboured had been achieved, that Christendom had become one. While under this delusion, during one of his sleepless nights, 'he wrote upwards of sixty pages to his cousin Sibthorp[1] . . . stating that he could now again embrace his previously unfortunate brother—that there was now but one Church—no distinct Roman Catholic, Anglican, nonconformist, or other denomination, and he drew imaginary cheques to be given to clergymen and others for distribution to the poor of their neighbourhood.'[2]

Undoubtedly, Pugin had 'been too hurried'. The over-wrought brain had lost its grip on reality; and an imaginary wrong seared it like heated iron on undefended flesh. The misunderstanding with Minton led to his writing a letter withdrawing from him his confidence and threatening to transfer all commissions to other manufacturers, and to his refusing either to see Minton or to receive his letters.

Minton, who was innocent of all offence and was deeply grieved at Pugin's sufferings, dealt with the situation with tact and delicacy, writing to Mrs. Pugin saying that he was not only innocent but ignorant of any cause of offence, and offering to withdraw any expressions and make any apology rather than lose Pugin's friendship.

The message was delivered, and on 14th February 1852, Pugin replied[3] :

'My dear, ever dear Minton,

Your capital letter to my wife has just arrived, thus leaving nothing, my dear friend, but a perfect reconciliation between us. You must attribute a great deal to the dreadful

---

[1] See Appendix II., under *Lincoln.*   [2] *Ferrey;* p. 266.
[3] *Ib.;* pp. 254-5.

irritation of nerves left by this terrible fever under which I suffered; but nothing would contribute so much to the final re-establishment of my improved health, as a real and hearty reconciliation with you. It is ridiculous, and a delight to the many to see two such men as you and I quarrelling. We cannot afford it long, let us cut the row and embrace. I will endeavour when sufficiently restored to settle it over a leg of mutton at Huntfield; and if you will come and see me I will give you a better reception at St. Augustine than the Emperor; for all my things are in the true style, which is more than you can say for the fancy patterns. I have written to Mr. Barry by this post that we are quite reconciled; it would be too affecting to see us really embracing over a happy combination of four tiles, so it must pass in imagination, though not less real.

Your devoted old friend,
A. W. Pugin.'

Appended to the letter was a rough sketch, showing Pugin and Minton embracing over an altar inscribed: '*Pax Pugin et Minton*'; and on each side a crowd of people shouting: '*Pax Minton et Pugin*'. And at the foot there was placed in old characters as a border tile: '*Pax in eternum*', and: '*A. W. Pugin, Fecit.*'

It was to be eternal peace. There was to be only one more letter to Minton; and seven months later he was dead. On 16th February, the last letter was written[1]:

'Many thanks for your kind letter, my dear friend. I don't think I have been myself. This nervous fever is a dreadful delusion: since I wrote I am no longer an *architect*, that is in a general way. After I wrote to you I was taken with a terrible relapse and a *stagnation of blood*. I soon became cold in all the vital parts, and I felt that without instant relief I must die.

---

[1] *Ferrey*; pp. 255–6.

I ordered three strong glasses of brandy :—my doctor came
in :—and by the mercy of God, and by about half a pint of
sal volatile which I drank off, and by my dear wife putting
on hot flannels all over me, with rubbing, in which others
assisted, at last the circulation returned. My medical man said
this could not go on any longer, and he had a consultation of
all the first medical men, who declared that I could not live a
week if I did not give up my profession. There was no
hesitation on my part: I immediately relinquished all my
buildings except Lord Shrewsbury's and Sir C. Barry's, and
of course yours, which will not kill me ; but I am a private
gentleman, a grand fellow. The relief of mind, as the doctors
predicted, was instantaneous, and succeeded perfectly, and I
am, thank God, out of danger. I shall enshrine your kind
letter among my most esteemed epistles. My mind has been
deranged through over exertion. The medical men said I had
worked one hundred years in forty. I have not time to say
more : I am ordered to Italy as soon as possible.'

It was characteristic that, though on the verge of insanity
through overwork, when ordered a complete rest, he should
make exceptions for his friends and for a public work.

On the same day as the last letter to Minton, Sir Charles
Barry wrote [1] :

' My dear Pugin,—Your electric message on Saturday gave
me a shock that I shall not easily forget. All yesterday I was
in an agony of suspense about you, and you may imagine,
therefore, that the sight of your handwriting this morning
was indeed an immense relief to my mind. . . . Do not, I
beseech you, think of anything you may have offered to do
for me, except so far as it may afford you amusement. . . .
I have been very glad to shake hands with Hardman this
morning on his way to you. I have begged of him to use his
persuasive eloquence with you to take things *calmly* and

[1] *Art-Architect;* pp. 55–6.

quietly for the future. *You have really already done enough for the world and for your own repose here and hereafter.'*

But Pugin had not done enough for Sir Charles Barry. On the 23rd of the same month he wrote to him again [1] :

' My dear Pugin,—I have received your joyous letter of this morning, and was rejoiced to find that you are restored to health again . . . *I am much pressed respecting the Clock Tower and the new front in Old Palace Yard, as the building is at a stand in respect of those portions of it, for working drawings.* I cannot bear that you should be bothered upon the subject, particularly as several new thoughts have occurred to me respecting it.'

The trouble was that Pugin could not bear it either.

In the following month Pugin received a letter which, complimentary as it was to him personally, was distinguished as much by its lack of tact as by its sincerity of tone :

' Cannon Row, Westminster ;
March, 1852.

' Sir,

We are trying to establish a museum of architecture, and a school of art for artist workmen, *i.e.* a school for all the workmen in any way employed in carrying out architectural works ;—to do, indeed, for the men just what the Royal Academy does for students and painters. I enclose you a prospectus I have drawn up, which, as you will see, has been approved by many architects and others, and thought capable of realisation. If you will kindly read it and tell me what your opinion of it is, I shall feel greatly obliged, and I feel sure that your opinion when repeated to others will greatly help me (if you approve of it), in the very difficult task of inducing people to assist such an undertaking. It is, as you will at once see, capable of almost indefinite expansion.

[1] *Art-Architect ;* p. 56

We intend to include all styles, but have commenced our collection with the Gothic as the one of churches and ecclesiastical structures. As I am quite a novice at this work, I trust, Sir, you will pardon my writing without introduction.

I am,

Faithfully yours,

C. Bruce Allen.'

Perhaps if Mr. Allen had not been 'quite a novice' he would have refrained from mentioning the Royal Academy to a man who, put up for election by his friends without his knowledge, had been refused membership of that institution; nor would he have asked assistance, for a school which was to instruct in 'all styles', from a man who upheld with passionate conviction that Gothic was not a 'style' but a 'principle'; nor would he have referred to Gothic as being the style 'of churches and ecclesiastical structures' to a man who had long striven to impress on his generation that it was not merely an ecclesiastical style ('MELANCHOLY, and *therefore fit for religious* buildings ! ! ! '), but a suitable method for all structures.

Pugin's reply was characteristic, both of his manner and of his belief that religion was the foundation-stone of art [1] :

'Sir,

I have just returned home and received your prospectus and letter. I wish you every success, but it appears to me you are going to work on too extensive a scale in bringing up men to work in all styles. Practically, I expect you will find no end of difficulties. Workmen are a singular class, and from my experience of them, which is rather extensive, are generally incapable of taking a high view on these subjects, —and ready at a moment to leave their instructors and

[1] *Ferrey;* pp. 259–61.

benefactors for an extra sixpence a day for the first bidder that turns up. I have been all my life instructing men, while others profited by the result of my labours. In the present state of society, and the total absence of anything like the faith and religious feeling that actuated men in past ages, I believe it is impossible to do much good; however, I have no doubt your inclinations are excellent, and time will show if they are attended with practical benefit.

I am yours most sincerely,

A. W. Pugin.'

The first definite manifestation of Pugin's insanity occurred, curiously enough, ' in the presence of Sir Charles Barry and his family '.[1] Sir Charles promptly ' called in a most eminent physician ',[2] and Pugin was ' removed to the Golden Cross in Wellington Street, Strand, and put under proper restraint '.[3]

His violence increasing, it was considered that the best hope of a cure lay in placing him in the practised care of the authorities of Bethlehem Hospital. Immediately it was assumed that his removal thither was caused by lack of funds, owing to his having ruined himself in his religious zeal; the Catholic body was bitterly reproached for allowing this degradation to befall one who had sacrificed so much for the Church, and the Editor of *The Builder* suggested that subscriptions be appealed for with the object of placing him in a private asylum. Edward Pugin promptly denied that poverty was the cause of his removal to Bedlam, and protested against a public subscription being opened without some authority. In the meantime, on 10th July 1852, Lord John Russell had given the first response to the appeal by offering £10 in the

---

[1] *Ferrey;* p. 248.
[2] *Ib.*; p. 248. Dr. Alexander Tweedie, ophthalmic surgeon; part author of *A Practical Treatise on Cholera,* and author of *Clinical Illustrations of Fever,* and other works.
[3] *Ib.;* p. 267.

event of a subscription being raised. ' For the rest,' Edward
Pugin said, ' I trust I may be able to carry out my father's
professional engagements ; and with the continued assistance
and encouragement of his friends, to maintain the family till
such time as it may please God to restore him to us.' [1]   He
was at that time seventeen years old.

The methods employed in the Bethlehem Hospital effecting
no improvement, Mrs. Pugin, with the help of an old friend,
the Rev. Mr. Glennie, transferred her husband to a house in
The Grove, Hammersmith, where he lived for some time with
his family under the care of Dr. Samuel Dickson.[2]   While
there, his health improved, and, on 11th September, he was
well enough to be taken back to The Grange at Ramsgate.
On the 12th, he was quite lucid and cheerful, and revisited
with delight the various parts of his home and buildings.
Great hopes were entertained of his complete recovery ; for
the only distressing episode had been his anger on finding his
original drawings missing from the library.   However, when
it was explained that they were safe in the possession of his
son Edward at Birmingham, he became calm, and expressed
the hope that they might help him in his profession.

This innate love of architecture had already once before
served to calm him when, while at the Golden Cross, in a
frenzy he had attacked Mr. Myers. With remarkable presence
of mind, in order to distract his attention, Myers reproached
him for keeping the scaffolding up at Beverley while they were
waiting for his drawings. " Give me a pencil," Pugin said,
and drew a vane, clear and precise, on the back of a large
envelope. It was afterwards placed on a corner pinnacle of
St. Mary's Church.

---

[1] *Ferrey ;* p. 270.

[2] Author of *Hints on Cholera and its Treatment*, and various other works, including *Fallacies of the Faculty, with the principles of the Chrono-thermal System*, ' in which he cast ridicule both on the intelligence and on the honesty of contemporary practice by way of recommending his original views.' [*Dict. Nat. Biog. ;* XV., p. 44.]

On the night of 13th September all hopes of recovery were finally dispelled. He sank into convulsions, which continued through the night, and he was already too much weakened by previous attacks to rally. On the morning of the 14th, he died. The immediate cause of death was apoplexy. On the same day, in the same county, almost in sight of The Grange, and almost at the same hour, the Duke of Wellington also died. It was the Feast of the Exaltation of the Holy Cross.

On the afternoon of Monday, 20th September, the Vespers of the Office of the Dead were chanted in St. Augustine's, and were followed by Matins and Lauds of the same Office. The cantors were John Hardman of Birmingham and John Lambert of Salisbury, the builder of St. Osmund's, who had already, with the Rev. Henry Formby, founded the St. Chad's Gregorian Choir.

On the following morning the Gregorian Mass of Requiem was sung by Bishop Grant, who also preached the funeral sermon, taking as his text the sixth verse of the forty-fourth chapter of *Ecclesiasticus* :

' Rich men in virtue, studying beautifulness : living at peace in their houses.'

Feelingly he drew attention to the fact that it was but just that these funeral ceremonies, carried out with the greatest perfection which they had been able to achieve, should be so offered for the soul's repose of one who, in that same church of St. Augustine which he had raised out of the earnings of a laborious profession, had spared no trouble while alive to arrange for the same rites on behalf of the poor.

' To some it has happened ', he said, ' that they have rested upon the works of their own hands, and have forgotten that the ability to plan, and the strength to perfect them had come from Him. . . . '

' There are others ,' he went on, ' whom He has inspired to understand that His gifts are His own, and that to Him alone belongs the fruit thereof, and He has made them feel that their talents are to be returned to Him with usury. Such men feel that their minds are elevated and their undertakings are ennobled, if He is willing to accept them for His own glory, and they exclaim in rapture and gratitude, "Lord, I have loved the beauty of Thy house, and the dwelling-place of Thy glory" . . .

'When we knew him in the days of his ardent youth and buoyant manhood we were too much dazzled by the brilliancy of his genius and the boldness of his aspirations, to recollect what was hid under that quick speech, and that sudden adaptation of means, great or little, to extraordinary ends or noble purposes. . . .

'A future age will look upon these monuments, and will ask how one man could have achieved so much, and posterity will envy to us the possession of a man who could accomplish undertakings in a few years that would have been wonderful if they had extended over many, and that were so various that they would have shed lustre over more than one, and seem incredible and almost fabulous in him. The explanation of the difficulty will be read in the words addressed by him to one of his friends, "I have done the work of a hundred years in forty, and it has worn me out." ' [1]

Thus were committed to the grave, in the vault beneath his own chapel of St. Lawrence, the remains of one who might truthfully have applied to himself, in so far as any such application be lawful, the terrible Biblical words: '*Zelus domus tuæ comedit me.*'

[1] *The Tablet ;* 2 October 1852.

CHAPTER XXI

AFTERMATH

Baligant well resembled a proud baron, with beard as white as the blossom. In the law that he held, he was a wise man, and in battle proud and terrible.

The Song of Roland.

It might have been thought that the fame of such industry and achievement, of so vivid and powerful a personality, would have remained. Some familiar image, even, might have been expected to linger ; as, perhaps, of a short, dark-haired, full-bodied man, sitting at a table, laughing, talking, joking with friends, while from a stub of pencil in his hand there spread out on the paper before him, with incredible rapidity, in an unending stream, designs of an exquisite freshness and grace.

But it is not so. Apart from those places, such as Oscott, the Church at Derby, Scarisbrick, the firm of John Hardman, and the Hall of John Halle, with which Pugin was especially associated, and in which is still cherished a kind of family affection, there is no general tradition of Pugin in the English mind.[1] 'Pugin ? ' a man might say, ' Pugin ? Oh, yes, he was one of those silly Sham Gothic people. And wasn't there some row about him and the Houses of Parliament ? . . . '

It is not enough. On the other hand, the fact that Pugin has not received the fame which is his due is a matter of no real importance : for fame was the last thing which he himself desired : even in connection with the Mediæval Court at the Great Exhibition, where advertisement might have been had

---

[1] A correspondent, a man of wide reading and culture, mentioning the undertaking of this biography, referred consistently to the architect as ' Pusey.' This, a mere slip of the pen, though repeated, may be taken as symptomatic of the oblivion which, outside the bounds of the narrow tradition, has fallen on the name.

for the asking, his name never once appeared in any official document.

Yet the reasons why that fame did not come to him repay enquiry.

Some of the causes of this oblivion, such as the financial limitations under which he worked, and the unkind fate which has mutilated or destroyed so many of his buildings, have been already touched upon. Two others remain: the tendency to associate Pugin solely with the Gothic Revival, together with the ill-esteem which has fallen upon that movement; and the hostility of John Ruskin.

Pugin's true position and the means of his overshadowing, are well summed up by Mr. J. D. Crace, the decorative artist who carried out many of his designs in the Palace of Westminster.

' I am not blind,' he wrote,[1] ' to the great services rendered by other men now living. But it was Pugin who laid down the road and pointed the way. To identify Pugin only with the Gothic Revival is to do him much less than justice. By defining for the first time in the history of Art what are the immutable laws which must govern all constructive design, if it is to appeal successfully to human intelligence; and by doing this in vigorous, manly, and fearless language; and best of all, by himself breaking through all difficulties, and putting his own principles into constant practice, he compelled everyone engaged in architecture or design to listen to him. The principles of adjusting design to requirement and ornament to construction seem obvious enough now. They have been preached with every refinement of language; and the writer who, eight or ten years after Pugin's vigorous promulgation of them, adopted them as his own, and held Pugin up to ridicule, if more widely read, practically carried

---

[1] *Crace.*

the arguments no further. . . . We of the present day can hardly understand how much we owe to his teaching. He brought order out of chaos, taught how much delight is to be found in the smaller allied arts, as well as in the noble art of architecture. Above all, he taught—so successfully that a younger generation has come to regard it as a truism, self-evident from the very beginning—that there are laws connecting design with constructive motive which must remain true for all time and for all styles. The younger men cannot conceive a time when no such truth had been expressed or recognised, and even the criticism of all design was supposed to be simply a question of taste. Where they have brought themselves to admit that there was such a time, they attribute the change to the silver tongue of Ruskin. But the truth had been driven home by the plain fearless expressive English of Pugin years before. Thousands of workers had learnt what he meant, and had been daily practising what he taught; the Palace of Westminster already stood in evidence of his principles; the House of Lords was in use in 1847. Pugin's *True Principles* was published in 1841; Ruskin's *Seven Lamps* not until 1849 (when Pugin's work was nearly done); *The Stones of Venice* only in 1851. Nor was it case of priority only. The vigour of Pugin's language, the enthusiasm of the man himself, had carried the day. The purchase of the Solages collection—from which resulted the Kensington Museum—was mainly effected by Pugin's disciples. The Architectural Museum was founded by Pugin's disciples; and if his name has since been overlaid by those whose success had its roots in his perception and enthusiasm, he remains, none the less, the prophet who revived architecture, and lifted design out of the ash-heap.'

Truly Pugin was 'the prophet who revived architecture'. But there was another prophet. There was the appearance in the intellectual life of England of the curious and unprecedented phenomenon, a Nonconformist aesthete. He came from Scotland, and his name was John Ruskin.

In addition to the advantages commonly supposed to lie in the possession of Scottish ancestry, Ruskin had a wealthy father,[1] and a mother the intensity of whose 'protestantism' excelled even that of Pugin's mother[2] ; and, rarer advantage still, his parents were of the opinion that they had had the pleasure of giving to the world a genius. Whether this opinion was the cause, or the result, of the little Ruskin's producing a work entitled *Eudosia, Or A Poem On the Universe*, at the age of nine, it now seems impossible to determine. However this may be, one result of their opinion is plain enough : the little Ruskin, and the adolescent Ruskin, and the full-grown Ruskin were each in turn—as long as he lived with his parents, which was till he was fifty-two—kept as far as might be 'unspotted from this world' : to wit, from anything, whether normal human contacts or literary or artistic indulgence, which could lessen the value of the elder Ruskins' gift of genius to the world ; and, in particular, from the meretricious gauds and spirit-sapping creeds of Rome.

John Ruskin the Aesthete looked out from his sterilised

[1] 'Although engaged in commercial pursuits, the father of John Ruskin was no mere city drudge. He was a man of considerable culture, and familiar with literature and art.' [*John Ruskin ;* by Marshall Mather ; p. 2.] There is a certain resemblance to Pugin's father in this. 'John Ruskin's maternal grandfather', however, unlike Pugin's, 'was a seafaring man, making frequent, and at times long, voyages from Yarmouth.' But Pugin did better : he went to sea himself.

[2] 'My mother forced me by steady, patient, daily toil, to learn long chapters of the Bible by heart, as well as to read it every syllable through, aloud, hard names and all, from Genesis to the Apocalypse, about once every year . . .' However, when it came to waving the Bible as a sort of exorcist's wand over the dangerous matter of Art, this early discipline had its advantages. For there was no respectable family in Protestant England which would not have implicit trust in a man who could write : 'I opened my oldest Bible just now . . . yellow, now, with age, and flexible, but not unclean, with much use, except that the lower corners of the pages at the viii. ch. of 1st Book of Kings and the xxxii. ch. of Deuteronomy are worn somewhat thin and dark, the learning of these two chapters having caused me much pains. My mother's list of chapters with which, learned every syllable accurately, she established my soul in life, has just fallen out of it, as follows : " Exodus xv. and xx. ; II. Samuel i. ch. from 17 v. to end ; I. Kings viii. ; Psalms xxiii., xxxii., xc., xci., ciii., cxii., cxix., cxxxix. ; Proverbs ii., iii., viii., xii. ; Isaiah lviii. ; Matthew v., vi., vii. ; Acts xxvi. ; I. Corinthians xiii., xv. ; James iv. ; Revelation v., vi." ' [Quoted in *John Ruskin ;* by Marshall Mather ; pp. 9 –10.]

high eyrie at the works of long dead Papist hands, and, to
his disquiet, saw that they were good.

John Ruskin the Nonconformist looked out from the same
fine vantage-point and, to his extreme disquiet, saw that the
finest work in that admired line that was then being produced, in practice and in theory, was the work of one who
was not only a Papist but was a renegade Nonconformist too.

Now John Ruskin, like Disko Troop in *Captains Courageous*,
was one of those who liked to 'keep things sep'rate'. Duty
and inclination called: John Ruskin the Nonconformist-
Aesthete stepped boldly to the fray. What made this boldness
easier was that the earlier expressions of Ruskin's enthusiasms,
before he had seen below the surface fully into the perils of
Catholicism, had appeared over the signature 'Kata Phusin'
in the short-lived *Architectural Magazine*.[1] But John Ruskin
knew better now. The result was *The Seven Lamps of
Architecture*. There might, of course, have been many more;
but seven, with its many respectable associations ranging
from the seven pillars of Wisdom's house to the seven-
branched candlestick, was a good enough number to start
with. Even with the number so limited, however, Puginism
would keep breaking in, although one of the purposes of *The
Seven Lamps* was to dissociate Gothic from its lamentable
Romish tendencies.

But that, however, could not be helped; and in the meantime the obvious way to begin the process of dissociating
Gothic art and Romanism was not to mention Pugin. Ruskin
took it.[2] There is no mention of Pugin in *The Seven Lamps
of Architecture*. But there was a footnote to page 67,[3] which

---

[1] *Clark;* p. 252.
[2] In all the thirty-five (counting Letters, Bibliography, and Index, there are thirty-
nine) volumes in the Library Edition of Ruskin's Works, Pugin is mentioned only
on three separate occasions; and one of these is merely a slight (or, more accurately,
slighting) footnote. Refusal to advertise a person of whom one disapproves could
hardly be carried further.
[3] References are to the Library Edition, edited by E. T. Cook and A. Wedderburn.

could only have been adorned by a reference to Pugin's *True Principles*, page 8, or to his *Apology*, page 41. Naturally enough, because of this and other passages, charges of plagiarism were made. It was expressed, for instance, in *The Ecclesiologist* of August 1851, in a review of the first volume of *The Stones of Venice* :

'Mr. Pugin himself might learn from Mr. Ruskin, had not (as is not improbable) Mr. Ruskin learnt it from him, to loathe all that is false and mean and meretricious in art.'

The charge stung. In Appendix III. ('Plagiarism') to the third volume of *Modern Painters*, Ruskin found it necessary to give a definite denial :

'It is also often said that I borrow from Pugin. I glanced at Pugin's Contrasts once, in the Oxford architectural reading room, during an idle forenoon. His "Remarks on Articles in the *Rambler*" were brought under my notice by some of the reviews. I never read a word of any other of his works, not feeling, from the style of his architecture, the smallest interest in his opinions.'

However, the charge of plagiarism was not to be so easily rebutted. Even the impressive exactness with which his reading of *Contrasts* was limited to one time and place was not enough. The charge followed him embarrassingly into private life, and to Frederick Furnivall he felt it necessary to write :

'I wish you would explain something to the Wedgwoods for me ; I have never been quite at ease with them since it happened, and yet it was so absurdly trifling that I never liked to write about it. One day at their dinner-table Mr. Wedgwood said to me across it, "So you have taken up Pugin's idea of comparisons." I could not at the instant determine with myself whether Mr. Wedgwood really supposed that I never could have had the idea of putting an ugly and a pretty thing side by side, and saying, "Which is best ?"

unless I had borrowed it from Pugin, or whether he merely meant that I had been carrying out the same idea; and as I never like to appear sensitive on the point of originality, and did not like to enter into a long assertion of my own independence across a dinner-table, I simply bowed, in a very confused manner, which I have often thought since must have appeared to all the company like the confusion of a person detected in a plagiarism—whereas it was, in fact, the confusion of a person not knowing whether it was worth while, or a proper occasion, to assert his non-plagiarism. I do not know what Mr. Wedgwood's impression was, but I wish you would now explain to him, and assure him that whatever I owe— and it is at least two-thirds of what I am—to other people, I certainly owe nothing to Pugin,—except two *facts*, one about Buttresses, and one about ironwork. I owe, I know not how much, to Carlyle, and after him to Wordsworth, Hooker, Herbert, Dante, Tennyson, and about another dozen of people. But assuredly *Nothing* to Pugin.'

One cannot do other than believe him. One would not wish to do so. But it would have been at the least a graceful action to admit that his path, or at any rate part of it, had been trodden, and well trodden, before him.

However, the silence of contempt was not enough. As Mr. E. T. Cook has it in his Introduction to the second volume of *The Stones of Venice* :

'Pugin hoped to convert his countrymen to Rome by Christianising their architecture; and the High Church Party, who were pioneers in the revival of Gothic, sought to revive also ritual ceremonies and observances. Ruskin put the movement on a Protestant basis, and thus won for it a hearing in circles where it had hitherto been suspected.'

In order to 'put the movement on a Protestant basis' it was necessary to remove from it both Pugin and Catholicism. It was a considerable purge to undertake, for it entailed

removing both its leader and principal exponent and the
reasons which were the mainspring of that leader's activity.
There was only one man in England who could do it. It was
done in Appendix 12 ('Romanist Modern Art') to *The
Stones of Venice* :

'It is of the highest importance, in these days, that
Romanism should be deprived of the miserable influence
which its pomp and picturesqueness have given it over the
weak sentimentalism of the English people ; I call it a miserable
influence, for of all the motives to sympathy with the Church
of Rome, this I unhesitatingly class as the basest : I can, in
some measure, respect the other feelings which have been the
beginnings of apostasy ; I can respect the desire for unity
which would reclaim the Romanist by love, and the distrust
of his own heart which subjects the proselyte to priestly
power : I say I can respect these feelings, though I cannot
pardon unprincipled submission to them, nor enough wonder
at the infinite fatuity of the unhappy persons whom they have
betrayed. . . . But of all these fatuities, the basest is the
being lured into the Romanist Church by the glitter of it, like
larks into a trap by broken glass ; to be blown into a change
of religion by the whine of an organ-pipe ; stitched into a
new creed by the gold threads on priests' petticoats ; jangled
into a change of conscience by the chimes of a belfry. I know
nothing in the shape of error so dark as this, no imbecility so
absolute, no treachery so contemptible. I had hardly believed
that it was possible, though vague stories had been told me
of the effect on some minds, of mere scarlet and candles, until
I came on this passage in Pugin's *Remarks on Articles in the
Rambler* :

' " Those who have lived in want and privation are the
best qualified to appreciate the blessings of plenty : thus, to
those who have been devout and sincere members of the
separated portion of the English Church ; who have prayed

and hoped and loved, through all the poverty of the maimed rites which it has retained—to them does the realisation of all their longing desires appear truly ravishing. . . . Oh ! then, with what delight ! what joy unspeakable ! when one of the solemn piles is presented to them in all its pristine life and glory !—the stoups are filled to the brim ; the rood is raised on high ; the screen glows with sacred imagery and rich devices ; the niches are filled ; the altar is replaced, sustained by sculptured shafts, the relics of saints repose beneath, the Body of our Lord is enshrined on its consecrated stone ; the lamps of the sanctuary burn bright ; the saintly portraitures in the glass windows shine all gloriously ; and the alb hangs in the oaken ambries, and the cope chests are filled with orphreyed baudekins ; and pix and pax, and chrismatory are there, and thurible and cross."

' One might have put this man under a pix, and left him, one should have thought ; but he has been brought forward, and partly received, as an example of the effect of ceremonial splendour on the mind of a great architect. It is very necessary, therefore, that all those who have felt sorrow at this should know at once that he is not a great architect, but one of the smallest possible or conceivable architects[1] : and that by his own account and setting forth himself. Hear him :

' " I believe, as regards architecture, few men have been so unfortunate as myself. I have passed my life in thinking of fine things, studying fine things, designing fine things, and

---

[1] One is reminded of Ruskin's own estimate of himself in his early years : ' I had in my little clay pitcher vialsful, as it were, of Wordsworth's reverence, Shelley's sensitiveness, Turner's accuracy, all in one. A snowdrop was to me, as to Wordsworth, part of the Sermon on the Mount ; but I never should have written sonnets to the celandine, because it is of a coarse yellow, and imperfect in form.' [Quoted in *John Ruskin ;* by Marshall Mather ; p. 14.] Ruskin would seem to have progressed considerably since those early days : reverence, sensitiveness, and accuracy would seem to have dropped from him ' all in one ' on contact with a precursor who happened also be a Papist. ' One of the smallest possible or conceivable architects ' . . . A snowdrop probably was to Ruskin (we have his assertion for it), ' as to Wordsworth, part of the Sermon on the Mount ' ; but his words were ' of a coarse yellow ' : the yellow of bile.

realising very poor ones. I have never had the chance of producing a single fine ecclesiastical building, except my own church, where I am both paymaster and architect, but everything else, either for want of adequate funds or injudicious interference and control, or some other contingency, is more or less a failure. . . . St. George's was spoilt by the very instructions laid down by the committee, that it was to hold 3,000 people on the floor at a limited price; in consequence height, proportion, everything, was sacrificed to meet these conditions. Nottingham was spoilt by the style being restricted to lancet,—a period well suited to a Cistercian abbey in a secluded vale, but very unsuitable for the centre of a crowded town. . . . Kirkham was spoilt through several hundred pounds being reduced on the original estimate; to effect this, which was a great sum in proportion to the entire cost, the area of the church was contracted, the walls lowered, tower and spire reduced, the thickness of walls diminished, and stone arches omitted " (*Remarks, etc.*, by A. Welby Pugin: Dolman, 1850).

'Is that so? Phidias can niche himself into the corner of a pediment, and Raffaelle expatiate within the circumference of a clay platter, but Pugin is inexpressible in less than a cathedral. Let his ineffableness be assured of this, once for all, that no difficulty or restraint ever happened to a man of real power, but his power was the more manifested in the contending with or conquering it; and that there is no field so small, no cranny so contracted, but that a great spirit can house and manifest itself therein.' [1]

In parenthesis it may be noted that Pugin's 'great spirit' did practically nothing else but manifest itself in small fields and contracted crannies, and that 'his power was the more

---

[1] 'We have little time enough in human life, to watch men who are doing right, and to help them.' John Ruskin: additional footnote to that part of *The Stones of Venice* called " Infidelitas " (XCIX.).

manifested in the contending or conquering' his difficulties.
But that was not the point so far as Ruskin was concerned.
The point was that, while those who placed the stones of
Venice one upon another were, alas, Catholics, but dead,
Pugin was not only a Catholic but was alive, and, as such, his
spirit could be allowed no manifestation. Ruskin's feelings
towards Pugin would seem to have been well enough summed
up in his poetic address to his own heart, written at the age
of twelve :

> *' Oh, stay thee now,*
> *Oh, stay thee now,*
> *Thou little bounder, rest !'*

When that Appendix was written, the time was close at hand
when Pugin perforce would rest. His hundred years work in
forty was drawing to a close. Even his sea-hardened frame
could hold out no longer against the fire that burned within.
Only a little longer could that exacerbated brain answer to
the goad.

The Appendix, to Ruskin's credit omitted in later editions
after he had learned of Pugin's tragedy, goes on, first with a
little windy rhetoric, and then with a more direct attack :

'. . . Was it in parsimony that you buried its [St. George's]
paltry pinnacles in that eruption of diseased crockets ? or in
pecuniary embarrassment that you set up the belfry fools'
caps with the mimicry of dormer windows which nobody
can reach nor look out of ? Not so, but in mere incapability
of better things.'

It is related that,[1] when Pugin's attention was drawn to
Ruskin's strictures, he merely said : ' Let the fellow build
something himself' ; and then turned back to his work.
' Le critique d'art,' Huysmans wrote,[2] ' est généralement un
homme de lettres qui n'a pu produire de son propre cru un

---

[1] Inf. of Mr. S. Pugin Powell.   [2] *Certains* ; p. 11 (*Du Dilettantisme*).

véritable œuvre.' Ruskin's strictures might have appeared less graceless if he had been a man of greater practical experience.

However, Ruskin was not content to end his Appendix with a vicious snarl at the results of Pugin's labours, though ' the withering sarcasm of these remarks can scarcely be said to be warranted under any circumstances.'[1] The Pugin-Romanism combine had been kicked, as it were, but not yet killed. The transition from Pugin's incapability to Roman abuses was easy. It was made; and well made. But it is of more interest as illustrative of Ruskin than of Pugin. Yet the last sentence deserves quotation. It is a magnificent example of an appeal to what the modern daily press would doubtless call ' the sturdy common sense of the British Public'; to that spongy sentimentalism which was an insuperable barrier in the way of the religious aspirations of Pugin and his peers :

' I have but this exhortation for all who love them [' painted glass and coloured tiles '],—not to regulate their creeds by their taste in colours, but to hold calmly to the right, at what-ever present cost to their imaginative enjoyment; sure that they will one day find in heavenly truth a brighter charm than in earthly imagery, and striving chiefly to gather stones for the eternal building, whose walls shall be salvation, and whose gates shall be praise.'

It is believed among Catholics that ' the Gates of Hell shall not prevail ' against the Church. But, in England, the Church itself is not able to prevail against that kind of rhetoric. For the English mind, for the most part, tends to lap up that sort of thing. The same phenomenon might be seen in those newspaper religions recently ably handled by the Rev. Ronald

---

[1] *Ferrey;* p. 166. He adds : ' It so far exceeds the bounds of fairness, that thoughtful people feel shocked at finding a man of Ruskin's ability descending to such gross personalities, in order to embody in them the expression of his bitter aversion to Romanism.'

Knox in *Caliban in Grub Street*. One might be tempted to surmise that the English mind has two instinctive prayers : to be freed from exact thought and from the Catholic Church.

Ruskin was an answer to both. He was just what the public wanted. He could give it untainted Art ; and at that time the public, having seen the possibility of the spread of beauty, was avid for æsthetic indulgence. But Ruskin could do more than that. To those who still found Art a little difficult, he could give himself : his works themselves were an æsthetic indulgence. As Sir Edmund Gosse quaintly put it[1] in a sentence of Ruskinian flavour in *The London Mercury* : ' Ruskin for instance, above all the Victorian prose writers, shouts like the morning star.' Pugin merely shouted like an earnest man, and a Papist at that.

Puginism, in consequence, was not only dead but damned. Gothic architecture was disinfected. From that time onwards any respectable Protestant parent could allow his child to go into a mediæval cathedral without fear of his being dragged over to Rome by a suddenly unleashed ambry, or lured thither by the seductive charms of an orphreyed baudekin.

It may be doubted if Ruskin himself, having risen on the ashes of Pugin's dead self to higher things, whole-heartedly desired the result which he had brought about. At any rate, he toned down some of the more Protestant passages for the 1880 edition of *The Seven Lamps*, and even at one time underwent a ' Romeward' tendency himself. For Ruskin was a man with a divided mind : Nonconformity and æsthetics are uneasy bedfellows, as is shown by an entry in his diary of 1843 [2] :

' Curious essay of Newman's, full of intellect, but doubtful in tendency. I fear insidious ; yet I liked it.'

Gothic architecture, too, was insidious, and he liked it. So it had to be accepted and at the same time purged. The feat

---

[1] Essay on *George Eliot*.   [2] Quoted in *Clark* ; p. 259.

was not without precedent : Dr. Bowdler in another sphere
had done his work. But Ruskin was to perform a more
surprising feat than Bowdler. Child of the Gothic Revival,
he went through a mental struggle followed by a meta-
morphosis, and blossomed out as that movement's patriarch.
The process was four-fold : he shouted like the morning star ;
he thrust Pugin contemptuously to oblivion ; he slandered
the Catholic Church ; and, curious piece of homœopathic
healing, he imported Italian Gothic.

The refusal of Balliol to make use of Pugin's drawings was
symbolical : even his ideas had to be expounded by a non-
Catholic before they could receive general acceptance, being
changed in the process. The fact that the introduction of
Italian Gothic was part of that change was not only ironic :
it was also both disastrous and symbolical. That it was
disastrous may be judged by anyone who cares to examine
almost any of its many manifestations.[1] It was symbolical,
for it showed that Gothic had once more lost touch with
simplicity, and had become again a thing of fashion.

Mr. E. T. Cook neatly sums up that aspect of the matter in
his Introduction to the second volume of *The Stones of
Venice* :

' The Gothic Revival in England did not originate with
Ruskin, but he gave to it a stimulus and an extension ; he
made it popular, and gave to it the force derived from his
incomparable resources of argument, imagination and
eloquence. " We do not remember anything in the history
of art in England," wrote a reviewer in the year following the
completion of *The Stones of Venice*, " at all corresponding in
suddenness and extent to the effect which the works of Mr.
Ruskin have already exercised upon the popular taste directly,

---

[1] Its shameful flower may conveniently be studied in north Oxford. ' A man
who paganizes *in the Universities* deserves no quarter ' : what they deserve who
dropped their architectural mongrels along the Woodstock and Banbury Roads, no
man can tell. Pugin might, perhaps, have given some hints.

and through popular taste on the taste and theories of artists themselves." '

This is not the place, however, to trace the ponderous decline of the Gothic Revival. The introduction of Italian Gothic was a means of that decline, not a cause. The cause of the decline is to be found in the nature of the Revival itself : Ruskinism, as it were, was only the crest of a wave which was already doomed to break.

The Gothic Revival was fundamentally unsound. All that Pugin could do was to discover ' true principles ' and use them to uphold an unsound edifice. ' As Herr Bruno Taut says, " the work of the architect lies in the interpretation of a new social order." ' [1] Pugin's error lay in not realising that the social order was new. To his mind, the ' pagans ' were but an invasion ; as it were merely an iridescent scum on the clear pool of social life. Clear away the scum, and, like a pool freed from a film of oil, the underlying mediæval life would once more thrust up its natural growths into the air— St. Mary Redcliffe, Salisbury. . . . But there was no under- lying mediæval life. There was nothing, as it were, in which his work could strike deep roots. This is not to say that masterly Gothic work was not done, is not being done, nor will be done ; only that Gothic could never again become the permanent and normal mode of expression. And that was what Pugin desired.

Because this was so, and quite apart from Ruskinian con- tempt, Pugin tends always to be seen (if looked at at all) in the wrong perspective. For he set out, as it were, to restore a whole neglected country to cultivation, and, owing to a change in the nature of the soil, was only able to cultivate a garden. When a man attempts the gigantic and impossible, and fails, it tends to be overlooked that he has achieved anything at all : Pugin was relegated merely to a position

[1] E. Prentice Mawson, in *The Studio ;* vol. 97, p. 362.

among those 'who spell it chaunted', among those early æsthetes who only were not adequately willowy because Rosetti's Blessed Damosel had not yet arrived to show them the correct postures. That is false.

'The modern world,' Mr. Chesterton writes,[1] 'is largely divided into two sorts of mediævalists : the silly æsthetes who think it very modern to be mediæval and the good craftsmen who have realised that it is very mediæval to be modern.' That was even truer in Pugin's time than it is to-day. But before Pugin began his life-work, only the first class existed. He was the first man to realise that it is very mediæval to be modern. His mistake lay in not being quite modern enough.

But he was modern enough for one thing : he reinstituted sincerity and good craftsmanship. The Gothic Revival as such might change and falter and decay ; but the spirit that could say in an age of artistic frippery that a man must go out of his way to make a thing badly was not to perish.

It has not perished yet.

In the long gallery of those who, in the last hundred years, have saved, and increased, and handed down whatever there is of artistic life in England, one picture has been badly hung. It deserves to be hung in a better light. It contains the figure of a tough little man, with dark hair, and flashing eyes, and a hearty laugh, dressed in semi-nautical clothes.

[1] *The Resurrection of Rome* ; p. 29.

APPENDICES

APPENDIX I

WORKS CITED

WITH certain exceptions, mentioned in the text, the works cited are as follows :—

Apology.	A. Welby Pugin : *An Apology for the Revival of Christian Architecture in England ;* 1843.
Art-Architect.	Edward Welby Pugin : *Who was the Art Architect of the Houses of Parliament ? A Statement of Facts,* founded on the letters of Sir Charles Barry and the diaries of Augustus Welby Pugin ; 1867.
Barry.	Rev. Alfred Barry, D.D. : *The Life and Works of Sir Charles Barry, R.A., F.R.S. ;* 1867.
Bumpus.	T. Francis Bumpus : *London Churches Ancient & Modern. Second Series : Classical & Modern.*
Cheetham.	F. H. Cheetham : Art. in *Lancashire & Cheshire Antiquarian Society ;* Vol. XXIV.
Clark.	Kenneth Clark : *The Gothic Revival ; an Essay in the History of Taste ;* 1928.
Crace.	J. D. Crace : *Augustus Welby Pugin and Furniture ;* an article in *Journal R.I.B.A.*
Eastlake.	Charles L. Eastlake : *A History of the Gothic Revival ;* 1872.
Ferrey.	Benjamin Ferrey : *Recollections of A. N. Welby Pugin, and his father, Augustus Pugin ; With Notices of their Works. . . . With an Appendix by E. Sheridan Purcell, Esq. ;* 1861.
Gillow.	Joseph Gillow : *A Literary and Biographical History or Bibliographical Dictionary of the English Catholics,* &c. ; 1885.
Gwynn.	Denis Gwynn : *Cardinal Wiseman ;* 1929.
Kelly.	Bernard W. Kelly : *Historical Notes on English Catholic Missions ;* 1907.
Lingard.	Martin Haile & Edwin Bonney : *Life and Letters of John Lingard, 1771–1851.*
Oscotian, 88.	*The Oscotian ;* Jubilee Number, 1888.
Oscotian, 19.	*The Oscotian ;* Vol. XIX., Part 3, 1919.
Phillipps.	Edmund Sheridan Purcell : *Life and Letters of Ambrose Phillipps de Lisle ;* edited and finished by Edwin de Lisle ; 1900.

Present State.   A. Welby Pugin : *The Present State of Ecclesiastical Architecture in England ;* 1843.

Q. R.   *The Quarterly Review.*

Rambler.   *The Rambler ;* Vol. V. New Series ; 1861.

Rood Screens.   A. Welby Pugin : *A Treatise on Chancel Screens and Rood Lofts,* &c. ; 1851.

St. Edmund's Chapel.   Bernard Ward : *St. Edmund's College Chapel ;* 1903.

St. Edmund's College.   Bernard Ward : *History of St. Edmund's College, Old Hall ;* 1893.

Sequel.   The Right Rev. Bernard Ward : *The Sequel to Catholic Emancipation ;* 1915.

Sirr, F.R.I.B.A.   Harry Sirr : *Augustus Welby Pugin : a Sketch ;* an article in *Journal R.I.B.A. ;* August, 1918.

Some Remarks.   A. Welby Pugin : *Some Remarks on the Articles which have recently appeared in the ' Rambler,'* &c. ; 1850.

True Principles.   A. Welby Pugin : *The True Principles of Pointed or Christian Architecture,* &c. ; 1841.

W. G. Ward.   Wilfrid Ward : *William George Ward and the Catholic Revival ;* 1893.

Ward (Oxford).   Wilfrid Ward : *William George Ward and the Oxford Movement ;* 1889.

Weedall.   Rev. Henry Weedall, D.D. : *A Funeral Discourse, delivered in the domestic chapel of Alton Towers, after the Solemn Requiem Mass celebrated for John, Earl of Shrewsbury, on Tuesday, the 14th of December,* 1852 ; 1852.

Wickham.   Rev. W. A. Wickham : Art. in *Transactions of the Historic Society of Lancashire and Cheshire.* New Series. Vol. XXIII.

Wiseman.   Wilfrid Ward : *The Life and Times of Cardinal Wiseman ;* 1912.

APPENDIX II

BUILDINGS, &C.

[This list is in no wise complete, but may serve to give an idea of the extent and variety of Pugin's labours. My thanks are due to many people, but for whose courteous response to requests for information it would have lacked still more in completeness and accuracy.]

A volume of *sixty-four drawings* of an (imaginary) ' *St. Marie's College*,' 1833–4; now (with six more books containing *designs* for church buildings and various church furniture, and a great number of *water-colour drawings* and *pencil sketches*) in the possession of Mr. Charles Henry Purcell, a grandson of Pugin, and partner (with Mr. Sebastian Pugin Powell) in the firm of Pugin & Pugin, of London and Liverpool. Also another large collection of *drawings* and *sketches* in the possession of Mr. Sebastian Pugin Powell.

BERKSHIRE.

DANESFIELD. *Church of St. Charles*. Middle Pointed. 1851. Built for Mr. Charles Robert Scott-Murray, of Danesfield, and since demolished. ' This was the last work which Pugin executed.' [*East-lake; p. 389.*]

READING. *Church of St. James*. Foundation-stone, 14 Dec. 1837; opened, 5 Aug. 1840. Originally a very simple Norman Church (nave and chancel) built of rubble from the ruins of the Abbey. ' In the autumn of 1883 it underwent considerable improvements under the direction of Messrs. Westlake.' [*Kelly; p. 329.*] New works begun in 1925 : large porch with baptistery at west end ; ambulatory round High Altar ; sanctuary enlarged ; new communion rails ; Lady Chapel added on south side, the southern wall being pierced with low Norman arches.

BUCKINGHAMSHIRE.

GREAT MARLOW. *Church of St. Peter*. Foundation-stone, 2 July 1845. Spire, 70 feet high. Built for Mr. Charles Robert Scott-Murray, of Danesfield.

CAMBRIDGESHIRE.

CAMBRIDGE. Restoration of *Jesus College Chapel*. This work is a notable embodiment of the mediæval spirit. For a full account, see *The Architectural History of Cambridge*, Vol. II., p. 147; by Willis and Clarke.

CAMBRIDGE. *East window* (by Hardman) in *Magdalene College Chapel*.

CAMBRIDGE. *Church of St. Andrew.* 'Great indignation was manifested at this in the University when the project became known. On November 5 a large body of students assembled to tear up the foundations, but retreated at the prospect of an encounter with a body of burly Irishmen and a force of special constables under the command of the mayor, Thomas Fisher, Esq.' [*Kelly;* p. 115.] Opened on Feast of St. George, 1843. Pronounced by the Camden Society 'a hidden gem.' Very small; since demolished, and replaced by the present larger church of Our Lady and the English Martyrs.

CHESHIRE.

MACCLESFIELD. *Church of St. Alban.* Begun, 1839; opened, 26 May 1841. East window given by Lord Shrewsbury.

NESTON. *Church of St. Winifride.* Opened, 29 Nov. 1843.

CUMBERLAND.

WARWICK BRIDGE. *Church of St. Mary.* Begun, 1840; opened, Nov. 1841.

DENBIGHSHIRE.

CHIRK. (1) Alterations at *Chirk Castle,* for Col. Robert Myddelton-Biddulph, about 1844, including an outside corridor of freestone, with front door, running the whole length of the courtyard on the east side of the Castle, and giving entry to various rooms. This, which is thought to have taken the place of a sort of arched verandah, still exists as built. (2) *Girls' School,* 1844, for Mrs. Myddelton-Biddulph, including the room to the south of the Bell Turret and the Schoolmistress' House. A porch, to the north of the Bell Turret, and two rooms were added between 1852 and 1874. Infants' Dept. added about 1905. The part with the south aspect by Pugin is a very good example of his work.

DERBYSHIRE.

DERBY. *Church of St. Mary.* Begun, 1838; dedicated, 9 Oct. 1839. Redecorated, 1892 and 1930. 'It is without exception the most magnificent thing the Catholics have yet done in modern times in this country, and is quite worthy of ancient days. The church is all of stone with three aisles, a glorious tower and a very rich sanctuary ornamented with beautiful stained windows and rich broad hangings, all given, as well as very splendid vestments, by Lord Shrewsbury. . . . On the whole it would not have done dishonour to Rome.' [*Wiseman;* I., p. 310; quoting letter from Wiseman, 11 Oct. 1839.] 'It is, we believe, one of the finest modern structures in England, and being the first entire work of Pugin, has excited general interest.' [*The Catholic Magazine;* Sep. 1839; p. 629.] See Chapter XI.

DURHAM.

STOCKTON-ON-TEES. *Church of St. Mary.* 1842. Early English. 'A small but elegantly proportioned church, of which the design is considerably in advance of its date.' [*Eastlake;* p. 379.]

Ushaw College. (1) St. Cuthbert's Church. Foundation-stone, 23 Apr. 1844; solemn opening, 11 Oct. 1848; demolished, 1882, as it had become too small, the old materials being largely used in the new building; Pugin's high altar and reredos now in the chapel of the Sacred Heart. (2) Chapels of the Holy Family and of St. Joseph, 1852, the altar and reredos in the latter being Edward Pugin's first work after his father's retirement. (3) Brass paschal candlestick; made by Hardman; shown at Great Exhibition, 1851, and at Dublin Exhibition. (4) Raising and improving the refectory, including a new fireplace and the massive oak tables and benches. The room has since been lengthened 40 feet, and otherwise altered.

EDINBURGH.

EDINBURGH. *Victoria Hall*, Castle Hill, in collaboration with James Gillespie Graham (for whom see Chapters IV. and IX.). Foundation-stone, 3 Sep. 1842. The tower is not by A. W. N. P. and J. G. G.

FRANCE.

DOUAI. Chapel and refectory of *St. Edmund's College* (afterwards Abbey). Foundation-stone, 1840. 'Pugin at first intended this to be at least sixty feet in height; but he was overruled by Superiors, who caused him to modify his plans, and beneath the chapel to design the refectory, which was almost a replica of the exquisite little structure above it.' [*Tercentenary of St. Edmund's Monastery,* &c.; ed. by Very Rev. F. C. Doyle, O.S.B.; p. 52.] Decorated by Hardman, 1851. Since 1903, when the Religious Orders were expelled from France, it appears not to have been used. It suffered from bombardment during the late War, and is falling into decay.

GALWAY.

BALLINASLOE. *Church.*

GLOUCESTERSHIRE.

WOODCHESTER PARK. (1) Plans (never carried out) for a fine *manor house*, an *abbey*, and a *church* with clerestoried nave, north and south aisles, separate chancel with rood-loft, and a north tower and low spire, for Mr. William Leigh, of Woodchester Park. (2) Design for a *tea and breakfast set* ordered by Mr. William Leigh for the priest at the mission which he had started at Nympsfield. It is a simple design of trefoils in dark blue on white china, and some of it is still in the possession of Miss Leigh at Scar Hill, Woodchester Park.

GUERNSEY.

ST. PETER PORT. *Church of St. Joseph & St. Mary.*

HAMPSHIRE.

CHRISTCHURCH. (1) *Communion Table* in the chancel of the Priory Church, on the site of the monastic High Altar; incised in black letter on the front chamfer (' . ' here standing for crosses pommée) : ' . this . table . was . made . and . presented . to . this . church . by . Augustus . Welby . Pugin . A + D . 1831 . ' A resolution of thanks for the gift was passed by the Vestry on 20 May 1831. [*Christchurch Miscellany ;* 1930; p. 558.] The Table was probably made at the Hart Street Works a month or two before the failure of that undertaking. See Chapter IV. (2) *Tombstone* over the grave of his first wife, in the north chancel aisle of the Priory Church. See Chapter IV.

SOUTHAMPTON. *Church of St. John.* Begun early in 1843 ; opened, Oct. 1843. Owing to the bankruptcy of the builder, and the failure of the building fund, only the chancel was completed to Pugin's designs. The chancel arches were raised by Leonard Stokes in 1888, who also raised the roof of the sanctuary, put in a larger window behind the high altar, and extended the sanctuary (which had ended at the middle pillars) to the front imitation-marble pillars. In 1911, Pugin's altar was replaced by an expensive but unsuitable attempt by Canon Scoles.

HERTFORDSHIRE.

WARE. (1) *St. Edmund's College Chapel.* See Chapter XVI. (2) A *house*, now St. Hugh's Preparatory School, near St. Edmund's College, built for Mr. William George Ward in 1846. See Chapter XVII.

KENT.

RAMSGATE. *Church of St. Augustine* (opened on the Vigil of the Assumption, 1851) and *The Grange.* See Chapter XVIII.

KERRY.

KILLARNEY. *Cathedral of St. Mary of the Assumption.* Founded, 1842 ; consecrated, 22 Aug. 1855 ; completed, 1912. 'I am exceedingly delighted to perceive from your last Tablet that public attention is at length drawn to the lamentable state of the new cathedral at Killarney. . . . The glazing, flooring, and I believe some external doors, are the *only indispensable works* which remain to be completed. . . . Now, it is a grievous pity to see a structure which, by its arrangement and detail, fully recal the ancient ecclesiastical edifices of Ireland in the days of her Catholic glory, left not only in a useless but in a decaying state, for the want of a comparatively small amount of well-directed expenditure.' [Pugin : letter to *The Tablet*, 23 March 1850.]

KILDARE.

MAYNOOTH. *Plans* for *St. Patrick's College.* See p. 111

LANCASHIRE.

BURNLEY. *Reredos* of high altar of St. Mary's Church (Hadfield & Weightman, archts.). Pugin's ' work here, it must be confessed, suffers by comparison with that of the architects of the church. . . . The *west window*, supplied by Messrs. Hardman & Co., from a design by Pugin, is very good for its date [about 1844 ?] and indeed superior to those put up at a later period by the same firm. The masonry of this and other churches erected by Mr. Hadfield exhibits evidence of an appreciation of those " true principles " of constructive detail which were then more preached than practised. The window arches, &c., instead of being turned in large blocks of stone, according to the prevailing custom, are executed in small and numerous voussoirs, which give scale and significance to the work.' [*Eastlake;* p. 243. And see also *True Principles;* p. 17, quoted in Chapter XIV.]

CLAUGHTON-ON-BROCK. A strengthening *calix* fitted at the base of the bowl of a pre-Reformation chalice now at St. Thomas's Chapel.

KIRKHAM. *Church of St. John the Evangelist,* commonly called the Church of the Holy Cross. Consecrated, 22, opened, 23 Apr. 1845. ' Its peal of bells was the first heard from a Catholic church in England since the Reformation.' [*Kelly;* p. 436.] Spire, 110 feet high. Seats 500–600. Owing to the lowering of the floor, an undue amount of the bases of the piers is exposed, giving them an ungraceful appearance. Chancel altered, 1897. The high altar has been removed to a side altar, an excessive marble erection taking its place. Both side altars now cut off a large part of the windows at the east ends of the aisles. The rood screen has been removed to the west end of the church, and glazed. Redecorated, 1931. See p. 322.

LIVERPOOL. *Church of St. Mary.* Decorated. Foundation-stone, 1 May 1844; opened, 1 July; consecrated, 18 Aug. 1845, when ' the solemnities connected with the opening were continued for eight days.' [*Cath. Rec. Soc.;* IX., p. 191.] In 1883–4 the site was bought by the Lancs. & Yorks. Rly. Co. for the Exchange Station, and the church was pulled down and rebuilt, by Edmund Peter (commonly known as ' Peter Paul ') Pugin, third and youngest son of Pugin by his third wife, in High-field Street, being shortened 14 feet in the process. ' An excellent example of a *town* church.' [*Eastlake;* p. 377.] The tower is a recent addition.

LIVERPOOL. *Convent of Mercy,* Mount Vernon Street, 1841–3. The first convent in Liverpool. *New wing* (cloister, corridor, and novice-ship), 1847. He also designed the *Girls' Orphanage* near by, which no longer exists.

LIVERPOOL. *Church of Our Lady of the Annunciation, Bishop Eaton.* Rebuilt by Edward Welby Pugin, some of Pugin's work being incorporated.

LIVERPOOL. *Church of St. Oswald, Old Swan.* Foundation-stone, 1840; opened, 7 Aug. 1842. Cost £5,000. Has been slightly extended to the west on either side of the tower, and has been redecorated. Rood screen removed to western end and the rood hung at entrance to chancel. The handling seems to have been sympathetic throughout, and the church remains as a good example of what Pugin could achieve on a limited outlay. It contains some fine and characteristically solid examples of his craftsmanship in wood and metal. Two of the three side-windows in the chancel are later insertions, Pugin's being that nearest the altar on the south side.

MANCHESTER. *Church of St. Wilfrid, Hulme.* Early English. Begun, 1839. 'How far he [Pugin] succeeded in this endeavour [to prove that Gothic was no more expensive than ' classic '] may be inferred from the fact that the entire cost of the church (which will hold a congregation of about 800 persons) and of the priest's house attached to it, did not exceed 5,000*l*.' [*Eastlake;* p. 160.] The cost thus works out at £6 5s. per head. The scale of expenditure on which Pugin too often had to work is shown on comparing this with St. Luke's, Chelsea, designed by Savage in 1824, which was for a congregation of 2,500 and cost £40,000, i.e. £16 per head. [*Ib.;* p. 141.] See also p. 110.

SALFORD. *Plans* for *St. John's Cathedral;* 'which building was afterwards erected by Mr. Hadfield, as Pugin could not be induced to give way on some point of principle.' [*Ferrey;* pp. 275–6.]

SCARISBRICK HALL. See Chapter X.

SOUTHPORT. *Church of St. Mary.* Foundation-stone, 22 July 1840; dedicated, 20 May 1841. Lord Shrewsbury gave the stained glass window over the altar. 'I built a solemn church at Southport. It was opened with a perfectly disgusting display and a bill ending with an Ordinary at 2 o'clock, 3/6 each.' [Pugin to March-Phillipps, 18 Dec. 1840; *Phillipps;* II., p. 214.] The church has been entirely rebuilt, part of the original material being used.

WAVERTREE. *House* (then named *Oswaldcroft*) and *furniture* for Mr. Oswald Sharples. Now used by the Sisters of Nazareth as a home for incurables. It adjoins the Church of Our Lady of the Annunciation in Woolton Road.

WHALLEY. *Window,* executed by Hardman, 1847, at the east end of the Lady Chapel in *St. Mary's Church :* three lights (St. John, Virgin & Child, St. Anne) and tracery-lights above.

WINWICK. Rebuilding *Chancel* of *St. Oswald's Church,* 1847–8; 'a fine and well-designed work with a high-pitched leaded roof, a four-light east window, and three-light windows on north and south.' [*Vict. County Hist. Lancs.;* IV., p. 124.[1]] 'One of his finest works.' [*Ferrey;* p. 275.] 'I am always glad to see your handwriting, and you know the great interest I take in this work, which is the first chancel that has been properly carried out.' [Pugin to Rev. James John Hornby, 1847; *Wickham,* p. 145.] 'I never so [*sic*] Mr. Pugin so particular in my life to make a fine job.' [G. Myers to Hornby, 17 Mar. 1847; *ib.,* p. 152.] *Glass* (by Hardman) also designed by Pugin. Of the east window he wrote : 'I never took so much pains with a window in my life.' [P. to Hornby, 26 May 1848; *ib.,* p. 153.] 'This Chancel, impaired by time and injured in the Great Rebellion, was rebuilt on its old foundation and restored to its original form, in more than its original beauty, in the years of Our Lord MDCCCXLVII and MDCCCXLVIII. James J. Hornby, Rector. A. Welby Pugin, Master of the Work. George

---

[1] The Church of St. Mary, Little Crosby, is also stated in *Vict. County Hist.* to be Pugin's work; but erroneously. [Inf. of Mr. F. N. Blundell, of Crosby.]

Myers, Builder. Laus Deo.' [Brass plate in Winwick Chancel.] Pugin also designed a *carpet* for the sanctuary.

LEICESTERSHIRE.

COALVILLE. *Monastery* of *St. Bernard*. Early pointed. 1839–42. ' These buildings, which are picturesquely situated, consist of a cloister, church, chapter-house, refectory, dormitory, guest-house, prior's lodgings, &c. The design of the whole is simple to severity, the massive walls of rubble granite, long narrow windows, steep roofs, and gables being thoroughly characteristic of old monastic architecture.' [*Eastlake;* p. 379.] See Chapter XII.

GARENDON. (1) *Designs* (never carried out) of a ' gorgeous church' for Mr. Ambrose Lisle March-Phillipps. [*Phillipps;* II., p. 320.] (2) ' a series of exquisite drawings, preserved in the Library at Garendon, which, if carried out, would have made old Garendon, then a ramshackled rats' castle, into a miniature palace of Westminster, with the twenty-seven old fish-ponds artistically connected one with another, to form a complete moat of defence, which was to have been approached by a drawbridge and gateway.' [*Ib.;* p. 286.]

GRACE-DIEU MANOR. (1) *Alterations & additions to St. Mary's Chapel.* ' He soon pursuaded his host to allow him to put in a better gothic chancel-arch of the decorated period, and a beautiful screen of carved oak was added. The Rood was painted and gilded all over, glorified as a Rood should be, for " Christ dyeth now no more, death shall have no more dominion over him." Lord Shrewsbury gave the figure of the Crucified, which was treasured as the Rood of Zion Abbey before the Reformation, carried to Spain by the fugitive nuns, and brought back by the great Duke of Wellington ; and Pugin had figures of S. John and the Blessed Virgin carved to suit.' [*Phillipps;* II., p. 289.] (2) *Altar* with stone canopy, or *ciborium*, in the chapel of the Blessed Sacrament. 1848. ' [It] is one of the handsomest works of Pugin that I have seen anywhere, at least for the size.' [Letter from March-Phillipps, 13 Dec. 1848 ; *Ib.;* p. 334.] ' This ciborium Pugin always considered his best effort in the reproduction of that most beautiful feature of early and mediæval church architecture so seldom seen except in the Roman basilikas.' [*Ib.;* p. 290.]

HIGH CADEMAN. *Chapel of the Holy Sepulchre.* ' It was in 1837 that the first Catholic procession of a ritual kind was attempted, since the Reformation, along the public highways. It took place at Whitwick and started from the chapel of the Holy Sepulchre on the rocks, near High Cademan, which had lately been erected in imitation of the wayside chapels of the Tyrol by Augustus Pugin. It is in the early English Gothic style . . . and when it was first erected excited the superstitious fears of the inhabitants of impending woe for the family upon whose lands it had been placed.' [*Phillipps;* II., p. 312.]

SHEPSHED. *Church of St. Winifride,* ' I hope before many months are over Pugin will have erected there a neat little £300 chapel.' [Letter from March-Phillipps, Jan. 1841 ; *Phillipps;* I., p. 108.]

WHITWICK. *Chapel of the Holy Cross.* Accommodation for about 200. Consecrated, 12 Oct. 1837. Demolished, and replaced by a larger building, 1905.

WYMESWOLD. *Restoration of St. Mary's Church :* '.the first of the old parish churches to be restored upon Catholic lines with return-stalls and rood-screen.' [*Phillipps ;* I., pp. 340–1.]   See Appendix III. (21).

LIMERICK.

ADARE MANOR. Work there for the second Earl of Dunraven & Mount-Earl, of which two mantelpieces probably now alone remain.

LINCOLNSHIRE.

LEADENHAM. *Decoration of chancel roof of St. Swithin's Church,* 1841, for Rev. Bernard Smith—' a most glorious man.' [*Wiseman ;* I., p. 424.] Together with Mr. Smith's service, it was declared by the Bishop of Lincoln to be ' unmistakably Roman.' [*Wiseman ;* I., p. 411.] Mr. Smith was shortly afterwards received into the Church and collaborated with Pugin in his *Glossary.* See Chapter XVIII. Pugin did the work himself. It has never been touched since, and is still in excellent preservation, though somewhat hidden by an elaborate screen put up about 1891.

LINCOLN. *St. Anne's Bede Houses.* Founded by Rev. Richard Waldo Sibthorp (1792–1879), who became a Catholic late in 1841, returned to the Church of England in Oct. 1843 (causing Dr. Wiseman to spend the day in bed), and returned to the Catholic Church in 1865. It is probably to him that Pugin wrote in his last illness (see p. 304), though the justification for calling him ' cousin ' is not clear. The chapel is by Butterfield. The houses for the porter and nurse were added about 1929.

LONDON.

BERMONDSEY. *Convent of Mercy.* First occupied, 19 Nov. 1839, two rooms being then finished. The first Convent of Mercy in England. ' Mother McAuley was no great admirer of the famous Pugin style. Bermondsey Convent she described as not likely to be dry for three years. . . . " Mr. Pugin [she wrote] was determined we should not look out of the windows, they are up to the ceiling. We could not touch the glass without standing on a chair. We have one good room finished with brown walls and a long table. There is too much room in some places, and too little in others. The noviceship is very small, the kitchen fit for a castle. It is nearly the best room in the house. I have seldom seen such a general favourite as Mr. Pugin is in this part of England. Nothing is perfect, that he does not plan and execute. Yet I do think, though he has certainly manifested much taste, that some of his plans would admit of improvement. For example, he has brought the Cells close to the Chapel door. I do not admire his gilded figures of Saints. They are very coarse representations, and by no means calculated to inspire devotion." ' [*Life of the Foundress of the Sisters of Mercy* (Catherine Elizabeth McAuley).] The buildings have received additions.

The original wood-block of Pugin's drawing of them is still in the possession of the Convent.

FARM STREET. *High altar* (Caen stone, painted and decorated with gold leaf) in the *Church of the Immaculate Conception*; with inscription: 'Pray for the good estate of Monica Tempest, of whose goods this altar was made, 1848.'

FULHAM. *Church of St. Thomas of Canterbury*. 1847. A fine specimen of Pugin's work, but extensive alterations are contemplated. The tower has been cut down, but its restoration is proposed. The painting on the altars is modern.

ST. PANCRAS. *Designs* for *glass*, executed by Hardman, in the great seven-light east window of *St. Mary Magdalene's Church*. He 'considered this about the best window which, up to that period, the Revival had succeeded in producing.' [*Bumpus*; p. 204.]

SOUTHWARK. *Cathedral of St. George*, including Petre and Knill Chantries. Decorated. See Chapter XVI.

WANDSWORTH. *Church of St. Thomas of Canterbury*; 'a new and elegant structure in the Perpendicular style' [quoted in *Kelly*; p. 413]; foundation-stone, 25 May 1847; opened, 3 Nov. 1847. Pugin's original plan (which he supplied, with estimates, in a few days) was for a church costing £3,000 without fittings. This being too costly, he was asked to design a school which might serve as a church until funds could be raised, a purpose which it served for nearly fifty years, being turned into a school on its supersession by the present larger church of St. Thomas.

WESTMINSTER. *Houses of Parliament*, in conjunction with Mr. (afterwards Sir Charles) Barry. See Chapters IX. and XIX.

WESTMINSTER. *Design* (never carried out) for 'an *archiepiscopal cross*, to stand always in the house, and be borne in procession' for the Archdiocese of Westminster. 'It ought to be worthy of the re-establishment of the Hierarchy, and to record its history (but I must be content with something plain from Belgium, though Pugin has made a splendid design).' [Letter from Wiseman, 17 Oct. 1850; *Wiseman*; I., p. 532.]

WOOLWICH. *Church of St. Peter*. Begun, 20 Oct. 1842; opened, 26 Oct. 1843. Accommodation, about 2,000. Very much altered.

NORFOLK.

KING'S LYNN. *Church of St. Mary*. 1844–5. Built on sand; foundations gave way; new church built, 1896, some of Pugin's work being incorporated.

NORTHUMBERLAND.

NEWCASTLE-UPON-TYNE. *Cathedral of St. Mary*. Opened, 21 Aug. 1844. The spire is not Pugin's work. Completely redecorated, 1881.

NOTTINGHAMSHIRE.

NOTTINGHAM. *Cathedral of St. Barnabas* and *Bishop's House*. Early English. Almost entirely paid for by Lord Shrewsbury. 'A large cruciform church, in which the choir and high altar are surrounded by aisles, with a Lady Chapel beyond. Beneath the choir is a crypt, of which the vaulting is carried on two rows of short columns. The interior is sumptuously fitted up with a large rood-loft, and oak screens of open tracery and panelled work enclosing the chapels, &c. The choir and sanctuary are paved with encaustic tiles.' [*Eastlake*; p. 379.] ' Nottingham was spoilt by the style being restricted to lancet, a period well suited to a Cistercian Abbey in a secluded vale, but very unsuitable for the centre of a crowded town. If fine tracery windows, admitting a due proportion of light, had been introduced, it would have been a grand and satisfactory building; but this was impossible to obtain, and even the width of the lights was regulated, so there was nothing left but to make the best of it under the circumstances, and the result has been what might be expected, the church is too dark, and *I am blamed for it.*' [*Some Remarks*]. The cathedral has since been lengthened, and this, added to its former gloom, causes it to be known familiarly as ' the Tunnel.'

NOTTINGHAM. *Convent of Mercy*, including Chapel and School (St. Catherine's). Stained glass, and decoration of chapel, by Hardman. Opened, though only north and east sides then completed, 26 Oct. 1846.

OXFORDSHIRE.

OXFORD. *Gateway to Magdalen College*. Temp. Henry VI. 1840. ' A pure and graceful example of the architect's skill.' [*Eastlake*; p. 377.] See p. 140.

OXFORD. *Memorial windows in the Church of St. Mary the Virgin*. (1) At the east end of the south aisle, to Thomas William Bartley, who died 18 May 1843. ' In less than a quarter of an hour he had made two or three masterly sketches for the subject of the window, to the astonishment of all present.' [*Ferrey*; p. 189.] (2) In the south aisle, to his sister, Sophia Catherine Bartley. Money was left to keep these windows cleaned and in good repair.

RADFORD. *Chapel of the Holy Trinity*. Opened, 21 Jan. 1841. See p. 126.

SOMERSET.

STRATTON-ON-THE-FOSSE. Two *designs* (never carried out) for *Downside Priory* (afterwards Abbey): (1) 1839. ' It preserved the building of 1823, but remodelled the Old House, and carried thence northwards, over the ground now occupied by the gymnasium, a monastery wing, 300 feet long, facing the Fosse Road; at the end another wing at right-angles contained kitchens, workshops, etc. This plan provided no new school buildings and no church besides the Old Chapel.' [*The Downside Review*; June 1914, p. 46.] (2) 1842. ' The style adopted for this structure is early lancet, as combining simplicity with true ecclesiastical character. Each alley of the cloister will measure above one hundred and fifty feet in length, the refectory eighty by thirty, the wall three and four feet thick; which may afford some data by which the extent and solidity of the buildings can be imagined. They will be constructed on the ancient principle of convenience and strength combined, without affectation of forced regularity or unnecessary features. Each portion of the edifice will bespeak its purpose, from the chapter-house to the kitchen. Roofs and chimney shafts stand forth undisguised in all the unadorned grandeur produced by their extent and solidity; and, when completed, this building will furnish an admirable proof of the vast superiority of effect which is produced by the *natural architecture of our Catholic ancestors* over the *mock-regularity system of modern builders.*' [*Present State;* pp. 106–7.] ' The plans were accepted, and a beginning was actually made—at least of cutting the stones'; but ' a will, under which it had been hoped to build the first portion, was disputed, and a lawsuit ensued; and thus it came to pass that the stones were used for new farm buildings, and the monastery was postponed.' [*The Downside Review;* June 1914, p. 48.] See p. 265.

STAFFORDSHIRE.

ALTON. (1) *Alterations and additions,* including Entrance Lodge, at *Alton Towers.* See Chapter XI. (2) *Hospital of St. John the Baptist.* Perpendicular. 1840–4. ' Erected for the Earl of Shrewsbury, on a steep rock some hundred feet in height. The buildings were planned to surround three sides of a quadrangle, but the design was never carried out in its entirety. They include a chapel, school, warden's lodgings, cloister, &c., all built of stone; the principal roofs, floors, &c., being of English oak. The chapel is richly decorated internally.' [*Eastlake;* p. 379.] See Chapter XI. (3) *Rebuilding Castle* on Alton Rock.

BREWOOD. *Church of St. Mary.* Begun, 1843; opened on Octave Day of Corpus Christi, 1844.

CHEADLE. *Church of St. Giles.* Early Decorated. Consecrated, 1 Sep. 1846. ' This church, erected at the expense of the Earl of Shrewsbury, was perhaps the most costly one for its size which Pugin executed. The interior is completely covered with decorative painting. The rood screen is of a very elaborate design. The east window is of five lights. In the wall, on either side, are stone niches richly canopied, and containing statues of the Blessed Virgin and St. Giles. Over the altar is placed a stone screen of tabernacle work, with figures of the Apostles. The church has a lofty tower and broached spire at its west end.' [*Eastlake;* p. 383.] Spire, 200 feet high. See Chapter XI.

COTTON. *Church of St. Wilfrid,* now the Chapel of Cotton College. Lord Shrewsbury contributed £1,000. ' Pugin says it will be " the only perfect church in England," with " an east window he could die for ".' [Letter from ' Brother Wilfrid ' to Michael Watts-Russell, 5 Oct. 1846; *The Life and Letters of Frederick William Faber, D.D.,* etc.; by John Edward Bowden; p. 315.]

STONE. *Chapel of St. Anne.* Now in the grounds of the Dominican Convent. Built by the Ven. Dominic Barbieri, C.P., the cause of whose

Beatification has been introduced.   Used as a school for a short time after the new church was built in 1854.

UTTOXETER.   *Church of St. Mary.*   Begun, 1838.   Enlarged, 1913–4, the main features being retained.   See Chapter XI.

SURREY.

PEPER HAROW.   Cherubim *Reredos and restoration* of the chancel arch and squint in *St. Nicholas's Church ;* also the *gateway* arch into Peper Harow Park, the *restoration* of the ruined wall of Oxenford Lay Monastery, and the *summer-house* at Bonbell Spring in the woods nearby. 'That unhappy man Lord Middleton' [i.e. Midleton] 'has at last destroyed himself.   I gave up all hopes of him when he put up the old pews in the new aisle I built for him.   I thought he would come to a miserable end.' [Pugin to Rev. J. J. Hornby, 11 Nov. 1848, referring apparently to work at St. Nicholas's; *Wickham*, p. 148.]   Also *barn*, etc., near southern gateway of the Park.

SUSSEX.

MAYFIELD.   At the Church of the Good Shepherd, Five Ashes : a pair of brass *candlesticks*, designed for Richard Partridge, F.R.S., and given by Mr. & Mrs. Lothian Nicholson, of Skipper's Hill, Five Ashes.

WARWICKSHIRE.

BILTON GRANGE.   *Additions* for Mr. John Hubert Washington Hibbert ; probably about 1840–1.

BIRMINGHAM.   *Internal fittings* and *detail* for *King Edward's Grammar School*, designed by Charles Barry, 1835.

BIRMINGHAM.   *Cathedral of St. Chad,* and *Bishop's House.*   Middle Pointed.   1839–41.   156 feet long, 58 feet wide, 75 feet high.   Re-decorated by John Hardman & Co., 1904–5.   Pugin's work in it includes the three sanctuary windows (given by Lord Shrewsbury), the canopy (nearly 30 feet high) over the Archbishop's throne, and the monument (carved by George Myers) to Bishop Walsh, the founder of the Cathedral. See Chapter XVI.   'I have just given up all hope now of that church coming to anything *really good :* it will look very well, *but it will not be the thing.*' [Letter to March-Phillipps, 7 Feb. 1841 ; *Phillipps ;* II., p. 225.]

BIRMINGHAM.   *Convent and Church of the Sisters of Mercy, Handsworth.* Begun, 1840.   'This foundation owes its existence to the piety and munificence of Mr. John Hardman, sen., aided by a large grant from the Earl of Shrewsbury,—both great benefactors to the religious edifices lately erected in this town.' [*Present State ;* p. 109.]   'The Convent is beautiful and fully furnished for twenty Sisters.   Mr. Pugin would not permit cloth of any kind on the parlours.   We have rush chairs and oak tables, and all is so admirable and religious, that no want could be felt. The building cost but three thousand pounds.   I would say six without hesitation.' [Letter from the Foundress, dated : Birmingham, 1841 ; *Life of the Foundress of the Sisters of Mercy* (Catherine Elizabeth

McAuley).] Church consecrated, 26 July 1847. When the convent was built, there were only two Catholic families in the neighbourhood, and the convent chapel, which held about thirty-six people, including the nuns, was adequate. It soon ceased to be so, and the church was built, and served as the parish church for forty-six years, being in turn superseded by the larger church of St. Francis. The convent church is now closed to the public except on special occasions. Pugin made the entire drawings for it in one morning, on two sheets of paper, in time to get the mid-day boat. [Inf. of Mr. S. Pugin Powell.]

KENILWORTH. *Church of St. Augustine.* Begun, 1841; finished, summer, 1852. Restored, 1904.

OSCOTT. *Work at St. Mary's College;* for which see Chapter XIII.; also designs (never carried out, and now hung in the Professor's Common Room) for a 'Milner Chauntry.'

RUGBY. *Church of St. Marie.* Opened, 8 Sep. 1847. Built for Mr. John Hubert Washington Hibbert, of Bilton Grange. It has been incorporated as an aisle in the present church.

SOLIHULL. *Church of St. Augustine of Canterbury.* Opened, 6 Feb. 1839. 'The Service began at 10½ with a Procession, Mr Pugin carrying the Cross, followed by Dr Weedall, officiating Priest . . . the Kyrie and Gloria of one of Mozart's Masses, and Agnus Dei etc from Haydn were sung without instruments by Rev Mr Chudah and Messrs Jeffries and Bens from Oscott, and Mr J. Hardman of Birmingham, standing on the left hand side of the Sanctuary. . . . The building is 50 feet by 22. The Altar, Font, Piscina, and Holy Water stoups are carved from designs of Mr Pugin in Gloucester stone, by Mr Roddis, of Sutton. The Tabernacle was designed by Mr Pugin, and got up by Mr Hardman. Mr Pugin gave his services gratuitously.' [*The London and Dublin Orthodox Journal,* 16 Feb. 1839.] Church originally austerely simple, and consisted of nave only. Sanctuary and porch added, 1878. Reredos added in 1876, replacing brass rods and red curtains. Recently replastered and redecorated throughout by Messrs. Hardman, Powell, & Pippet. Stated, with others, to be Pugin's 'first church.'

WATERFORD.

WATERFORD. *Presentation Convent. Chapel* (with rood screen), and *School.* Foundation-stone, 3 May 1842; opened, 14 Sep. 1848. Simple and handsome in design, the buildings, of cut stone, enclose a cloistered quadrangle, and remain as built.

WEXFORD.

BELLEVUE. *Private Chapel* for Mr. Anthony Cliffe of Bellevue. Fortunately not attached to the house, and so escaped destruction when the house was burned in the political disturbances in Ireland about ten years ago.

EDERMINE. *Private Chapel* for Sir James Power, second Baronet, M.P., of Edermine.

ENNISCORTHY. *St. Aidan's Cathedral.* Begun, 1843; finished (except the spire), 1848. Work completed, and spire added, to Pugin's plans, 1872–3. 175 feet long; 78 feet across transepts. [See also p. 109.]

GOREY. (1) *Church of St. Michael the Archangel.* 1839–42. Norman, with massive square central tower, nave, two aisles, two transepts, and fine rounded apse. Recently redecorated, &c., at a cost of £2,000–£3,000. (2) *Convent of Our Lady of Loreto;* attached to the Church; has received additions.

TAGOAT. *Church.* Severe thirteenth-century style. Opened, 1846.

WEXFORD. *Church and College of St. Peter.* Foundation-stone of church, 18 June 1838; dedicated 1840. The first of Pugin's Irish buildings.

WILTSHIRE.

CLARENDON PARK. A *lodge* for Sir F. H. Hervey-Bathurst. See Chapter VII.

Plans (never carried out) *for additions and alterations* to *Longford Castle*, and for a *bridge* near by over the Avon. See Chapter VII.

SALISBURY. (1) *Restoration of the Hall of John Halle.* See Chapter V. (2) *St. Marie's Grange.* See Chapter VII. (3) *Church of St. Osmund.* Decorated. Begun, 1847. Accommodation, 300. Cost, between £2,000 & £3,000. Organ gallery over sacristy at south side of chancel. Enlarged, 1894. See Chapter V.

WORCESTERSHIRE.

DUDLEY. *Church of Our Blessed Lady & St. Thomas of Canterbury.* Begun, 1839; consecrated, Easter Monday, 1842. 'The church at Dudley is a compleat facsimile of one of the old English parish churches, and nobody seems to know how to use it.' [Pugin to March-Phillipps, 18 Dec. 1840; *Phillipps;* II., p. 214.]

YORKSHIRE.

ACKWORTH GRANGE (near Pontefract). The *Jesus Chapel.* Opened, 12 Oct. 1842. Built for Mrs. Tempest (Elizabeth, dau. of Henry Blundell, of Ince Blundell, co. Lanc.), of Broughton, co. York. But for the additions of central heating, a porch, brass gates in the rood screen, and an organ-loft, it remains as built. There is a tradition that Pugin was very proud of it and called it the gem of the north.

BEVERLEY. *Restoration of St. Mary's Church.* Among Pugin's last works. Glass in great west window is by Hardman from his designs. See p. 310.

BOLTON ABBEY. *Restoration of nave,* and *designs for glass* in south windows.

KEIGHLEY. *Church of St. Anne.* In the *Apology* it is erroneously called St. Mary's. Opened, 21 Nov. 1840, and then described as ' by far the handsomest building in Yorkshire.' [*Kelly;* p. 231.] 'Keighley was opened the other day with a most horrible scene. Not only was all decorum violated, but a regular Row took place between the musicians, who quarrelled about their parts in the church, and after an hour's delay one priest drew off his singers and a Miss Whitwell—whose name appeared in the bills in gigantic letters—quavered away in a most extraordinary style. There was *no procession.* Every building I erect is profaned, and instead of assisting in conversions only serves to disgust people.' [Pugin to March-Phillipps, 18 Dec. 1840; *Phillipps;* II., p. 214.]

Plans (never carried out) for the complete *restoration of Hornby Castle* for the seventh Duke of Leeds.

'He also designed many churches for Australia and the colonies.' [*Ferrey;* p. 276.]

ADDENDA

BERKSHIRE.

WINDSOR CASTLE. *Furniture.* See pp. 23–4.

FLINTSHIRE.

PANTASAPH. *Completion* of *Church of St. David.* Begun, 1849; opened, 13 October 1852. On the conversion of the eighth Earl of Denbigh in 1850, ' Pugin was called in to give a Catholic finish to the design of the original architects.' The high altar, font, pulpit, and various statues were among Pugin's works at the Exhibition of 1851. Archdeacon Manning preached at the laying of the foundation-stone. [*Franciscan Annals;* Vol. VI., No. 70, October 1882.]

NOTTINGHAMSHIRE.

NOTTINGHAM. *St. Barnabas's Cathedral* was consecrated, 27 Aug. 1884. Lord Shrewsbury contributed £10,000. Pugin's altar and reredos have been removed, and another, with canopy, substituted.

SURREY.

ALBURY. *South transept* of the (now disused) Church of St. Peter & St. Paul.

APPENDIX III

(1) A Letter to A. W. Hakewill, Architect. 1835.

(2) Gothic Furniture in the style of the 15th Cent^y, designed & etched by A. W. N. Pugin. Lond. Ackermann, 1835, 4to, 25 plates; *ib.* 1836, roy. 4to. [According to Talbot Bury (*The Builder;* 25 Sep. 1852), Pugin's motto of 'En Avant' was adopted owing to the success of this book.]

(3) Details of ancient timber houses of the 15th & 16th Cent^{ries} selected from those existing at Rouen, Caen, Beauvais, Gisors, Abbeville, Strasbourg, etc., drawn on the spot & etched by A. Welby Pugin. Lond. 1836, 4to, 21 plates; *ib.* 1864.

(4) Designs for Iron and Brass work in the style of the XV and XVI centuries, drawn and etched by A. W. N. Pugin. Lond. Ackermann, 1836, 4to, 27 plates, engr. title without letterpress.

(5) Designs for gold and silver smiths drawn and etched by A. Welby Pugin. Lond. Ackermann, 1836, 4to, 28 plates, in 2 pts., the 2nd being for church plate, engr. title without letterpress.

[The four last-mentioned thin volumes were also sold together as 'Pugin's Ornaments of the XVth and XVIth Centuries.' New edn. 1904.]

(6) Contrasts; or a parallel between the noble edifices of the four-teenth and fifteenth centuries, and similar buildings of the present day; showing the present decay of taste: Accompanied by appropriate Text. By A. Welby Pugin, Architect. London: printed for the author, and published by him at St. Marie's Grange, near Salisbury, Wilts., 1836; 2nd edn. Lond. 1841, improved and with extra plates, title altered: . . . edifices of the Middle Ages and corresponding buildings. . . .

(7) An Apology for a work entitled 'Contrasts'; being A Defence of the Assertions Advanced in that Publication, against the various attacks lately made upon it. By A. Welby Pugin Author of the Book in Question. Birmingham, R. P. Stone, 1837, 12mo, pp. 33, followed by 'Some Observations on the State of the Arts in England; showing that the degraded condition to which Art has fallen is owing to the Absence of Catholic Feeling among its professors, the loss of all Ecclesiastical Patronage owing to a Protestant Church Establishment, and the Apathy with which a Protestant Nation treats the higher branches of Art,' pp. 35–49.

(8) A Reply to Observations which appeared in *Fraser's Magazine* for March 1837, on a work entitled 'Contrasts.' Lond. 1837, 12 mo.

[Rev., *Dublin Review*, Oct. 1837. See also Chapter VI.] The 'observations' included the following : ' That the profession must now regard him as an insolent reviler, admits of little dispute ; whether the Roman Catholic Church will greatly admire him as its advocate, is not quite so certain, since his attachment to it seems to arise quite as much from his admiration of its outward splendour, as from conviction of the soundness of its doctrines. . . . We shall merely observe that he does not seem to be aware that the Romish Church has been reproached with —perhaps, the more suitable term would be convicted of—having engrafted many of the rites of paganism upon Christianity . . . nor is it likely that when perusing it,' [Hope's *History of Architecture*] ' he should have somehow missed the seventeenth Chapter, which treats expressly of the " heathen customs kept up or emulated by the Christians "—those corruptions of the apostolical church, and those interpolations in its doctrine, which it was reserved for the Reformation to root out. So far, he must consent to appear either very ignorant, or not a little disingenuous : when he attempts to fix upon the Reformation the stigma of having occasioned the decline and disuse of the Gothic style, he is palpably absurd.' It also refers to him as ' too much of a Smelfungus.'

(9) A Letter on the Proposed Protestant Memorial to Cranmer, Ridley, and Latymer, addressed to the Subscribers to and Promoters of that Undertaking. Lond. Booker & Dolman, 1839, 8vo. [It elicited from the anti-Catholic writer, Rev. Thomas Lathbury, ' The Protestant Memorial. Strictures on a Letter addressed by Mr. Pugin to the Supporters of the Martyrs' Memorial at Oxford.' 1839, 12mo.]

(10) Illustrations to the Missal. Designed and engraved by A. Welby Pugin, Esq., Professor of Ecclesiastical Antiquities at St. Mary's College, Oscott. Lond. Dolman, 1839, 12mo. [These formed 6 illustrations in ' The Missal for the use of the laity . . . arranged and in great measure Translated by the Rev. F. C. Husenbeth ', Dolman, of which the 3rd edn. was in 1840 and the 4th in 1843.]

[Between 1839 and 1844 were issued : ' Penny Book and Sheet Almanacks ', embellished with devotional engravings by Pugin and others ; the ' Ladies' and Gentlemen's Annual Catholic Pocket-books and Diary ', with beautiful engravings by Pugin and others ; and ' The Cath. Wkly. Instructor ' with an engraving by Pugin.]

(11) Elevation of the Cathedral Church of St. Chad, Birmingham. Lond. 1840.

(12) The True Principles of Pointed or Christian Architecture : set forth in two lectures delivered at St. Marie's, Oscott, by A. Welby Pugin, architect, and professor of ecclesiastical antiquities in that college. Lond. 1841, 4to, pp. 67, with plates and cuts ; 2nd edn. 1853. [' Les Vrais Principes de l'Architecture Ogivale ou Chrétienne, avec des remarques sur leur renaissance au temps actuel. Remanié et développé d'après le texte Anglais . . . par T. H. King, et traduit en Français, par P. Lebrocquy.' Bruxelles et Leipzig (Bruges, pr.), 1850, 4to.]

(13) An Apology for The Revival of Christian Architecture in England. By (as above). Lond. John Weale, 1843, 4to, pp. 51, besides title and dedn. to Earl of Shrewsbury, &c., with plates ; 2nd edn. Lond. Bohn, 1853, 4to ; originally pub., with illustrns. from his works, in *The Dublin Review*, 1841–2.

(14) The Present State of Ecclesiastical Architecture in England. By A. Welby Pugin, Architect. With Thirty-six Illustrations. Lond. Dolman, 1843, 8vo ; repr. from *The Dublin Review*, 1841–2.

[Pugin's works published before ' 1844 were illustrated with etchings by himself ; from that date the illustrations were redrawn for lithography and have lost much of their character in the process.' (Bryan's *Dictionary of Painters and Engravers*).]

(15) Glossary of Ecclesiastical Ornament and Costume, [setting forth the Origin, History, and Significance of the various Emblems, Devices, and Symbolical Colours peculiar to the Christian Design of the Middle Ages, with especial reference to the Decoration of the Sacred Vestments and Altar Furniture formerly used in the English Church, illustrated by nearly 80 plates, splendidly printed in gold and colours by the new Lithochromotographic process, containing Examples of the Ecclesiastical Costume of the Roman, English, French, and German Bishops, Priests, and Deacons ; Altar Furniture ; Embroidery ; Diaperings ; Bordures ; Powderings ; Floriated Crosses ; Holy Emblems ; Holy Monograms ; Examples of the Nimbus ; Conventional Forms of Animals and Flowers for Heraldic and Church Decoration ; Funeral Palls, &c. &c., also a variety of Ornamental Alphabets of Church Texts of various dates. The details of many of the Ornaments are given of the full size ; the whole drawn, coloured, adapted, and described from Ancient . . .] Compiled and Illustrated from Antient Authorities and Examples, by A. Welby Pugin, Architect, Professor of Ecclesiastical Antiquities at St. Maries College, Oscott. With extracts from the works of Durandus, Georgius, Bona, Catalani, Gerbert, Martene, Molanus, Thiers, Mabillon, Ducange, etc. Faithfully translated by the Rev. Bernard Smith, of St. Maries College, Oscott. Lond. Bohn, 1844, roy. 4to [the words in brackets above do not appear on the title-page of the 1st edn.] ; 2nd edn., revised and enlarged by Rev. Bernard Smith, *ib.*, 1846, *ib.* ; 3rd edn. Lond. 1868, 4to.

(16) A Statement of Facts relative to the Engagement of marriage between Miss [. . .] and Augustus Welby Pugin, Esq. of S. Augustins, Isle of Thanet. Lond. 1848, 8vo, pr. for private circulation, and repr., with the omission of names and a few passages, in *Ferrey*, pp. 193–222.

(17) Floriated Ornament : A Series of Thirty-one Designs By Augustus Welby Pugin, Architect. Lond. Bohn, 1849, roy. 4to, with 30 plates in gold and colours. [Entitled ' Floral Ornament ' on the original drawing of the frontispiece. The drawings were reduced to scale, &c., by John Hardman Powell (Inf. of Mr. S. Pugin Powell)] ; new edn. Lond. 1875, roy. 4to.

(18) Some Remarks on the Articles which have recently appeared in

the ' Rambler,' relating to Ecclesiastical Architecture and Decoration. Lond. Dolman, 1850, 8vo, pp. 25.

(19) An Address to the Inhabitants of Ramsgate. Ramsgate, 1850, 8vo.

(20) An Earnest Appeal for the Revival of Ancient Plain Song. Lond. Dolman, 1850, 8vo, pp. 10. [Rev., *Tablet*, xi., 667, 715; *Dub. Rev.*, xxxi. Extracts from this pamphlet were made up as an anti-Catholic tract and printed by the *English Churchman* (a paper which stated of itself that while ' avoiding the errors of Latitudinarianism and Dissent on the one side, and of Romanism on the other, it seeks to promote a strict and faithful obedience to the Doctrines and Practices of the Book of Common Prayer.'), under the title of ' Present State of Public Worship among the Roman Catholics. By a Roman Catholic.']

(21) History of the restored Church of St. Mary, Wymeswold. Lond. 1850, 4to, plates. [Rev., *Tablet*, xii, 165, 172.]

(22) A single-sheet address to the ' Catholics of England,' issued before the ' Earnest Address ' (printed by T. Maher, Birmingham), in which he appealed to all Catholics to set aside a fixed sum every year for the support of the new hierarchy. Also printed as a letter in *The Tablet* of 8 March 1851.

(23) An Earnest Address on the Establishment of the Hierarchy. Lond. Dolman, 1851, 8vo, pp. 32; ' Church and State; or Christian Liberty. An Earnest Address on the Establishment of the Hierarchy. By A. Welby Pugin.' Lond. 1875, and edited by E. W. Pugin. ' With an introduction and notes by his son ' (E. W. P.). Lond. 1875, 8vo, 2nd edn.; ditto, 3rd edn., ' together with Letters from Dr. Newman, Canon Liddon, and the Rt. Hon. W. E. Gladstone,' Lond. 1875, 8vo; *id.* 4th edn. 1875.

(24) An answer to an attack on his *Earnest Address*, by ' a Catholic Priest ' in *The Tablet* of 8 March 1851, in a letter to *The Tablet* of 15 March 1851. Also separately printed. Similar to his letter of justification to Cardinal Wiseman, dated ' Ramsgate, February, 1851,' and printed in his son's edn. of the *Earnest Address*.

(25) A Treatise on Chancel Screens and Rood Lofts, Their Antiquity, Use, and Symbolic Signification. By A. Welby Pugin, Architect. Illustrated with figures copied on stone from drawings by the author. Lond. Dolman, 1851, 4to. [Rev., *Tablet*, xii., 314, 330; *Lamp*, ii., 363.]

(26) Photographs from Sketches by Augustus Welby N. Pugin. . . . By S. Ayling. Lond. 1865, 2 vols. 8vo, 500 sketches, ed. by E. W. Pugin. [The collection, chiefly of sketches done on the Continent, is incomplete, and the reproductions are too small to do full justice to the skill and delicacy of Pugin's work. There is an interesting note on this publication on pp. 132–3 of *The Cathedrals and Churches of Belgium* by T. Francis Bumpus.]

(27) Pugin helped his father in the following works :—

(a) Specimens of the Architectural Antiquities of Normandy. Lond. 1825–8, 4to, 80 plates; *ib.*, 1833.

(b) Gothic Ornaments selected from various Ancient Buildings in England and France. Lond. 1831, 4to, 91 plates; *ib.*, 1854, roy. 4to.

(c) Paris and its environs, displayed in a series of two hundred picturesque views, from Original Drawings, taken under the direction of A. Pugin, Esq. The Engravings under C. Heath, Esq. Lond. 1831.

(d) Examples of Gothic Architecture, selected from various Antient Buildings in England, &c.; with Accounts by Aug. Pugin and Aug. Welby Pugin. Lond. 1831–8, 4to, 3 vols., 226 fine plates.

(28) Pugin is said also [*Dict. Nat. Biog.*; LI., p. 3] to have published in 1828 ' two sheets of classic detail, drawn by F. Arundale from sketches by Parke and Scoles in 1823.'

(29) Contributions :—Lectures on Ecclesiastical Architecture, delivered to the Students of St. Mary's College, Oscott, *The Catholic Magazine*, 1838–9, ii. 193–214, 321–7, iii. 17–34, 89–98; letters and articles, *Orthodox Journal*, vi. 1838, vii., ix., & x.; *Dublin Review*, Feb. 1842; *Weekly Register*, 1849, i; *Rambler*; *Tablet.*

(30) In the 1875 edn. of the *Earnest Address* the following notification appears :—' *Preparing for Press*. A New View of an Old Subject: or, the English Schism impartially considered. By A. Welby Pugin. A large portion of this work has lately been discovered, and will shortly be issued.—E. W. P.' This book, which was also announced as in preparation in the original edition of the *Earnest Address*, has never been published.

(31) ' Preparing for publication in parts at intervals, richly illustrated, An Apology for the separated Church of England since the reign of the Eighth Henry. Written with every feeling of Christian charity for her children, and honour of the glorious men she continued to produce in evil times. By A. Welby Pugin. Many years a Catholic-minded son of the Anglican Church, and still an affectionate and loving brother and servant of the true sons of England's Church.' Never published. For a discussion of this projected work, see Edmund Sheridan Purcell's ' Appendix ' to Ferrey's *Recollections*. Perhaps identical with the *New View*; or the one may have formed a part of the other. ' In consequence of the religious commotion of the times the work, by the advice of the author's ecclesiastical superiors, was delayed; he was admonished indeed " not to go on with his promised publication without a *sound*, theological adviser, nor before he had cleared up the objections and the scandal which was feared to have resulted from his former work on the Hierarchy —a work so taken up by the hostile papers, and by whom certainly it was hoped Pugin could not wish to be considered as a friend." ' [Edmund Sheridan Purcell: ' Appendix ' to Ferrey's *Recollections*; p. 431.]

[This list of publications is taken (but with some additions and corrections) from Gillow's *Bibliographical Dictionary*.]

(32) An illustrated letter (' On Spires and Towers ') dated ' Feast of St. Aldhelm, 1843,' with a long appendix (' Notices of Spires and Towers in England '), printed in the *Architectural Review*, 1908, vol. xxiii., pp. 3–9.

APPENDIX IV

SONG ON PUGIN'S 'CONTRASTS'

['By Mr. M'Cann, an Irishman' (*Ferrey*, pp. 115–6)]

OH ! have you seen the work just out
   By Pugin, the great builder ?
'Architect'ral Contrasts' he's made out
   Poor Protestants to bewilder.
The Catholic Church, she never knew—
   Till Mr. Pugin taught her,
That orthodoxy had to do
   At all with bricks and mortar.

But now it's clear to one and all,
   Since he's published his lecture,
No church is Catholic at all
   Without Gothic architecture.
In fact, he quite turns up his nose
   At any style that's racent,
The Gracian, too, he plainly shows
   Is wicked and ondacent.

There's not a bit of pious taste
   Iver since the Reformation ;
'Twas Harry the Eighth, the nasty baste,
   That introduced the Gracian.
When they denied the truth outright
   Of Transubstantiation,
They built them in the Composite—
   That great abomination.

Next thing their frien's to build dozing pews
   In the most systematic way go ;
They'd be kilt, they say, the other way,
   With rheumatics and lumbago.

Some raise a front up to the street,
   Like ould Westminster Abbey ;
And then they think the Lord to cheat,
   And build the back part shabby.
For stuccoed bricks, and sich like tricks,
   At present all the rage is,
They took no one in ! those fine ould min !
   In the ' pious Middle Ages ! ! !'

APPENDIX V

HANDWRITING, &c.

In one of his letters to Lord Shrewsbury, Pugin wrote : ' I am very sorry for my bad writing, but really I have so many letters to write, so much work to do, and get so driven up for time, that my ideas go so much faster than the pen, I fear I cut the syllables short, but I will be more careful in future.' [*Ferrey ;* p. 125.] Lord Shrewsbury's complaint would not have been without justification, for Pugin's handwriting degenerated into a form of shorthand, most of the letters being completely unformed, and the smaller letters being little more than wavy horizontal lines joining the larger letters. Even more symptomatic of haste was his punctuation, which consisted chiefly of full-stops and short dashes, commas appearing but rarely, and a larger space between words frequently being employed where normal usage would demand a comma, dash, or even bracket ; a full-stop followed by a larger space, though no capital, was a frequent introduction to a new sentence. The result was a flowing and decorative script, almost illegible in detail, but surprisingly easy to read if taken sentence by sentence or line by line. It was adorned, too, by small crosses such as Catholic Bishops write before their signatures. But Pugin, in his devotional enthusiasm, outdid the hierarchy, and put his cross before the address and date as well as before his name.

APPENDIX VI

ARCHITECTS were not the only people who made profitable use of Pugin's work without acknowledgment. Sometime towards the end of the nineteenth century, an extremely fine water-colour of a procession moving in a cathedral of almost incredible magnificence was exhibited for sale. It was marked: *Interior of Munich Cathedral; by Charles Rousse.* To a discerning Catholic eye, the costumes and behaviour of the members of the procession is peculiar, and to anyone with any knowledge of architecture it seems strange that a procession, immediately after passing up the chancel steps and under the rood-screen and organ-loft, should find itself in the open air. In addition, it bears no resemblance to Munich Cathedral. It so happened that it was seen by a great-grandson of Pugin, who purchased it, not only because it was of singular beauty, but because, with the exception of the unorthodox procession and the open-air chancel, it was taken almost line for line from a drawing of the chapel of an imaginary 'St. Marie's College' with the designing of which Pugin had amused himself in 1833–4. The drawing, which is entitled *view of organ screen and antechapel*, shows a piece of perpendicular Gothic of almost fantastic splendour.[1] By the time the painting was made, Pugin was but a memory; but his work still had financial value for those who knew how to make use of it. Charles Rousse ' took his wages, and,' it may be assumed, ' is dead.' His work remains, in the possession of its purchaser, Mr. Humphrey Watts, at Sion House in Worcestershire, together with a photograph of the original drawing, which shows, with the other drawings of ' St. Marie's College,' that Pugin was well capable of producing designs for the Houses of Parliament: he had, in fact, been doing that sort of thing for his own amusement a year before Barry and Graham decided to enter for the great competition.

[1] It is reproduced opp. p. 404 of *The Burlington Magazine* of March 1906. (Art. by Robert Dell; which see also for a detailed discussion of the extent of Pugin's work on the new Houses of Parliament.)

APPENDIX VII

(1) IN childhood. Full-length; full-face; life-size; digging in a garden. In the possession of Mr. Sebastian Pugin Powell, at 7 Norham Gardens, Oxford.

(2) In early manhood. Head & shoulders; three-quarter face. Drawn from recollection by Joseph Nash. Published in *Ferrey*, opp. p. 26: ' Lynch, lith. Hanhart, Impt.'

(3) Ditto. In National Portrait Gallery. Head & shoulders; three-quarter face; 24″ × 19½″; coat of arms. ' Purchased in 1905 from Messrs. Shepherd's Gallery. The date of the painting may be about 1830–5, or alternatively posthumous since the words " R.I.P." are painted on the top, in which case it would be based on an earlier portrait. It has been suggested that it is the work of George Richmond ; there is, however, no record of Richmond ever having drawn or painted Pugin. It has also been suggested that it is the work of a Mr. George Mackay, but this has not been confirmed.' [Inf. of Mr. John Steepmann, of the Nat. Port. Gall.]

(4) In late life. Formerly in the possession of Pugin's grandson, Mr. A. W. Pugin, at Woodford Wells, Essex. Half-length; full-face; seated at table ; coat of arms. By John Rogers Herbert, R.A. ' His left hand is upon a parallel rule, an instrument with which he invariably worked in preference to a T-square, and compasses are held in the right hand. The portrait was photographed by the Arundel Society for the record of the National Portrait Exhibition, 1868.' [*Sirr, R.I.B.A.*] Herbert repeatedly asked Pugin to sit to him, but was refused because of pressure of work. Eventually he yielded so far as to ask how long it would take, and Herbert, anxious to get at any rate something done, said twenty minutes. Pugin then sat down at a table with his watch in front of him, and left the room at the end of the twenty minutes. Herbert had done the head in that time. The rest was done from memory about ten years later. This is the reason for the undecipherable costume, which itself is one of the sources of the story that Pugin worked in a special ' architect's robe.' Actually, he worked in his usual semi-nautical costume, the trousers of which were vividly patched where necessary. [Inf. of Mr. S. Pugin Powell, in whose possession there is a copy of the portrait and another copy of the head and shoulders only.]

(5) Full-length effigy in stone on his cenotaph in the Pugin Chantry in St. Augustine's, Ramsgate. ' He lies wrapped in a mantle of mediæval shape, with prayer-clasped hands, the Pugin martlet supporting his feet.

The features have been faithfully reproduced by the sculptor. The tomb is of altar shape, supported by pillars of green marble, the ends and sides being divided into panels which contain kneeling effigies in miniature of the great architect's sons and daughters. An inscription surrounding the tomb—painted on tiles in Gothic lettering,—requests a remembrance for his soul's health :

" Pray for the soul of Augustus Welby Pugin, founder of this Church." ' [*St. Augustine's, Ramsgate ;* by the Rt. Rev. Abbot Egan, O.S.B.]

(6) Full-length statue at N.E. corner of the Albert Memorial. He wears a flowing garment, reaching to the ground—probably another source of the ' architect's robe ' story. The presence of the statue is owing to the generosity of Gilbert Scott, who insisted that Pugin had a better right to be represented there than himself. [Inf. of Mr. S. Pugin Powell.] In consequence, Scott only appears in low relief on a medallion at his left shoulder. The arrangement of the figures is not without ironic implication : for, owing to being placed at a corner, Pugin is ' cut ' by his fellow immortals, his immediate neighbours having their backs to him. On his right, Decamps looks over Delaroche's shoulder. On his left, Cockerell looks as though a joke of Sir Charles Barry's were not really funny. Only Scott, self-exiled to the background, turned in inconspicuous homage, even looks at him.

POSTSCRIPT

It remains, to express my thanks to those without whose help and sympathy this book would have been a far less complete treatment of its subject. Of these, among Pugin's descendants, I would especially mention Mr. Sebastian Pugin Powell, Mrs. Watts of Sion House, Mr. Humphrey Watts, the Rev. Philip Watts, S.J.; of others, Mr. and Mrs. Everard Scarisbrick of Scarisbrick, Major C. J. Chichester-Constable, Mr. James Roskell Reynolds, Major T. B. Trappes-Lomax.

The sources from which this book has been drawn are referred to throughout; but particular reference is due to two books: Mr. Kenneth Clark's *The Gothic Revival* and Benjamin Ferrey's *Recollections*. My debt to the latter is only what must be owed by any biographer of Pugin; for although, as Mr. Clark points out, 'it must be one of the worst arranged biographies ever written,' yet, as he adds, 'it contains most of the material.'

The chapter-headings from *The Song of Roland* and *The Saga of Grettir the Strong* are from the translations respectively of Mr. John Harrington Cox and Mr. George Ainslie Hight.

INDEX

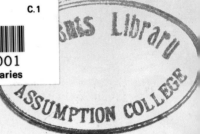
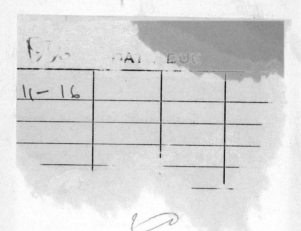